MW00804437

PLATO'S *LETTERS*

A volume in the series

Agora Editions

General Editor: Thomas L. Pangle
Founding Editor: Allan Bloom

A list of titles in this series is available at cornellpress.cornell.edu.

PLATO'S *LETTERS*

THE POLITICAL CHALLENGES OF THE PHILOSOPHIC LIFE

Translated, with Introduction, Notes, and Interpretive Essay by

ARIEL HELFER

CORNELL UNIVERSITY PRESS
Ithaca and London

First published 2023 by Cornell University Press

Library of Congress Cataloging-in-Publication Data

Names: Helfer, Ariel, author. | Plato. Epistles. English (Helfer)
Title: Plato's Letters : the political challenges of the philosophic life / Ariel Helfer.
Description: Ithaca : Cornell University Press, 2023. | Series: Agora editions | Includes bibliographical references and index.
Identifiers: LCCN 2023006805 (print) | LCCN 2023006806 (ebook) | ISBN 9781501772894 (hardcover) | ISBN 9781501772900 (epub) | ISBN 9781501772917 (pdf)
Subjects: LCSH: Plato. Epistles—Criticism and interpretation. | Plato—Political and social views.
Classification: LCC B391.E83 H45 2023 (print) | LCC B391.E83 (ebook) | DDC 184—dc23/eng/20230608
LC record available at https://lccn.loc.gov/2023006805
LC ebook record available at https://lccn.loc.gov/2023006806

To Tom Pangle

Contents

Preface

Consensus eludes scholars on virtually every aspect of Plato's *Letters*. Prominent figures in every branch of Platonic studies have pronounced drastically differing opinions on these epistles, individually and as a collection, with regard to their authenticity, significance, and interpretation. This confusion, which has surrounded the *Letters* for so long, has had the unfortunate effect of creating a barrier between the student and the text. To open any existing edition of the *Letters* is to find oneself thrown at once upon an academic battlefield, caught in the dizzying cross fire of arguments over arcane matters of historiography and philology. Before long one is bound to become unsure not only of *how* to approach and to read Plato's *Letters*, but even *whether* the text is worth reading.

This volume seeks in a number of ways to make it easier for the student, whether amateur or expert, to see the value and importance of reading the *Letters*. Most crucially, it provides a new translation of the *Letters*, of which the purpose is to allow the English-speaking reader without knowledge of ancient Greek to come as close to the literal meaning of the original text as possible, with footnotes to supply insight into historical context and linguistic subtleties where necessary or helpful. My hope is that this will enable generations of readers to judge for themselves, in a way not hitherto possible, as to the character and worth of this fascinating text.

There is a further and more ambitious goal at which this volume also aims: to rehabilitate what I call the "literary unity thesis," according to which the *Letters* is a single, authentic, unified work of Platonic political philosophy. While my defense of this argument in the introduction necessarily threatens to involve the reader in the forbidding fray of scholarly debate to which I referred above, I have done my best to remain above that fray, first by explaining the origins of the various disputes over the *Letters*, and then by showing how the literary unity thesis resolves, with admirable parsimony, many of the historical puzzles and interpretive paradoxes that have emerged from these fraught disputes. But since the proof of this pudding, as I insist in the introduction, is in the eating, I have also provided a long, three-part interpretive essay treating the whole *Letters*, so as to give some idea of what it would be to study Plato's *Letters* as a coherent Platonic work.

I have placed the interpretive essay after the translation in order to convey my intention that the reader should take up a careful, independent study of the *Letters* before turning to my interpretation. Aside from the fact that the essay is written for readers who have the details of the *Letters* fresh in their minds, I believe that the study of Plato is more fruitful when one can first form one's own ideas about the text's major themes and puzzles with minimal prejudice for or against any particular line of interpretation. In any case, since the literary unity thesis has been so widely overlooked for so long, the interpretive essay in this volume constitutes what I believe to be the first attempt at such a complete and detailed interpretation of the whole *Letters*, and I have no doubt that I have missed numerous important points in my exploration of this remarkably uncharted territory. My hope is that students of Platonic philosophy more capable and more talented than I, spurred on by my insights and by my mistakes, will produce still more penetrating and persuasive interpretations of the *Letters* in the years to come.

As a graduate student at the University of Texas at Austin, I participated in a reading group on Plato's *Seventh Letter* in the spring of 2012. The discussions I had with my professors and fellow students during that time planted the seed that at length grew into this book. Along the way, friends, colleagues, and students continued to indulge me by agreeing to form reading groups with me on the *Letters* in whole or in part. For this, I owe thanks in particular to Tom and Lorraine Pangle, Loren Rotner, Zachary Bennett, and Derek Foret, as well as to the lively group of Wayne State University graduate students in political science who attended regular, virtual meetings on the *Seventh Letter* in the fall 2020 semester. I am grateful moreover to many friends and colleagues whose discussions with me about the *Letters* provided valuable insights over the years. Devin Stauffer on several occasions made time to help me think through various substantive and strategic issues in my work on the *Letters*. More than once while I was at Michigan State University, a conversation with Dustin Sebell helped me to see the *Letters* in a new and insightful way.

I received some significant financial support for the production of this manuscript. A full year of research was funded by a fellowship from the National Endowment for the Humanities. Further summer research funding was provided in the form of a University Research Grant from Wayne State University. In addition, my thanks are due to Chantel Raymond, to whom Wayne State awarded a special Graduate Research Assistantship to aid in the preparation of my manuscript during the 2019–2020 academic year.

There are a few people whose generosity in agreeing to review and discuss my manuscript saved me from many embarrassing mistakes. Keith Whitaker did me an enormous kindness, which I did nothing in particular to deserve, by reading a draft of my translation and returning it thoroughly annotated with his suggestions and feedback. Tom Pangle, to whom my debt grows ever greater, provided invaluable editorial guidance on every part of this book, dramatically improving the readability of the translation and helping me to refine and to clarify my thought throughout the interpretive essay. Erik Dempsey and Gregory McBrayer also helped me to improve early drafts of my translation. Without the help of these friends, I would not have been able to raise the quality of this book to the level it has reached; I alone bear responsibility for the deficiencies that remain.

I owe a special thanks to my brother, Joseph Helfer, who shared his brilliance with me in two totally different ways. He helped me translate Franz Dornseiff's article on the *Letters* from the original German and wrote a computer program to help me compile the index to the translation.

I am also grateful to Bethany Wasik at Cornell University Press, who helped guide me smoothly through the publication process, and to the anonymous peer reviewers, who made a number of helpful suggestions.

During my years of working on this project, various people under various auspices kindly invited me to present aspects of my research, which invariably helped me to work out my own thoughts and allowed me to receive helpful feedback from intelligent audiences. My thanks to Debra Nails, Emily Katz, and the Michigan State University's History of Philosophy Circle, Yumin Sheng and Wayne State University's Political Science Colloquium Series, David Ramsey and the Reubin O'D.Askew Department of Government at the University of West Florida, and Dustin and Lauren Sebell with the LeFrak Forum on Science, Reason, and Modern Democracy at Michigan State for these opportunities. In addition, I presented working drafts of parts of my interpretive essay at academic conferences for almost seven years, receiving valuable feedback from my discussants who took the time to read and respond to my work. Lorraine Pangle, Peter Ahresndorf, Laura Rabinowitz, Eric Buzzetti, Gregory McBrayer, and Michael Hawley all helped my work on the *Letters* in this way. My thanks are also due to Sean Stidd and Josh Wilburn, who allowed me to co-coordinate the Wayne State Plato Symposium with them in 2021, where I was able to share my work on the *Letters* with, and receive feedback from, an impressive interdisciplinary group of Plato scholars.

Through it all, my wife, Cassie, was by my side. Over and again, she performed the miraculous feat of making time for me to work when there was no time to spare, taking care of our home and our two beautiful boys (as well as her own career) so that I could achieve this goal of mine, which seemed so distant for so long. I cannot say what would have become of this project, or of me, without her endless encouragement and support; I only know that I owe her more than I can repay.

Note on Translation

In producing this translation, I have made use of both John Burnet's edition of the Greek, first published in 1907 for Oxford Classical Libraries, and that of Joseph Souilhé, first published in 1931 by Belle Lettres for their Guillaume Budé series. The latter is the more complete, in that its collation and critical apparatus include some manuscripts to which Burnet does not refer, but here and there Burnet includes a variant left out by Souilhé. I have also referred regularly to the digital images of the original manuscripts made available online by the libraries in which they reside.

In cases of substantive disagreement between manuscript readings, I have generally tried to translate according to the main text of the oldest and best manuscripts—especially Parisinus Graecus 1807 and Vaticanus Graecus 1 (Bekker's A and O, respectively)—avoiding the emendations of later scribes and scholars when reasonable and above all when justified by the principle of *lectio difficilior potior*. I have used the footnotes to record important manuscript variants as much as considerations of conciseness and ease of reading would allow. Whenever I have transliterated Greek words in footnotes or in the interpretive essay, I have employed the *ē* and *ō* symbols for *eta* and *omega*, and represented *theta*, *phi*, *chi*, and *psi* as "th," "ph," "ch," and "ps," respectively. When the second person plural is employed in the Greek, I have usually written "you [pl]" in the translation, lest the plural be mistaken for a singular.

My guiding principle in rendering the text into English has been to enable the reader who does not possess knowledge of ancient Greek to come as close as possible to the precise and literal meaning of the text. This often requires a sacrifice of fluidity and gracefulness in the English; the reader will have to navigate many long and complex sentences and learn to think about the text's subject matter in terms of categories and ideas belonging to a worldview rather distant from our own. But all this has been done for the sake of ensuring that the original author's careful choice of words and composition of sentences are respected and preserved in translation. I feel certain that the resulting translation, among other advantages, can be trusted more than any of its predecessors to translate key terms consistently: words related to *dikē* are always given by some form of "justice," words related to *phusis* by some form of "nature," and so on. I have indicated in footnotes where context has compelled me to deviate from this principle of consistency in regard to words I consider significant within the *Letters*.

For all that I believe my translation constitutes an improvement on past attempts, I must acknowledge my debt to the fine translations to which I have referred continuously in the course of my work. First and foremost, I have learned a great deal from the translation of J. Harward (1932), who provides copious footnotes on difficult points in the grammar and syntax of the Greek. I have also benefited from the English translations of Glenn R. Morrow (1962), L. A. Post (1925), and R. G. Bury (1929), as well as the French translations of Joseph Souilhé (1931) and Luc Brisson (1993).

Introduction

It is a distinctive and essential feature of Plato's political philosophy that, at its peak, its theme is the relationship between philosophy and politics as such. The *Republic*'s doctrine of the philosopher-king is a stunning answer to the challenge that philosophy is poisonous to the healthy community, that its irreverent skepticism corrodes the pious and patriotic spirit upon which the city relies, especially among the young, whom philosophy is most apt to seduce. The bewildering claim for which Plato is justly famous is that if one carefully attends to the distinction between philosophy and its corrupted counterpart, sophistry—personified in the *Republic* itself by Socrates and Thrasymachus, respectively—one learns that philosophy suffers unjustly from the reputation belonging properly to its sinister or misguided doppelgänger. The true philosopher is so far from being a pernicious or parasitic presence in the city that he is in fact the city's, nay, humanity's only hope of bringing an end to the ills that beset us, of creating the just community, and of bringing meaningful happiness into the world. In short, the solution to the most profound and comprehensive political problem is, according to Plato's Socrates, the rule of true philosophy. And yet this most famous Platonic doctrine has from the start been the object of intense controversy. For, as it has seemed to many, the *Republic*'s proposal for a regime of philosophic rule amounts to a call for

Plato's followers to become utopian dreamers doomed to quixotic failure. Inevitably, various readers have come to doubt Plato's seriousness in proposing this regime as a blueprint for political action: some see the *Republic* rather as a didactic exercise in studying the elements of political life, others see an attempt to defend philosophy amid the hostile Greeks who had only recently executed Plato's own teacher for philosophizing, and still others allege a propagandistic agenda aimed at elevating Plato's way of life, his friends, and his school. The effect of the *Republic*, then, has been to *deepen* the puzzle it seeks to address about the relationship between philosophy and politics. If it is meant as a serious political proposal, should its author be judged a visionary or a fool? If it is not, what was his purpose in writing it?[1]

There is one source of information that would seem to promise wondrously direct access to Plato's inner thoughts and opinions on these matters. Along with the philosophic dialogues making up the bulk of the Platonic corpus, the manuscript tradition has also preserved a collection of thirteen letters addressed from Plato to a variety of correspondents across the Greek political world of his day. And it so happens that in all these letters, Plato either actively engages in, or discusses circumstances in which he has previously engaged in, practical political dealings and decision-making, mostly as one whose wise counsel has been sought by men in powerful political positions. Above all, Plato's infamous entanglements and dramatic misadventures in Syracuse, where it seems that he attempted to turn the young tyrant Dionysius toward the study of philosophy, feature prominently in these letters: all but three of the thirteen are addressed to people connected to the events in Sicily, and Letter Seven—by far the longest, most famous, and most extensively studied of the thirteen—contains a lengthy and detailed account of Plato's actions and reasoning throughout the decades-long affair, albeit from the point of view of an interested party in a series of contentious and controversial historical episodes. In these documents, then, it would seem that we are afforded a glimpse of Plato in action, not as the hidden author of philosophic dramas in which he himself has no role, but as political adviser to real people regarding real cities and events. To the extent that deeds offer more reliable evidence of a person's inner thought than do their

---

1. For major statements of a few of the most important positions in the debate over the seriousness of Plato's apparent political proposals in the *Republic*, see Strauss 1964, 121–24, 127–29; Lane 1999; Burnyeat 1999; Schofield 2006, 195–97, 239.

words,[2] these letters—as providing ostensible documentation of Plato's political actions—present themselves as an ideal source of confirmation and clarity regarding Plato's genuine answers to some of the great political-philosophic questions, and indeed regarding the question of philosophic kingship itself. A careful study of the Platonic letters therefore has the potential to illuminate Plato's understanding of the highest theme of his political philosophy, the relationship between philosophy and politics, and therewith the many weighty problems involved in this theme that he seems to address in the *Republic*: the nature of justice, the good of the human soul, the good of the political community, the good as such, and the possibility of knowledge, among others.

Such hopes regarding these documents, which have survived together in the manuscript tradition under the single heading *Epistolai* (*Epistles* or *Letters*), are, however, not likely to remain intact once we have begun to review the existing scholarship pertaining to them. The *Letters*, like the rest of the Platonic canon, has been scrutinized over the past two centuries by philologists, historians, and students of philosophy, all harboring grave doubts as to the authenticity of many of the texts that have been attributed to Plato since antiquity. For the most part, the *Letters* is now viewed as a motley collection of jewels and scraps from within and without Plato's literary estate—with considerable disagreement as to which are which. Its contents are seen as ranging from genuine Platonic private and open letters that were somehow preserved or retrieved to forgeries by counterfeiters writing centuries after Plato's death. Accordingly, while some of the letters seem to be inconsequential and utterly mundane, others have struck readers as being tinged with Platonic genius, bearing the marks of carefully constructed narratives, well-executed rhetorical or apologetic purposes, and subtle irony. Clearly, our assessment of whether and how the Platonic letters can be used as evidence of Plato's true views concerning philosophy and politics will hinge on our determination regarding the provenance and intended purpose of each or all of them.

It is my hope that the present volume will bring what has been until now a minority view concerning the *Letters* to the forefront of active debate, a view according to which the *Letters* would gain tremendous new importance for the study of Platonic political philosophy. According to this view, which I call the "literary unity thesis," the *Letters* is not at all

2. Consider Plato, *Apology of Socrates* 32a4–5; *Letters* 355c5–8; cf. Hobbes, *De cive*, Preface 11.

what it has seemed to most modern readers, but is rather a single work, written with a unity of purpose and coherent teaching, marked throughout by Plato's subtlety, artfulness, and political philosophic insight, and intended to occupy an important place in the Platonic corpus. The literary unity thesis posits that the *Letters* is something like an epistolary novel—though an unusual one to be sure—a manner of semi-fictional, semi-autobiographical literary experiment, and, for its time, a brilliant innovation of literary form. Most important among the implications of this thesis is that Plato decided to produce a text of which the purpose must be, at least in part, to provide his most demanding and attentive readers with some guidance in thinking more deeply about the practical difficulties that necessarily beset the philosophic political actor who would take his bearings by the claims made famous in the *Republic* and the *Laws*.

This volume is intended to advance a threefold strategy in the service of the literary unity thesis. To begin with, the present introductory essay will provide a review of the scholarly history pertaining to the Platonic letters so as to explain how such a strong critical prejudice has built up against what I take to be an undistorted view of the whole collection. Second is a new English translation of the *Letters*, prepared with a view to the student who wishes to assess the literary unity thesis. This means a highly literal translation that is scrupulous with respect to the consistent rendering of key words, and an apparatus consisting of hundreds of footnotes to supply background information ranging in subject matter from manuscript variants, to historical context, to indications of Platonic idioms or wordplay lost in translation. Third and most important is an interpretive essay that will attempt to bring out the political philosophic lessons revealed in the *Letters* when read and interpreted according to the literary unity thesis.

Indeed, the interpretive essay really has two intended purposes. Primarily, the point is to attempt to blaze an interpretive trail into what must seem in many ways uncharted literary territory, with the hope of discovering a new source of insight into Platonic political philosophy. In doing just this, however, I will also hope to demonstrate by deed that the *Letters* bears being read in accord with the literary unity thesis, and thus to offer that thesis the best possible support. Yet because the plausibility of this thesis is still so little acknowledged, there is need here at the start for some preliminary engagement with the prevailing views of the *Letters*, to survey and to understand the scholarly work that has been done thus far and to explain why conclusions reached and accepted by so many impressive and respectable readers of the Platonic corpus are in need of such radical revision.

Ancient Views of Plato's *Letters* and the Influence of Richard Bentley

The third-century CE biography of Plato by Diogenes Laertius remains the most important extant source of information on the Platonic canon in antiquity (Hackforth 1913, 1). By way of discussing two bygone librarians' attempts to order and organize Plato's works, Diogenes lists the thirty-six texts that, according to him, were held to comprise the Platonic corpus in his day. Included in one of the trilogies into which the third-century BCE librarian Aristophanes of Byzantium organized Plato's texts, and in one of the tetralogies arranged by the first-century BCE librarian Thrasyllus, was the *Letters*, a text comprising the same thirteen Platonic epistles contained in the best manuscripts extant today.[3] This strongly suggests that ancient readers of Plato considered the *Letters* to be a genuine article of Platonic writing deserving of careful philosophic study.[4] Both Cicero and, much later, Plutarch quoted freely from the *Letters* with evident confidence in its authenticity.[5] We may add to those

3. The individual epistles are identified by their addressees. It has been claimed that the number and identity of the epistles is noted only with respect to the Thrasyllean canon and that we cannot know whether the earlier catalog of Aristophanes contained the same collection (Hackforth 1913, 1–2; Morrow 1962, 5–6; Brisson 1993, 11–12; Burnyeat and Frede 2015, 17). But this seems to me a distortion of Diogenes's text. His enumeration of the letters, though it comes at the end of his discussion of the Thrasyllean tetralogies, is not specific to Thrasyllus but is rather Diogenes's own cataloging of the contents of the *Letters*. He gives us no reason to think that he knows of any question as to which epistles belong in the collection; on the contrary, by mentioning without further note that Aristophanes included the *Letters* in one of his trilogies, he implies that, to his knowledge, Aristophanes's text was the same as Thrasyllus's (just as we assume that Aristophanes's editions of the *Republic* and *Laws* contained ten and twelve books, respectively); evidently, this is also the opinion of Bentley (1838, 411). Were it otherwise, as Taylor noted, "we should have heard more about the matter" (1926, 16).

4. For another statement of this view, see Pangle 1987, 4n6. The fact that Aristophanes and Thrasyllus placed the *Letters* where they did in their arrangements of Plato's works could itself be seen as reflecting their endorsement of it as a single work of Platonic philosophy; see Dornseiff 1934, 223 and 225n1.

5. Morrow (1962, 5) notes another fifteen ancient authors, not mentioned here, who refer to Plato's *Letters*. In general, it seems that greater stock ought to be put in the judgment of ancient readers than is typical. Thus Harward: "Surely more attention should have been paid by the iconoclasts to the fact that the Epistles were read without suspicion by the Greek writers on style, Demetrios and others, who have referred to them, that Plutarch knew them intimately and treated them as a classic without feeling any doubt, and that a sceptic like Lucian quotes them with respect. . . . Cicero admired the 7th Epistle, was fond of the 9th, and evidently had

well-known examples the second-century CE Platonists Albinus and Alcinous, whose introductions to Platonic philosophy each treat the *Letters* as a Platonic work worthy of careful study, and the tenth-century Islamic philosopher al-Farabi, who describes the *Letters* as Plato's final work, in which he "gave an account of how to abolish the ways of life of nations and the corrupt laws that prevail in the cities, how to move the cities and nations away from them, and how to reform their ways of life" (1962, 70).[6]

It is common to trace the origins of suspicion regarding the *Letters* back to the *Dissertation upon the Epistles of Phalaris* written by Richard Bentley in 1697.[7] In proving the spuriousness of the collection of letters traditionally ascribed to Phalaris, a Sicilian Greek tyrant of the sixth century BCE, Bentley's tour-de-force display of philological acumen (from which the epistles of Phalaris have never recovered)[8] made two crucial contributions to the critical study of ancient epistolography. First, drawing upon a passing remark of the philosopher-physician Galen, Bentley identified an important age and motive for the forgery of documents under the names of famous authors: at the height of the competition for preeminence between them, the libraries of Pergamum and Alexandria "gave great rates for any treatises that carried the names

---

no suspicion of the others. He had studied Plato under the best Greek teachers, and was a good judge of a letter" (1932, 78).

6. Albinus 1865, 318; Alcinous 1865, 312–13. Al-Farabi's description of the *Letters* is reminiscent both of Alcinous's and of the description in the *Anonymous Prolegomena to Platonic Philosophy* (25.43–45).

7. Hackforth 1913, 3; Souilhé 1931, xviii n1; Syme 1972, 5; Burnyeat and Frede 2015, 7. Here and there, a doubt was expressed in the time before Bentley: (1) Most significant is a note in all the manuscripts of the *Letters*, which, according to all modern readers, reports the claim that the very short Letter Twelve is not by Plato, but the value of this note is doubtful (Hackforth 1913, 5; Dornseiff 1934, 225n1); recently, an elaborate argument specifically against the authenticity of Letter Twelve gave almost no weight to the authority of this note (Burnyeat and Frede 2015, 6, 19–25); Wohl (1998, 86) provides interesting speculation as to the note's origin (see also Howald 1923, 17ff.). It is my view that this note actually pertains to Letter Thirteen and not to Letter Twelve, but if anything this only further weakens any case built upon it; see my note ad loc. (2) The writer of the *Prolegomena to Platonic Philosophy* says that Proclus rejected the authenticity of the *Letters* on stylistic grounds, but this is of little importance, since it is said in the same breath that he rejected the *Republic* and *Laws* as well (26.5–9). (3) Lastly, Ficino thought Letter One had written by Dion (a view since refuted; see Hackforth 1913, 36n1; Harward 1932, 162; Bury 1929, 393; Brisson 1993, 7), and rejected Letter Thirteen outright, but cited no firm grounds for doing so. This leaves only Cudworth's rejection of Letter Thirteen in 1678 on the basis of an argument too lame to recapitulate here (see Hackforth 1913, 5), and roundly refuted by Bentley himself (1838, 409–13).

8. Rosenmeyer 2001, 195.

of celebrated authors" (1874, 78).[9] By teaching them the significance of this remark, Bentley has assisted generations of scholars seeking to allege the spuriousness of ancient texts—especially such relatively short and simple texts as letters tend to be—in their concoction of provenance hypotheses; forgers out to dupe the librarians for the sake of money, as well as students in the schools of rhetoric who, in subsequent centuries, were assigned to write speeches and letters in the voices of famous figures of antiquity (79, 583), have become the imagined authors of spuria hastily granted the imprimatur of librarians eager to incorporate "lost" works of famous writers into their exclusive collections. Second, Bentley's arguments not only set a standard of learning and rigor that subsequent generations of European classicists would strive to emulate;[10] they gave a blueprint for the demonstration of spuriousness that is still recognizable in contemporary scholarship. It is in fact hard to imagine that any attempt at this genre of criticism could be carried out with comparable force and influence—so much so, that it will be instructive to review Bentley's original procedure as a model, so that we may understand what would be required to establish the inauthenticity of part or all of the Platonic collection.

Bentley's proof of the spuriousness of the epistles of Phalaris proceeds in the following, meticulous way. First, he marshals every piece of evidence of which he is aware—which, as his exposition often provokes the reader to assume, must very nearly amount to every piece of evidence in existence—for the dates of Phalaris's birth and death and the general course of his life. He then advances his arguments, which we may group broadly into three categories. Most important are the arguments whereby Bentley identifies elements of the epistles that bespeak either a date of composition much later than Phalaris's death (i.e., an anachronism) or an author unacquainted with details Phalaris could not but have known. There are many examples of this: some epistles make use of words or phrases known to have taken on the intended meaning only centuries after Phalaris; others seem to mistake the geography of Sicily or fail to take note of its distinctive mode of currency; still others seem to be quoting from tragic or comic poetry, which, as Bentley seeks at great length to demonstrate, did not exist at all in

9. Galen, *In Hippocratis De natura hominis comm. III* 108–9. See Pangle (1987, 9) for a critique of Zeller's use of this same testimony of Galen; Bentley, in responding to a similar criticism leveled by his rival Boyle, gives a possible response (1874, 81–83).

10. See Wagner's 1874 introduction to the *Dissertations* (Bentley 1874, x)

Phalaris's day. But the most important argument from anachronism is that whereas Phalaris himself must have spoken Greek in the Doric dialect of his native land, the epistles bearing his name are written in (a rather late form of) Attic. "If we had wanted this argument," Bentley speculates in an earlier letter, "there had been nothing else to be done, but to let [the great defender of these epistles, William Temple,] enjoy his own opinion *sine rivali*" (1874, 582).

And yet, while they cannot have the same force to compel any reasonable mind, there are other arguments to be made: "In a disquisition of this nature, an inconsistency in time and place is an argument that reaches everybody. All will cry out that *Phalaris*, etc. are spurious, when they see such breaches upon chronology. But I must profess, I should as fully have believed them so though the writers had escaped all mistakes of that kind" (Bentley 1874, 560). Here, then, we may place the remaining two categories of argument. One type infers from evidence external to the text itself: had the epistles of Phalaris been extant in the centuries following his death, there are other authors whom we might expect to have referred to them, authors who spoke about the writings of tyrants or who tried to fix the age of the art of letter-writing. The absence of such references will seem, or can be made to seem, damning. But it is the category of argument I have reserved for last that is most subject to debate and controversy. These are the arguments contending that the style or diction of the text does not match the purported author's, or that what Bentley calls the "matter" it contains would not have been discussed thus or at all if they were genuine. Hence we have three modes of argument: from anachronism (or anatopism), from external evidence, and from style and matter.[11]

Where, then, do the epistles of Plato stand? It is significant that Bentley himself, who wrote further *Dissertations* claiming to prove the inauthenticity of the collections of letters attributed to Themistocles, the Socratics, and Euripides in like manner, saw nothing objectionable in our collection. In the words of J. Harward, "Bentley was prepared to pull down any idol: and no other scholar has had an equal knowledge of Greek epistolary literature," yet he actively *defended* the authenticity of the Platonic epistles (1932, 78).[12] But Bentley's seal of approval was powerless to protect the *Letters* from being swept up in the storm of

11. For similar categorizations of arguments concerning authenticity with different emphases, see Syme 1972, 4–13; Brisson 1993, 20–21; Lewis 2012, 68.

12. For his defense of Plato's *Letters*, see Bentley 1938, 409–13; 1874, 390, 465, 551.

scholarly suspicion that was to descend on the Platonic corpus some hundred years following, and greatly inspired by, his *Dissertations*. And aside from, or in addition to, the disfavor into which Thrasyllus's judgment regarding Plato's dialogues would precipitously fall, Bentley had shown how easily and how often forgers had succeeded in duping casual and scholarly readers for centuries on end by the production of spurious letter collections. By the nineteenth century, all letters purporting to have been penned by celebrated ancient Greek writers or statesmen were, as it seemed, presumed guilty of inauthenticity until proven innocent. Plato's were no exception.[13]

It must be noted that "the sceptical attitude in the extreme form in which it was held almost universally in Germany and England" (Harward 1932, 71) in the mid-nineteenth century is now generally seen as having been unduly harsh,[14] just as the pendulum is seen as having swung too far in the opposite direction with those who argued *for* authenticity in the first decades of the 1900s.[15] But it would be too much for our purposes here to attempt to trace the long and winding path of scholarly debate regarding the authenticity of the *Letters* through the twentieth century and up to the present day.[16] As will be evident, it suffices for us to take note of where there has been consensus, and where debate has continued to simmer and even to rage.

Prominent Arguments Concerning Provenance and Authenticity

We begin with the most important fact. No argument of the truly definitive type—which means, above all, argument from anachronism—has ever been leveled with any force or credibility: the *Letters* contains no references to people, events, or places about which Plato could never

13. This view concerning ancient letters has undergone some refinement, but remains in large part unquestioned. The most recent major study of Plato's *Letters* postulates that "there is reason to initially suspect letters and collections of letters as being spurious in a way in which there is no reason to suspect writings like dialogues or treatises" (Burnyeat and Frede 2015, 7). See also Syme 1972, 5.

14. See, e.g., Friedlander 1969, 236–37.

15. Harward 1932, 59–60; Morrow 1962, 9; Wohl 1998, 87n1; Lewis 2012, 68–69; Burnyeat and Frede 2015, 5–6; Kahn 2015. Hackforth (1913, 1–19) provides a good review of the history of the authenticity debate in the nineteenth and early twentieth centuries.

16. The literature is extremely voluminous. There are several helpful, recent lists and tables cataloging the major scholars who have been for or against authenticity of the whole collection or parts of it: Brisson 1993, 70; Huffman 2005, 42–43; Sanders 2008, 1–3n1; Altman 2012, 264n30; Burnyeat and Frede 2015, 100n6.

have known, and as for the collection's dialect and diction, "it is generally admitted by all scholars who have examined the letters from this point of view, that the language in which they are written is definitely the language of the fourth century" (Field 1930, 198).[17] Likewise, the known history of letter-writing can accommodate the existence of a genuine Platonic *Letters*: the extant letters of his contemporary and rival Isocrates, widely agreed to be genuine, confirm for us that Plato does not antedate the genre.[18]

As for external evidence against the *Letters*, arguments have been advanced, but they are characteristically inconclusive. The only ones to generate any sustained debate have been those that point to disagreements between the account of Sicilian history given in the *Letters* and those of some later historians, especially Diodorus Siculus and Cornelius Nepos.[19] The obvious difficulty with these arguments, however, is that a disagreement between two historical accounts tells us nothing more than that at least one of them must be wrong. There is no reason to privilege Diodorus and Nepos over the *Letters* (or Plutarch, who appears to draw heavily from the *Letters*); in fact, if the *Letters* is genuine, it would contain the only extant account from a source contemporary with the events it narrates, and so would have an important claim to greater authority. At any rate, the history in question is full of contentious issues that were bound to be presented in different lights by observers and participants on different sides, so that disagreement

17. See also Richards 1911, 271–72. Both Richards and Field are inclined to reject a number of the Platonic letters, but not on the grounds of any hard evidence such as anachronism.

18. See Harward 1932, 65–68. In any case, it is unclear that it would be of decisive importance even if we were to determine that no other genuine collection of letters had been preserved intact until long after Plato's death. This point has been made in recent debates about the *Letters*: "In the end, it simply does not follow that because—putting Plato's letters aside—we do not have any authentic *philosophical* letters before Epicurus, Plato's letters cannot be authentic" (Lewis 2017, 356; emphasis added). See also Dornseiff 1934, 226.

19. There is one other argument that may deserve mention under this heading: it has seemed suspicious to some that no known reference to Plato's *Letters* can be traced to any earlier date than that of the record made by Aristophanes of Byzantium, perhaps as much as 150 years following Plato's death (however, cf. Grote 1867, 132–69, 393–95n2; Souilhé 1931, vi). In particular, Gulley (1972, 110–12) finds it suspicious that Aristotle, despite a number of opportunities, never so much as mentions Plato's involvement in the Syracusan political drama that occupies most of the *Letters*. But even he concludes that, while he "consider[s] this *argumentum ex silentio* to have some weight," he does not think that it, or *any* of the arguments "drawn from the kind of external evidence" he reviews, can justify "any firm conclusion either in favour of, or against, the authenticity of the *Epistles*." Some interesting alternative explanations of Aristotle's silence are considered in the discussion of Gulley's essay by von Fritz (1971, 432–35).

among the historical accounts, including the lost accounts from which our later sources were derived, was inevitable.[20]

There is one specific argument falling under the heading of "external evidence" that must be mentioned because it is the only one to have produced truly widespread agreement. Letter One has been decried as spurious for longer and more consistently than any of the others, the main reason being that in it Plato says he had served under Dionysius at Syracuse as *autokratōr* (309b2-3)—evidently the title of a plenipotentiary political or military position—which fact is recorded nowhere else.[21] One could ask whether the argument outlined just above does not apply: Why should the inclusion of a detail in the *Letters*, even a major detail, not carry greater weight than its absence from later historical accounts?[22] Perhaps, however, the problem is not only the lack of external attestation: perhaps doubts about Letter One have arisen from misgivings about the very notion that Plato would have agreed to take on such a position in a tyrannical government. Is that what lies, for example, behind R. G. Bury's statement that "Plato *could never* have described himself as the 'sole Dictator' (*autokratōr*) of Syracuse" (1929, 393; emphasis added)?[23]

But here we enter the realm of "style and matter," wherein the question is always whether one believes that Plato *would have* or *could have* written such and such a letter given what we know about Plato independently of the letter in question. This is indeed the realm in which the vast majority of discussion and debate has taken place, and the outcome has provided confirmation through experience of what Bentley opined long ago—namely, that arguments of this kind cannot produce

---

20. The arguments in this paragraph summarize in extremely broad strokes the definitive study undertaken by Morrow, who examines each disagreement among the historical narratives and attempts to determine the lineage of sources from which the later histories were directly and indirectly derived, noting especially where the *Letters* itself appears to have influenced the later tradition (1962, 17-44). See also Brisson 1993, 16-19.

21. Hackforth 1913, 37; Post 1925, 130; Bury 1929, 393; Field 1930, 199; Souilhé 1931, lxxxvii; Burnyeat and Frede 2015, 5.

22. It must be noted that many doubters of Letter One cite its inconsistency not only with other sources but above all with the other Platonic letters, especially Letter Seven (Edelstein 1966, 133-34; Brisson 1993, 77; Morrow 1962, 191 [citing both Letter Three and Letter Seven]). Of course, one would need independent reasons for preferring one letter over another. But this takes us to the question of the *unity* of the *Letters*, which I address below.

23. Consider in this context the opinion of Field, who denies that "supposed incompatibilities of particular passages with some preconceived idea of Plato's character [are] of any real weight, considering that the letters are almost the only material we have for the formation of an idea of his character" (1930, 197).

firm and compelling conclusions regarding authenticity.[24] By way of elaboration, we highlight here two problems often encountered. First, how are we to evaluate passages in the *Letters* that, in style, phrasing, or substance, either echo or diverge from passages in Plato's dialogues? Does a similarity discovered between two texts indicate the work of a single hand or merely a forger's attempt at imitation? Does an obvious disagreement between a dialogue and a letter betray a forger's carelessness or a variation explicable only if the author had no fear of being discovered for an imposter? Hardly a piece of evidence of this kind has been advanced on one side without a critic on the other alleging that it is perfect proof of the opposite conclusion.[25] Second, our answer to the question whether Plato would or would not have written a given letter depends upon our understanding of what he *thought*. But we arrive at this understanding mainly by way of the notoriously difficult task of interpreting Plato's dialogues, which has been dividing his readers into hostile camps since antiquity.[26] Arguments from the style and matter of

---

24. Hence, Ledger: "The arguments *pro* and *contra* [the] epistles . . . are based mainly on exegetical uncertainties and personal preferences, not on any indubitable historical fact or incontrovertible philosophical principles. The assertions of stylistic merit, or lack of it, are just as wild and varied in this field as in that of any other of the dubious dialogues" (1989, 78).

25. On these issues, see Field 1930, 197; Solmsen 1969, 29–30; Syme 1972, 10. The paradox is articulated compellingly by Momigliano in his defense of Letter Seven: "We may remind ourselves that K. Latte persuaded many scholars by his observation that Sallust's letters are not authentic because they are so Sallustian. May we not suspect that the converse is also true, that Plato's *Letter 7* is authentic because it is so un-Platonic?" (1971, 61). Beginning with the likes of Campbell, Dittenberger, and Ritter in the late nineteenth century, classicists have attempted to make use of stylometric methods to remove any subjective elements from comparisons of Plato's style. The quantitative methods gradually became more involved, sophisticated, and sensitive to nuance, reaching a high-water mark with the nearly simultaneous, computer-assisted works of Ledger and Brandwood in 1989 and 1990, respectively, after which the stylometric approach faced a flurry of criticism (Howland 1991; Kahn 1992; Keyser 1992; Nehamas 1992; Nails 1993). Of the two, only Ledger takes up the question of the *Letters'* authenticity (as opposed to chronology; Brandwood 1990, ix). He examines the five longest letters, concluding that Letters Three, Seven, and Eight are stylistically very close to Plato's *Laws*, with Letters Two and Thirteen exhibiting such variation as could plausibly be explained by "peculiarity of subject and genre" (1989, 168–69). It is generally agreed that the other letters—perhaps all the letters but Letter Seven—are too short, and too different in form and purpose from the dialogues, to admit of this type of statistical analysis (Hackforth 1913, 16–17; Ledger, 78–79).

26. See Tigerstedt 1974 for a compendious review of interpretive debates since the Neoplatonists. The enigmatic character of Plato's writing is treated thoughtfully by Howland, who quotes the following anecdote from Olympiodorus: "When he [Plato] was about to die, he saw in a dream that he had become a swan and was going from tree to tree, and in this manner he caused the greatest trouble for the bird-catchers. Simmias the Socratic judged that Plato would elude those after him who wished to interpret him. For the interpreters who attempt to hunt out what the ancients had in mind are similar to bird-catchers, but Plato is elusive because it is possible to hear and understand his words in many ways, both physically, and ethically,

the *Letters*, then, are bound to persuade only those who are in agreement about the interpretation of Plato as a whole.[27] W. K. C. Guthrie's description of the situation more than four decades ago remains perfectly apt today: "Throughout the literature on the letters one is baffled by the way in which Dr *A* will recognize unmistakably 'the hand of the Master' in passages which to Dr *B* are trivial, absurd and quite unworthy of P[lato]" (1978, 402n1).[28]

Franz Dornseiff and the Idea of Literary Unity

We have seen that arguments against the authenticity of the *Letters* generally come down to highly debatable claims about Plato's philosophic and political outlook. Yet perhaps those inclined to athetize the *Letters* will seek to make progress along the following lines. Even if two readers disagree on which of the letters are "Platonic" in their style and content, will they not perhaps agree that, differing *from one another* as the various letters do, they cannot *all* be genuine? And if we can be sure that they are not *all* genuine, then the reliability of all those ancient witnesses who vouched for the whole collection, however astute they may have been, has been positively undermined.[29] Indeed, there have been

---

and theologically, and literally, just like those of Homer as well" (1991, 190). Cf. Plato, *Letters* 341b7–342a6; *Second Alcibiades* 147b7–c5; *Protagoras* 316d–e.

27. See, for example, the varied and conflicting views regarding the regimes of Plato's *Republic* and *Laws*, which are variously adduced to support or reject authenticity of one or more Platonic letters: Gulley 1972, 113ff.; Aalders and Wzn 1972, 151–52; De Blois 1979; Lewis 2000; Burnyeat and Frede 2015, 43ff.; Hull 2019.

28. See also Harward 1932, 59.

29. This tack is taken by Frede in the most recent major study of the *Letters*: Frede claims to demonstrate that Letter Twelve must be a forgery of the late second century BCE, and therefore cannot have been present in the collection of Aristophanes of Byzantium (Burnyeat and Frede 2015, 18ff.; cf. n. 3 above), and hence that we cannot trust Thrasyllus's judgment. The precariousness of this attempt, however, lies in the fact that Frede's whole approach to the *Letters* depends upon a few fine points, which may be, and have been, disputed or refuted (see Burnyeat and Frede 2015, 24–25, 90, 106n30, 107–8n37; Pappas 2017, 40–41). Bentley, for his part, was generally satisfied to show that some few members of a collection were spurious in order to conclude that the whole collection was tainted by association. Here we may take note of what has probably been the biggest departure from Bentley in the evaluation of authenticity in epistolary literature: according to the present view, in Morrow's words, "it is essential to recognize that each letter must be examined on its own merits, and its claims to authenticity must not be prejudiced by the manifest spuriousness of some of its companions in the collection" (1962, 13). Of course, as Morrow himself acknowledges, one still needs to consider the connections between the letters in a collection: in *some* cases, the genuineness or fraudulence of one will serve as evidence in the case of another (14; see also Field 1930, 198–99; Edelstein 1966, 121). But it may well be that attempts to save some of the Platonic letters while disavowing others have been more vulnerable to the argument I will sketch below than has

many scholarly allegations to the effect that the author of one letter has merely (and poorly) imitated another, or that some two letters give irreconcilable accounts of the same historical events.[30] As Ludwig Edelstein puts it in his momentous rejection of the whole *Letters*, "One fact emerges clearly from my brief analysis of the so-called Platonic letters: they do not form a unity. . . . For the Plato of the letters has a chameleonic personality" (1966, 156).

Often overlooked or forgotten, however, is the fact that Edelstein's denial that the *Letters* forms a unity is in direct response to an earlier scholar's claim that they *do*. During the first decades of the twentieth century, when debate over the authenticity of the *Letters* was at its most intense and prolific, the German classicist Franz Dornseiff advanced an astounding and original hypothesis in a short 1934 article entitled "Platons Buch 'Briefe'" ("Plato's Book, 'Letters'"). Dornseiff held that if one resists the critical injunction to treat each letter separately and instead "reads through the whole [*Letters*] in order" as we have it in the manuscripts, one finds that the apparently disparate epistles actually "play off one another" and contain "certain motifs that are methodically developed" over the course of the text (223–24). As the title of his article suggests, Dornseiff argues that the *Letters* was in fact "published as a book," the individual letters being either pieces of pure Platonic invention and hence fictional representations of events that may or may not have taken place in reality, or else versions of real letters Plato had sent in the past, heavily edited for adaptation to their new purpose (225). The thirteen letters, then, have been carefully arranged, not in chronological order or by addressee, but in accordance with a more complex plan whereby themes, motifs, and lessons are developed or juxtaposed to suit

---

generally been noted, and that in truth Lloyd is correct in his judgment that, given the "cross-references between them, or at least large groups of them, . . . the letters in question stand or fall together"—whether or not we, like Lloyd, conclude that they "probably fall" (1990, 159).

30. We can cite only a few of the more extensively debated examples here. We have already noted above the inconsistency that has been alleged between the claim in Letter One and the rest of the *Letters* (see nn. 21 and 22 above). The so-called "enigma" of Letter Two is often said to be a poor imitation of the philosophical digression of Letter Seven or of the religious conclusion to Letter Six (Hackforth 1913, 45–49; Bury 1929, 399–400; Field 1930, 200–201; Souilhé 1931, lxxx; Harward 1932, 165; Edelstein 1966, 134–38). Likewise, the discussion with Dionysius recalled in Letter Two has seemed to some incompatible with the timeline of events given in Letters Three and Seven (Field 1930, 199–200; Harward 1932, 166–68; Brisson 1993, 83). Finally, Plato's demeanor and relationship to Dionysius in Letter Thirteen have been thought inconsistent with what is indicated in the rest of the *Letters* (Bury 1929, 610; Souilhé 1931, lxvii–lxvviii; Edelstein 1966, 132–33; Brisson 1993, 276). See Edelstein for further examples and for a review of previous scholarly debates about them (1966, 121–55).

the author's various intentions.[31] Dornseiff was the first to postulate what I have called the "literary unity thesis."

For many years, Dornseiff's work did not receive the attention it deserved, but in the last few decades scholars have begun to recognize his perspicacity. There are now several studies postulating that the *Letters* has long been misunderstood by the great majority of its readers, that it forms a "corpus," a "unified whole" arranged with literary, philosophic, or didactic purpose—and this in spite of Edelstein's allegation of the author's "chameleonic personality."[32] But those who claim to have discovered some connecting threads running through the *Letters* tend to stay away from the authenticity debate. Each finds the appropriate moment to announce his or her educated guess—that the text is a genuine work of Plato, or a post-Platonic piece of pseudepigraphy, or else the production of some redactor drawing entirely, partly, or not at all from Plato's real correspondence—but focuses primarily on the considerable task of interpretation.[33] That is, the literary unity thesis has been found by its various proponents to be compatible with each of several different answers to the question of authorship. It does not depend on any particular view regarding the *Letters*' authenticity. What is more, the proof of the pudding is necessarily in the eating: it is the careful examination and literary or philosophic analysis of the *Letters* taken together that reveals its unity. And with so much pudding to eat, most lack the time to engage in lengthy speculations as to the identity of the chef.

---

31. On the ordering of the *Letters*, see also Morrison 2013, 112–14.

32. The first to pick up the thread from Dornseiff was Holzberg (1986, 30–31; 1994, 7–8). Others include Pangle (1987, 4n6), Wohl (1998), Christy (2010, 20–60), Altman (2012, 259–75), and Morrison (2013). Strauss (2001, 585–86) appears to have come to the same conclusion on his own, but never published on this subject. Harward (1932, 64–65), writing before Dornseiff, suggests a precedent for viewing the *Letters* as "something in the nature of a 'Briefroman'" in the nineteenth-century studies of Sauppe and Susemihl, but he does not give precise references. Perhaps he has in mind Sauppe 1866, 890–91 and Susemihl 1891, 281–85.

33. For example, Altman (2012, 45n38) thinks the *Letters* was written by Plato himself, Christy (2010, 30–34) postulates that the *Letters* "grew up around" the central Letter Seven as an attempt to strengthen the defense of Plato's political activity at Syracuse (see Szlezak 2019, 262n2 for a similar idea), and Wohl (1998, 87n1) remains agnostic; see also Morrison (2013), who declines to engage in the debate over authenticity, but believes that the *Letters* is thoughtfully composed and can teach us about the genre of the epistolary novel. Dornseiff himself, though his conviction never wavered regarding the *Letters*' unity and literary character, eventually changed his mind about its authorship. In 1939, he wrote that the *Letters* was more likely to have been written by a member of the Academy around 300 BCE than by Plato himself. But the point is that Dornseiff still saw in the *Letters* the intentional work of a single author. The identity of the author is a separate question, and Dornseiff's reasons for changing his mind are as disputable as the question of authenticity must always be: whether Plato could have written the *Letters* depends on who Plato was and what he thought.

Partly because of this, growing interest in the possibility of the *Letters*' literary unity has not impacted the authenticity discussion, which still proceeds according to the precept that, to begin with at least, each letter must be examined and evaluated on its own.[34] Hence, in the course of their assessments of authenticity, scholars sometimes note Dornseiff's or Niklas Holzberg's opinion that the *Letters* constitutes a *Briefroman*, only to dismiss it.[35] The flimsiness of these denials on the part of so many competent researchers can only be attributed to a stubborn inertia in the discussions of authenticity stretching back as far as Bentley: by now, it has long been taken as gospel that a collection of epistles purported to be from the fourth century BCE can consist of only two things, authentic letters or imitations thereof. The literary unity thesis can be rebuffed with perfect equanimity, it is made to seem, because there is no evidence that the genre of the epistolary novel had become popular even by Cicero's time, much later than even the latest proposed dates of composition for any part of the *Letters* (Harward 1932, 64–65).

Dornseiff recognized the challenge to reigning orthodoxies that the adoption of his view must entail: "That such a cyclically ordered book, with parts from different fictitious drafting dates, existed as early as 350 B.C. is indeed important for the history of literary forms" (1934, 226). Yet he maintains that this is the most plausible explanation, and the only way "to save the phenomena," once one has recognized the character and unity of the work (226). Thus Dornseiff concludes that the *Letters* was "probably Plato's last publication and shows his literary-artistic enterprising power still at its full height" (225). And is it, after all, so great a stretch to think that the greatest literary innovator in the history of philosophy produced one last, grand stylistic innovation? Indeed, the authenticity debate has been focused for so long on fine points of language or Platonic doctrine that many have lost sight of the most significant problems—problems that are immediately solved if these letters were written by Plato. Take, for example, the recent conclusion of Myles Burnyeat who claims that the author of Letter Seven, despite being "philosophically incompetent" and therefore not Plato, should nonetheless be "hail[ed] . . . as a distinctive, original, and interesting creative mind" who "borrowed the idea of a tragedy in prose" from Plato's *Laws* "to make a tragedy in epistolary form out of Plato's

34. The most recent major treatment of the question of authenticity (Burnyeat and Frede 2015) never even mentions the possibility that the *Letters* could be read as a literary whole.

35. E.g., Edelstein 1966, 121; Friedlander 1969, 236.

own life" (Burnyeat and Frede 2015, 136–37).[36] One reviewer, otherwise persuaded by Burnyeat's argument, has felt compelled to raise the question "Who *is* that masked writer," the "astonishing figure who invented autobiographical correspondence and who all but invented the prose tragedy," and who seems to have understood the nuanced distinctions between the political philosophy of the *Republic* and *Laws* better than any reader of Plato until the nineteenth century (Pappas 2017, 45)? Is attribution of the letter to Plato himself not by far the most parsimonious and credible explanation in this regard?[37]

The same goes, indeed, for the rest of the *Letters*. As Harward has put it, "If [the Platonic Epistles] are not genuine, we can only account for their existence by crediting their author with a dramatic power which is not likely to have been found at that age except in a writer of original genius. . . . Those who think it likely that such a work as the 3rd Platonic Epistle issued from a school of rhetoric at that period, or was produced by an unknown rhetorician, show a want of literary perception which is remarkable in scholars of taste and ability" (1932, 69). Likewise, L. A. Post: "The writer of the Platonic Epistles must have been the greatest historical novelist that ever lived, and that while unknown to fame, or else no other than Plato" (1925, 61). As for Edelstein's breezy rejection of Dornseiff on the grounds of the variety of personalities Plato appears to assume in the various letters, it seems quite to miss the point. Edelstein pretends to consider the literary unity thesis but fails to consider how much it must change the way we approach the question of authenticity. If we are to evaluate the hypothesis that the whole *Letters* has been constructed as a dramatic fiction (however much it may draw from real events), then we must treat the author's apparently "chameleonic personality" as a literary device whereby the book's protagonist, "Plato," is presented in varying circumstances and hence from a variety of perspectives. Edelstein continues to think in terms of historical criticism when the task is one of literary-philosophic interpretation. Here again, Post is helpful: "Plato has several tones; the rhythm of his utterance varies

---

36. Burnyeat and Frede's conclusions regarding Letter Seven remain the most important and authoritative recent contribution to the authenticity debate. See Price 2016, 453; Pappas 2017, 39–40.

37. Certainly, this is the view of Momigliano: "We do not know of any autobiographical letter comparable to Plato's *Seventh Letter* before Plato. I am reluctant to admit that forgery preceded reality in the matter of autobiographical letters. The letter seems to me an exceptional creation by an exceptional man, namely Plato" (1971, 60–61).

with his moods. An analysis of the rhythms in the *Letters* and in the *Laws* shows how individual Plato's later style was" (1925, 5).

The fact is that if one really takes the time to consider the interpretive possibilities concerning the *Letters* that open up under the literary unity thesis, one begins to wonder whether there is *any* serious question in the authenticity debate that does not collapse into irrelevance.[38] For instance, one important critique against those who would defend the *Letters* as containing the genuine remains of Plato's correspondence concerns the means of the letters' preservation: How, why, and by whom would copies of these particular epistles have been kept and, later, collected?[39] This problem, of course, disappears entirely under the literary unity thesis—Plato himself assured the preservation of the *Letters* along with the rest of his corpus. Still more to the point is the fate of arguments derived from stylistic or substantive comparisons between the letters. Parallel passages in two different letters need no longer raise suspicions of imitation: it is only natural that Plato should have returned to key themes over the course of the work, creating intratextual references that connect the individual letters to one another. Nor should it deter us to find the same theme, event, or person treated differently in different places. Just as the utterances of Plato's Socrates must always be interpreted with a view to the context, such as the characters to whom he speaks and the concerns that motivate the conversation, so by having the letters directed to a variety of addressees in a variety of scenarios does Plato require that we examine the content of each letter in *its* own context.[40] By triangulating from the disparate perspectives afforded to us in the *Letters*, we may be able to grasp Plato's true view of a subject, the view that would cause him to characterize things one way to one correspondent in a given circumstance and otherwise to others in others.[41]

---

38. Dornseiff (1934, 225) made exactly this point with respect to the debate taking place in his own day, particularly that between Egermann and Hell.

39. Among those who raise this concern, which probably does not receive enough attention from the *Letters'* defenders, are Bury (1929, 390–91), Field (1930, 198–99), and Burnyeat and Frede (2015, 15). Harward's (1932, 69–70) is the best attempt at a response.

40. See Dornseiff: "[Plato] now represents himself, for the first time, dialogically, albeit in a one-sided dialogue, just as he had represented Socrates dialogically throughout his life" (1934, 225).

41. Moreover, readers who have made the attempt to interpret the *Letters* as a work worthy of careful attention tend also to find effective rebuttals to the many arguments against authenticity focusing on the wording or content of specific passages. To give only one example, consider that even the problematic passage in Letter One noted above (see n. 21), on account of which the letter is all but universally maligned, becomes merely an interpretive puzzle, and

There must be some concern over the difficulty of falsifying such a thesis. How are we to distinguish between two letters of different provenance, on one hand, and two chapters of an epistolary novel written in different tones and making incompatible claims for the sake of an unspecified literary or didactic purpose, on the other? It is precisely here that, as we have already noted, there is no proof but in the pudding. Any assertion of the literary unity thesis must stand or fall with the particular interpretation of the *Letters* it accompanies. But what we have been at pains to argue here is that, despite the impression one would receive from the existing literature, there is *nothing that precludes* the consideration of our thesis as a serious possibility, and indeed much that recommends it. A crucial element of what Dornseiff saw in 1934 was that the idea of an epistolary novel with Plato as the semi-fictional protagonist was perfectly Platonic:

> Is this so psychologically convoluted for a writer who, in every other one of his writings, hides himself to a great extent in the background, as only Homer before in all of Greek literature had done? Likewise here, then, he once more built a new kind of wall around himself, so that even after reading [the *Letters*] no one could say, "Now I have read a writing by Plato himself, in which he speaks to every reader ex cathedra." (226)

It is therefore precisely when we cease naively to presume that the *Letters* can only be authentic if the letters are themselves naive Platonic self-representations that we recognize how profoundly Platonic a text we have before us. Arnaldo Momigliano, in his defense of Letter Seven, has captured the crucial point with penetrating force:

> The Socratics were infuriating in their own time. They are still infuriating in our time. They are never so infuriating as when approached from the point of view of biography. We like biography to be true or false, honest or dishonest. Who can use such terminology for Plato's *Phaedo* or *Apology*, or even for Xenophon's *Memorabilia*? . . . The fact we have to face is that biography acquired a new meaning when the Socratics moved to that zone between truth and fiction which is so bewildering to the professional historian. We shall not understand what biography was in the fourth

---

by no means intractable, to proponents of the literary unity thesis: Wohl 1998, 67–68; Christy 2010, 33–34; Altman 2012, 267.

> century if we do not recognize that it came to occupy an ambiguous position between fact and imagination. Let us be in no doubt. With a man like Plato . . . this is a consciously chosen ambiguity. The Socratics experimented in biography, and the experiments were directed towards capturing the potentialities rather than the realities of individual lives. (1971, 46)

It is a strong mark in favor of the literary unity thesis that scholars who otherwise refuse or neglect to entertain it, including Momigliano, often acknowledge or adopt its key premises. Bury, for example, in dealing with the much-discussed question of Letter Seven's intended audience, considers it "probable"

> that not only is this letter an "open" letter addressed rather to the general public than to the parties named in the superscription, but that superscription itself is merely a literary device. The letter was never meant to be sent to Sicily at all. . . . So that what Plato is doing in this letter is to indulge in a literary fiction which enables him to publish in epistolary form what is at once a history, an apology and a manifesto. (1929, 473–74)[42]

If this can be imagined of one particular letter, why not of the whole collection? Only a bona fide attempt to interpret the whole *Letters* together, as a literary unity, can determine whether the text can bear such an interpretation.

The Story and Structure of the *Letters*

The *Letters* is unique in the Platonic corpus—indeed, it may be unique in the whole history of philosophic literature. However comfortable we may have become in the world of Plato's dialogues, however accustomed to its characters and formulas, to the tone and rhythm of its conversations, we are in bewildering new territory in the *Letters*. It is helpful, therefore, even before turning to the text itself, to orient oneself by taking a survey of the whole work, in an attempt to understand its basic structure and to acquaint oneself with the people, places, and events to which the text regularly refers. What follows is intended to provide the reader with just such an orientation, but no more. I present my own, lengthy attempt to

42. See also Heidel 1976, 28–29.

interpret the *Letters* only after the translation, in order to encourage the reader first to study and think about the text independently.

The thirteen letters in the collection vary greatly in length. Eight of them (Letters One, Four, Five, Six, Nine, Ten, Eleven, and Twelve) are less than 425 words long; four more (Letters Two, Three, Eight, and Thirteen) are between 1,200 and 1,700 words; at some 8,800 words, Letter Seven dwarfs the others. In fact, the first six letters taken together and the last six taken together each comes out to just about half the length of the seventh. The arrangement of the *Letters* thus presents a pleasing and intriguing symmetry: Letter Seven, flanked on either side by four short and two longer letters, occupies the central half of the whole work. But the *Letters'* centerpiece commands our attention for reasons more interesting than its length and position. Letter Seven is something of a literary masterpiece unto itself—complex, layered, and sometimes tortuous—and has enjoyed the most durable reputation for authenticity of all the Platonic letters. Moreover, owing to the wealth of autobiographical details it contains, in addition to a famous "philosophic digression" that appears to elucidate Plato's famous theory of the Forms, Letter Seven has received by far the most scholarly attention of any of the Platonic letters.

More important still, Letter Seven could be said to contain a road map to the *Letters* as a whole. Out of the thirteen letters, ten deal directly or indirectly with Plato's connection to the political drama that unfolded in the major Sicilian city of Syracuse in the first half of the fourth century BCE—a drama that culminated in a chaotic and destructive civil war. The Syracusan story line thus dominates the *Letters*, and Letter Seven is largely structured around Plato's autobiographical narration of his long relationship, spanning some three decades, with the two men who would eventually become the major antagonists in the struggle over the regime: the hereditary tyrant Dionysius the Younger and the tyrant's uncle Dion. The historical and other contextual information offered by Letter Seven, then, provides a way for us to get our bearings with respect to the chronology, characters, subject matter, and significance of most of the other letters.

It is therefore possible for us to extract a helpful narrative from Letter Seven. But we wish to do so in a way that imports a bare minimum of historical and biographical information from other sources. For we are seeking to understand the story told by the *Letters* itself; other accounts, *especially* where they supplement or contradict the details provided in the *Letters*, threaten to confuse matters by distracting us from what is internal to Plato's text. In the summary account that follows here, then, we are informed by such outside sources only in regard to the dates of, and corresponding lengths of time between, Plato's visits.

Plato made three trips to Sicily. It was during his first visit, at the age of forty, that Plato encountered a twenty-year-old Syracusan named Dion, brother-in-law to Dionysius the *Elder*, who was then still the ruler of Syracuse (324a–b). From this fateful meeting in about 387 BCE, Dion became a zealous proponent of Plato's moral and political teachings (327a–c). Twenty years later, when Dionysius the Elder was succeeded by his son, Dionysius the Younger (and Plato was now sixty years of age), Dion called upon Plato to return to Syracuse as the new tyrant's tutor and adviser, evidently in hopes of realizing the dream of philosopher-kingship or something like it—an idea made famous by Plato's *Republic*, which had in all likelihood been written and published by this time (327c–328a). Despite some misgivings, Plato decided to accept the invitation and journeyed to Syracuse for the second time (328b–329b). But slanderers in Dionysius's court whispered in the tyrant's ear of conspiracy between Dion and Plato, and Dion was exiled to the Peloponnesus in the fourth month following Plato's arrival (329b–c). Dionysius at first compelled Plato to remain, but when Syracuse went to war with Carthage, the two men settled upon terms for Plato's and Dion's future recall to Syracuse, and Plato was at last allowed to go home to Athens (329d–e, 338a–b).

About half a decade later, Plato now being older than sixty-five, Dionysius's summons for Plato to return again to Syracuse came riding a wave of reports that the young tyrant was consumed with desire for philosophy (338b–c). In response, Plato departed in 361 BCE on his third and final journey to Sicily with the intention of "testing" Dionysius's purported passion for philosophy; but their relationship deteriorated further following Plato's arrival, and Plato incurred the tyrant's ill will by repeatedly taking sides against him—especially in regard to the status of the still-exiled Dion and of his highly valuable estate, which was under Dionysius's control (340b–341a, 346a–349e). Having fallen into clear and dangerous disfavor, not only with the tyrant but also with some of his angry mercenaries, Plato engineered his escape from the city, in which he had been trapped for about a year, with the help of Archytas, ruler of the nearby city of Tarentum, whose friendly relations with the Syracusan court Plato had orchestrated on his previous visit (350a). In the final episode recounted in Letter Seven, Plato and Dion crossed paths at Olympia, evidently on the occasion of the

Olympic games of 360 BCE: Plato was on his way home to Athens, but Dion, having at last run out of patience with Dionysius, had in mind a homecoming of a different and defiant kind (350b–c). He invited Plato to join him on a campaign to march on Syracuse and depose the tyrant. But Plato would have no part in the revolution (350c–d). Dion did succeed in overthrowing Dionysius, only to be assassinated in the following months by a pair of brothers he had befriended in Athens during his exile and whom he had brought with him on his campaign against Dionysius (333d–334a).

This sketch of Plato's dealings in Syracuse, taken from Letter Seven, brings the arrangement of the whole *Letters* more clearly into focus. The first four Platonic letters belong to the period following Plato's third and final return from Syracuse to Athens. In Letter One, Plato writes briefly and stormily to Dionysius, chastising the tyrant for having treated him so shabbily. In Letter Two, he writes to Dionysius again, but this time at greater length and with much greater goodwill: although there are signs that Dionysius is catching wind of Dion's tyrannicidal machinations, it seems in Letter Two that the embers of Dionysius and Plato's relationship are still glowing rather more than we might have expected. In Letter Three, however—yet another letter to Dionysius—those embers have more or less been extinguished: Dionysius has evidently denounced Plato as the mastermind behind Dion's plot to overthrow the Syracusan dynasty, and Plato writes vigorously in his own defense. Letter Four is from Plato to Dion himself, ostensibly in the midst of Dion's initial success in deposing Dionysius.

Letters Five and Six form a kind of digression from the narrative of Plato's affairs in Syracuse. In Letter Five, Plato writes to the young Perdiccas, ruler of Macedon, with some political counsel and a recommendation to take on Plato's associate Euphraeus as an adviser. In Letter Six, he writes jointly to Hermias, ruler of Atarneus, and two of Plato's own students who live in the vicinity of Atarneus, in an attempt to establish a mutually beneficial friendship between the three of them. In Letter Seven we return to Syracuse, but the setting is now the dark period following Dion's assassination. Plato writes in reply "to the intimates and comrades of Dion," that is, to the anti-tyrannical party carrying on the fight for Dion's political vision in the ongoing Syracusan civil war, who have apparently sent to Plato to ask him to aid in their cause. The long and complex Letter Seven is quite obviously meant to serve more purposes than just Plato's reply to this request. Letter Eight, however, *also* addressed to the "intimates and comrades of Dion," is rather more to the point in this regard. Plato does his best here to counsel the Syracusans as to how they might put an end to their suffering and woe.

After Letter Eight, the *Letters* no longer follows such a neat trajectory. Four brief and varied letters now follow, which (like Letters Five and Six) we cannot so easily place on the timeline of events in Syracuse. Letter Nine is addressed to Archytas, the philosophic ruler of Tarentum, whom Plato had put on friendly terms with Dionysius during his time in Sicily; Letter Ten, the shortest in the collection, is a note to a companion of Dion's whom Plato has never met; Letter Eleven is a response to a man named Laodamas, who has invited Plato to help in the founding of a new colony; and Letter Twelve is another to Archytas, briefer still and more puzzling than Letter Nine.

Letter Thirteen, which is prefixed in all the manuscripts with a note denying Plato's authorship, concludes the *Letters* with a flabbergasting return to the Syracusan drama. This letter, addressed to "Dionysius, Tyrant of Syracuse," evidently belongs to the months immediately following Plato's *second* visit to Syracuse, which is to say his *first* stint as prospective teacher of Dionysius the Younger. Whereas all the other letters pertaining to Plato's activity in Syracuse had followed Plato's *final* departure, this one belongs to a much more active and apparently hopeful period of his relationship to Dionysius. What the reader learns in this letter will cast much of what has preceded in a new light. The *Letters* thus shares with so many of Plato's works that charming quality of making the reader think, just when a first study of the text has been completed, that all this has only been the necessary preparation to study the text anew.

Plato's Letters

Letter One

309a Plato to Dionysius:[1] Do well![2]

---

1. Plato writes to Dionysius the Younger (c. 397–343 BCE), who took over the tyranny of Syracuse upon his father's death in 367 and ruled for ten years until being ousted by Plato's zealous disciple Dion. Letters One, Two, Three, and Thirteen are all addressed to this Dionysius, and the whole *Letters* revolves around the events arising out of Plato's relationships with Dionysius and Dion. Letter Seven in particular famously provides a long and detailed account of Plato's activities in Syracuse, and may be consulted for the sake of giving context to many of the other letters. For a brief summary, see the last section of the introduction, above.

2. This greeting, which appears to have been peculiar to Plato (see Lucian, *Pro lapsu inter salutandem* 4; Diogenes Laertius 3.61), opens each of the thirteen letters except the third, which instead begins with a discussion of the greeting (see also 339b8–c2, 352b1–4, 360a1–4). (To Dornseiff [1934, 223], this is a sign of the *Letters*' artful composition.) No English translation captures the ambiguity of the Greek *eu prattein*: it is unclear whether Plato bids his addressees to "do good," i.e., to "act well" in a moral sense, or rather to "fare well" in the sense of "to prosper." Harward suggests the salutation "covers the two meanings" (1932, 163n1; cf. Morrow 1962, 191n2; Post 1925, 139n1). A kind of reflection on this ambiguity is contained in Plato's *Alcibiades* (116b2–d6); see also *Charmides* 171e7–172a3; *Gorgias* 507b8–c7; *Republic* 353e1–9 and 621d2–3; Xenophon, *Oeconomicus* 11.8; Aristotle, *Nicomachean Ethics* 1095a14–22; *Politics* 1325a34–b21.

After I had been occupied[3] for such a long time with you[4] and had become most trusted of all in managing your rule,[5] you were receiving the benefits while I was enduring the slanders, which were vexatious.[6] For I knew that it would not seem as though I had gone along with you in any of the more brutal things that were done; for all those
309b taking part in the regime with you are my witnesses, many of whom I fought alongside, relieving them of no small losses. But, having often kept guard over your city as a ruler with full powers,[7] I was sent away more dishonorably than would be proper if you were dispatching a vagrant and directing him to sail away after having been occupied for so long a time with you. I, therefore, will henceforth deliberate in a less humane[8] way concerning myself, whereas you,[9] "being such a tyrant, will dwell alone."[10]

---

3. The first word of the *Letters* following the salutation is *diatripsas,* the aorist participle of *diatribein,* "to be occupied." It refers to one's spending time in something, but can range in meaning from the negative sense "to waste time" or "to lose time" to the more neutral "to be busy" with something, and even the more specific "to be engaged in teaching" (see Burnyeat and Frede 2015, 147–49). Plato marks the significance of this word by making it begin the *Letters*: the question of Plato's habitual "occupation" or "pastime," and of why he "spent so much time" in Syracuse, is thematic. I have generally used some form of the word "occupy" to translate forms of this word, indicating exceptions in footnotes.

4. Plato employs the second-person plural for the first several lines of the letter, up to and including "spent so much time with you" at 309b5. It should be noted that this is not a sign of formality or deference in Greek, but a true plural: "The Greek address system contains no trace of any type of T/V distinction. There is only one 2sg. pronoun, *sú*; its plural, *humeîs*, is never used for a singular addressee in ordinary language" (Dickey 1997, 7). See Morrow 1962, 162; Souilhé 1931, n. 3 ad loc.; Bury 1929, 395n2.

5. "Rule" translates *archēn,* which can range in meaning from "office" to "empire," or, in other contexts, "origin" or "beginning."

6. Or "disgusting," "hard to take" (*duschereis*). The word is not related to *aganaktō,* which is the word I have elsewhere translated with forms of the verb "to be vexed," but rather to *duscherainō,* which I have consistently translated by the verb "to be disgusted."

7. "Ruler with full powers," here and throughout the *Letters,* translates the single word *autokratōr*; see the introduction for the significance of the claim Plato makes here.

8. "Less humane" is an attempt to split the difference between the possible readings of *apanthrōpoteron*—literally "further from human," but this could mean "more *in*human" as in "crueler" or "more misanthropic," "more unsocial." The line appears to be the source of a tradition that held Plato to have been misanthropic and solitary (Harward 1932, 163n3; Brisson 2004, 79n6).

9. Here and for the rest of the letter, Plato switches to the second-person singular.

10. "Apparently a 'tag' from some tragedy" (Bury 1929, 395n2). Harward suggests the lost drama from which this line appears to be quoted may also have been the source of the phrase "in a less humane way" (*apanthrōpoteron tropos*) (1932, 163n3).

309c As for the shining gold, which you gave in dispatching me, Bacchius,[11] the bearer of this letter, is bringing it to you; for it wasn't even sufficient as a travel allowance, nor was it advantageous as any other means of livelihood, since it would occasion the greatest disrepute for you, the giver, and not much less for me, too, the receiver—wherefore I do not accept it. But it is clear that to receive or to give such an amount makes no difference to you, so take it back and tend to some other one of your comrades 309d as you did to me; for I myself have been sufficiently tended to by you.

And it is a propitious moment for me to quote the saying of Euripides, that when other problems someday converge upon you,

You will pray to have such a man standing by you.[12]

And I wish to remind you why the majority of the other tragedians, too, whenever they bring forward a tyrant being put to death by someone, make him shout:

310a Bereft of friends, O woeful me, I perish!

Not one has made him perish for a scarcity of gold. And this poem doesn't seem bad to those who have intellect:

It is not glittering gold that is scarcest in the life of mortals, hard of hope;
Nor does adamant, nor do couches of silver, set before a human being, upon inspection, dazzle the sight;
Nor are the fertile fields of the broad earth, when laden with crops adequate
As is the intellect of good, like-minded men.

310b Be strong,[13] and recognize how greatly you have erred with us, so that you may bear yourself better toward others.

---

11. We know nothing of this Bacchius. His name is reminiscent of the name "Dionysius," in that Bacchus was another name for the god Dionysus.

12. The verse and all the others to follow are unattested outside of this letter.

13. This is the literal translation of a valediction so common it is often translated simply "farewell." It also occurs at the end of Letter Ten (358c7) and near the end of Letters Two (314c4) and Thirteen (363c9).

Letter Two

Plato to Dionysius: Do well!

I heard from Archedemus[1] that you hold not only that I ought to keep quiet concerning you, but also that my associates ought to keep from 310c doing or saying anything nasty concerning you—but that you make an exception for Dion only.[2] But this statement,[3] "Dion is an exception,"

1. This Archedemus, not to be confused with any other from Greek history (e.g., Archedemus of Pelekes, of Athens, or of Tarsus), is known only from the *Letters*. We are to learn later in this letter that he is serving as letter carrier and go-between for the present epistolary exchange (313d–e), and in later letters we learn of other important roles he played in Plato's Syracusan drama (319a, 349d). He appears to have been an associate of Archytas (339a–b), himself an important figure in the *Letters* (see n. 86 to Letter Seven below).

2. Dion of Syracuse (408–354 BCE), a brother-in-law of Dionysius the Elder, is a character of central importance in the *Letters*. He is the addressee of Letter Four, and his "intimates and comrades"—those who carried the torch of Dion's political vision after he was assassinated—are the addressees of Letters Seven and Eight. The *Letters* may be said to revolve around Dion's ardent hopes of bringing the Syracusan regime into alignment with the principles of Platonic philosophy. For a brief overview of his role in the drama of the *Letters*, see the summary of Letter Seven presented in the opening section of the introduction.

3. "Statement" translates the first instance in the *Letters* of the Greek word *logos*. *Logos* generally refers in some way to the human capacity for reasoned speech, and can mean "reason," "speech," "language," or "reckoning"—in each case, either as a faculty or as a specific instance of its use, such as the "statement" referred to here—as well as "account," "argument," and "definition," among other things. The word is too common and multifaceted to be rendered

signifies that I do not rule my associates.[4] For if I were thus ruling the others, and you, and Dion, then would there be more good things for us and all the other Greeks, as I claim. As it is, I myself am great by rendering myself a follower of my own reason. And I say these things on the grounds that Cratistolus and Polyxenus[5] have said nothing sound to
310d you—one of whom, they say, says that he heard many of those with me accusing[6] you at Olympia. Now, perhaps he hears more keenly than I do, for I did not hear it. But it seems to me that, in the future, you ought to do as follows: whenever someone says some such thing about anyone among us, send me a note to ask. For I shall neither shrink from, nor be ashamed of, speaking the truth.

Well then, here is how things happen to stand for you and me with respect to each other. To no one among the Greeks, so to speak, are we
310e ourselves unknown, nor is our intercourse being passed over in silence. Let it not escape your notice that it will not be passed over in silence in the time to come either—such are those who are getting news of it, given that it came to be no short time ago, and not without commotion. Well then, why do I say this? I will say, beginning from the top.

By nature, practical wisdom[7] and great power come together in the same place, and they always pursue and seek each other and come to be together. And then, human beings also enjoy both conversing about

---

consistently throughout; I have used the word "speech" to translate it wherever possible, but also "reason," "account," "argument," "definition," "word," and in this case only, "statement."

4. The meaning here is not very clear. This letter probably belongs to the period of time during which Dion is planning or executing his assault on Syracuse (cf. the reference to "Olympia" at 310d1 with the story Plato tells at 350b6–351e4). "Dion is an exception" suggests that Dionysius does not expect Plato to be able or obligated to restrain Dion.

5. This is the only known mention of Cratistolus. Polyxenus is mentioned again at the end of this letter (314c7) and in Letter Thirteen, where we learn that he was a pupil of the sophist Bryson (360c5).

6. Reading *katēgorountōn* ("accusing") with the best manuscripts. Burnet and Souilhé both prefer *kakēgorountōn* ("speaking ill of"), which differs by only a letter and is suggested as an emendation by a second hand above the line in manuscript O. Souilhé also cites the later manuscripts Z and V as containing his preferred reading, but from my examination he appears to be mistaken in the former case. Neither Burnet nor Souilhé notes that, e.g., the fifteenth-century manuscripts L, e, and f all, like A, give only *katēgorountōn*, with no suggested emendation.

7. "Practical wisdom" translates the Greek word *phronēsis*, which is traditionally rendered in English as "prudence." It is to be distinguished from *sophia*, "wisdom" as such, i.e., from the primary object of *philosophia* ("love of wisdom"). My choice of the phrase "practical wisdom" is thus meant to suggest a distinction from "theoretical wisdom." Yet *phronēsis* has as its root a word related to "mind" and "thought" (cf. *phrēn*, *phronein*). It generally refers to the possession of that knowledge and good sense that enable one to direct private or political affairs successfully toward a given end. Consider Aristotle, *Nicomachean Ethics* 6.5–8; and cf. [Plato], *Definitions* 411d5–7 with 414b5–9; see also Strauss 1952, 148n2.

these themselves and hearing others do so, both in private intercourse 311a and in poems. For example, whenever human beings converse about Hiero and Pausanias the Lacedaemonian, they enjoy bringing up their intercourse with Simonides, what he did and said with regard to them.[8] And they are wont to sing the praises[9] of Periander the Corinthian and Thales the Milesian together,[10] and of Pericles and Anaxagoras,[11] and

---

8. Hiero was tyrant of the Sicilian cities of Gela and Syracuse from 485 and 478 BCE, respectively, until his death in 467 BCE; tradition holds him to have been a lover and patron of the arts, which flourished under his reign (Aelian, *Varia historia* 4.15, 9.1). He is mentioned again at 336a8 below. His association with Simonides of Ceos (c. 556–468 BCE), the prolific and illustrious lyric poet remembered for his love of gain and pleasure (Aristotle, *Rhetoric* 1391a8–12; Plutarch, *An seni respublica* 786b; Aelian, *Varia historia* 9.1; Athenaeus, *Deipnosophistae* 12.5, 14.73; Strauss 2000, 184–85; cf. 50), is memorably portrayed in Xenophon's *Hiero* (see also Cicero, *On the Nature of the Gods* 1.22, with Strauss 2000, 104–5). Pausanias was the leading Spartan general in the Persian Wars of the early fifth century BCE, infamous for treasonously conspiring with the Persians thereafter (Thucydides 1.128–34). Some Simonidean verses are speculated to have been commissioned by Pausanias (Molyneux 1992, 198; Boedeker and Sider 2001, 38–41, 98–104), but there is virtually no extant evidence of any interaction between them outside of the present Platonic suggestion (see Plutarch, *Consolatio ad Apollonium* 6; Aelian, *Varia historia* 3.41). Plato's Socrates twice engages in interpretive discussions of Simonides's poetry (*Republic* 331d4–332c3, 335e1–336a7; *Protagoras* 338e6–347a5; cf. 316d3–9).

9. "Sing the praises of" translates *humnein*, related to the English "hymn." This is different from the word translated "sing of" below (311b7), *aidousi*, related to the English "ode." Both words can range in meaning from "sing of" to "celebrate," though *humnein* gravitates a bit more strongly to the latter meaning. For the relationship between the two, consider Plato, *Laws* 700a7ff.

10. Periander, tyrant of Corinth from 627 to 585 BCE, was known for being violent, harsh, and lawless (Herodotus 3.48–54). Yet he is also remembered, not only as an effective ruler, but even as a wise man, and he is traditionally included among the legendary "Seven Sages of Greece" (see Diogenes Laertius 1.97–98; cf. Aristotle, *Politics* 1284a26–36, 1313b22–24, 1315b11–39). Thales of Miletus (c. 624–546 BCE) is often regarded as the first of the pre-Socratic philosophers (Aristotle, *Metaphysics* 983b17–984a3). In Plato, Thales is described as having been so completely absorbed in theoretical contemplation as to be hopelessly unaware of imminent practical affairs (*Theaetetus* 174a3–b1; *Greater Hippias* 281c3–8; cf. Plutarch, *Convivium* 2), though other reports indicate that he was willing and able to turn his theoretical knowledge toward profitable application (Herodotus 1.74–75, 170; Aristotle, *Politics* 1259a6–19; but cf. *Nicomachean Ethics* 1141b2–8). There is no evidence that Periander and Thales ever associated or even met; they are connected only by the tenuous bond of their inclusion among the "Seven Sages." See also *Protagoras* 343a1–5.

11. Pericles (c. 495–429 BCE), one of the most influential and celebrated statesmen and generals in Athenian history, oversaw the ascent of Athens' imperial splendor to its peak during its golden age in the mid-fifth century; see Thucydides's presentation of Pericles's speeches and deeds in the first two books of his history of the Peloponnesian War, and cf. Socrates's discussions of him in Plato, *Phaedrus* 269a5–270a8, *Alcibiades* 118b6–119a6 and 124c, *Gorgias* 515c4–519a7, *Meno* 94a4–95a1, 319d–320b, and *Menexenus* passim; for a more comprehensive biography, see Plutarch's *Pericles*. Anaxagoras (c. 510–428 BCE), a pre-Socratic philosopher famous for his impious claims about the material nature of the heavenly bodies (*Apology of Socrates* 26d1–6; *Cratylus* 409a7–c2), played an important role in the Platonic Socrates's philosophic development as described in the *Phaedo* (95e8–99d2). The friendship between Pericles and Anaxagoras appears to have been mutually beneficial. Pericles's Anaxagorean education made him a

again of Croesus and Solon as wise and Cyrus as one in power.[12] And
11b the poets, imitating these things, bring together Creon and Tiresias,[13] Polyidus and Minos,[14] Agamemnon and Nestor and Odysseus and Palamedes[15]—and as it seems to me, the first human beings brought

---

shrewder statesman and an abler orator (Plato, *Phaedrus* 269a5–270a8; Plutarch, *Pericles* 6, 8.1). In turn, Anaxagoras, who appears rather to have *lacked* a certain measure of prudence (Plato, *Greater Hippias* 281b5–283b3; Xenophon, *Memorabilia* 4.7.6–7), is said to have found support and protection for his theoretical pursuits from the powerful Pericles, especially when he at last came to be tried for impiety by the city of Athens (Plutarch, *Pericles* 16.5–7, 32; *Nicias* 23.3). Plutarch draws a direct comparison between Anaxagoras's education of Pericles and Plato's of Dion; see *Maxims* 1, 4; and cf. *Nicias* 23.2–4 with *Dion* 24.1–2.

12. The word for "one in power" is *dunastēn*, so translated because of its relation to *dunamis* ("power" at 310e5 above). "Wise" translates *sophous*; see n. 7 above.

Croesus (c. 595–546 BCE), king of Lydia from 560 until, near the end of his life, his armies were defeated by Cyrus, conquered vast territories in Asia Minor and was the possessor of legendary wealth. Solon (c. 638–558 BCE), Athenian poet, lawgiver, and one of the "Seven Sages" along with Thales and Periander, is often credited as the founder of Athenian democracy (see Aristotle, *Athenian Constitution* 6–14; and cf. *Politics* 1273b34–1274a21; see also Plutarch, *Solon*; Diogenes Laertius, s.v.). Cyrus (c. 600–530 BCE), usually styled "Cyrus the Great," was the conqueror and founder of the vast Persian Empire. Stories of all three are chronicled by Herodotus, whose portrayal of the relationship between Croesus and Cyrus in particular is reimagined by Xenophon in his *Education of Cyrus*, a philosophical-historical fiction based on the life and rise to power of the Persian monarch. Despite Plato's suggestion here, no extant sources tell of any meeting between Solon and Cyrus, though Solon's wisdom is conveyed to Cyrus *through* Croesus in Herodotus's telling (1.30–33). In that version, Croesus becomes a political adviser to Cyrus (1.85–90, 154–56; see also 1.46–56; and cf. Xenophon, *Education of Cyrus* 7.2).

13. Creon was the uncle (and brother-in-law) of Oedipus, the fabled ruler of Thebes, and features prominently in Sophocles's Theban plays. Tiresias was a blind Theban seer famous from a variety of episodes in Greek mythology and literature (notably, his encounter with Odysseus at *Odyssey* 11.90–150). For Sophocles's portrayals of their bitter confrontations, see *Antigone* 988–1090 and *Oedipus Tyrannus* 300–462; cf. Euripides, *Phoenician Women* 834–959. Of these, the Euripidean encounter is the only one ever mentioned by Plato: Socrates likens himself and Alcibiades to Creon and Tiresias, respectively, at the end of *Second Alcibiades* (151b4–c2).

14. Minos, the legendary Cretan lawgiver, was known in Greek mythology as a son of Zeus (Homer, *Iliad* 13.449–50, 14.321–22; *Odyssey* 11.568–71, 19.178–79) and a judge in the underworld (Plato, *Apology of Socrates* 40e7–41a6; *Gorgias* 523e6–524a7, 526c1–d2). In Plato, he is presented as having created the Cretan law code with direct guidance from Zeus (*Minos* 318c4ff.; *Laws* 624a1–b3; cf. Thucydides 1.4, 8). The only well-preserved story concerning the fabled seer Polyidus is the one connecting him to Minos (Pseudo-Apollodorus, *Biblioteca* 3.3; Hyginus, *Fabulae* 136). In this story, Minos compels Polyidus to bring his son back to life, but Polyidus thereafter evades the king's attempt to compel him to share his art of divination. This story, and others concerning Polyidus, may have been the subject of a number of lost tragedies, such as Sophocles's *Manteis* and Euripides's *Polyidus* and *Bellerophon*.

15. Agamemnon and Nestor are among the heroes of Homer's *Iliad*, kings of Argos and Pylos, respectively. Agamemnon commanded the entire Achaean army in the siege of Troy; Nestor is portrayed as beyond the age of fighting strength by the time of the Trojan War, valued more for the counsel drawn from his long experience than for his strength or bravery. Yet while Nestor was undoubtedly a persuasive speaker (Plato, *Laws* 711d6–e7; and cf. Homer, *Iliad* 1.247–49 with Aristophanes, *Clouds* 1055–57), he often appears long-winded and vain, and some of his advice proves questionable. Odysseus, king of Ithaca, is another Homeric hero of the *Iliad* and

together Prometheus and Zeus in the same way[16]—and of these, they sing of some coming into conflict with each other, others into friendship, and still others into friendship at one time and into conflict at another, being like-minded about some things and conflicting about others.

311c I say all these things wishing to indicate the following: that when *we* meet our end, the speeches about *us* will not be passed over in silence either, so care must be taken over them. For it is necessary, as is likely, for us to care about the time to come, since, indeed, by a certain nature, the most servile happen to think nothing of it, while the most decent do everything in such a way that, in the time to come, they will hear well of themselves.[17] Indeed, I even make this out to be evidence that those who have

311d died have some perception of the things here; for the best souls divine[18] that these things are so, while the most depraved ones don't say so, but

the protagonist of the *Odyssey*, which recounts his tortuous journey and eventful arrival home from Troy. He is known above all for his wiliness. Palamedes was a fabled wise man, sometimes identified as the inventor of the alphabet among other things (Hyginus, *Fabulae* 277; Smith 1867, 92–93). A certain tradition holds that Palamedes exposed the ruse by which Odysseus had hoped to avoid joining in the expedition against Troy (Hyginus, *Fabulae* 95; Pseudo-Apollodorus, *Epitome* 3; Philostratus, *Heroicus* 33–34). Plato and Xenophon both suggest that Palamedes was killed unjustly, comparing his fate to Socrates's (Plato, *Apology* 41b1–3; Xenophon, *Apology* 26; *Memorabilia* 4.2.33; see also Diogenes Laertius 2.5.44).

There is an ambiguity in Plato's list regarding these last four characters. While it is natural to think of them as representing two pairs, the use of particles in the Greek strongly suggests a single grouping with Agamemnon as the powerful man and Nestor, Odysseus, and Palamedes as a triad of prudent associates (Harward 1932, 170n6). Odysseus thus comes to sight as another of the Platonic examples whose designation on the list is uncertain. For Odysseus as loyal friend to Agamemnon, see Aeschylus, *Agamemnon* 841–42. For the relationship of Palamedes to Agamemnon, consider Euripides, *Orestes* 433 and Plato, *Republic* 522d1–8. See also *Phaedrus* 261a7–e5.

16. The stories of the adversarial relationship between Zeus and the Titan Prometheus (whose name means "forethought") are among the most famous of Greek myth. The most important extant account from antiquity is probably that of Hesiod's *Theogony*: Prometheus steals Zeus's fire to give to man, and Zeus retaliates by chaining him to a rock to have his liver eaten every day by a great bird (507–615; cf. *Works and Days* 42–105). Prometheus is sometimes represented as giving to man not only fire but some or all of the most useful arts, as, for example, in the famous retelling of the myth of Prometheus by Plato's Protagoras (*Protagoras* 320c8–322d5; see also Aeschylus, *Prometheus Bound* 476–506). For contrasting depictions of Prometheus's motives, consider Aristophanes, *Birds* 1547 and Plato, *Gorgias* 523d5–e1. Plato's Socrates seems to identify himself with Prometheus in a way: see *Protagoras* 361c2–d6 with *Philebus* 16b4–17a5 and *Phaedo* 99d4ff., as well as Strauss 1952, 143n1 in context.

17. I.e., they will be well spoken of.

18. The verb for the act of divining here is *manteuontai*, just as "divinations" later in the sentence is *manteumata*—related words appear three more times in the *Letters* (317e7, 323c4, 340a2–3). There is no etymological connection between these terms and the adjective *theios*, which appears later in this sentence ("the divine men"), and which in all other cases is the word translated "divine."

the divinations of the divine men are more authoritative[19] than those of the men who aren't. I at least suppose, with respect to the figures from the past about whom I am speaking, that if it were possible for them to correct their intercourses, they would very seriously strive to be better spoken of than they are now. For us, therefore, to speak with god,[20] it is still possible, if something has not been nobly[21] done in our past intercourse, to correct it by speech and by deed. For I myself say that 311e opinion and speech about the true philosophy will be better if we are decent, but if we are petty,[22] the opposite. And in fact, about this thing, we could act no more piously[23] than to take care, nor more impiously than to be careless. That this needs to happen, and where the just lies,[24] I will explain.

I myself came to Sicily with a reputation of being quite distinguished 312a among those in philosophy; and I wished, by coming to Syracuse, to get you as a fellow-witness in order that, through me, philosophy would be honored even among the multitude. But this turned out for me not to be favorable.[25] As for the cause, however, I do not say the same thing that

---

19. Or "more sovereign" (*kuriōtera*); I have generally tried to use some form of the phrase "sovereign authority" for words related to *kurios*.

20. The phrase *sun theōi eipein* is idiomatic, expressing something like the sentiment of "god willing." But the literal meaning, "to speak with (a) god," should be emphasized, as meaning "to say things that are consonant with the will/meaning/existence/desire of (a) god"; cf. *Protagoras* 317b7 in context. The phrase is used twice more in the *Letters* (320b3, 320c7).

21. The adverbial form of *kalos*, one of the most important terms in Platonic philosophy. *Kalos* encompasses a range of meanings not captured by any one English word. Most simply, it means "beautiful" in an aesthetic sense; but the domain of "beautiful" things designated by *kalos* extends seamlessly beyond the aesthetic to encompass a variety of traits and activities of the human soul, especially those that we generally denote as "noble" in a moral sense. I have used the words "beautiful" and "noble" exclusively to translate words related to *kalos*.

22. The word for "petty" is *phaulōn*, which I have generally translated "paltry."

23. *Eusebesteron*, "more piously," is the comparative form of *eusebēs*, one of several Greek words that may describe the pious, sacred, or religious; this is the first occurrence of any of them in the *Letters*. *Eusebēs* in particular carries the sense of pious *veneration* or *duty*; it and related words appear twice in this line, and then twice in Letter Seven (325c1, 344d7). Apart from these cases, I will reserve the English words relating to "piety" for forms of *hosios*. In general, I try to follow the example set and explained by Pangle 1980, 518–19n7.

24. "That this needs to happen" might quite naturally be read as "*how* this needs to happen," but what follows leads me to prefer the translation I offer in the text. "Where the just lies," by which is meant something like "what justice demands," could also be read as "to what extent it is just."

25. The word is *euagēs*, which has more than one possible meaning. As well as "favorable," the word can mean "clear" or "illuminated," which would in this context suggest a lack of impediment or obstacle. But it may also mean "unpolluted" or "undefiled" in a religious sense (cf. *Laws* 956a2), indicating that Plato's venture was in some way impure. In either case, the sentence conveys that Plato's mission to Sicily did not meet with success.

many would say, but rather that you came to light as not much trusting me, {wishing} to send me away somehow {and to send for others to replace me,}[26] and seeking out what my business[27] is, since you were distrustful, as it seems to me. And those making noise about these things were many, saying that you disdained me and were serious about other things. Indeed, much noise has been made about these things.

312b

Hear, then, what it is just to do after these things, so that I may also answer what you ask as to how you and I ought to be disposed toward one another. If you have come to disdain philosophy altogether, bid it farewell. If you have heard from someone else, or if you yourself have discovered, better things than from me, honor those. But if the things from us[28] are agreeable to you, then I also should be honored most. Now, then, as in the beginning, you lead the way and I will follow. For if I am honored by you I will honor you, but if I am not honored I will keep quiet. Moreover, if you honor me and take the lead in this, you will seem[29] to honor philosophy, and the very fact that you have carefully examined others too will bring you good repute in the view of many as being a real philosopher. But if I honor you without you giving honor, I will seem to admire[30] and pursue riches, and we know that this, among everyone, has no beautiful name. In summary: if you give the honor, it is an adornment[31] to us both, but if I do, it is a reproach to us both. So much, then, concerning these things.

312c

312d

26. It is not clear whether the words in braces belong in the text. They appear only as marginal additions or emendations in the best manuscripts. Still, there is good evidence that the text just above was corrupted at some point (311d4–e2—I have rendered those lines according to the correction given in the margins of the manuscripts and accepted by all the editors), and that the transcribers' marginal corrections are based on older and superior manuscripts no longer extant. Without the bracketed words, the clause would have to read "sending me away somehow."

27. *Pragma*, generally "affair" or "matter of concern," may refer specifically to philosophic problems, as at 341b8ff.; cf. *Apology of Socrates* 20c4–5; *Alcibiades* 104d3–5; and see n. 37 below and n. 101 to Letter Seven.

28. Presumably, the philosophic teachings of Plato and his followers. Plato speaks about his philosophic doctrines or conclusions in extraordinarily vague terms throughout this letter, often apparently referring to them simply as "they" or "these things." See n. 44 below.

29. Or "be reputed" (*doxeis*).

30. "To admire" is *thaumazein*, which I have otherwise translated "to be amazed."

31. "Adornment" translates *kosmos*, the meaning of which is broad, as suggested by its English descendants "cosmos" (an ordered whole) and "cosmetic" (beautifying, adorning). Words related to *kosmos* appear twice more in the *Letters*, at 336a4 and 340e1.

The little sphere is not in the correct condition;[32] Archedemus will clarify this for you when he comes. But now, about that which is both more honored and more divine than this—that on account of which you sent, being at a loss[33]—it must very much be clarified by him. For according to his account, you claim that the nature of the first[34] has not been sufficiently demonstrated to you. It must indeed be explained to you through riddles, so that "if the writing-tablet should suffer something in the folds of sea or earth"[35] the reader will not understand it. 312e

It is like this: all things are around the king of all things and all things are for the sake of him, and that is responsible for all the noble things.[36]

---

32. It is not possible to know precisely to what this "little sphere" (*sphairion*) refers. Every scholar addressing this question plausibly suggests that it may be an "orrery," a model for studying or predicting the apparently erratic motions of the "planets" (including sun and moon) against the smoothly rotating background of the stars. For evidence that Plato thought the motions of the heavenly bodies were regular and calculable, consider *Republic* 529c7–530c7 and also 616b6–617b7 in light of the interpretation suggested by Bloom (1991, 427–28, 471–72n15), as well as the view of Plato's Timaeus concerning the prediction of eclipses using "models" (*mimēmata*) (40c3–d5). But compare the Platonic Socrates's denigration of knowledge of the "divine sphere" at *Philebus* 62a2–b4. See also Plutarch, *Dion* 19.4 and Cicero, *De republica* 1.14.

33. Or "being perplexed" (*aporoumenos*); see n. 45 below.

34. The following discussion of "the nature of the first" has received a great deal of attention over the centuries. It is generally assumed, reasonably, that "the first" means the first cause of all things; I have striven for a literal translation throughout, which reflects the cryptic or "enigmatic" manner of Plato's presentation. The "king of all things," as Plato will call "the first" he is describing, has been identified by various readers with the cosmic creator of Plato's *Timaeus* (28c3, 37c7, 41a7); with *nous,* said in the *Philebus* to be "king" of heaven and earth according to the wise (28c7); with "the one who cares for the whole," referred to as "our king" by Plato's Athenian Stranger (*Laws* 904a4–6); with the "idea of the good," said in the *Republic* to "rule as king (*basileuein*) over the intelligible species and place" and through which "both being and substance are attached to" the known things (509b6–8, d2); and, of course, given the triad of which "the king" here forms a part, with one-third of the Holy Trinity by early Christian theologians; see Harward 1932, 172–73, Bury 1929, 400–401, and Morrow 1962, 115–16 for reviews of various interpretations.

35. Regarding this unusual flourish, Harward explains, "Plato has worked into his sentence fragments of a passage in a lost tragedy. . . . It is not possible to say whether the word δέλτος [i.e., "writing tablet"] is a part of the quotation; but in any case the word belongs to the poetic coloring" (1932, 171n16). Cf. Euripides, *Iphigenia in Tauris* 755–65; Aristotle, *Rhetoric* 1407b34–35. Note also that Euripides more than once speaks of the "folds" (or "leaves" or "plates") of the writing tablet, using forms of the same word Plato here uses to speak of the "folds of sea or earth" (*ptuchē*) (Euripides, *Iphigenia in Tauris* 727, 760, 794; *Iphigenia in Aulis* 98, 112).

36. Some notes on the precise wording of this vexed sentence are necessary. In the phrase "that is responsible," the word "that" translates the demonstrative pronoun *ekeino.* The same pronoun was translated four Greek words earlier as "him" in the phrase "for the sake of him," which seems to have led most translators to prefer the reading "*he* is responsible for all the noble things." But whereas the first use of the pronoun appears to be in the masculine gender to accord with "the king," the second is unambiguously in the neuter; and while it is not impossible to refer to a masculine subject with a neuter demonstrative pronoun, this does not

The second things are around a second, and the third things around a third. So the human soul reaches out to learn about them, what sort 313a of things they are, looking to the things akin to itself, of which none is in sufficient condition. Indeed, about the king and the things of which I spoke, there is no such thing, and the soul says after this, "Well then, but what sort of thing?" This, child of Dionysius and Doris, is the question that is responsible for all evils—or rather the labor pains coming to be in the soul about this are responsible, and until one is relieved of them, one never really hits upon the truth.

But you yourself said to me, in the garden, under the laurels, that 313b you had thought of this and that it was your discovery. And I said that if this appeared to you to be so, that you would have released me from many speeches. I said that I had never encountered anyone else who had discovered this, but that the great trouble[37] for me was about this. Perhaps you heard it from someone; maybe you set out for it by divine fate—then, as though you had the demonstrations of it firmly,[38] you did not tie them down,[39] but they dart about,[40] now one way, now another,

---

seem a likely instance of that. I have therefore translated in the spirit of Post (1925), whose version reads "*that fact* is the cause of all that is beautiful" (emphasis added). The more typical reading, however, is also possible and should be considered. Also consider Tarrant, who suggests, "the king appears to be neuter!" (1993, 170).

Post's translation brings out two further points. First, the word I have translated "noble things" is *kalōn*, which includes also the "beautiful things"; see n. 21 above. Second, "responsible" in my version translates the adjective *aition*. Originally a legal term meaning "culpable," *aition* came to have another prominent meaning without the negative connotation—namely, to be "responsible" for something in the sense of being its "cause"—and hence became an important term in Greek philosophy. Thus translators (including Post) have generally preferred some version of the phrase "he is *the cause* of all the noble things." But the reader might take note of the fact that Plato does not use the definite article here—he does not strictly say that "he" (or indeed, "that") is *the* cause, but rather says that "he" (or "that") is *responsible for* all of *tōn kalōn*, though admittedly, this may well amount to the same thing. The same word is used a few lines below, again without the definite article, in the phrase "responsible for all evils."

37. The word *pragmateia*, translated "trouble" here, can also mean "business" or "concern," much like its more common relative, *pragma*; but unlike *pragma*, *pragmateia* likely implies an ongoing or long-standing preoccupation. It occurs only once more in the *Letters*, at 314a7, where I have translated it "diligent activity." See also n. 101 to Letter Seven.

38. "Firmly" is *bebaiōs*, the adverbial form of a word I elsewhere translate either "stable" or "steadfast."

39. Scholars have noted the similarity between the description of Dionysius's opinion as "not tied down" and the "fugitive slave" metaphor at *Meno* 97e6–98a3; see, e.g., Harward 1932, 173n21; Bury 1929, 412n2; Souilhé 1931, 9–10n2. Souilhé and Bury also point to *Theaetetus* 151aff., Socrates's famous claim to be a midwife of knowledge, as parallel to the mention of "labor pains" earlier in this passage (though, more specifically, reference should be made to 148e7); *Symposium* 206e1, in context, is of equal significance.

40. There is disagreement among the major manuscripts here, several of which seem to indicate that the text has suffered some corruption. I follow the suggestion of Novotny to read

313c around the imagined thing,[41] but there is no such thing. And this has not happened to you alone, but know well that no one, after hearing me for the first time,[42] has ever been in any other state than this at the beginning: and though one has more problems and another has fewer, they are rid of them only with difficulty—and almost no one has few.

So then, given that these things have taken place, and now stand, in this way, we have nearly discovered, in my opinion, what you sent a letter[43] about: how we need to be disposed toward one another. For since you are testing them, both in getting together with others and comparing them 13d with the others', as well as themselves by themselves, they will now, if the test is true, grow naturally in you and you will be an intimate both with them and with us.[44]

---

aittousi ("they dart about"), but there are at least two alternatives. The vulgate has *aitteis*, "*you* dart about, etc.," while Burnet suggests *aittei soi*, "it darts at you, etc."

41. The word for "imagined thing" is *phantazomenon*, which could refer, however, to something appearing to the physical senses as well as the appearance of something called up or produced by the imagination. It is in accordance with the former possibility that Post (1925, ad loc.) overtranslates "never getting away from the appearances of things," clarifying a possible interpretation, however, in doing so; similarly, Harward (1932, ad loc.) has "in the region of the apparent."

42. Given the context, the Greek here could conceivably be construed as "after hearing about 'the first' from me."

43. "Sent a letter" translates *epesteilas*, related to *epistolē*, "letter" or "epistle," as in the title of the work. Regardless of whether that title was affixed to the *Letters* by Plato himself or a later editor, the reader may wish to track Plato's use of these words on account of the *Letters*' literary form. There are some difficulties in translation, however, regarding the verbal form *epistellō*. In many cases, it would be most natural to render this word "write" or "send" (i.e., in the present case, "what you wrote/sent")—the latter could be especially apt, since technically the verb *epistellō* need not refer to the transmission of a *written* message, but could indicate the giving of an order or the sending of a messenger. However, the English "write" is usually reserved for *graphō* and "send" for *pempō*, both common Greek words. So that the English reader may be sure of when Plato is using *epistellō*, then, I have opted to use the phrase "send a letter" for this word wherever possible, even at the cost of some awkward formulations, and have indicated deviations from this principle in footnotes.

44. The meaning of this sentence is particularly unclear because Plato specifies neither what "things" of his Dionysius is "testing" nor who the "others" are whose counterpart "things" are to serve as a point of comparison. Other translators render the sentence intelligible by specifying that Dionysius is testing Plato's "doctrines" or "principles," and that he is comparing those to the principles of other "teachers." This is likely the meaning (see n. 28 above), but I have left my own translation unclear so as to reproduce the bewildering effect of the original. See also n. 4 to Letter Thirteen. Note also that "grow naturally" translates *prosphusetai*, which literally refers to a biological outgrowth (of any kind); thus Morrow (1962, ad loc.), for example, uses the phrase "take root." I have tried with my translation to keep the reader in mind of the relation to *phusis*, the scientific or philosophic word for "nature" (cf. n. 130 to Letter Seven). Elsewhere, I have consistently used some version of the phrase "grow naturally" to translate the related verb *phuein*, "to grow."

How, then, will they and all the things we've said be realized? You acted correctly in sending Archedemus now; and in the future, when he comes to you and reports the things from me, after these, perhaps other perplexities[45] will seize you. You'll send Archedemus to me again if you deliberate correctly, and once he's transported [the message] he'll return again. And if you do this two or three times, and sufficiently test the things sent from me, I would be amazed if the things that are presently perplexing will not come to be very different for you than they are now. Take heart, therefore, and do thus;[46] for never did you dispatch,[47] nor will Archedemus ever transport, a thing nobler and dearer to the gods than this cargo.

313e

314a

Beware, however, lest these things ever be exposed to uneducated human beings; for, as it seems to me, there are for the many almost no more ridiculous things to be heard than these, nor indeed for those of good natures any more amazing and more inspired.[48] But being spoken often[49] and for many years, they are with difficulty, like gold, purified with much diligent activity.[50] But hear the amazing thing that has come to be from it. For there are human beings, and plenty of them, who have heard these things—who are, on one hand, capable of learning, and on the other hand, capable of remembering and judging by testing altogether in every way—who are now old and have been listening for no fewer than thirty years, who just now are saying to themselves that the things that once seemed to be most untrustworthy[51] now appear most

314b

45. "Perplexities" translates *aporiai* (just as "perplexing" translates part of *aporoumena* in the sentence after next). There is something of a play on words in the uses of *aporia* and *emporia* in this paragraph. The root word, *poros*, refers to a means of "passage" through or across an obstacle, often a river or body of water, but can also mean simply "journey." *Aporia*, then, is to be without recourse, to have "no way out" of a difficulty, while *emporia* is merchandise or cargo that is quite literally "imported," especially by sea. The words "transport" and "cargo" in this paragraph all translate some word related to *emporia*. The suggestion is that Archedemus's traveling and transporting, that is, his *emporia*, will provide the resolution to Dionysius's *aporia*.

46. These imperative verbs are in the second person plural; presumably, Plato addresses himself to both Dionysius and Archedemus.

47. The verb for "dispatch" (*steilēis*) is the root word of *epistolai*, the title of this work. See n. 43 above.

48. "More inspired" translates *enthousiastikōtera*, which is from *entheos*, "divinely inspired," "having a god within." In this context, the word may also mean "inspiring."

49. Marginal notes in the best manuscripts suggest the insertion here of the words "and always/constantly (*aei*) heard," which are included in the text of some later manuscripts as well as in the quotation by Eusebius (*Praeparatio evangelica* 12.7).

50. "Diligent activity" is *pragmateia*; see n. 37 above.

51. I have generally used words related to "worth" or "worthy" only to translate forms of the Greek word *axios* (including "unworthily" in the following sentence). The three occurrences of words related to "trustworthy" in this sentence, however, translate forms of the word *pistos*.

trustworthy and clearest,[52] and those which then seemed most trustworthy now appear to be the opposite. So beware in examining these things lest you come someday to regret their having been unworthily exposed now. A very great safeguard is not to write but to learn by heart; for it is not possible for things written not to be exposed. Because of these things, I have never written anything at all about these things, nor are there written works of Plato, nor will there be any at all, but those now spoken of are of a Socrates become beautiful and young.[53] Be strong and be persuaded, and as soon as you have read this letter many times, burn it up. So much for these things.

314c

314d

As for Polyxenus, you were amazed that I would send him to you. But I give the same account now as before concerning Lycophron as well as the others who are around you:[54] with respect to conversing,[55] you altogether surpass them, both in nature and in method[56] concerning speeches, and no one of them is refuted voluntarily, as some assume, but involuntarily. And indeed, you seem to have made use of them and to have given them gifts in a very measured way. So much concerning them—a great deal, given that it concerns such as them!

314e

With respect to Philistion,[57] if you yourself have a use for him, by all means make use of him; but if you're able, send him off and lend him to Speusippus.[58] Speusippus too begs this of you. And Philistion promised me that, if you let him go, he will come to Athens with eager spirit.

---

52. Or "most splendid" (*enargestata*).

53. "Beautiful" might also be "noble" or "fine" (see n. 21 above); "young" might also be "new."

54. This Lycophron may be the sophist mentioned by Aristotle in, e.g., *Politics* 1280b8–12; *Physics* 186b25–32. Polyxenus was mentioned earlier in this letter (310c7).

55. "Conversing" translates *to dialechthēnai*. This articular infinitive does not appear elsewhere in Plato, but it is of course closely related to the important Platonic theme of "dialectic" (e.g., *Republic* 533a1ff.).

56. "Method" is hardly more than a transliteration of *methodōi*, and does not in fact capture the full meaning of the Greek term. Composed of *meta-* ("with/after") and *hodos* ("road," "path"), the original meaning of the word was something like "pursuit." More commonly, especially in philosophy, *methodos* means either the pursuit of a given inquiry or rather the *mode* in which one conducts such an inquiry; hence the sense of the English "method." The phrase *methodōi tōn logōn* in this passage, then, might be translated "mode of inquiry into speeches."

57. Apparently the noted Locrian-Sicilian physician and teacher of Eudoxus; see Diogenes Laertius 8.86. Not to be confused with the Syracusan historian Philistus (see n. 8 to Letter Three).

58. Plato's nephew, who became the head of the Academy after Plato's death; Harward, citing Diogenes Laertius 4.1 and the thirty-fifth Socratic Epistle, notes that "Speusippus suffered from very poor health" (1932, 175n29). He is mentioned again in Letter Thirteen (361e2).

You did well to let the [man] go from the rock quarries;[59] the entreaty[60] concerning both his household slaves and Hegesippus, son of Ariston,[61] 315a is easy. For you sent a letter to me saying that, if anyone should do injustice either to him or to them and you should perceive it, that you would not let it stand. And concerning Lysiclides, it is worth saying the truth: for he alone of those who arrived at Athens from Sicily did not change his position at all concerning the intercourse between you and me, but to the end continues always to say something good and with a view to the better things concerning the things that happened.[62]

---

59. The rock quarries at Syracuse were used as prisons; Thucydides describes the miserable hardship of the thousands of Athenians imprisoned there after the failure of the Sicilian Expedition (7.86-87). See also Plutarch, *Nicias* 28.2; *On the Fortune and Virtue of Alexander* 2.1.

60. The noun translated "entreaty" here (*deēsis*) is virtually the same word as the verb translated "begs" just above (*deitai*).

61. Hegesippus and Ariston are both common Athenian names (Nails 2002, 158)—indeed, Ariston was the name of Plato's father—but nothing is known either of these men or of the Lysiclides mentioned in the letter's final sentence.

62. For the last portion of this sentence (after the comma), I follow the suggestion of Burnet, who combines part of the reading from the main text of the best manuscripts, which appears to be corrupt, with part of the emendation offered in the margin of two of them. No available version of the sentence reads very smoothly; the only alternative might be something like "continues always to say something good, and things still better, concerning the things that happened."

Letter Three

"Plato to Dionysius: Rejoice!"[1]–if I sent such a letter, would I correctly hit upon the best salutation? Or rather by writing, in accordance with my customary usage, "Do well!" as I have habitually greeted my friends in the letters? For you indeed addressed even the god in Delphi, as they who then went to see [the oracle][2] reported, by wheedling him with this very same phrase: you wrote, as they say, "Rejoice and preserve a tyrant's life of having pleasure!" I, on the other hand, would not, in a call to a

315b

315c

1. "Rejoice" here translates *chairein*, the most common word of greeting in ancient Greek. It is so common a greeting that it is often translated simply "hail," but the literal meaning related to joy and gladness is important in what follows. Cf. *Charmides* 164d6–e5. Elsewhere in the *Letters*, the same verb is mainly used not as a greeting but as the valediction that I have translated "farewell"; it is also rendered "enjoy" twice in Letter Two (310e and 311a). Since Plato begins this letter with a question about how to address Dionysius, this is the only letter of the thirteen that lacks a salutation.

2. "They who went to see [the oracle]" translates the participle *hoi theōrountes*. The verb *theōrein* is most often used to mean "to observe" or "to contemplate," whence the English "theory" and "theorize." But Plato here employs the word in another sense–namely, "to be a *theōros*," an envoy sent to consult an oracle, or "to be a spectator" at a religious festival. For the practice of submitting questions to the Delphic Oracle in writing via *theōrountas*, see Fontenrose 1978, 217. The only other use of this word in the *Letters* occurs at 350b7, where it refers to Dion "being a spectator" at the Olympic games.

human being—let alone[3] to a god—encourage anyone to do this: to a god, because I would be commanding against nature, for the divine lies far away from pleasure and pain; to a human being, because pleasure and pain engender much harm, the pair of them begetting badness at learning, forgetfulness, imprudence, and hubris in the soul. And let these things have been said in such a way by me about the mode of address; but you, in reading them, take them in whatever way you wish to take them.

Not a few are claiming that you were saying to some of those who came 315d to you as ambassadors that, when I once heard you saying that you were going to colonize the Greek cities in Sicily[4] and to unburden the Syracusans by replacing the rule of tyranny with kingship, I then prevented you, as you claim, though you were intently eager to do these things; and that now I would teach Dion to do these very things, and that we, 315e by means of your own intentions,[5] are taking your rule away from you. Whether you are deriving some benefit because of these speeches, you yourself know,[6] but you do injustice to me by saying the opposite of the

3. Accepting *mē hoti dē*, the marginal correction found in the manuscripts instead of the difficult *outi*. Burnet's further emendation to *mēti dē* seems unnecessary.

4. Referring to the Greek cities of Sicily as opposed to those inhabited by the Carthaginians. The inhabitants of the former had been conquered or expelled during Dionysius the Elder's wars with Carthage in the late fifth century or subsequently displaced by Dionysius the Elder himself, and Dionysus the Younger evidently had ambitions of reclaiming and repopulating them with Greek colonists. See Harward 1932, 9–10; and cf. 319c7–d2, 331e2–32a3.

5. "Intentions" translates *dianoēmasin*; it is the first appearance of this or any related word in the *Letters*. While I have used "intention" and "intend" to translate words in this family wherever possible (indicating deviations from this practice in footnotes), there is another dimension of meaning that should be carefully considered, especially given the importance of this word in the *Letters*. The prefix and root of, for example, the abstract noun *dianoia*, suggest something that has been "thought through"; it comes to mean "intention," then, rather, as in the English phrase "to have in mind." That is, the word refers to a process of thought that has culminated in the conception of a plan and the resolution to execute it. However, especially in the philosophic writings of Plato's era, it was at least as common for *dianoia* to have the more purely theoretical sense of a mental "understanding." Hence, Plato uses the word *dianoia* to describe the "affection arising in the soul" in the soul's grasp of "the mathematical things" in his "divided line" metaphor (*Republic* 511d). In the *Letters*, words in this family occur most of all in Letter Seven—a letter much to do with the relationship of theory and practice, of thought and action—though also here in Letter Three and elsewhere in Letters Eight and Eleven. These uses span the range of possible meanings, and one should always consider the alternative possible translation related to a theoretical "understanding" wherever a word related to "intention" appears in my translation.

6. "Know" here is *gignōskeis*, "recognize" or "understand," as opposed to the word I have usually reserved for the English "to know" (*eidenai*).

things that happened.[7] For I was slandered enough by Philistides[8] and many others to the mercenaries and among the majority of Syracusans on account of my staying in the acropolis, and as for those outside, if there was any error, they made everything turn on me, asserting that you obeyed me in all things. But you yourself know most clearly that I was voluntarily engaging in a few of the political things in common with you at the beginning, when I supposed I could do something more; I was taking seriously, in a measured way, some other, minor things and the preludes to the laws,[9] separate from the things which you or someone else wrote in addition; for I hear that some of you were later revising them, though it will be clear which [parts are which] to those capable of discerning my style.[10] But therefore, as I just said, I have no further need of slander, either among the Syracusans or any others you persuade by saying these things; rather, I am in need much more of a defense speech[11] against both the slander that occurred before and that which is now naturally growing greater and more vehement after it. For these two, it is necessary for me to make the defense speeches double: first, that I appropriately avoided sharing in common with you in the affairs of the city, and second, that you have not spoken [truthfully] of my counsel,

316a

316b

7. Plato puts this accusation in the language of a legal charge.

8. It is generally accepted that this is Philistus, the Syracusan historian who wrote influential histories of Sicily (no longer extant) and who helped to establish the tyranny of Dionysius the Elder. Though he fell into that tyrant's disfavor, it seems he came to be an important figure in the court of Dionysius the Younger and generally an opponent of Plato and Dion. See especially Plutarch's *Dion* 11–14, 19, and 35–36, as well as Nepos, *Dion* 4. Philistus's historical works are thought to have painted Plato in a negative light (Morrow 1962, 22) and may for all we know have begun to circulate in some form by the time Plato composed the *Letters*. The appellation "Philistides" in the text here has suggested to some the ignorance of a forger (Nails 2002, 240), but Harward notes that "the interchange between the patronymic and the simple name was common at Athens" (1932, 179n5), and Morrow that "proper names were often abbreviated in the manuscripts and hence variant readings could easily arise" (1962, 200n3).

9. For the Platonic notion of "preludes to the laws," see *Laws* 722c6ff.

10. Or "to those capable of judging my character" (*tois to emon ēthos dunamenois krinein*). *Ēthos* can refer to traits of moral character (as in the titles of Aristotle's *Nicomachean* and *Eudemian Ethics*), and more generally to character traits or manners developed and sustained through habitual activity (see Aristotle, *Nicomachean Ethics* 1103a14–18). Thus the word can also mean "usage" or "custom"—or, as in the present passage, a habitual "style" of writing. I have tried to use "character" to translate *ēthos* wherever possible.

11. Here and in the next sentence, as well as at 318e7 below, the word for "defense speech" is *apologia*, the same word that is usually translated "apology" in the title of Plato's *Apology of Socrates*. It can refer to any speech one might make in one's own defense, but particularly to such speeches made in legal cases. Apart from these three places in Letter Three, I have reserved all forms of the word "defend" for translations of forms of the Greek word *amunō* (i.e., "defend against," "ward off").

nor of my prevention, in saying that I had come to be standing in your way when you were going to recolonize the Greek cities.

316c Hear first, then, the beginning, concerning the things I spoke about first. I came to Syracuse, having been called by both you and Dion. He had undergone my inspection, having long ago become a guest-friend,[12] and was in the midst of his prime and middle-aged, which things are altogether needed[13] by those possessing even a little intelligence[14] who are going to deliberate concerning things so great as yours then were. You, on the other hand, were very young, there was great inexperience around 316d you of the things in which one needed to have become experienced, and you were very unknown to me. After this, either a human being, or a god, or some fortune together with you cast Dion out, and you were left alone. So do you suppose that I then had a partnership with you in political things, when the sensible partner had been destroyed, and I saw the senseless[15] one left behind with many and wicked human beings, not ruling but supposing he ruled, and being ruled by, such human beings? In these circumstances, what ought I to have done? Wasn't it the very 316e thing I did by necessity: to bid farewell to the political things for the remainder of the time and to beware of the slanders of the envious; and as regards you [pl] altogether, though you [pl] had come to be split from one another and were at odds, to attempt to make you [pl] friends with each other as much as possible? Of these things even you are a witness: that I never gave up straining for this very thing, and, though with dif- 317a ficulty, it was nevertheless agreed by both of us that I would sail home,

---

12. The important Greek notion of *xenia*, roughly translated "guest-friendship" here and throughout, has no exact counterpart in modern Western culture. The unwritten rules of *xenia* entailed a pious obligation to extend favors of hospitality to travelers far from home, and a similar obligation upon the traveler readily to repay those favors if an occasion to do so should later arise. To have been hosted as a *xenos*, a "stranger" or "guest-friend" in a foreign city, therefore, was to have been hospitably received and to have incurred a debt of gratitude. Moreover, bonds of *xenia* might be established in other ways: two families could come to share such a relationship across generations, and a person or family could be granted a kind of diplomatic status within the framework of *xenia* by a city, regime, or ruler. The reciprocal obligations of guest-friendship were believed to fall under the jurisdiction of Zeus (hence the epithet Xenios; see 329b4), and transgressions could be punished by the Furies (see 357a4).

13. "Needed" translates the Greek word *chreia*. Generally, I have reserved words related to "need" for the translation of words related to the Greek *dei*, whereas the word *chrē* (related to *chreia*) is translated "ought."

14. Lit. "those possessing a mind—even a small one."

15. "Sensible" and "senseless" here translate *emphrona* and *aphrona*. The latter could well be translated "imprudent," as it is equally the antonym of *phronimon*, the adjectival form of *phronēsis*, "prudence" or "practical wisdom" (see n. 7 to Letter Two). The prefix *em-* on the word *emphrona* here suggests something like "in one's senses."

since war had taken hold of you [pl], but that when peace should again come to be, both Dion and I would come to Syracuse, and that you would call us.

This is how these things came to be concerning my first voyage to Syracuse and my safe[16] return back home. As for the second: when peace had come to be, you did not call me in accordance with the agreements but sent a letter telling me to come alone and claimed that you would send for Dion in his turn. Because of these things I did not go, though 317b I then incurred even Dion's hatred, for he supposed that it was better for me to go and to hearken to you. One year after these things, a trireme arrived with letters from you. At the beginning of the things written in the letters was that, if I should come, all Dion's affairs would come to be to my liking,[17] but if I should not come, the opposite. I am ashamed to say how many letters then came from you, and from others because 317c of you, from Italy and Sicily, and to how many of my intimates and acquaintances, all directing me to go and begging me to obey you in every way. It seemed to everyone, beginning with Dion, that I needed to sail and not become soft. But I was making a point of my age to them, and, concerning you, I was asseverating that you would not be able to withstand those slandering us and wishing us to come to enmity—for I both saw then and see now, with respect to the great and extravagant property[18] of private men and monarchs, that in general, the greater it 317d is, the more numerous and greater are the slanderers and indulgers in shamefully harmful pleasure whom it nourishes; riches and the power of the rest of excessive property[19] engender no greater evil.

---

16. Ordinarily, I reserve the word "safe" to translate words related to the Greek *asphalēs*, keeping these distinct from the noun *sōtēria* and the verb *sōizein* ("salvation" and "to save," respectively). Here, however, the word *sōtēria* is used to mean something like "safe arrival." There is a parallel case in Letter Seven, where the verb *esōthēn* means something like "arrived safely" (338e5).

17. "To my liking" translates the common Greek idiom *kata noun ton emon*, literally "according to my mind."

18. Lit. "substance." The Greek *ousia* has both the mundane meaning intended here, which refers to wealth in the form of property and financial assets (as in "a man of substance"), and a highly abstract ontological meaning, which refers to the substance of a being in the sense of its essence, i.e., that which underlies its accidental qualities, or indeed to "being" as such. *Ousia* is used seven times in the *Letters*: here, just below at 318a6, and five times in Letter Seven. Only once is the philosophic meaning intended ("being" at 344b2). All other instances have been translated "property." The related word *exousia* appears just below at 317d4, and is translated "excessive property."

19. Or "the other [forms of] license" (*hē tēs allēs exousias*).

Nevertheless, having bid farewell to all these things,[20] I went, having resolved[21] that there was need that no one of my friends ever accuse me on the grounds that, because of my faintness of heart, all that was

317e his, though it might not have been lost, was utterly destroyed.[22] Having got there—for you yourself know everything that happened thereafter—I was of course requesting, in accordance with the agreement of the letters, that you first reconcile[23] with Dion and recall him. I was pointing the way to reconciliation,[24] which, had you then obeyed me, would perhaps have been better than the things that have now come to pass for you, and for the Syracusans, and for the other Greeks, as my opinion divines. And then, I was requesting that Dion's relatives[25] have his [prop-

318a erty], and that it not be apportioned by those apportioning it among themselves—you yourself know who. In addition to these things, I supposed that, once I had come to be there, you needed to be sending what you had been in the habit of providing him each year and more besides, not less. Hitting upon none of these things, I requested to leave. After these things, you were trying to persuade me to remain for the year, asserting that you would sell off all of Dion's property, send half the

318b proceeds to Corinth, and leave the rest to his son. I could say many things that you promised but in no way did; I cut them short on account of their multitude. For indeed, having sold off all the property[26] without persuading Dion (though you asserted you would not sell it without persuading him), you most impetuously added the pièce de résistance, you amazing one, to all your promises. For you found a contrivance neither noble, nor refined, nor just, nor advantageous: to frighten me, as though I was ignorant of the things then going on, in order that I should not

318c seek for the money to be sent back. For when you cast out Heraclides,

---

20. I.e., "having dismissed the preceding considerations."

21. Or "intending." The word is *dianoētheis*; see n. 5 above.

22. The words for "lost" (*apolesthai*) and "utterly destroyed" (*diōleto*) are closely related.

23. "Reconcile" translates *oikeiōsamenon*, the mending of a relationship between kinsmen or similarly close friends. I translate *oikeiotēta* in the following line "reconciliation" to indicate the etymological link, but that word refers more simply to the relationship itself, not to its restoration. Most important, one should note the connection between these words and *oikeios*, an "intimate" or "relative," which appears in the following line (as well as in the addresses of Letters Seven and Eight; see n. 1 to Letter Seven). A different cluster of words (*katallagē/diallagē/diallaxis*) is translated "reconciliation" in Letters Seven and Eight (350d6, e1, 356c7).

24. "Pointing [the way]" translates the word *phrazōn*, which I have usually rendered "explaining."

25. Or "Dion's intimates," as I have usually translated *oikeious*.

26. The word for "property" here is not *ousia* as elsewhere but *chrēmata*, which I usually translate "money" or "wealth."

seeming just neither to the Syracusans nor to me—wherefore, together with Theodotes and Eurybius, I begged you not to do these things—you, taking this as a sufficient pretext, said that even long ago it was clear to you that I thought nothing of you,[27] but rather of Dion and Dion's friends and intimates, and since now Theodotes and Heraclides were 318d being slandered, who were intimates of Dion, I was employing every contrivance so that they should not pay the just penalty.[28]

And that's how it is concerning the political things in the partnership between you and me. And if you observed any other estrangement of me from you, it is appropriate for you to suppose that all these things came to be in this way. And don't be amazed, for I would justly appear bad, to a man with mind at least, if I were persuaded by the greatness of your rule to betray an old friend and guest-friend who was doing badly because 318e of you—someone in no way worse than you, if I may say so—and choose you, the doer of injustice, and do everything in whatever way you commanded, clearly for the sake of money; for nothing else would anyone claim was responsible for my change, if I had changed. But these things, having come to be in this way, produced my and your wolf-friendship[29] and lack of partnership, because of you.

My speech, which is nearly continuous with the one from just now, has reached a speech concerning that about which I was saying that a 319a second defense must be made for me.[30] Examine, then, and in every way turn your attention toward, whether I seem to you to be lying about anything and not to be speaking the truth. For I claim that, when

---

27. The verb for "think" in this case is not related to *noeō*, the word usually rendered "think," but rather *phrontizō*.

28. Heraclides was to become an important ally of Dion during the latter's campaign against Syracuse, which eventually ousted Dionysius the Younger. In the turbulent time following that victory, a political rivalry developed between Dion and Heraclides—to which Plato alludes in Letter Four (320eff.)—which itself degenerated into military conflict. In the end, Dion's reluctant acquiescence to the assassination of Heraclides appears to have precipitated his own assassination in turn. Our primary source for the details of Heraclides's role in the history of Syracuse is Plutarch's *Dion* (especially 32ff.); Harward's (1932, 29–53) summary, tailored to a study of Plato's *Letters*, is excellent and considers the relevant historiographical questions. Theodotes is said by Plutarch to have been Heraclides's uncle (*Dion* 45); Eurybius appears to have been another companion of Heraclides. These two are otherwise unknown, but the incident involving them to which Plato refers here in Letter Three is presented again and in greater detail in Letter Seven (348b–349e).

29. *Lukophilia*, "wolf-friendship," may be Plato's coinage. See Harward 1932, 180n15.

30. The structure of this sentence in the Greek is unusually convoluted, even if the sense is tolerably clear. See Harward 1932, 180–81n16.

Archedemus was present in the garden, as well as Aristocritus,[31] nearly twenty days before my voyage homeward from Syracuse, you were blaming me for the very things you now speak of: that I cared for Heraclides and all the others rather than you. And you questioned me in front of them as to whether I remembered directing you, when I came at the 319b beginning, to recolonize the Greek cities. And I conceded that I did remember, and that it even still seemed to me that these things were best. But it must also be told, Dionysius, what was said after this at that time. For I asked you whether I had counseled you to do this very thing only or also something else in addition to this. And you answered me, very much enraged and hubristically, that you supposed—wherefore what then was your act of hubris has now become a waking reality rather 319c than a dream—you said, with very feigned laughter if I remember, "You directed me to do all these things once I had been educated, or else not to do them." I said that you remembered most beautifully.

"So it's once I had been educated," you said, "to do geometry? Or what?" And I did not say what it occurred to me to say in response, fearing lest, for the sake of a little phrase, the prospect of my sailing away, which I was anticipating, should narrow after having been wide open.

But I have said all this for the sake of the following things: don't slander me by saying that I didn't allow you to colonize the Greek cities 319d wiped out by barbarians or to relieve the Syracusans by replacing the tyranny with a kingship. For no falsehoods you could ever speak of me befit me less than these. And I would give speeches of refutation in addition to these and still clearer than them, if an adequate trial were to manifest itself somewhere, to the effect that I directed you to do things, but you weren't willing to do them. And indeed, it is not hard to say clearly that 319e these would have been the best things to do—for you, and for the Syracusans, and for all Siceliotes.[32]

But, sir, if you, having said these things, claim not to have said them, I have my just penalty.[33] But if you agree, then after this, holding

31. This Aristocritus is unknown outside of Plato's *Letters*. It is presumably the same Aristocritus to whom Plato refers at 363d2. On Archedemus, see n. 1 to Letter Two.

32. Siceliotes were the Greek inhabitants of Sicily.

33. I.e., if Dionysius would claim victory in this imagined judicial contest simply by denying the truth of Plato's defense, then Plato has his punishment already: the ill repute resulting from Dionysius's slanders.

Stesichorus to be wise and imitating his palinode, replace the lie with the true speech.[34]

34. The legend of the poet Stesichorus told that he was blinded for maligning Helen of Troy but had his sight restored when he wrote his palinode, retracting his criticism. *Palinōidia* literally means a "recanting." Plato's Socrates famously follows the example of Stesichorus's palinode in the *Phaedrus* (243a2ff.).

Letter Four

Plato to Dion the Syracusan: Do well!

320a I suppose that during the whole time my eagerness has been manifest concerning the actions that have occurred, and that I was very serious about their being resolved, for the sake of love of honor for the noble 320b things more than anything else. For I believe it to be just that those who are in truth decent and who do such things hit upon the proper reputation. Now, things up to the present, to speak with god,[1] are in a noble condition; but the greatest contest concerns things yet to come. For to be distinguished in courage, and speed, and strength would seem to belong also to certain others, but in truthfulness,[2] and justice, and 320c magnificence, as well as decorum concerning all these things—anyone would grant that those who claim to honor such things would appropriately be distinguished above the rest.

What I now mean to say, then, is clear, but we need nonetheless to remind ourselves that it is proper for the you-know-who [pl][3] to be

1. See n. 20 to Letter Two.

2. Or simply "truth."

3. An unusual phrase generally thought to refer either to philosopher-kings or to members of Plato's Academy, but this is necessarily speculative. It is hard to understand, for example, how Post claims to know that "Plato expects those who have been initiated by him into the mysteries of the true philosophy to be a tribe of supermen" (1925, 144n1).

distinguished among the other human beings more than among children.[4] It needs therefore to become manifest that we are the very sorts we claim to be, especially since, to speak with god,[5] it will be easily done. 320d For it has turned out to be necessary for others to wander far and wide if they were going to become recognized; but the situation around you now is such that people from every inhabited region (even if this is to speak rather exaggeratedly[6]) are looking toward one place, and in this place, upon you most of all. Since, then, you are being watched by all, be prepared to show up Lycurgus himself as outdated,[7] as well as Cyrus,[8] and anyone else who ever seemed to be distinguished for his character 320e and regime, especially since many, and almost all those here, are saying that there is a great expectation[9] that, Dionysius having been done away with, your affairs will come to ruin on account of your love of honor as well as that of Heraclides, Theodotes, and the other notables.[10] Above all, then, may no one of you be of this sort. But if indeed someone comes to be this way, manifestly provide a doctor's treatment and you [pl] would proceed toward what is best.

321a Perhaps my saying these things appears ridiculous to you, since indeed you yourself are not ignorant; but even in the theaters, I see that those competing [for the actors' prizes] are spurred on by the children—to say nothing of their friends—if one should suppose that they shout their encouragements in seriousness and with goodwill. So be yourselves competitors now,[11] and if there is need of anything, send us a letter. Things here are in much the same state as they were when you 321b were here. But send a letter also relaying anything that has been done by you or that you happen to be doing, as we hear many things but know nothing; even now, letters from Theodotes and Heraclides have come to

---

4. A proverbial phrase. The general meaning is clear enough, but there is some disagreement among scholars over the exact sense of the wording. Plato's Socrates employs the same idiom in describing Isocrates's superiority to his rivals at *Phaedrus* 279a6–7.

5. See n. 20 to Letter Two.

6. Or "impetuously" (*neanikōteron*) as at 318b5 and 347d8.

7. Lit. "ancient" or "old," though *archaios* can have the pejorative sense of "outdated" or "worn out" as it does here and at *Hippias Minor* 371d4.

8. Lycurgus was credited with founding Sparta's renowned militaristic and austere political institutions, probably in the late ninth century BCE. For Cyrus, see n. 12 to Letter two.

9. Or "a great hope."

10. On Heraclides and Theodotes, see n. 28 to Letter Three.

11. From here until the end of the paragraph, every appearance of the second person is plural, including the imperatives "be competitors" (*agōnizesthe*) and "send a letter" (*epistellete*). Beginning in the next paragraph, with the imperative "take to heart," Plato returns to the second-person singular.

Lacedaemon and Aegina, but we, as I have said, hear many things about things here, but we know nothing.

But take to heart also that you seem to some to be rather lacking in the proper courtesy. Let it not escape your notice that it is through being 321c agreeable to human beings that it is possible to act, but stubbornness dwells with loneliness. Good luck.[12]

---

12. I render the one-word valediction *eutuchei* (lit. "be fortunate") into English as "good luck" here and throughout, but it should be noted that I have consistently translated the root word *tuchē* as "fortune" in hope of reminding the English reader that *tuchē* for the Greeks was more likely to evoke the idea of *divine* fortune (or the goddess Tuchē, i.e., Fortuna) than mere "dumb luck" (even if the latter falls within the word's scope of meaning). Note also that the verb *tugchanein*, which I translate "to happen to be" or "to hit upon," shares the same root.

Letter Five

Plato to Perdiccas:[1] Do well!

I counseled Euphraeus, just as you sent a letter instructing me to, to take care over your affairs and to occupy himself with them. But it is just of me[2] also to counsel you with what is called the guest-friend's and 321d sacred counsel—concerning both the other things you would point out[3]

1. Perdiccas III was the king of Macedon from 365 to 360 BCE, some three decades before the ascension of his nephew, Alexander the Great. It seems Perdiccas was still young enough to be under the regency of his brother-in-law, Ptolemy of Alorus, for three years before the latter's assassination initiated Perdiccas's own reign (cf. Diodorus Siculus 15.60.3, 71.1–2, and 77.5 with Aeschines, *On the Embassy* 26–27). The historicity of Euphraeus's relationship to the Macedonian court is attested by Demosthenes's *Third Philippic* (59–65), which provides information that neither confirms nor contradicts anything in this letter. More relevant are the details presented in the *Deipnosophistae* of Athenaeus (fl. c. 300 CE), who professes to quote from Carystius (fl. late second century BCE). There we learn that, under the influence of Plato's student Euphraeus, Perdiccas became so enamored of philosophic pursuits that "participation at [Perdiccas's] common meals was not allowed unless one knew how to do geometry or philosophy," and that Euphraeus himself rose to considerable power and prominence as a result of their relationship (*Deipnosophistae* 11.119). Moreover, the story is reported that it was Euphraeus who first persuaded Perdiccas to give Philip II (father of Alexander the Great) his political start in Macedon, resulting in the widespread opinion that "Philip first obtained the kingship through Plato" (11.115). But even Athenaeus, who is hardly one to shy away from gossip-mongering, is quick to cast doubt on the truth of those rumors.

2. Lit. "I am just."

3. "Point out" translates *phrazēis*, which I have usually rendered "explain."

and how you should make use of Euphraeus now. For the man is useful in many respects, but the greatest is that of which you too are now in need, both because of your age and because there are not many counselors for the young concerning the matter.

For there is a certain voice of each of the regimes just as of certain animals:[4] one of democracy, another of oligarchy, and yet another of monarchy. Very many would claim to know[5] them, but for the most part they fall short of understanding them, except for a very few. Whichever of the regimes, then, makes utterance in its own voice, both to gods and to human beings, and makes its actions follow its voice, always flourishes and is saved, but by imitating another is ruined. Not least of all with respect to these things, then, Euphraeus could come to be useful to you, and indeed with respect to other things as well, since he is courageous; for I hope[6] that he, not least of those who are concerned with your occupation, will assist in finding out the speeches befitting monarchy. Using him for these things, then, you yourself will profit and you will benefit him most.

321e

322a

But if someone, having heard these things, should say, "Plato, it seems, pretends to know what things are advantageous to a democracy, but when it was possible to speak to the demos and to counsel the things best for it, he never went up to utter a sound," say in response to these things that Plato was born late in [the life of] the fatherland and came upon the demos already elderly and habituated by those who came before to do many things unlike to his own counsel—since, of all things, it would be most pleasant for him to give it counsel as to a father, if he didn't suppose that he would be taking risks in vain and doing nothing more. "So I suppose," [you'll say,] "he would have done the same thing also with his counsel to me. For if we should have seemed to be in an incurable state, he would have bid us a great farewell and distanced himself from counsel concerning me and my things." Good luck.[7]

322b

322c

4. Scholars have seen here a reference to *Republic* 493a6–c8.

5. "Know" here translates *epistasthai*. In contrast to *eidenai* (the word I have otherwise consistently translated "to know") *epistasthai* refers to a rigorous, even "scientific" form of knowing—that is, to the possession of *epistēmē*, scientific knowledge. This is the only instance of any form of *epistamai* or *epistēmē* in the *Letters* outside of Letter Seven; see n. 108 to Letter Seven.

6. Or "I expect."

7. On the valediction "good luck" (*eutuchē*), see n. 12 to Letter Four.

Letter Six

Plato to Hermias, and Erastus, and Coriscus:[1] Do well!

To me some one of the gods appears to be kindly and sufficiently preparing good fortune for you [pl], if you [pl] should accept it well. For you [pl] both dwell as neighbors and have such need[2] as to benefit 22d each other in the greatest things. For to Hermias, neither from a multitude of horses, nor from another military alliance, nor even from the further accrual of gold could a greater power come to be in all things

1. Hermias ruled the Ionian city of Atarneus in the mid-fourth century BCE. He is often said first to have been the eunuch or the slave of Eubulus, a banker who came to rule Atarneus and left the throne to him. Contrary to the testimony of this letter (322e6–323a1), Strabo (64/3 BCE–24 CE) records the story that Hermias was a pupil of both Plato and Aristotle in Athens before inheriting the rule of Atarneus around 351 BCE (*Geographica* 13.1.57). His relationship to Aristotle, who spent time in his court after Plato died, appears to have been the more extensive: Aristotle is said to have married Hermias's daughter, and it was through Aristotle that Hermias developed his political ties to Philip II of Macedon (Diogenes Laertius 5.1.3). The collapse of this alliance with Philip precipitated Hermias's ultimate downfall. Very little is known about Erastus and Coriscus outside of the *Letters*. They are said to have been from Scepsis, not far from Atarneus; Diogenes Laertius lists them among Plato's students (3.46), and Strabo calls them "Socratics" (13.1.54). Coriscus happens to have been the father of Neleus, the improvident inheritor of Aristotle's literary estate from Theophrastus (Strabo 13.1.54). Erastus is mentioned again in Letter Thirteen (362b2).

2. "Need" translates the Greek word *chreian*. Generally, I have reserved words related to "need" for the translations of words related to the Greek *dei*, whereas the word *chrē* (related to *chreia*) is translated "ought."

than from friends who are steadfast and who have healthy character. As for Erastus and Coriscus, in addition to this beautiful wisdom of the Forms,[3] I claim, "even though [I am] old,"[4] that they have further 322e need—of a wisdom that guards against the wicked and unjust, and of a certain defensive power. For they are inexperienced on account of having been occupied with us, who are measured and not bad, for a long part of their life. This is why I said they have need of these things in addition,[5] lest they be compelled to be careless of the true wisdom in order to take care over the human and compulsory [wisdom] more than they need to. 323a But Hermias appears to me (so far as is possible without my yet having met him)[6] to have acquired this very power both by nature and, through experience, by art.

What, then, am I saying? To you, Hermias, I—having made trial[7] of Erastus and Coriscus more than you have—claim, declare,[8] and bear witness that you will not easily find more trustworthy characters than these neighbors. I counsel you to hold fast to these men in every just way, holding this to be no peripheral issue. To Coriscus and Erastus, I am counseling that you hold fast to Hermias in turn and that you 323b attempt by this mutual holding of one another to arrive at a single braid of friendship. But if anyone among you should at some point resolve to dissolve this—for the human is not altogether steadfast—send [pl] to me and mine here a letter of accusation. For I suppose that, both by justice and by awe,[9] the speeches coming from us here, unless the dissolution

---

3. A reference to Plato's famous metaphysical, ontological, and epistemological doctrine. The word for "Form" appears only once more in the *Letters*, but in that case it is not obviously a reference to the doctrine of the Forms as it is here (354c5). The long "philosophic digression" in Letter Seven, however, is usually taken to be a summary and explanation of this doctrine despite Plato's never using the word in that passage (341b3–345c3).

4. Post (1930a) has proposed that this is a quotation from Sophocles's lost *Thyestes*, of which the relevant fragment (Nauck fr. 239) has been preserved by Stobaeus. The full fragment reads "even though [I am] old; but wont to accompany old age are mind and deliberation as to what is needed."

5. This reading appears in the text of some manuscripts, and as a marginal correction in the best ones. The main text of the best manuscripts has instead only "This is why I spoke."

6. The word for "having met" (*suggegonoti*) is literally "having come to be together with." It might mean instead something like "having spent time in conversation with."

7. The word translated "having made trial of" is *pepeiramenos*, the same verb I have elsewhere translated "attempt." The connection should also be noted to words like *empeiros* ("experienced") and *apeiria* ("inexperience") appearing elsewhere, including in this letter.

8. Or "reveal," as of a secret (*mēnuō*).

9. "Justice" (*dikē*) could also be "just penalty." "Awe" translates *aidōs*, "that feeling of reverence or shame which restrains men from wrong" (Evelyn-White 1914, 17n2). Both Dikē and Aidōs were often deified as goddesses; in Plato's *Laws*, the Athenian Stranger claims that Dikē is rightly said to be the virgin daughter of Aidōs (943e1–2). This seems to have been a deliberate

happens to have been great, would, more than any incantation whatsoever, naturally implant,[10] and bind [you] together again in, the preexisting friendship and community; and with respect to this, whenever we all—both we and you [pl]—shall philosophize insofar as we are capable and as is appropriate to each of us, the oracles just now delivered will come to be authoritative.[11] But if we should not do these things—I will not speak to this. For I deliver a good prophecy, and I claim that we will do all these good things, if a god should be willing.

323c

This letter all of you, being three, ought to read—most of all as a group, but otherwise in twos—in common[12] as often as, within your power, you are able; and use[13] it as a compact and sovereign law, which is just, swearing with seriousness that is not unmusical,[14] and at the same time, with the playfulness that is a sister of seriousness, and swearing by the god who is leader of all the things that are and the things that will be, sovereign father of the leader and cause, whom, if we really philosophize, we all shall know as clearly as is within the power of happy human beings.

323d

---

twist on a line from Hesiod: "Dikē was born the virgin daughter of Zeus, who is renowned and reverenced (*aidoiē*) by the gods who hold Olympus" (*Works and Days* 256–57).

10. The main text in all the manuscripts, which I follow, has *emphusai*, "would naturally implant." Most editors and translators, however, have followed the suggestion of scribes who indicate that the word should be *sumphusai*, "would naturally unite" or "would naturally heal [as a wound]." On this reading, the line would run something like, "would, more than any incantation, naturally unite [you] and bind [you] together again" or perhaps "would, more than any incantation, naturally heal [your wound] and bind [you] together again." Cf. n. 44 to Letter Two on my translation of words related to *phusis*, "nature."

11. Or "sovereign" (*kuria*); see n. 19 to Letter Two.

12. The word for "in common" (*koinēi*) is related to the word for "partnership" above (323c1).

13. Or perhaps "consult," in the sense of consulting an oracle (*chrēsthai*).

14. "Unmusical" translates *amousōi*, literally "without the Muses," and so can mean more generally "tasteless," "uncultured," or "unrefined."

Letter Seven

Plato to the intimates[1] and comrades of Dion: Do well!

You [pl] sent a letter saying I need to believe that your [pl] intention is the same as that which Dion also had, and you [pl] directed me more-
324a over to join in common [with you], insofar as I am able, in deed and in speech. If you [pl] have the same opinion and desire as him, I grant that I will join in common [with you]; otherwise, I will deliberate at length.[2] But as to what his intention and desire were, I could speak as someone who is hardly conjecturing but rather knows clearly. For, when I arrived at Syracuse in the beginning, I was about forty years old, and Dion was at the age at which Hipparinus[3] is now; and the opinion of which he

1. As a rule, I have translated the word *oikeioi* as "intimates." The word literally refers to ones with whom one shares a household, and thus often specifically to family members (as it does sometimes in the *Letters*). However, Plato clearly uses the word in some cases to refer to a broader class of very close relationships (e.g., 313d2).

2. Lit. "often" (*pollakis*).

3. Three men connected to the Syracusan royal family were named Hipparinus: Dion's father, Dion's son, and Dion's nephew. There has been considerable debate as to which of the latter two men Plato is referring to here; see, e.g., Nails 2002, 166–68; Burnyeat and Frede 2015, 187–88n143; Harward 1932, 195–96; Post 1930b; Brisson 1993, 211–12n7; Souilhé 1931, xlv–xlvii. Of the two candidates, only Dion's son would have been of such an age as to match Plato's description (around twenty years old in about 354 BCE). The primary difficulty is that this Hipparinus is said by Plutarch (*Dion* 55.2) and Nepos (*Dion* 6) to have committed suicide

324b then took hold was the same one he continued holding to the end: he supposed that the Syracusans should be free, dwelling under the best laws. So it will be in no way amazing if some one of the gods should make this man too [i.e., Hipparinus] come to be of the same mind with the other's opinion about their regime. As for the way of [the opinion's] coming to be, it is not unworthy of being heard for him who is young and him who is not young, and I will attempt to go through it for you [pl] from the beginning; for now is a propitious moment.

When I was young, I underwent the same thing as many do: I supposed that, as soon as I should become my own master,[4] I would engage 324c straightaway in the common affairs of the city. And certain strokes of fortune from among the affairs of the city befell me, such as the following. The regime of that time being reviled by many, there came to be a change, and from the change fifty-one men came to the fore as magistrates, eleven in the town and ten in the Piraeus—each group to manage as many things as were needed concerning the agora and the things 324d in the districts—and they set up thirty rulers over everything as rulers with full powers.[5] Of these some happened to be intimates and acquaintances of mine, and they straightaway called upon me as toward my own

---

shortly before Dion himself was assassinated, in which case he could never have been alive at the time of the writing of Letter Seven. The other candidate, Dion's nephew, was a more noteworthy historical figure. This Hipparinus was the son of Dionysius the Elder and went on himself to become the leader of Dion's party, winning back rule over Syracuse from Dion's murderer Callippus and ruling the city as a tyrant himself for two years (Diodorus Siculus 16.36). But he was some ten years too old to match Plato's description here. Those who say that Plato could never have been ignorant either of the suicide of Dion's son or of the age of Dion's nephew allege that the reference to Hipparinus at 324a7 gives away the author of Letter Seven as a forger—some adding that neither Hipparinus was deserving of the hopeful description at 324b3–4. Others, defending the letter's authenticity, have thought it plausible either that Plato might not have received word of the younger Hipparinus's untimely death or that he might have become confused as to the elder Hipparinus's age. Of course, it may also be that the confusion in chronology lies with the sources of Plutarch's and Nepos's biographies. Nor is it impossible, though I consider it unlikely, that Plato was intentionally feigning ignorance of the death of Dion's son. Letter Eight also appears to have been written under the impression that Dion's son was still alive (355e5).

4. Lit. "authority" or "sovereign"; see n. 19 to Letter Two.

5. Plato refers here to what is known as the regime of the Thirty Tyrants, which ruled Athens for eight months after its defeat in the Peloponnesian War in 404 BCE. Plato's account of the Thirty here is unusual in several respects, beginning with his reference to the broader group of "fifty-one" rulers as opposed to the most infamous "Thirty"; for parallels, see Aristotle, *Athenian Constitution* 35 and Xenophon, *Hellenica* 2.3.54. Furthermore, Plato gives a notably softened and even biased account of the Thirty's rise to power by attributing it to a "change" (*metabolē*) in the previously "reviled" regime and not to the victorious Spartans' imposition upon their defeated foes (see Aristotle, *Athenian Constitution.* 34; cf. Xenophon, *Hellenica* 2.2.20, 23; 2.3.1–3, 11). The strangeness of this account has been noted by Richards (1911, 278–79).

proper affairs. And it was no wonder what I underwent, on account of my youth; for I supposed that they would manage the city by leading it from a certain unjust life to a just way, so that I was intently focusing my mind upon them as to what they would do. But then, seeing these men in a short time show the previous regime to have been golden—both in 324e other matters and, especially, when they sent a man who was my friend, the elderly Socrates, whom I would scarcely be ashamed to say was the most just of those in that time, with some others, to carry off one of the 325a citizens by force to be put to death, in order that he should participate in their affairs whether he should wish to or not—but he did not obey, but risked suffering everything rather than become a partner in their impious deeds[6]—seeing distinctly all these things and still others such as these that weren't slight, I was disgusted and I withdrew myself from the evils of that time.

It was not a long time before the affairs of the Thirty and the whole regime of that time fell; and once again, though more slowly, nevertheless 325b the desire to be active in the common and political things began to draw me. Well, many things were happening in these times too, troubled as they were, with which one would be disgusted, and it was in no way anything amazing that, in times of change, some came to impose great vengeful penalties on some of their enemies; yet those who then returned [from exile] employed great decency indeed. But by some fortune, some of those in power again brought this comrade of ours, Socrates, into 325c court, laying a most impious accusation against him and one that was proper least of all with respect to Socrates. For these brought him in on grounds of a lack of pious veneration, and others condemned and killed him—he who had formerly not been willing to participate in the impious arrest of one of the friends of those in exile at the very time when they themselves were in exile and suffering bad fortune.

I was examining both these things and the human beings who were doing the political things, and also the laws and customs, and the more I carefully examined and advanced in age, the harder it appeared to me 325d to be to manage the political things correctly. For one is not able to act without men who are friends and faithful comrades—and these were not already there and easy to find, for our city was no longer being managed according to the ways and practices of our fathers, and it was impossible to acquire other, new [friends and comrades] with any ease—and both

6. A reference to the arrest of Leon of Salamis, an episode known to us especially from Plato's *Apology of Socrates* 32c3–e1; cf. Xenophon, *Hellenica* 2.3.38–39.

the written laws and the customs were being corrupted and increas- 325e ing to such an amazing degree that, while at first I had been full of a great impulse toward doing the common things, when I looked at these things and saw them being borne about everywhere in every way, I ended up becoming dizzy; and though I did not leave off examining in what way something better might ever come to be, both concerning these 326a very things and moreover concerning the whole regime, yet with respect to acting I was always waiting for propitious moments, and ended up thinking, concerning all of the cities now, that all of them are being governed badly—for what is of their laws is in a nearly incurable state without some amazing artifice[7] together with fortune—and I was compelled to say, praising correct philosophy, that on the basis of this it is possible to see distinctly both the just political things and all in private matters; 326b therefore the human tribes[8] will not cease from evils until either the tribe of those philosophizing (correctly and truly, that is) should come into the positions of political rule, or that of those who are in power in the cities should, by some divine fate, really philosophize.[9]

Having this intention, I went to Italy and Sicily—when I arrived the first time. But when I got there, the life that is there called happy, one full of Italiote[10] and Syracusan tables,[11] was agreeable to me in no way or manner—to live, stuffing oneself twice a day, never going to bed alone 326c at night, and all the practices that accompany this life; for neither could anyone of the human beings under heaven, practicing these customs from youth, ever be capable of becoming practically wise—there will be no blending by nature that is so amazing—nor would one ever go on to become moderate; and the same speech would hold, moreover, for the rest of virtue, and no city could be at rest under any laws whatso- 326d ever where men suppose that they need to spend away everything on excesses, and hold moreover that they need to become idle in everything except for feasts, drinking-bouts, and the serious toil of the Aphroditean

7. Lit. "preparation" (*paraskeuēs*).

8. "Tribes" translates the plural of *genos*, which can have the meaning of "family" or "stock," though it is evident enough even in this passage that it can also mean merely a "kind" or "group," as in the English "genus." "Classes" might well be the best translation here, if it were not apt to be misconstrued as indicating a socioeconomic class or caste.

9. This whole passage is an unmistakable reference to, and must be carefully compared with, *Republic* 473c11–e2; see also 499a11–d6.

10. Italiotes were the Greek inhabitants of Italy.

11. Morrow (1962) notes ad loc. that "Syracusan tables were proverbial," and refers to Plato, *Republic* 404d, as well as Athenaeus, *Deipnosophistae* 527d.

things;[12] and it is by necessity that these cities never cease changing—tyrannies, oligarchies, and democracies[13]—and those in power in them won't put up with hearing the name of a regime of justice and equality under the law.

Having these things in mind, in addition to those from before,[14] 326e I crossed into Syracuse, perhaps by fortune, but it's likely that, by some one of the mightier ones contriving,[15] a beginning was then laid down of the problems that have now come to be concerning Dion and of those concerning the Syracusans—and, it is to be dreaded, of still more, unless you would now obey my counsel, given now for the second time.

327a In what way, then, do I mean that my arrival in Sicily at that time came to be a beginning of everything? I'm afraid that, having come to be together at that time with a young Dion, revealing to him through speeches the things that seemed to me to be best for human beings and counseling him to do them, I was ignorant that I, without noticing myself, was in a certain way contriving what would come to be a dissolution of a tyranny. For Dion being indeed very much a good learner, about other things too but especially the speeches that were then spo- 327b ken by me,[16] he hearkened keenly and intently such as none of the young I have ever met,[17] and was willing to live the rest of his life in a manner differing from that of the many Italiotes and Siceliotes,[18] having come to cherish virtue more than pleasure and the rest of luxury; from which point he led his life, until the event of Dionysius's death, in a manner that was rather aggravating to those living according to what is lawful convention in a tyranny.

327c After this, he had in mind that this intention,[19] of which he himself took hold from correct speeches, would never have come to be in

12. I.e., sexual activity.

13. The phrase might also mean "never cease changing between tyranny, democracy, and oligarchy."

14. The word for "having in mind" is *dianooumenos*, which I have tried to render "intending" as much as possible. See n. 5 to Letter Three. Plato seems to refer back in this sentence to the *dianoia*, "intention," he had in mind in traveling to Sicily in the first place at 326b5.

15. The gender of *tōn kreittonōn* is ambiguous. It could refer to "the mightier people" or "gods," or if it is neuter, to "the mightier things."

16. The reading of one of the two best manuscripts. The other reads "the speeches that then came into being from me."

17. "Met" translates *prosetuxon*, which is related to *tuchē*, "fortune"; see n. 12 to Letter Four.

18. I.e., the Greek inhabitants of Italy and Sicily, as noted above (n. 32 to Letter Three and n. 10 above)

19. "He had in mind" and "intention" translate the related words *dianoēthē* and *dianoian*; see n. 5 to Letter Three.

him alone, but he apprehended that he saw it coming to be in others too—not in many, but it was coming to be in some, and he held that even Dionysius could perhaps become one of these with the assistance of gods, and if such a thing should in turn come to pass, that both his life and that of the other Syracusans would turn out to become one of indomitable bliss.[20] In addition to these things, he supposed that 327d I needed to come, by every means, to Syracuse as quickly as possible as a partner in these things, remembering how easily his and my intercourse had succeeded in bringing him to a desire for the noblest and best life;[21] and if he could now accomplish in Dionysius what he was undertaking, he had great hopes of establishing, without slaughters, deaths, and the evils that have now come to be, a happy and true[22] life throughout the whole land.

Correctly intending these things, Dion persuaded Dionysius to send for me, and he himself sent to me begging that I come as quickly as 327e possible by every means, before some others encountered Dionysius and turned him away to a life other than the best one. And he begged by saying the following things, though speaking at even greater length: "What propitious moments are we waiting for," he said, "greater than those that have now come to be at hand by some divine fortune?" He 328a went through the imperial rule over Italy and Sicily and his power in it, and Dionysius's youth and desire for philosophy and education, saying that he was intent on this, that his nephews[23] and intimates would easily be called toward the reason and life of which I am always speaking and would be most sufficient to join in calling Dionysius toward the same, so that, now if ever, there was every hope of bringing to completion the outcome that philosophers and rulers of great cities would be the same.

328b These and other such encouragements were very numerous, but as for my own opinion, on one hand I was fearful as to the way in which

---

20. "Indomitable" translates *amēchanon,* which is related to the word I have usually translated by a form of the word "contrive." The literal sense is something like "against which no contrivance could prevail."

21. "Noblest and best" translates *kallistou te kai agathou*, the superlative form of *kalos te kai agathos*, "noble and good." (see n. 21 to Letter Two on the meaning of *kalos*). The contracted form *kalos k'agathos* is a formula that refers to a morally and civically upstanding member of the Greek political community; it is often translated "gentleman." There is only one other use of this phrase in the *Letters*, at 359b7–8. The phrase is important in Platonic philosophy generally; see, e.g., *Apology of Socrates* 21d1–8 in context as well as *Alcibiades* 114e7–116b1.

22. Or "truthful" (*alēthinon*).

23. "The masculine noun [*adelphidous*] may well be generic, so that it includes Dion's nieces" (Burnyeat and Frede 2015, 146n25).

things would ever come to be concerning the young—for the desires of such as them are flighty and are often borne into their opposites—but on the other hand I knew,[24] concerning the character of Dion's soul, that it was by nature weighty and that it had already reached its middle age. Hence, though I was examining and waffling as to whether I must go and hearken or else what, nevertheless the need [to go] prevailed:[25] if ever 328c someone was going to undertake to bring these intentions concerning both laws and regime[26] to completion, it must be attempted also now; for if I should sufficiently persuade just one, I would be achieving all good things.

With this intention and daring, then, I set out from home—not in the way that some were opining, but ashamed of myself in the highest degree lest I should ever seem to myself to be altogether, solely, and artlessly a certain speech,[27] voluntarily taking hold of not one deed ever, 328d and to be in danger of betraying, in the first place, the guest-friendship and comradeship of Dion, who had really come to be in no small dangers. Whether indeed he should suffer something, or whether, having been thrown out by Dionysius and his other enemies, he should come to us in exile and ask, "Plato, I have come to you as an exile, not needing hoplites,[28] nor having come to be in need of cavalrymen for defense against enemies, but of speeches and persuasions, by means of which, as I myself have known,[29] you most of all are capable on every occasion of setting up young human beings in friendship and comradeship with each other by turning them toward the good things and the just 328e things; it is out of need for these things from your side that I am here now, having left Syracuse behind. Now, what pertains to me carries

---

24. Or "I knew scientifically" (*ēpistamēn*); see n. 5 to Letter Five.

25. There is a connection, difficult to render in consistent idiomatic English, between the words I have translated "waffling" and "prevailed" in this sentence. The former, *distazonti* ("doubting," "hesitating"), is literally a "dripping" on both sides of something (*dis-* = "both" + *stazein* = "to drip, trickle"). The latter, *errepse* ("inclined," "preponderated"), has as its primary meaning "tipped the scale." Plato's image, then, is of a balance in which his two options were being weighed; initially, his considerations gave equal weight to each side, but finally the scale was tipped in favor of departure to Syracuse.

26. It should be noted that *Laws* and *Regime* (usually translated *Republic*) are the titles of Plato's two longest books and the two that most explicitly and extensively describe purportedly ideal and philosophically informed political communities.

27. "Speech" translates *logos*, which could also be rendered "argument" or "reason." Its contrast in this sentence with "deed" (*ergou*) is a common one. In idiomatic English, we might say, "all talk and no action."

28. Heavy-armed foot soldiers, who would compose the core of a typical polis's army.

29. Or "as I myself have known scientifically" (*ēpistamēn*); see n. 5 to Letter Five.

relatively little reproach for you; but philosophy, which you always extol and which you claim is held in dishonor by the rest of human beings—how has it not been betrayed at this point, together with me, insofar as a 329a part of what has come to pass was up to you? And if we happened to be dwelling in Megara,[30] surely you would have come to my aid on account of the things for which I was calling upon you, or else you would hold yourself to be pettiest[31] of all; but as it is, do you suppose that by blaming the length of the journey and the magnitude of the sailing and of the toil you will ever escape a reputation for vice? Far from it,[32] indeed."—if these things had been said, what decorous answer would I have to them? There isn't [one].

329b But I went, in accordance with reason and in justice as much as can be for a human being, and because of such things I left behind my occupations, which were not indecorous, [to go live] under a tyranny that didn't seem to be fitting with respect to my things[33] or to me. In going, I both acquitted[34] myself in relation to Zeus Xenios[35] and rendered the philosopher's part unimpeachable—it would have come to be a matter of reproach had I participated in shamefulness and vice by in any way becoming soft and being cowardly.

But when I went (for there is no need to go on at length) I found 329c everything around Dionysius full of strife and slanders about Dion in relation to the tyranny. To be sure, I was defending him to the extent I was capable, though I was able to do only small things, but in about the fourth month, Dionysius, accusing Dion of plotting against the tyranny, put him in a small boat and cast him out in dishonor.

Indeed, after this we friends of Dion were all fearful lest Dionysius should avenge himself upon someone by accusing him of being an accomplice in Dion's plot; and a certain speech concerning me even got around among the Syracusans to the effect that I had been put to death

30. A city some twenty-five miles from Athens.

31. Or "paltriest," as I otherwise try to render words related to *phaulos*.

32. Lit. "there would be need of much." The main verb, *deēsei*, is related to the words for "need" and "lack" that appear in this same passage.

33. The best manuscripts include the word *logois* in the margins here, suggesting the reading "didn't seem to be fitting with respect to my speeches or to me." But it is not clear whether the marginal note indicates a preferable reading from other manuscripts since lost or merely a later scribe or editor's explanatory gloss on the text.

34. *Ēleutherōsa*, which is literally "I freed," as in "freed from blame" and hence "acquitted," or indeed "freed from debt."

35. "Xenios" is an epithet of Zeus indicating his responsibility for overseeing, and punishing transgressions of, the obligations of *xenia*, "guest-friendship"; see n. 12 to Letter Three.

by Dionysius on the grounds that I was to blame for all the things that 329d had happened up to that point. But he, perceiving that we all were disposed this way and fearing lest something greater should come to be from our fears, began to pick back up with everyone in a friendly manner; and with respect to me in particular, he was reassuring me, directing me to take heart, and begging me in every way to stay; for my fleeing from him would come to be no beautiful thing for him, but rather my staying, wherefore he pretended to beg very intently indeed. But we know that 329e the begging[36] of tyrants is mixed with compulsions, and he contrived to prevent my sailing away by bringing me into the acropolis and settling me whence not a single ship captain would any longer lead me out—not that Dionysius was [actively] preventing this; rather, not unless he himself should give the order[37] by sending someone with directions to lead me out was there a merchant, or a single one of the officers ruling at the land's exits, who, if they knew that I was leaving alone, wouldn't have seized me straightaway and led me back again to Dionysius, especially 330a since it had already been proclaimed at some point, contrary to before, how amazingly fond Dionysius was of Plato.

So then, what indeed was the state of things? For one needs to explain the truth. While he did grow ever fonder of me as time went on during his intercourse with my way and character, he also wished for me to praise him more than Dion and to hold him to be more especially[38] a friend than him, and he had an amazing love of victory with regard to such a thing. But as for the way in which it might have come to be 330b that way (if indeed it was to come to be that way) most nobly—in learning from and listening to speeches concerning philosophy, to become familiar[39] with me and come to be together with me—he shrank from it, fearing, on account of the slanderers' speeches, lest he should become ensnared in some way and Dion come to accomplish everything for himself. But I endured everything, guarding the first intention with which

36. I have translated *deēseis* here with the word "begging," since it is related to the verb *deō*, "I beg," which appears several times in the surrounding text. Elsewhere, I have rendered the noun *deēsis* with the English "entreaty."

37. A rare case in the *Letters* in which the verb *epistellein*, which I usually render with the phrase "to send a letter," means instead "to give an order"; see n. 43 to Letter Two. Of course, it is possible even here that Plato is describing Dionysius sending his messenger with a written letter.

38. "Especially" translates *diapherontōs*, which I usually translate with some form of the word "different," "distinguished," or "surpassing" (or, in other contexts, "conflict").

39. *Oikeiousthai* might be translated "become an intimate of," to render the word's relationship to *oikeios*, which I have translated as "intimate"; see n. 1 above.

I had arrived in case he should somehow come to a desire for the life of philosophy; but he, resisting, won out.

330c And the time of my first visit and occupation in Sicily came out thus, because of all these things. And after this I voyaged back, and returned when Dionysius sent for me in all seriousness. As to why, and how many things I did, that they were appropriate and just—after having first counseled you [pl] with respect to what [you] ought to do on the basis of the things that have now happened, I will later go through thoroughly what concerns those things, for the sake of those repeatedly asking what indeed I was wishing when I went the second time, so that peripheral issues do not turn out to be spoken of by me as the main issues.

Here is what I mean. One who is counseling a sick man adhering to 330d a regimen that is depraved with respect to health ought first to change his life into something else, and if he is willing to obey, at that point to suggest other things too; but if he is not willing, I would hold one who flees from counseling such a one to be both a man and a doctor, and one who remains to be the opposite: unmanly and artless. It is indeed the same with respect to a city as well, whether it has one sovereign authority or more.[40] If, while duly proceeding on the correct path, he should 330e seek counsel regarding something advantageous for the regime,[41] then it belongs to one with intelligence[42] to give counsel to those of this sort. But as for those who are deviating altogether from the correct regime and are in no way willing to go in its tracks, who declare beforehand to 331a the counselor that he is to let the regime be and is not to change it and that he will be put to death if he should change it, and who direct their servants to give counsel as to how their wishes and desires would most easily and most quickly come to be [satisfied] for all time—I would hold the one who remains to give such counsels to be unmanly, and the one who does not remain to be a man.

This is the intention I hold whenever someone should seek counsel from me concerning any of the greatest things in his life, such as the 331b acquisition of money or the care of body or soul; if he should seem to

40. Throughout the following passage, Plato seems to shift between the singular and the plural in referring to the one needing counsel.

41. A variant reading in the manuscripts, differing by only one letter and accepted by several editors and translators, has the word "proceeding" in the feminine so as to accord with "regime" rather than "sovereign." The clause then would read "if, the regime proceeding duly on the right path, he should seek counsel regarding something advantageous."

42. Lit. "one having a mind."

me to be living daily in a certain way[43] or to be willing to obey once I have counseled him concerning those things about which he is consulting in common, I eagerly give counsel and do not stop at the perfunctory discharge of duty.[44] But if he does not seek counsel from me at all, or if it is clear that he will in no way obey me when I do counsel him, I will not go to counsel such a one on my own initiative, nor will I use force, even if he should be my own son. Now, to a slave I would give counsel and, if 331c he were unwilling at least, I would use force; but I hold it not to be pious to use force upon a father or a mother unless they are out of their senses due to illness; but if they are living a certain life, which has been set up to be agreeable to them but not to me, I do not make myself hateful by admonishing in vain, nor do I serve them by flattering, furnishing fulfillments of desires which, if I myself were fond of them, I would not be willing to live.

Indeed, one who is sensible ought to live intending this same thing 331d concerning his city as well: he should speak, if it does not appear to him to be nobly governed, if he is neither going to be talking in vain nor to be put to death for speaking; but he should not bring force against a fatherland to produce a change of regime when it is not possible for it to come to be the best without exile and slaughter of men; rather, he should keep quiet and pray for the good things for both himself and the city.

In this same way, indeed, I would counsel you [pl], and as I, with Dion, was counseling Dionysius too: first, to live each day in such a way that he 331e was going to be as much in control of himself as possible, and to acquire faithful friends and comrades so as not to suffer the very things his father suffered, who took many and great Sicilian cities that had been pillaged by barbarians but, having recolonized them, was not able to set up in each of them regimes of men who were his comrades,[45] neither 332a foreigners from anywhere else, nor his brothers, whom he himself had raised when they were younger, and whom he had made from private persons into rulers and from poor into surpassingly rich. None of these was he able successfully to make into a partner in his rule, whether by

---

43. I.e., in the way of which Plato approves.

44. "Perfunctory discharge of duty" translates the participle *aphosiōsamenos*, the literal meaning of which refers to religious purification from pollution. The metaphorical meaning, "to do something in a perfunctory way" may have evolved from use of the word in reference to the routine performance of rituals.

45. Marginal emendations in the two oldest and best manuscripts add the adjective "faithful" (*pistas*) to this line, so that it would read "was not able to set up in each of them faithful regimes of men who were his comrades." This emendation also appears in the main text of later manuscripts.

persuasion, teaching, benefactions, or ties of kinship. Rather, he came to be seven times paltrier than Darius, who, trusting neither in brothers nor in anyone raised by him but only in his partners in the subduing of the Mede and eunuch, apportioned among them seven regions, each greater than all of Sicily, made use of them as faithful partners who attacked neither him nor each other, and gave demonstration of a model of what sort the good lawgiver and king ought to become; for by establishing laws, he has preserved the Persian empire even up to the present day.[46]

32b

In addition to these things, moreover, the Athenians, having taken over many Greek cities that they had not colonized themselves, which had been invaded by barbarians but were still inhabited, nevertheless kept guard over their empire for seventy years by having acquired men who were friends in each of the cities.[47] But Dionysius, having gathered all of Sicily in a single city, in his wisdom trusting no one, with difficulty saved himself; for he was poor in men who were friends and faithful—and there is no greater sign of virtue and vice than this, whether one is bereft of such men or not.

32c

So Dion and I together counseled these things to Dionysius too, since from his father it had turned out that he had come to be unacquainted with education and unacquainted with the proper associations:[48] [we counseled him] first . . . ,[49] and then, once he had set out in this way, to acquire other friends for himself from among his intimates[50] and his agemates and those who were in accord with respect to virtue, but most

32d

46. Darius the Great ruled the Persian Empire from 522 BCE until his death in 486 BCE. The "Mede and eunuch" to whom Plato refers would be the ruler of the Persian Empire preceding Darius, whose identity is a matter of long-standing debate. Plato seems to be the only one to suggest he was a eunuch (a detail not compatible with Herodotus's account). Yet Plato makes the same claim even more clearly at *Laws* 695b2–c4; cf. that passage (in the context of the Athenian Stranger's condensed history of the Persian empire; 693d–696a, 697c–698a, 698c–699d) with Herodotus 3.28–30 and 61ff.

47. According to Harward (1932, 203n 43), "The 'seventy years' describes roughly the period 478–404 B.C.," i.e., from the formation of the Delian League to the defeat of Athens in the Peloponnesian War.

48. The word translated "associations" here and "intercourse" elsewhere (*sunousia*) is most literally a "being together"; in this instance, it should be noted that the word can have the specific meaning of "intercourse *with a teacher*" and thus "attendance at his teaching" (LSJ, s.v.).

49. The word "first" (*prōton*) being followed immediately by the word "next" (*epeita*) in the best manuscript, as well as disagreements between other manuscripts, indicates some corruption of the text here. The reading I have favored suggests some kind of lacuna in the text. Souilhé and Novotný have proposed emending *epeita tautēi* to *epi tauta*, denying any further missing text; the sense would then be "first, in service of these [goals]."

50. Or "relatives" (*oikeiōn*); see n. 1 above.

of all himself with himself, for he had come to be amazingly in need of this. We were not saying it as clearly as this, for it was not safe, but we were speaking in riddles and contending by way of speeches that every man would thus save both himself and those of whom he would come 332e to be a leader, but that by not turning himself in this direction, he would bring everything to the opposite completion; and that by proceeding in the way we were saying and successfully making himself sensible and moderate,[51] if he should then resettle the desolated Sicilian cities and bind them together by laws and regimes so as to be intimates to him and to each other with a view to aiding each other against the barbar- 333a ians, he would then make his father's empire not only twice as great, but in fact many times greater. For if these things should come to pass, he would then be ready to enslave the Carthaginians to a much greater extent than the slavery that had come to be for them in Gelon's time—as opposed to how it is now: his father ordered that a tribute be paid to the barbarians.[52]

These were the things said and encouraged by us, the plotters against Dionysius, according to such speeches as were spreading from many places and indeed which, by prevailing over Dionysius, cast Dion out 333b and cast us down into fear. But—that we may wrap up in a short time no few affairs—Dion, coming from the Peloponnese and Athens, admonished Dionysius by deed.[53] But when he twice set the city free and gave it back to them, the Syracusans then suffered the very same thing with

51. "Sensible and moderate" translates the phrase *emphrona te kai sōphrona*; the two adjectives are closely related. The latter word refers to one of the four Platonic cardinal virtues; both share their root with *phronesis*, "practical wisdom" or "prudence." See n. 7 to Letter Two and n. 15 to Letter Three. For the importance of this phrase to the sense of the whole letter, see Harward 1932, 204n45.

52. Gelon, who ruled the city from 485 BCE until his death in 478 BCE, was the first of an earlier series of Syracusan tyrants. In 480 BCE, he scored a decisive victory over Hamlicar I's Carthaginian army in the Battle of Himera, and granted peace on terms that included the payment of 2,000 talents of silver in reparations (Diodorus Siculus 11.26.2). But this proved to be only the beginning of centuries of wars over Sicily between Carthage and Syracuse. In 376 BCE, Dionysius the Elder was defeated by Himilco Mago's forces at the Battle of Cronium, agreeing thereafter to pay 1,000 talents of silver as reparations (15.17.5). These reparations are apparently what Plato here refers to as the payment of "tribute" to the barbarians established by Dionysius (see Harward 1932, 204n46).

53. In 357 BCE, the exiled Dion sailed to Sicily with a small mercenary force to depose Dionysius the Younger. His campaign was successful, but, as is implied by the next sentence, the exercise soon needed to be repeated. In the aftermath of his victory, Dion lost his power over the Syracusans to his military ally turned political rival Heraclides, who was advancing more popular political proposals (see n. 28 to Letter Three). Not long after leaving, however, the Syracusans found themselves once more in mortal peril and called for Dion to return and save them, which he did. See Plutarch, *Dion* 22ff.

respect to Dion as Dionysius had when [Dion] undertook to educate him and to raise him to be a king worthy of rule so as to partner with 333c him in all of life. Dionysius [listened][54] to the slanderers and to those who were saying that Dion, plotting at the tyranny, was doing everything he did at that time in order that Dionysius, having had his mind beguiled by education, would not care about his rule and turn it over to him, while Dion usurped it and cast Dionysius out from the rule by trickery. These things were victorious at that time; and also the second time, when they were being said among the Syracusans, by means of a victory that was very strange and shameful for those responsible for 333d the victory. And those who are calling upon me in regard to the current affairs ought to hear what sort of thing has happened.

I, an Athenian man, Dion's comrade and his ally, came to the tyrant so that I could make friendship take the place of war between them; but I was defeated in contending against the slanderers. Dionysius was trying to persuade me by means of honors and money to join with him as a witness and friend, with a view to lending seemliness to his casting out of Dion. Of course, he altogether missed the mark in these things. But 333e later, when Dion was coming back home, he brought with him a pair of brothers from Athens who had come to be [his friends][55] not from philosophy but from the promiscuous comradeship belonging to most friends, which they work out through hosting someone as a guest-friend or through initiation into the lesser and greater mysteries.[56] In this case, the pair of friends who together brought him back had come to be his comrades both from these things and from providing the service of his 334a return; but when they came to Sicily, since they perceived that Dion had been slandered among the Siceliotes who had been freed by him to the effect that he was plotting to become tyrant, they not only betrayed their comrade and guest-friend but came to be, as it were, perpetrators of his murder, themselves holding weapons in their hands as they stood by

54. The main verb in this sentence appears to be missing; Harward, whom I follow in supplying the word "listened," calls it a "violent anacolouthon of the nominativus pendens type" (1932, 205n49).

55. The word for "friends" (*philō*) appears in the margins of the best manuscripts and in the main text of some others.

56. "Initiation into the lesser and greater mysteries" translates the phrase *muein kai epopteuein*. These two verbs refer to different stages of initiation into the Greek mystery cults and particularly into the Eleusinian Mysteries. Initiation into the "lesser mysteries" (*muein*) granted one the status of *mustēs*; by initiation into the "greater mysteries" (*epopteuein*), one graduated to the status of *epoptēs*.

as auxiliaries for the murderers.[57] And I, for my part, neither pass over the shameful and impious thing, nor do I say anything—for to harp on[58] these things is an object of care for many others and it will be the 334b object of their care in the time to come as well—but as for what is being said about them as Athenians, that they brought shame upon their city, I reject it. For I claim that he too is an Athenian who did not betray this very Dion, though he stood to obtain money and many other honors. For he had become a friend to Dion not through vulgar friendship, but through partnership in liberal education. In this alone ought one who possesses mind to trust, more than in kinship of souls and of bod- 334c ies; thus, I do not deem the pair who killed Dion worthy of bringing reproach upon their city, as though they had ever come to be men of any account.

All these things have been said for the sake of counsel to the Dionean friends and kin. Indeed, the counsel I give with respect to these things is the same counsel and the same speech that I am now saying for the third time, you [pl] being the third ones to whom I am saying it. Let not Sicily, nor any other city, be enslaved to human masters, but, as my speech has it at least, to laws; for otherwise it is better neither for the enslavers 334d nor the enslaved, not for them, nor for their children's children, nor for their descendants, but the attempt is altogether ruinous. It is the small and illiberal characters among souls who like to snatch up such gains, knowing nothing of the good and just[59] things, both divine and human, in the future and the present propitious moment.

Of these things I undertook first to persuade Dion, second Dionysius, and third now you [pl]. Now, then, be persuaded [pl] by me, for

---

57. It is well attested that Dion's murderer was Callippus, the Athenian who succeeded Dion as ruler of Syracuse and reigned there for just over a year (Diodorus Siculus 16.31.7; see also Plutarch, *Dion* 54ff., Athenaeus, *Deipnosophistae* 11.119, and Aristotle, *Rhetoric* 1373a18–20). Nepos's biography of Dion appears to be the only source to identify a brother of Callipus, a man named Philostratus who played a peripheral role in the assassination plot.

58. "To harp on" translates *humnein*, which was translated "to sing the praises of" at 311a; see n. 9 to Letter Two.

59. The word "just" (*dikaiōn*) is proposed in a sublinear emendation in one of the best manuscripts as well as in the main text of later manuscripts, and appears to be a necessary correction to *diōn* (as in the main text of the best manuscripts). Probably, the name "Dion" was miscopied from the next line. However, it could be that Plato actually wrote *diōn*, a rather poetic word for "divine" or "heavenly," which would also be a play on the name "Dion" (*Diōn*). Harward has noted that "the language" in this section, beginning at 334c8, "becomes impressive, and poetical words and phrases appear" (1932, 206n57).

the sake of[60] Zeus Third Savior,[61] and then looking to Dionysius and
34e Dion, of whom the one who was not persuaded now lives but not nobly, while the one who was persuaded has been nobly put to death; for to suffer whatever one may suffer while aiming at the noblest things, for both oneself and one's city, is altogether correct and noble. For neither is anyone of us naturally deathless, nor would one become happy if one should somehow turn out to be, as it seems to the many. For no bad or
35a good worthy of account belongs to the soulless, but this[62] will turn out to belong to each soul, either while it is with a body or after it has been separated. One really always ought to be persuaded by the ancient and sacred speeches, which indeed reveal to us that the soul is deathless, that it has judges, and that it suffers the greatest penalties whenever it is rid of its body; wherefore ought one to believe that it is a smaller evil to suffer even the great sins and injustices than to do them; which the lover of
35b money (who is a poor man with respect to his soul) either doesn't hear, or, if he does hear them, he ridicules, as he supposes is apt, and shamelessly[63] snatches from everywhere, like a wild beast, everything that he supposes will stuff him with eating, or drinking, or the furnishing of what concerns the servile and graceless pleasure said, incorrectly, to be "Aphroditean,"[64] since he is blind and does not see what accompanies the impious activity in his acts of plunder[65]—such a great evil always

---

60. Usually, I have reserved the phrase "for the sake of" to translate the preposition *heneka*, but here and in a few other places in Letters Seven and Eight, it translates instead the word *charin*. *Charis* means "grace," both as a human characteristic and in reference to the triad of goddesses known collectively as the Graces or Charites. In the accusative (*charin*), it was commonly used as a one-word formula meaning "in gratitude to" or "thanks to" and hence generally "for the sake of."

61. The third in a series—for example, the third cup of wine—was often dedicated to Zeus Sōtēr "Zeus Savior," which made for a superstitious belief in the propitious character of thirds (cf. "third time's the charm"). Plato makes this same reference again below (340a3–4) as well as elsewhere in his dialogues: *Charmides* 167a9, *Philebus* 66d4–5, *Republic* 583b2–3, and *Laws* 692a3; cf. *Laws* 960c8.

62. It is unclear whether "this" refers to "bad and good" or to death. Two interpretations illustrate some possible meanings. "Good and bad, which are defined in the end by knowledge, can come about only in the soul, the seat of knowledge" (Brisson 1993, 221n81). "The thought seems to be as follows: Nothing that possesses a soul can avoid death; people are wrong therefore in thinking that we should be happy if we did not have to die, for that would mean that we were creatures without souls and hence incapable of experiencing either good or evil" (Morrow 1962, 229n34).

63. The word for "shamelessly" is related not to *aischron* but to *aidōs*, "awe" or "reverence"; see n. 9 to Letter Six.

64. I.e., sexual pleasure. Cf. 328b–d above.

65. "Acts of plunder" translates the unusual word *harpagmatōn*, which appears here in the best manuscript. All the next best manuscripts have instead the more common word *pragmatōn*, "affairs."

together with each act of injustice—which necessarily drags along with the doer of injustice as he goes about upon the earth and once he has 335c returned below the earth on a journey that is altogether and in every way dishonored and wretched.

I, in saying these and other such things, was persuading Dion, and I would most justly be incensed at those who killed him—and at Dionysius, in a very similar way. For both inflicted the greatest harms on me and, so to speak, on all other human beings, the former having ruined the one wishing to make use of justice, the latter, though he held the greatest power, having been in no way willing to make use of justice 335d throughout his whole rule, in which, had philosophy and power really come to be in the same person, shining out among all human beings, both Greek and barbarian, he would have sufficiently set down in everyone the true opinion that neither a city nor any man would ever become happy who did not lead his life with practical wisdom under justice, either possessing [this][66] in himself or having been justly reared and educated in the ways of pious ruling men.

335e These are the things that Dionysius harmed; the others would be a small harm to me compared to these. But he who killed Dion does not know that he achieved the same thing by doing this. For of Dion I know clearly, as much as a human being is able to affirm confidently about human beings, that if he had taken hold of the rule, he never would 336a have turned toward another form[67] of rule than this: first, with regard to Syracuse, his fatherland, once he had delivered her from slavery and set her up free in form, then he would by every contrivance have adorned the citizens with the proper and best laws; following on these things, what he would have striven eagerly to do would have been to recolonize all Sicily and make it free from the barbarians, casting some out and subduing others more easily than Hiero;[68] and had these things in turn 336b come to pass through a man who was just and courageous, moderate, and philosophic, then the very same opinion concerning virtue would have come to be among the many that, if Dionysius had been persuaded, would have come to be among, so to speak, all human beings, and saved

66. No object whatsoever is given for the participle "possessing" (*kektēmenos*). The "true opinion" Plato has mentioned is one possibility; others are prudence, justice, or both.

67. Here and later in the sentence, "form" translates *schema*, literally "shape."

68. See n. 8 to Letter Two. Hiero repopulated the Sicilian cities of Naxos and Catana with Dorian Greeks, sending the previous inhabitants to settle in Leontini (Diodorus Siculus 11.49).

them. But as it is, either, presumably, some daemon,[69] or some avenging spirit,[70] falling upon them by means of lawlessness, godlessness, and most of all brazen[71] acts born of unlearnedness[72]—from which all evils to everyone take root, sprout up, and later culminate[73] in the bitterest fruit for those who bear it—this unlearnedness overturned and destroyed everything on the second occasion.

36c Well then, let us now speak reverently[74] for the sake of good omens for the third occasion. Nevertheless, I counsel you [pl], his friends, to imitate Dion, both in his goodwill for his fatherland and in his moderate regimen in regard to nourishment, and to attempt, upon more favorable auguries, to bring his wishes to their completion—what they were, you [pl] have heard clearly from me—but as for him among you who is 36d not capable of living in the Dorian[75] way according to your forefathers, who pursues the life both of Dion's slaughterers and of Sicily: neither call upon such a one nor suppose that he would ever do anything faithful and sound; but call upon the others with a view to a recolonization of all of Sicily and to equality under the law, produced from Sicily itself and from the whole Peloponnese—and do not fear Athens, for there are

69. Daemons occupied a somewhat ill-defined place among the spiritual or supernatural beings of Greek religion: beneath the gods themselves, it would seem, but above the heroes (see, e.g., Plato, *Laws* 717b2–4). The word *daimōn* occurs nowhere else in the *Letters*; but note the etymological link to *eudaimonia*, "happiness," literally a human state governed or overseen by a "good daemon."

70. "Avenging spirit" translates *alitērios*, which can simply mean "one who sins" or "one who is guilty," but in this context appears to carry the secondary meaning of a spirit who avenges injustice, especially murder (cf. Antiphon, *Third Tetralogy* 4.2.8). This reading is strengthened by the mention of the *xenikai erinues* ("guest-friend Furies") at 357a4 below (see note ad loc.); see Harward 1932, 208n65 and Burnyeat and Frede 2015, 155. There is only one other instance of a related word in the *Letters*: at 351c3, *alitēriōdē* is translated "accursed," indicating a pollution that attaches to the committer of sin worthy of vengeance.

71. The word for "brazen acts," here and at 336d, is *tolma*; all related words elsewhere in the text are rendered with some form of the word "daring."

72. "Unlearnedness" is a literal rendering of *amathia*. It could also be translated "stupidity," which conveys the word's sharply pejorative connotation, but the literal meaning is important to understand Plato's attribution to *amathia* of "all evils." Cf. *Alcibiades* 118b4ff. The same word occurs at 351d9 below.

73. Lit. "come to completion" (*apotelei*).

74. "Let us speak reverently" translates *euphēmōmen*, literally "let us speak well," a word whose meaning is well illustrated by taking note of its antonym, *blasphēmein*, "to speak profanely of sacred things," the root of the English "blasphemy." To "speak well," then, is not merely to "be positive" or "keep it light," but specifically to avoid blaspheming.

75. Syracuse was one of several major Sicilian cities said to have been founded by Dorian Greeks (see Thudycides 6.3.2, 7.57). The Dorian tradition to which Plato appeals here is best understood by reference to the famously abstemious way of life of the Spartans, leaders of the Dorian Greeks throughout the classical period.

some even there who are distinguished among all human beings with respect to virtue, and who hate the brazen acts of men who murder guest-friends. But if it should be that these [counsels] have come too 336e late, since the many and varied conflicts naturally growing each day among the factions are pressing upon you [pl], any man to whom some divine fortune has given even a small share of correct opinion ought presumably to know that there is no cessation of evils for the faction-riven until those who have prevailed by means of battles, casting out of 337a human beings, and slaughters should cease bearing grudges and turning to vengeance against their enemies, and, being self-controlled and giving common laws that are laid down no more properly for themselves than for those who have been defeated,[76] should compel them to be subject to the laws[77] by means of a pair of compulsions, awe and fear:[78] they would compel by means of fear by demonstrating that they are stronger than them with respect to force; and by means of awe, in turn, by being manifestly stronger concerning pleasures and by being more willing and capable of being slaves to the laws. But otherwise, it is not possible that 337b a city riven by faction within itself should put a stop to evils; rather factions, enmities, hatreds, and distrusts always like to arise in cities that are themselves so disposed with respect to themselves.

But those who have prevailed, whenever they should desire salvation, ought always, among themselves, to select from among the Greeks men whom they find through inquiry to be the best: first of all, elders, who possess children and wives at home, and whose own ancestors are as much as possible many and famous,[79] and all of them possessing suffi- 337c cient possessions—as a number, fifty such are sufficient for a city of ten thousand men. Indeed, they should send for these men from their homes by means of entreaties and the greatest possible honors, and once they have been sent for,[80] they should entreat and direct them to give laws, having sworn oaths to apportion more neither to the victors nor to the vanquished, equally and in common for the whole city. The laws having

76. The reading of one of the best manuscripts, attested also as a marginal emendation in the other. The alternate reading has *pros hēdonē*, "with a view to pleasure," instead of *prosēkon*, "properly," yielding the reading "giving common laws that are laid down no more with a view to their own pleasure than to that of those who have been overcome."

77. Lit. "to make use of the laws" (*chrēsthai tois nomois*).

78. On "awe" (*aidōs*), see n. 9 to Letter Six; on the combination "awe and fear" as a foundation for willing enslavement to the laws, see *Laws* 698a9–c3.

79. Marginal emendations in the best manuscripts (favored by Burnet and Souilhé) make the phrase "many and famous" read instead "many, good, and famous."

80. I.e., once they have arrived.

been given, everything comes down to this: if those who have won victory should render themselves, more than the vanquished, subservient 337d to the laws, everything will be full of salvation and happiness and there will be refuge from all evils; but if they do not, neither call upon me nor upon another partner for help against whoever is unpersuaded by the letter that has now been sent to you. For these things are siblings of both what Dion and what I undertook to do together, meaning well toward the Syracusans, though in fact they were second. First were the things undertaken to be done first, with Dionysius himself, which were common goods for all; but some fortune stronger than human beings 337e dissipated them. May you [pl] attempt with better fortune to do these things now, with good fate and some divine fortune.

Well then, let my counsel and message[81] have been spoken, as well as the account of my earlier arrival at the court of Dionysius; as for how the later journey and sailing came to pass at once appropriately and harmoniously, he who cares may listen to what is after this. For 338a indeed, my first period of occupation in Sicily has now been thoroughly described in what I said before my counsel to the intimates and comrades close to Dion.

After those things, then, I persuaded Dionysius, in whatever way I was ever capable, to let me go, and we came to an agreement on both sides for when there would come to be peace—for there was war in Sicily at the time.[82] Dionysius said that he would send for Dion and me to come back once he had set what concerned his rule back up in a safer state 338b for himself, but he was requesting that Dion should understand[83] what had then come to pass for him to be not an exile, but a removal;[84] and I agreed to the terms of these speeches.[85]

When there came to be peace, he sent for me; but he begged Dion to hold off for yet another year, though he was requesting that I come by all

---

81. Lit. "letter" or perhaps "command"; see n. 43 to Letter Two.

82. Reading and punctuating the text at 338a3–b1 according to the assertion of Harward, who claims that this is a hyperbaton characteristic of Plato's later style (1932, 209n74; cf. 89–90).

83. "Understand" translates *dianoeisthai*; see n. 5 to Letter Three.

84. Morrow explains the difference between "removal" (*metastasis*) and "exile" (*phugē*) as distinct legal concepts: "Μετάστασις, as distinct from φυγή, both technical terms in Greek law, did not involve the confiscation of the condemned person's property" (1962, 233n43). See also LSJ, s.v. "metastasis" (def. A.II).

85. Marginal emendations in the best manuscripts suggest the alternative reading "I agreed that I would come [back] according to the terms of these speeches" (*hēxein hōmologēsa* rather than *xunōmologēsa*).

means. Dion, then, directed and begged me to set sail; for indeed, word from Sicily was spreading far that Dionysius had at present returned amazingly to a desire for philosophy; hence Dion vigorously begged us not to disobey the summons. But I, while I had surely known many 338c such things to come to pass for the young with respect to philosophy, nevertheless it seemed to me safer, at that time at least, to bid a great farewell to both Dion and Dionysius, and I became hateful to both of them by answering that I was old and that none of the things that were now being done were coming to pass in accordance with the agreements.

Now it is likely that, after this, both Archytas[86] arrived at the court of Dionysius[87]—before sailing home, I had brought about a guest-relationship and friendship between Archytas (along with those in 338d Tarentum) and Dionysius—and there were some others among the Syracusans who had learned[88] some things from Dion, as well as still others [who had learned] from these ones, filled up with certain misunderstandings in philosophy;[89] they seemed to me to be attempting to converse with Dionysius about what concerned such things as though Dionysius had learned everything I thought.[90] He is not ill-natured

---

86. This is the first mention in the *Letters* of Archytas, the addressee of Letters Nine and Twelve. A contemporary of Plato, Archytas was born and lived in the Italian city of Tarentum. He was a man of extraordinary and diverse talents, and it was under his protracted rule that Tarentum reached its apex and dominated southern Italy (see Strabo 6.3.4). A follower of the Pythagorean school, Archytas was among the most brilliant mathematicians and scientists of his day, and Pythagorean philosophy flourished in Tarentum under his influence (Strabo 6.3.4; van der Waerden 1961, 110–12; Heath 1981, 246–49). Yet, although his encounter with Archytas cannot but have been highly significant for Plato, the character of their relationship is not entirely clear; see Cicero, *Tusculan Disputations* 1.17; *Republic* 1.10; Demosthenes, *Erotic Essay* 61.46; Plutarch, *Marcellus* 14.6; *Quaestiones Convivales* 8.2. Lloyd (1990) argues that Plato's adversarial relationship with Archytas motivated the writing of Letter Seven.

87. Lloyd points out the anacolouthic character of this sentence (1990, 162–63). The "both" (*te*) earlier in the sentence makes us expect a grammatically parallel clause that does not come.

88. With only one exception, the word "learn" throughout this paragraph translates the verb *diakouein*, literally "to hear out" or "to hear through to the end." Likewise, the word "misunderstandings" at 338d3 is *parakousmatōn*, "things misheard" or even "things overheard." Note also that "he had learned nothing" at 338e1, and "he did not learn" at 338e3, translate forms of the root verb *akouein*, "to hear," without the *dia-* prefix—not only had Dionysius not heard anything "through to the end," he had heard nothing *at all*. Only the phrase "the ability to learn" at 338d6–7 includes the verb normally translated "to learn," *manthanein*. The use of words of hearing to refer to intellectual rather than sensory apprehension is prevalent in the following pages.

89. An alternative reading of this part of the sentence would run "and there were some among the Syracusans who had learned some things from Dion, and some, different from these, filled up with certain misunderstandings in philosophy."

90. Or "intended" or "understood" (*dienooumēn*); see n. 5 to Letter Three.

with respect to the ability to learn, having an amazing love of honor. Perhaps, then, the things being said were agreeable to him, and at the 38e same time he was ashamed, as it was becoming manifest that he had learned nothing while I was visiting, and hence he came to a desire to learn more clearly, while at the same time the love of honor was pressing upon him—the reasons why he did not learn during my earlier visit, we went through in the speeches given above, just now. So when I returned home safely and denied him when he called the second time, as I said just now, Dionysius seems to me to have been altogether pursuing his 39a love of honor, lest I should ever seem to anyone to be disdaining his nature and disposition while also having had experience of his way of living, and to be, out of disgust, no longer willing to visit him.

It is just of me to speak the truth and to endure it if someone, having heard the things that happened, should disdain my philosophy and hold that the tyrant is intelligent. For Dionysius, the third time, sent me a trireme for the sake of an easy journey, and he sent Archedemus[91] 39b (the one of whom, Dionysius held, I thought most highly of those in Sicily, one of those who had spent time with Archytas) and other notables from among those in Sicily. And these were all reporting to us the same account, that it was amazing how far Dionysius had advanced in philosophy. And he sent me a very long letter, knowing how I was disposed toward Dion as well as of Dion's eagerness for me to set sail and go to Syracuse; for the letter was prepared with a view to all these things, and had a beginning that explained things in the following way: "Dionysius 39c to Plato"—and, having said the customary[92] things in addition to this, he immediately said, "If, obeying us, you should come now to Sicily, first of all, what is happening concerning Dion will start to be just the way you yourself would want it—and I know that you will want the measured things, and I will concede them; but should you refuse, none of the affairs concerning Dion, neither the other things nor the ones concerning [Dion] himself, will come out to your liking." Thus did he say 39d these things; to say the others would take long, and this is not a propitious moment. But other letters kept coming in from Archytas and those in Tarentum, extolling the philosophy of Dionysius, and saying that, if I did not go now, I would be altogether rending apart[93] their friendship

91. See n. 1 to Letter Two.

92. Lit. "lawful" (*nomima*).

93. The word for "I would be rending apart" here is *diabaloiēn*, which is the same word that I have translated "slander" elsewhere in the *Letters*.

with Dionysius, which had come to be through me, and was no small matter with respect to the political things.

At that time, with this summons having come to be such, and with some pulling me from Sicily and Italy, and others artlessly thrusting 339e me, as it were, out of Athens with an entreaty, yet again the same speech was coming, that there was a need not to betray Dion, nor my guest-friends and comrades in Tarentum; and lurking beneath this for me was that it is nothing amazing for a young human being, hearing about[94] affairs worthy of account, if he is a good learner, to come to a passionate desire[95] for the best life. There was a need, therefore, to put the matter clearly to the test[96] as to which way things stood after all, and, if indeed things should really be as had been said, in no way to betray this very thing, nor for me truly to become the cause of so great a reproach. 340a So I am carried off, veiled by this calculation, dreading many things and divining not very nobly, as is likely. At any rate, by going I really made this one, at least, "the third for the savior,"[97] for, fortunately, I was saved again, and for these things, at least, I ought to acknowledge gratitude to Dionysius next after a god, because he prevented many who wished to destroy me and gave some part of the affairs concerning me to awe.[98]

340b But when I arrived, I supposed I must first put the following to the test:[99] had Dionysius really been kindled by philosophy as by a fire, or had this great speech come to Athens in vain? Now, there is a certain way of attempting to grasp such things that is not lowborn but is really

---

94. *Parakouonta* here might also be translated "overhearing," "mishearing," or "misunderstanding"; see n. 88 above.

95. "Passionate desire" translates a form of *erōs*, whence the English "erotic." Though *erōs* can refer to what we would call "erotic" or "romantic" love, its scope of meaning is much broader. It refers in general to the human attraction to and desire for the beautiful or noble (*to kalon*; see n. 21 to Letter Two), in all its psychological complexity. Socrates's speech in Plato's *Symposium* brings out the connection of this passionate desire for *to kalon* with the human longing for immortality, and thus extends *erōs* beyond physical or romantic love by connecting it to the loftiest political, literary, and philosophic ambitions. It is indeed a quintessential feature of Platonic philosophy that the philosophic activity itself is characterized as "erotic"; see *Symposium* and *Phaedrus*, and cf. *Republic*, books 5, 6, and 9. The only other occurrences of any such words in the *Letters* are in Letter Eight, at 354d5 and 355d5.

96. The word for "put to the test" here is *exelegxai*, related to "elenchtic," the word that describes Socratic refutation. Indeed, *exelegxai* could also mean "to refute" even here, though the context seems to call for the translation I have chosen.

97. See n. 61 above.

98. That is, Dionysius allowed himself to be guided by *aidōs* ("reverence," "awe," "shame"; see n. 9 in Letter Six) in some part of his dealings with Plato.

99. *Elegchon*; see n. 96 above.

fitting for tyrants, especially those filled with misunderstandings,[100] which, as I indeed perceived right away when I got there, was very much what had happened to Dionysius. One needs to show such people both

340c what sort of thing the whole problem[101] is and through how many problems and how much toil it lies. For the one who has listened, if he should really be a philosopher, being both intimate with and worthy of the divine problem, will hold that he has heard of an amazing path, which one must immediately strain to follow, and that life would not be worth living for one who would do otherwise. After this, then, having strained both himself and his leader in following the path, he will not let up until he should either bring everything to completion or obtain such a power that, separately from the one who has shown him, he is incapable[102] of being a guide himself.

340d In this way and according to these intentions will such a person live, managing whatever will be his business, but, beyond everything, always holding on to philosophy and to the daily nourishment that would most of all succeed in making him a good learner, with a good memory, and capable of calculating, as one who is sober in himself; and the opposite of this, he continues hating to the end. But those who are not really philosophers, but have been tinctured by opinions just as those whose bodies have been burnt by the sun, once they have seen how many are

340e the subjects of learning, and the extent of the toil, and the ordered daily regimen that befits the problem, hold it to be hard and impossible for

341a themselves; they do not, indeed, come to be capable of engaging in the practice, but some of them persuade themselves that they have heard

---

100. Lit. "things misheard" or "overheard" (*parakousmatōn*); see n. 88 above.

101. The word *pragma*, here translated "problem," appears eight times in these three paragraphs (between 340b8 and 341c7), in addition to several instances of related words (*prattō*, *praxis*). A word I most commonly translate "affair," *pragma* can range in meaning from the extremely broad "thing" or "matter" to a variety of more specific connotations. In the present passage, Plato seems to use *pragma* to refer to the "problems" encountered in philosophic investigations, i.e., to the "matters of concern" for philosophers. Although the translation "problem" may sometimes mislead the reader where "affair" or "matter" might be more appropriate, I have consistently rendered *pragma* by "problem" from here through 341c in order to allow the reader to follow more easily Plato's use of this word in this context. See also *pragmatos* at 344a3 with my note there, and consider also 312a5–6 and 313b4 above, along with my notes there on *pragma* and *pragmateia*.

102. The best manuscripts here read "incapable," which seems to be contradictory to the sense of the passage. In one manuscript, a scholiast has suggested the emendation "capable" (removing the alpha privative), and Stephanus adopted the emendation "not incapable," both of which are plausible suggestions. But the reader should have the opportunity to consider whether the more challenging reading, which the manuscripts all contain, might be the correct one.

the whole sufficiently and have no further need of any problems. Now indeed this attempt comes to be the clear and safest one with respect to those who luxuriate and are incapable of enduring toil, since one of these can never cast the blame upon the one who is showing him the way, but rather upon himself, for his not being capable of engaging in all the practices advantageous for the problem. This is the way the things then spoken were spoken also to Dionysius. Neither, therefore, was 341b I going through everything, nor was Dionysius begging me to; for he pretended both to know and sufficiently to have a hold on many, even the greatest, things because of hearsay from others.[103]

I even hear that he has subsequently written about the things he then heard, composing as though it were his own treatise[104] and not at all made up of the things he heard; but I know nothing of these writings. I know some others have written about these same things, but as to who they are, they do not even know themselves. This much, at any rate, have 341c I to explain about all who have written or will write, and who claim to know about the things I take seriously, whether claiming to have heard them from me, or from others, or that they discovered them themselves: it is not possible, according to my opinion at least, that they understand[105] anything of the problem. Therefore there is no writing of mine, at least, concerning them,[106] nor will there ever come to be; for it is in no way speakable as are the other subjects of learning, but rather, from the coming to be of much intercourse concerning the problem itself, and 341d living together, suddenly, as from a jumping fire, a light is kindled, and, having come to be in the soul, it straightaway nourishes itself. And yet I know this much, at least: that in being written or said by me, these things would be said best; and that, if they were written badly, it would pain me not least. But had they appeared to me to be sufficiently writable and speakable to the many, what nobler thing could have been done in life by us than this, both to write what is a great benefit for human beings 341e and to lead nature forth into the light for all? But the undertaking[107]

---

103. The word for "hearsay" is *parakoas*, related to but distinct from *parakousma*, as at 338d3 and 340b6. This word could also mean "misunderstandings" or "things misheard." See n. 88 above.

104. "Treatise" here seems to be the correct translation of *technēn*, which more usually means "art." The translation "as though it were his own art" is also possible and should be considered.

105. Lit. "hear" (*epaïō*; see n. 88 above).

106. I.e., concerning the things Plato takes seriously.

107. "Undertaking" or "attempt" is the primary meaning of *epicheirēsis*, though in Aristotle the word can also mean a line of dialectical reasoning. Thus, "undertaking concerning them"

spoken of concerning them I do not hold to be good for human beings unless for some few—however many are themselves capable of finding them out through a small indication; of the others, it would fill some, in no way harmoniously, with incorrect disdain, and others with a lofty
342a and empty hope as though they had learned some august things.

It has come about that I have in mind to speak at still greater length about these things; for perhaps the things about which I'm speaking will be clearer once they have been stated in some way. For there is a certain true speech that opposes him who has dared to write of such things at all. And though it has often been said by me before, it is likely that it must be spoken now too.

There are, of each of the beings, three things through which it is necessary that scientific knowledge[108] comes to be, [the scientific knowl-
342b edge] itself [being] a fourth—and there is need to set down as fifth the very thing that is knowable[109] and is truly a being.[110] One is a name, second is a definition,[111] the third is an image, fourth is scientific knowledge. Take, then, what concerns one thing, if you wish to learn what is now being spoken of, and think in this way about all things. A circle is something spoken of, of which this very thing we just now uttered is a name. A definition of it is the second thing, being composed of names and phrases;[112] for "that which is everywhere equally distant from the

---

could mean something like a "disquisition on them," as Harward has it. See also Morrow's note, as well as Souilhé's, each ad loc.

108. "Scientific knowledge" translates the noun *epistēmē,* which appears five times in this section (between 342a7 and 343e2) and nowhere else in the *Letters. Epistēmē* refers to the kind of knowledge one obtains, not by mere familiarity with something, but on the basis of a rigorous understanding of its structure, causes, etc. See n. 5 to Letter Five.

109. "Knowable" is related neither to *oida* nor to *epistamai* (see n. 5 to Letter Five); rather, it translates *gnōston,* which gives the root, for example, of the English "cognition." Thus one might attempt to get hold of the sense of the Greek word by means of some such phrase as "available as an object of cognition."

110. Accepting the marginal emendations in the manuscripts favored by Burnet, Souilhé, and most translators (see Harward 1932, 214n96), which indicate that there were a pair of plausibly minor corruptions in transmission. Though one must strain the grammar a bit, one could render the unemended version "set down as fifth that thing on account of which it is knowable and truly exists."

111. The word "definition," occurring three times here in 342b, twice at 343b, and once at 344b4, appears from the context to be the correct translation for these instances of the word *logos,* a common and important Greek word with a wide range of possible meanings. See n. 3 to Letter Two.

112. "Names and phrases" is the commonsense reading of *onomatōn kai rhēmatōn* (here and at 343b4–5 below) and is supported by the discussion at *Cratylus* 399a6–c6, where Socrates clearly indicates that a *rhēma* is a multiword phrase that may be contracted to form a single *onoma.* However, the explicit definition of these same terms by the Eleatic Stranger in the *Sophist*

extremes to the middle" would be a definition for that very thing of
342c which "round" and "ring"[113] are names, as well as "circle." Third is what is drawn and erased, and what is turned on a lathe and destroyed—of these things the circle itself, which all these are about,[114] suffers nothing, as it is different from these. Fourth is scientific knowledge and mind and true opinion about these;[115] and all this must be set down in turn as one, being not in sounds, nor in shapes of bodies, but within souls, by which it is clear that it is different both from the nature of the circle[116]
342d and from the three spoken of earlier. Of these, mind has approached most nearly in kinship and similarity to the fifth, while the others are more distant. And it is the same way concerning both straight and at the same time round shape, and color, and concerning good and noble and just, and concerning every body, both artificial and having come to be according to nature (fire, water, and all such things), and concerning every animal, and character in souls, and about all things done and
342e suffered. For of these things, someone who did not somehow or other get hold of the four will never completely be a participant in scientific knowledge of the fifth. In addition, these things undertake to make
343a clear the "of what sort" about each thing no less than the being of each, because of the weakness of the speeches;[117] for the sake of these things,

---

(262a1–8) would suggest the translations "noun" and "verb" for *onoma* and *rhēma* respectively. Perhaps most ambiguous but most directly relevant is *Cratylus* 424e4–425a7, where Socrates speculates that, just as letters are combined to make syllables, so from syllables are composed "both *onomatōn* and *rhēmatōn*; and again, from the *onomatōn* and *rhēmatōn* we will compose something great and beautiful and whole, and just as earlier the animal [was made] by [the art of] painting, now *ton logon* [will be made] by *onomastikē*, or *rhētorikē*, or whatever the art may be." See also Burnyeat and Frede, who argue that *rhēmata* here means "descriptions" (2015, 123n7).

113. Two words that can each mean "circular" (*stroggulon* and *perpheres*), with subtle variations in connotation. See Harward 1932, ad loc.

114. The relationship between the circle itself and the "images" of it is stated in extremely vague terms (*hon peri estin*). Burnyeat and Frede (2015, 124) propose "which all these are to do with," noting the alternatives preferred by Morrow ("to which they all refer"), Post, Bury, and Brisson ("are related"), and Souilhé ("auquel on rapporte"). One might compare Letter Two, "All things are around the king of all things, . . . the second things are around a second, and the third things around a third" (312e1–4), where "around" translates the same construction (*peri* + accusative).

115. It is sensible to suppose that the adjective "true" (*alēthēs*) in this sentence would belong with "opinion" (*doxa*), as I have suggested. But if, as the text of the manuscripts seems to indicate, that part of the sentence runs *nous alēthēs te kai doxa*, and not simply *nous alēthēs te doxa*, it is harder to insist against the unexpected reading "true mind and opinion."

116. Or "from the circle of nature itself," where "itself" still refers to the circle (*autou tou kuklou tēs phuseōs*).

117. It is not clear whether "the weakness of the speeches" refers to a deficiency of language as such or should be read rather as "the weakness of the definitions (*logōn*)," i.e., of the second of "the five" identified at 342b2 (see n. 111 above).

no one with intelligence[118] will ever dare to put the things thought about by him into it,[119] and these into something unchangeable[120] at that, which indeed happens with what has been put in engraved writing.

One needs to learn again this thing that has just now been said. Each circle, of those drawn in actions or even turned on a lathe, is full of the opposite of the fifth—for it everywhere touches the straight—but the circle itself, we claim, does not hold in itself something either smaller or larger of the opposite nature. We claim that no name of any of these

43b things is stable at all,[121] that there is nothing to prevent the things now called round from being called straight and the straight round, and that it will be no less stable for those who make changes and call things oppositely. And moreover concerning definition, since the definition itself is indeed composed of names and phrases, it is in no way stable in a sufficiently stable way. And there is in turn a ten-thousandfold argument[122] for each of the four to the effect that it is unclear, but the greatest is the very one we said a short time ago: that, of the two beings—the

43c being, and the "of what sort"—when the soul seeks to know not the "of what sort" but the "what," each of the four, by holding out to the soul, both in speech and in relation to deeds, the thing that is not sought—each thing, both what is said and what is demonstrated, always being rendered easily refutable by the senses—fills every man, so to speak, with every perplexity and unclarity.

And so, in those cases wherein, by bad rearing, we have not been habituated to seek the truth, but rather whichever of the images is held out suffices, we do not become ridiculous to each other, the questioned

43d to the questioners, who are capable of tossing around and refuting the four. But in those cases wherein we compel someone to answer and clarify the fifth, he who wishes to confute[123] (of those who are capable) prevails, and makes the one expounding in speeches or writings or answers

---

118. Lit. "having a mind."

119. This "it" (*auto*) must refer to "the weakness of the speeches." "[T]he things understood" translates *ta nenoēmena*, a participle related to the word *nous* ("intelligence," "mind") occurring earlier in the sentence. Note also that the words "by him" (*hup' autou*) are reported only in the margins of the manuscripts.

120. Lit. "immovable."

121. "Stable" is *bebaios*, a word that appears four times here at 343b. The same word is translated "steadfast" throughout the rest of the *Letters* (with the exception of "firmly" at 313b6 and "assurance" at 346b8).

122. Note that, while *logos* seems to refer to "definition" as the second of "the four" in the previous sentence, Plato now employs the same word to mean something like an "argument" *about* "the four," and again to mean something like "in speech" later in the sentence.

123. Lit. "to overturn" (*anatrepein*).

seem to the many among the listeners to know[124] nothing of the things about which he is undertaking to write or speak; sometimes they are ignorant that it is not the soul of him who has written or spoken that is
343e refuted, but the nature of each of the four, being naturally poor.

But the way leading through all of them, shifting up and down to each one, does with difficulty give birth to scientific knowledge of the good-natured in the good-natured; but if it[125] grows by nature badly—either naturally, as with the disposition of soul among the many both
344a in learning and in the things spoken of as "traits of character,"[126] or if these are corrupted—not even Lynceus[127] could make such as these see. In one word,[128] neither goodness at learning nor memory could make him see who is not akin to the matter[129]—for it does not come to be to begin with in dispositions alien to it—so that neither those who are not naturally attached[130] and akin both to the just things and to the other things insofar as they are noble (though various ones may yet be good learners and rememberers of various things), nor those who *are* akin but are bad learners and forgetful—none of these could ever learn the truth
344b of virtue to the extent possible, nor of vice. For it is necessary to learn them simultaneously, and also the false and true of the whole of being[131] simultaneously, with total occupation[132] and a great deal of time, just as I said in the beginning. But with difficulty, when each of them has been rubbed against one another—names and definitions, sights and

---

124. Here, "to know" is *gignōkein*, "recognize" or "understand," and neither *eidenai* (which I most commonly translate "to know") nor *epistasthai* ("to know scientifically"). The word "ignorant" (*agnoountōn*) later in the sentence shares the same root.

125. I.e., "scientific knowledge of the good-natured," as it would seem.

126. Lit. "characters." *Ēthē* might even be rendered "traits of moral character." See n. 10 to Letter Three.

127. One of the Argonauts, Lynceus was a figure from Greek mythology whose extraordinary keenness of vision became proverbial (see, e.g., Aristophanes, *Wealth* 210; Pindar, *Nemean* 10.61.3; Apollonius, *Argonautica* 1.153.5). There does not appear to be any tradition, however, holding that Lynceus could bestow sight upon others.

128. Or "in one speech" (*eni logōi*).

129. I.e., to the matter being investigated in this way; specifically, Plato is now discussing the investigation of what is "good-natured" (*eu pephukotos*). But *pragmatos* here may refer again to the "problem" discussed above at 340b–341c. See n. 101 above.

130. "Naturally attached" translates the adjective *prosphueis*, which suggests that something has grown together with or sprouted out of something else. It is closely related to the verb *prosphuō*, which appears only once in the *Letters* (313d2). The two passages should be compared.

131. *Ousias*; see n. 17 above [317c].

132. "Total occupation" translates *tribēs pasēs*, "every occupation" or even "every study." The noun is *tribēs*, directly related and very close in meaning to *diatribēs*, for which see n. 3 to Letter One. The literal meaning of the word is "a rubbing against," just as the participle *tribomena* ("has been rubbed against") occurring later in the sentence.

perceptions—and has been refuted in kindly refutations, those making use of questions and answers being without envy, then practical wisdom concerning each shines forth, as well as mind, straining to the utmost 344c extent of human power. Wherefore every man who is serious about the serious beings is far from[133] ever having written [about them], lest he should cast them down amid the envy and perplexity of human beings. In one word, one needs to recognize, on the basis of these things, that whenever one sees someone's writings that have been written—whether laws of a lawgiver or in any other things at all—these were not the most serious things to him, if indeed he himself was serious, but that they lie somewhere in the noblest region he possesses.[134] But if, even though these things were really taken seriously by him, he put them in writing, 344d "then indeed"—not "gods," but mortals—"themselves destroyed the wits in you."[135]

He who has followed along with this tale and wandering[136] will know well that, if either Dionysius or someone lesser or greater wrote something of the highest and first things concerning nature, he had in no way heard or learned soundly the things of which he wrote, according to my argument; for he would then have venerated them like I do, and he would not have dared to cast them out into dissonance and unseemli- 344e ness. For he wrote not for the sake of[137] reminders—for there is no danger that someone would forget it once one gets hold of it in one's soul; for of all things it is posited in the fewest words—rather, for the sake of a shameful love of honor, either as though he was setting it down himself or indeed as though he was a participant in an education of

133. "Is far from" translates the idiom *peri pollou dei*, literally "has need of much."

134. Lit. "the noblest [or most beautiful] region of those that are his."

135. The line Plato here cites and alters appears twice in Homer's *Iliad*: it is spoken once by Paris to Antenor (7.360), and once by Hector to Polydamas (12.234). In each case, the speaker is responding to a piece of advice that, while prudent and prescient, is unwelcome because it opposes his own passionate desire. Also in each case, it is not only this line that is spoken verbatim, but also the three preceding lines (but for the name of the person addressed), which together make up the first four lines of the speaker's rebuttal. The full four lines are:

> [Antenor/Polydamas], these things that you advise are no longer dear to me.
> You know how to think of another tale, better than this one.
> But if you are genuinely advising this in seriousness
> Then indeed, gods themselves destroyed the wits in you.

136. "Tale" is *muthōi*, for which "myth" is not an altogether inappropriate translation; note the appearance of the same word in the Homeric passage alluded to by Plato in the preceding sentence (n. 136 above). "Wandering" (*planōi*) could mean "digression" in this context.

137. *Charin*; see n. 60 above.

345a which he was not worthy, cherishing the reputation that comes of this participation.[138]

If, then, this is what Dionysius got from our single intercourse, then perhaps it is so. But *how* that ever came to be, "Zeus knows!" as the Theban says;[139] for I myself went through what I said only once, and never again thereafter. As to what has happened concerning these things, then, whoever cares to discover the way in which it ever happened needs to think of what is after this: whatever was the cause of our not thoroughly going through it for the second and the third time, and more often? 345b Does Dionysius, having heard only once, thus suppose he knows? And does he sufficiently know, either by having made the discovery himself or even having learned beforehand from others? Or does he suppose the things said were paltry? Or, thirdly, does he suppose that they are not on his level, but rather greater, and that he would not really be capable of living while taking care of practical wisdom and virtue? For if he supposes they are paltry, he'll be battling many witnesses who say the contrary, who would be altogether more authoritative judges concerning such things than Dionysius; but if he supposes that he has discovered or learned them—and that they are worthy with a view to the education of a 345c free soul—how, unless he is an amazing human being, could he ever have dishonored so nonchalantly the leader and sovereign authority regarding these things? But how he dishonored, I shall explain.

No long interval of time having passed after this, though he had previously been allowing Dion to possess his own things and to reap the profits, he would now no longer allow Dion's stewards to send his wealth to the Peloponnese, as though he had altogether forgotten his letter; for he claimed that it was not Dion's wealth but his son's, who 345d was his nephew and of whom he was therefore the guardian by law.[140] These were the things that had been done up to this point in time; so, when these things had come to be in this way, I myself saw Dionysius's

---

138. Accepting the one-letter variant (from *genomenēs* to *genomenēn*) found, not in the main text of the best manuscripts, but as an emendation in one and in the main text of a later, important manuscript. The other version would read "cherishing the reputation that belongs to the coming-to-be of this participation."

139. Plato writes this exclamation—in spirit something like "God only knows"—in the Theban dialect (*ittō* instead of *istō*, "may he know"). The exact same expression is used by Socrates's Theban companion Cebes in Plato's *Phaedo* (62a8), but its significance is otherwise unclear.

140. The words "stewards" and "guardian" in this sentence are effectively the same (*epitropos*). As Harward explains, "Dionysius now abandoned the assumption that Dion was merely on his travels (*v.* 338b1), and treated him as an exile, so that the guardianship of Dion's son passed into his own hands" (1932, 219n121).

desire for philosophy with precision, and it would have been permissible for me to be vexed, whether I wished to or not.

For it was already summer then and the time for the ships to sail out; and it seemed that I needed to be hard, not any more on Dionysius than 345e on myself and on those who had forced me to go for the third time into the strait by Scylla,

so that I might once more measure back out the path to destructive Charybdis,[141]

and that I needed to say to Dionysius that it was impossible for me to stay, Dion having been thus trampled in the mud. But he was trying to reassure me and was begging me to stay, as he supposed that it would not go beautifully for him for me to go myself, as quickly as possible, as a messenger about such things. But as he wasn't persuading me, he said 346a he himself would prepare me a conveyance. For I was intending to set sail by embarking on the messenger ships,[142] as I had grown angry and was supposing that I needed to suffer whatever might come if I should be prevented, since it was entirely evident that I was committing no injustice, but was being done injustice; but he, seeing that I would not accede to staying put, contrived the following scheme to make me stay for the duration of that sailing season.

The day after these things, he came and gave me a speech of persua- 346b sion. "Let's me and you," he said, "get Dion and Dion's things out of the way and be rid of our frequent conflicts about them. On your account," he said, "I will do the following things for Dion. I request that he, taking what is his, dwell in the Peloponnese—not as an exile, however, but as one for whom it is possible to voyage here whenever it be so resolved in common by him, me, and you [pl] his friends. But these things are [conditional on] him not plotting against me; and you [pl], your [pl] intimates, and Dion's who are here are to become his guarantors in these things—let him render his assurance to you [pl]. As for the money that 346c he would receive, let it be deposited in the Peloponnese and at Athens among whoever seems good to you [pl], and let Dion reap the profits, but let him not come to have sovereign authority to make withdrawals without you [pl]. For I do not much trust in him that, if he should have the use of this money, he would come to be just concerning me—for it is

141. Homer, *Odyssey* 12.428.

142. It is not entirely clear what is meant by "messenger ships," but the phrase apparently refers to ships that came and departed at regular intervals.

no small amount—but I have rather come to trust in you and yours. See, then, if these things are agreeable to you, and stay for the year on these 346d terms; and then, when the season comes, go away and bring this money; and I know well that Dion will have a great deal of gratitude for you for accomplishing these things on his behalf."

When I heard this speech I was disgusted; nevertheless, after deliberating, I said that I would report my opinions about these things to him on the following day. These were the arrangements we made together at that time. Then after these things, when I came to be by myself, I was deliberating, very confused. First, the following speech led the way in 346e my deliberation: "Come now, if Dionysius intends to do nothing of the things he says, and if, when I leave, he should send a letter of persuasion to Dion—both doing so himself and directing many others of those with him to do so—saying what he now says to me, that he himself was willing, but that I was not willing, to do what he was proposing to me, but that I was taking altogether little account of Dion's affairs; and in addition to these things, if he were moreover not willing to send me out, 347a but, not even giving commands to any of the ship captains, he simply indicated to all that he did not wish for me to sail out—who then will be willing to lead me as a passenger on his ship as I set out from Dionysius's house?" For, in addition to the other bad things, I was then dwelling in the garden about his house, whence the porter would not be willing to let me go unless some instruction had been sent to him from Dionysius. "But if I should stay around for the year, I could send a letter to Dion relating these things, as well as the circumstances I am in and what I am doing; and then, if Dionysius should do something of the things he 347b says, the things done by me will not have been altogether ridiculous—for Dion's property, if one were to value it correctly, is perhaps not less than a hundred talents[143]—but if things turn out to be of such a sort as it is now starting to appear likely that they will, I am at a loss as to what I will do with myself; nevertheless, it is perhaps necessary, for this year anyway, to toil further and to attempt to frustrate by deeds the machinations of Dionysius."

It having been so resolved by me, on the following day I said to Diony- 347c sius, "I have resolved to stay. But I request," I said, "that you not hold me

143. The Attic talent was both a measure of weight (about 57 pounds) and a monetary value corresponding to that same weight in silver. In the fourth century, one talent corresponded to something like nine years' worth of wages for a skilled laborer such as a carpenter (Engen 2004).

to be a sovereign authority over Dion, but that, together with me, you send {him a note clarifying}[144] the things that have now been resolved, and ask whether these things satisfy him. And if not, but he wishes for and requests some other things, for him to send a letter relating these things as quickly as possible—but you must in no way make changes to the things that concern him until then."

These things were spoken; upon these things we agreed, nearly just as they have been said now. The ships sailed out after this, and it was no 47d longer possible for me to sail—at which point, indeed, Dionysius remembered and said to me that half of the property needed to be Dion's and half his son's. He said he would sell it, and that once it was sold he would give half to me to take away and leave the other half to his child, for in this way it would be most just. Stricken by what had been said, I supposed it would be totally ridiculous to say anything further; nevertheless, I said that we ought to wait for the letter from Dion and send a letter back about these very things. But right after these things, he alto- 47e gether impetuously sold all the property, on whatever terms, in whatever manner, and to whomever he wanted, but to me he was uttering absolutely nothing about these things, and thus I, in turn, likewise was no longer conversing at all about Dion's affairs with him; for I supposed there was no longer anything more to do.

Up until these things, my coming to the aid of philosophy and of friends had come to be in this way. After these things, we were living, 48a I and Dionysius, such that I was looking outward like a bird longing to fly up and away,[145] and he was contriving some way that he could frighten me away[146] while giving back[147] nothing of what was Dion's. Nevertheless, we claimed to all Sicily that we were indeed comrades.

Dionysius now undertook, against the customs of his father, to reduce the wages of his senior mercenaries; but the soldiers, having been angered, gathered together in a group and declared they would not let

---

144. The words in braces are suggested in marginal additions to the best manuscripts.

145. With the phrase "longing to fly up and away," Plato employs an alliterative flourish: *pothōn pothen anaptesthai*.

146. Plato here uses not the common word for "frighten," *phobeō*, but the considerably rarer *anasobeō*. I owe to Keith Whitaker the observation that this verb or its root appears several times in Aristophanes with the sense "to shoo away birds."

147. "Give back" translates the participle *apodous*, a form of the same word translated "sell off" at 318a6 and b3. Consideration of the respective contexts seems to require these different translations, but the divergence is worth noting because the relevant passages of Letters Three and Seven contain parallel accounts of the same events, and in both cases this verb is used to refer to some part of what Dionysius did or claimed he would do with Dion's property.

348b it stand. He was undertaking to use force by barring the doors of the acropolis, but they threw themselves right at the walls, shouting some barbarian and warlike paean; and Dionysius, having come to be in great dread from this, conceded everything and still more to the peltasts[148] then gathered together. A certain speech quickly got around that Heraclides[149] was responsible for all these things that had happened. When he heard this, Heraclides took himself out of the way unseen, and Diony-
348c sius sought to seize him but, being at a loss, sent for Theodotes to come to the garden. And I myself happened to be walking about in the garden then, so while there are other things from their conversation which I do not know and was not hearing, what Theodotes said before me with a view to Dionysius I both know and remember.

"Now Plato," he said, "I am persuading this Dionysius that, if I should come to be capable of bringing Heraclides here to us to speak about the charges that have now come to be against him, and if it be resolved that
348d he needs not to dwell in Sicily, then I would request that he sail away to the Peloponnese, taking his son and his wife, to dwell there while in no way harming Dionysius, and reaping the profit from his property. I sent for him even before, and I will send for him again now; whether from the earlier summons, then, or from the present one, may he hearken to me; but I request and beg of Dionysius, if someone should encounter
348e Heraclides either in the fields or within the city, that nothing else nasty happen to him, but that he be removed from the land until something else be resolved by Dionysius.

"Do you concede these things?" he said, speaking to Dionysius.

"I concede them," he said. "Not even if he should appear at your house will he suffer anything nasty contrary to the things that have now been said."

The day after this, Eurybius and Theodotes came to me in the evening in seriousness, both raising an amazing clamor, and Theodotes said, "Plato, you were present yesterday for the things to which Dionysius agreed, with me and you, concerning Heraclides."

"Of course," I said.

"Well," he said, "now peltasts are running around seeking to seize
349a Heraclides, and there is a danger that he is somewhere around here. By all means," he said, "follow along with us to Dionysius."

---

148. Light infantry troops named for their distinctive light shield (*peltē*).

149. On Heraclides, as well as Theodotes and Eurybius, who have parts in the story narrated here, see n. 28 to Letter Three.

So we departed and came before him, and the pair of them stood in silence, weeping, but I said, "These ones are frightened that you might do something new about Heraclides, contrary to the things agreed upon yesterday; for it seems to me that, having returned, he has been seen somewhere around here."

When he had heard this, he was inflamed and turned every sort of color one growing angry would emit; and Theodotes, falling before him 49b and taking his hand, wept and was supplicating him not to do any such thing; but I, interrupting and reassuring him, said "Take heart, Theodotes, for Dionysius will never dare to do anything else contrary to the things agreed upon yesterday."

And he looked at me and said, very tyrannically, "With *you*, I agreed to nothing, either small or large."

"By the gods," I said, "but you did, with respect to these things which he is now begging you not to do." And having said these things, I turned 49c around and departed. After these things, he was hunting for Heraclides while Theodotes was sending messengers to Heraclides directing him to flee. Dionysius sent out Tisias[150] and some peltasts, directing them to pursue. But Heraclides, it is said, reached the province of the Carthaginians, escaping by a small part of a day.

After this, the old plot of not giving back Dion's money seemed to Dionysius to hold out a persuasive argument for enmity against me. 49d And first, he sent me out of the acropolis, discovering as a pretext that the women needed to perform a certain ritual sacrifice for ten days in the garden in which I was dwelling;[151] so he commanded me to stay outside the acropolis at Archedemus's during this time.[152] While I was there, Theodotes sent for me, greatly vexed concerning the things that had been done then and blaming Dionysius; but when Dionysius heard 49e that I had gone to visit Theodotes, he made this yet another pretext, sister to the previous one, for his conflict with me, and he sent someone to ask me if I was really getting together with Theodotes upon his sending for me.

"Absolutely," I said.

---

150. This Tisias is otherwise unknown.

151. This women-only festival was the Thesmaphoria, parodied by Aristophanes in his *Thesmaphoriasuzae*, which the Sicilian women celebrated as a ten-day festival as opposed to the three-day version put on by Athens and other Greek cities (Diodorus Siculus 5.4). It would have taken place in October (Harward 1932, 220n135).

152. On Archedemus, see n. 1 to Letter Two.

"Well then, [Dionysius] directed me," he said, "to explain to you that you are acting in no way nobly in always making more of Dion and Dion's friends than of him." These things were said, and he no longer sent for me to come back to his house, as though I was now clearly a friend of Theodotes and of Heraclides, but of him an enemy, and he supposed that I did not have goodwill toward him because Dion's money

350a was completely running out. After this, then, I was dwelling outside of the acropolis among the mercenaries. Among others, those of the rowers[153] who were from Athens, my fellow-citizens, came to me and reported that I had been slandered among the peltasts and that some were threatening that, if they caught me, they would kill me.

I contrive a salvation such as follows.[154] I send to Archytas and my other friends in Tarentum, explaining the circumstances in which I happen to be. They, furnishing some pretext of an embassy, send from their

350b city a thirty-oared ship and one of their own, Lamiscus,[155] who, when he came, begged Dionysius concerning my case, saying that I wished to go away and telling him to do in no manner otherwise. He agreed and, having given a travel allowance, sent me away. Of Dion's money, neither was I asking for any, nor did anyone give it back.

When I came to Olympia in the Peloponnese and caught up with Dion, who was a spectator at the games,[156] I reported to him the things that had happened. He, calling Zeus as his witness, straightaway gave

350c word to me and to my intimates and friends to prepare to take vengeance on Dionysius on account, in our case, of the cheating of guest-friends[157] (for so he said and thought), and in his own case, for an unjust casting out and exile. Having listened, I directed him to call upon my friends if they were willing. "But as for me," I said, "you, together with the others, by force, in a way, made me a sharer of meals, and a sharer of hearth, and a partner in sacred rites with Dionysius, who may have believed many of

153. *Tōn huperesiōn* can mean either "the servants" or "the rowers in the fleet." Harward opts for the latter reading with the following explanation: "The ships' crews here mentioned belonged to the navy of Dionysius. The ships which he kept permanently in commission would be manned by paid crews, and it is interesting to observe that some of the men were enlisted at Athens" (1932, 221n137). However, it is also possible that Plato is referring to Athenian members of the Syracusan servant class.

154. Plato adds liveliness to his narrative here by use of the historical present.

155. This Lamiscus is otherwise unknown.

156. See n. 2 to Letter Three.

157. The compound word *xenapatia*, "cheating of guest-friends," i.e., of *xenous* (see n. 12 to Letter Three), appears to be a Platonic coinage. At any rate, it does not appear anywhere but here in any extant text.

the slanderers saying that I, together with you, was plotting against him
350d and the tyranny—and nonetheless he did not kill me, but was restrained by shame.[158] At any rate, I am hardly of an age any longer to be joining in war with anyone; and you [pl] have me in common should you [pl] ever, being in some need of friendship with each other, wish to do some good; but for so long as you [pl] should desire to inflict evils, call upon others." I said these things having come to hate my wandering about Sicily and ill fortune; but they were unpersuaded,[159] and, not having been persuaded by my conversations,[160] they came to be responsible for all the evils that have now come to be for them, none of which would ever have
350e come to be, so far as the human things go at least, if Dionysius had given back to Dion his money or been altogether reconciled[161] with him—for I would have been easily holding Dion back both by wishing it and by the power I held with him[162]—but as it is they, having set out against one another, have had their fill of every evil.

351a And yet Dion held the very same wish that I myself would claim is needed, for me as for anyone else: whoever is measured concerning his own power and friends, and concerning his own city, would intend, by doing the greatest benefactions, to come into the greatest power and honors. But this would not be possible if someone were to make himself, his comrades, and his city rich by plotting and by bringing together conspirators, if he is poor and does not have control over himself, defeated
351b by cowardice in the face of pleasures; or if he, killing the possessors of property and calling these enemies, should carry away their money and encourage his accomplices and comrades to do whatever they must so that no one should accuse him, claiming to be poor. And it is the same if someone is honored by the city for doing benefactions for her by apportioning to the many the things of the few by means of measures passed

---

158. Lit. "stood in awe" or "acted with reverence" (*ēidesthē*); see n. 9 to Letter Six.

159. Or "they disobeyed" (*apeithountes*), just as "not having been persuaded" later in this sentence could also be "not having obeyed" (*ou peithomenoi*).

160. "By my conversations" (*dialexesin*) is the reading of the best manuscripts. Marginal comments in these, adopted in the main text of later manuscripts, suggest "[attempts at] reconciliation" (*diallaxesi*) instead of "conversations."

161. The word for "reconciled" here is *katēllagē*, which could even suggest "atonement" in this context; it is to be distinguished from *oikeiotēta*, "reconciliation," at 317e above (see n. 23 to Letter Three).

162. The phrase *tōi boulesthai kai tōi dunasthai* ("both [merely] by wishing [it] and by the power [I] held [with him]") is hard to translate. The latter of the two verbs here is elsewhere translated "to be capable," though it is of course also related to the noun *dunamis*, translated "power" throughout. A very literal translation that would fail to convey the sense would be "both by wishing and by being capable."

by majority vote, or, having come to the fore of a great city, which rules many lesser ones, if he should apportion the money of the smaller ones to his own city not according to justice.[163] For neither Dion nor anyone else ever voluntarily goes for power that is accursed[164] for him and his tribe[165] for all time, but rather for a regime with the establishment of the most just and best laws to come to be through not even the fewest deaths and murders.[166]

351c

These things Dion was now doing, having preferred[167] the suffering of impious deeds above the doing of them, yet being very careful not to suffer them; nevertheless he stumbled, having come to the peak of his overcoming of his enemies—suffering nothing amazing. For, concerning the impious, a pious human being, both moderate and sensible,[168] would never be wholly deceived concerning the soul of such as they—but perhaps it would not be amazing if he should suffer the experience[169] of a good pilot: a coming storm would not altogether escape his notice, but the extraordinary[170] and unexpected magnitude of a storm could escape his notice and, having escaped it, inundate him by force. The same thing also brought down Dion; for it hardly escaped his notice that the ones who brought him down were evil, but the height of unlearnedness[171] to which they had attained, and of the rest of depravity and gluttony, did escape his notice,[172] and having been brought down by it, he lies, having engulfed Sicily in ten-thousandfold sorrow.

351d

351e

352a

The things that I counsel after what has now been discussed have pretty much already been spoken by me—and let them have been spoken.

---

163. Or "not according to a just penalty" or "a just judgment" (*mē kata dikēn*).

164. See n. 70 above.

165. Or "family" (*genei*); see n. 8 above.

166. Marginal emendations in the best manuscripts suggest the word "murders" (*phonōn*) should instead be "exiles" (*phugōn*).

167. Lit. "having honored more highly" (*protimēsas*).

168. "Moderate" and "sensible" here translate two words closely related in the Greek, *sōphrōn* and *emphrōn*. See n. 15 to Letter Three.

169. "Suffer" and "experience" here translate virtually the same word; the phrase is *pathos pathoi*. There is no word in this sentence related to *empeiron*, for which I usually reserve the word "experience."

170. Lit. "beyond what is ordained," "inauspicious" (*exaision*).

171. See n. 72 above.

172. Accepting the emendation offered by a second hand in one of the best manuscripts and preferred by Burnet and Souilhé. Note, however, that Souilhé mistakenly claims that his preferred reading also appears in the main text of the best manuscripts, which it does not. The main text reads *etuchon* instead of *elathon*, which might be translated "but the height of unlearnedness to which they had attained, and of the rest of depravity and gluttony, did happen [to escape his notice]."

As regards those things for the sake of which I took back up my second arrival in Sicily, it seemed to me that they necessarily needed to be discussed because of the strangeness and unreasonableness of the things that happened. And if what has now been said appeared rather reasonable to someone, and seemed to him to provide sufficient pretexts for the things that happened, then what has now been said would have been spoken in a measured and sufficient manner for us.

Letter Eight

352b Plato to the intimates and comrades of Dion: Do well!

What things, should you[1] intend them, you would most of all really "do well"—these I will attempt to go through for you as much as is in my power. I hope to counsel the things that are advantageous not for 352c you alone, but most of all, to be sure, for you, and second for all those in Syracuse, but third for your enemies and adversaries in war, except for any of them who may have become a doer of impious deeds; for these things are incurable, and one may never purge them away. And think about what I am now saying.

For you, throughout all of Sicily, the tyranny having been dissolved, all is battle concerning these very things: some wishing to take up the rule again, others to complete the escape from tyranny. Correct coun- 352d sel concerning such things seems to the many on each occasion to be counsel as to what is needed to achieve as many evils as possible for their adversaries in war and as many goods as possible for their friends; but it is in no way easy for one doing many evils to others not also to suffer many further evils himself. And there is no need to go anywhere far away

1. Plato employs the second-person plural throughout this letter.

to see such things clearly, but so many have now come to be in this way right there, all around Sicily—some undertaking to do them, others to 352e defend against the doers; and by telling the tales[2] about these things to others, you would come to be sufficient teachers on every occasion. Now about these things, there is hardly any perplexity; but about how many of them would come to be either advantageous for all, both enemies and friends, or as little evil as possible for both, these things are neither easy to see, nor, having been seen, to bring to completion, but such counsel and undertaking of speech resembles a prayer. Let it be altogether, then, 353a a certain prayer—for one ought always to speak and think, in all things, beginning from the gods—and would that it be brought to completion, signaling to us some speech such as the following.

Over you and pretty much over your adversaries in war, now and from the very moment the war came to be, one family continuously rules, which your fathers set up in the time when they had come to be altogether at a loss: when an extreme danger came to be for Greek Sicily, that it would be wholly overrun by Carthaginians and thoroughly bar- 353b barized. For they then chose Dionysius for the actions of war that befit him, on the grounds that he was young and skilled in warfare, and an elder, Hipparinus,[3] as a counselor, and both, for the salvation of Sicily, as "rulers with full powers," as they say, naming them tyrants. And whether one wishes to hold that it turned out to be divine fortune and a god, or the virtue of the rulers, or even both of these together with the citizens of that time that came to be the cause of salvation, let it be in whatever way one assumes; thus did there turn out to be salvation for those who 353c then came to be. Such things as these having come to be, then, it is presumably just for everyone to have gratitude for the saviors; but if in the time thereafter the tyranny has not correctly made use of the gift from the city, it has paid some of the just penalties for these things—let it pay others.

What just penalties, then, would necessarily come to be correct on the basis of their situation? If you were able to escape them easily and without great dangers or toils, or they to take back the rule without trouble, I would not be able to counsel the things that are about to be spoken. 353d But now, both of you ought to think of and to remember how often

2. I avoid the near transliteration "mythologizing" as a translation for *muthologountes*, though it would not be an altogether inappropriate alternative to "telling the tales."

3. Father of Dion; on the various Syracusan Hipparini, see n. 3 to Letter Seven.

you have each come to be in hope of at last supposing that you are in need—it is almost always this way—of some small further thing in order to do everything to your liking, and then this small thing turns out each time to come to be the cause of ten thousand great evils; and no limit ever puts an end to it, but an old end seems always to be joined to a new naturally growing beginning;[4] and both the entire tyrannical and the 353e popular tribe will be in danger of being utterly destroyed[5] by this circle; and all Sicily, if any of the likely and abominable things should come to be, will come to be nearly devoid of the Greek language, changing into some power and might of Phoenicians or Opicans.[6] All the Greeks ought to provide a remedy for these things with all eagerness of spirit. Now, if someone has something more correct and better than what will be said by me, he would be most correctly spoken of as a lover of the 354a Greeks if he brought it forward; but what now appears to me somehow, I will attempt to make clear in all frankness and by a certain common, just speech.

Indeed, conversing in a certain way as an arbiter with the two parties—those who tyrannized and those who were tyrannized—and to each as one, I speak my old counsel: even now, my speech at any rate would be a counsel to every tyrant to flee this name and deed and, if it should 354b be possible, to change into a kingship. But it is possible, as Lycurgus showed by deed, a wise and good man who, having seen the tribe of his intimates in Argos and Messene changing from the power of kings to that of tyrants, having corrupted themselves as well as the city of each, and dreading the same for his own city and tribe, he brought in as a remedy the rule of the old and the bond of the Ephors, a salvation for the kingly rule,[7] so as to save it with glory for so many generations now,

4. The word for "beginning" here, *archēi*, may carry a double entendre, since the same word also means "rule" or "empire." See n. 5 to Letter One.

5. There is disagreement among the best manuscripts as to whether the word here is *dioles-thai*, "utterly destroyed," or *dielesthai*, "divided," "broken apart."

6. To the south, the Carthaginians, who had long been the Syracusans' major rivals for power in Sicily, spoke a Phoenician language. The "Opicans," also called the Osci, were an Italic people to the north. Their Oscan language was also spoken by the Samnites, who at this time were competing with Rome for dominance over the central Italian mainland; in addition, Dionysius the Elder's practice of employing non-Greek Italian mercenaries may have led to the existence of some Opican presence in Sicily itself (see Morrow's note ad loc.). Plato's wording leaves unclear whether he is speaking of Phoenician and Opican *peoples* or *languages*.

7. Political power in the Spartan regime was shared between three major institutions: the two kings, the "Gerousia" or council of thirty elders, and the Ephorate, a council of five citizens elected by the full Spartan assembly. Plato's attribution to Lycurgus (see n. 8 to Letter Four) of the creation of the latter two offices agrees with the account of Herodotus (1.65.5), but not

354c since law became a sovereign king over human beings, and not human beings tyrants over laws.

Which, even now, my speech urges to everyone: it urges those aiming at tyranny to turn away in flight and flee the purported happiness[8] of insatiably hungry and mindless human beings, and to attempt to change into a form[9] of a king, and to be slaves to kingly laws, having acquired the greatest honors both from human beings voluntarily and 354d from the laws; and those pursuing free ways and fleeing the slavish yoke as being bad, I would counsel to beware lest they should ever fall into the disease of their ancestors out of insatiability for a certain unpropitious freedom, which disease they then suffered because of the excessive anarchy, making use of an unmeasured, passionate love of freedom.[10] For the Siceliotes before Dionysius and Hipparinus had ruled were living happily (as they then supposed), luxuriously, and at the same time ruling the rulers; and they, casting stones, lapidated the ten generals pre- 354e ceding Dionysius, in no way judging according to law, in order that they should in no way be enslaved with either justice or law as a master, but be altogether free in every way; hence did the tyrannies over them come to be. For slavery and freedom are each, if excessive, altogether bad, but if each is in measure, altogether good; and slavery to a god is measured, but to human beings unmeasured; and law is a god to moderate human 355a beings, pleasure [a god] to the imprudent.

These things naturally being this way, I encourage the friends of Dion to explain to all Syracusans what I counsel, which is his and my common counsel; and I will interpret what he would say to you now, if he were breathing and capable of speaking. "What speech, then," someone might say, "would Dion's counsel bring to light for us concerning the things that are present now?" The following.

---

with the account given by Plato's own Athenian Stranger in the *Laws* (691d8–692b1; see also Plutarch, *Lycurgus* 7.1). The claim that Lycurgus's lawgiving was prompted by his observation of what happened in the nearby cities of Argos and Messene is unique to the *Letters*, but cf. *Laws* 690d1–e5 in context.

8. The word for "purported happiness" (*eudaimonisma*) appears to be a Platonic coinage, and its intended meaning can only be inferred from the context. Strictly speaking, it is formed from the word for "happiness" (*eudaimonia*; see n. 69 to Letter Seven) and the suffix *-isma*, which generally denotes a finished product emerging from some productive process. Thus one might well translate *eudaimonisma* as "state of happiness," in which case the sense "purported" is conveyed by sarcasm rather than explicitly.

9. The word for "form" here is *eidos*, as in the famous Platonic doctrine of the "Forms" or "Ideas." The word occurs only once elsewhere in the *Letters*, at 322d5 above.

10. The phrase "passionate love" translates the word *erōs*. See n. 95 to Letter Seven.

355b "Accept, O Syracusans, first of all, laws which would appear to you not to turn your judgments, together with your desire, toward money-making and riches, but—there being three things, soul, and body, and then money—such as would make the virtue of the soul most honored, second that of the body, which lies under that of the soul, and third and 355c last the honor of money, which is a slave to both body and soul. And the ordained law that achieves these things would be laid down correctly for you, completing as really happy those who use it; but the speech that names the rich "happy" is both wretched itself, being a mindless speech of women and children, and achieves [wretchedness] for such as who are persuaded by it. That these things I encourage are true, you will recognize by deed if you shall taste the things now being said concerning laws, which seems to come to be the truest test concerning all things.

355d "And having accepted such laws, since danger has taken hold of Sicily and you are neither prevailing sufficiently nor, in turn, have you been surpassingly prevailed over, perhaps it would come to be just and advantageous for all of you to cut down the middle, both for you who are fleeing the harshness of rule and for those passionately desiring to hit upon rule again, whose ancestors then saved the Greeks from barbarians in the greatest way so that it is possible now to make speeches about regimes; had they then been wiped out, neither speech nor hope would have remained in any place or in any way.

355e "Now, then, let the former have freedom under kingly rule and let the latter have kingly rule for which they are accountable, with laws as masters both of the other citizens and of the kings themselves in case they should do anything illegal. And on all these terms, by means of judgment that is without trickery and sound, together with gods, set [each of the following people] up as king. First, my own son, for the sake of gratitude on two counts: for my contribution and for my father's. 356a For my father freed the city from barbarians in his time, and I from tyranny twice now, of which things you yourselves have come to be witnesses. Second, make a king of the one possessing the same name as my father, the son of Dionysius, in gratitude for his giving aid now and for his pious ways.[11] Though born of a tyrant father, he voluntarily sets the city free, acquiring honor for himself and his tribe that will live forever

11. See n. 3 to Letter Seven for a discussion of the three men named Hipparinus who figure in this story: Dion's father, Dion's son (both mentioned just above), and this one, the son of Dionysius the Elder, who had by the time of this letter become the leader of Dion's party at Syracuse.

instead of acquiring an ephemeral and unjust tyranny. Third, you ought to propose that he shall become king of the Syracusans, a willing king

356b of a willing city, who now rules the camp of your adversaries in war: Dionysius, son of Dionysius. If, that is, he should be willing voluntarily to be removed and changed into the shape of a king out of dread for his fortunes and pity for his fatherland and its neglected temples and graves, lest, on account of love of victory, he should destroy everything in every way, coming to be a source of joy to barbarians.

"Set up three kings, agreeing to give them either the Laconian power[12] or something less, and arrange matters in some way such as the follow-

356c ing (which has been said to you also earlier, but nevertheless listen now yet again). If the tribe of Dionysius and Hipparinus should be willing, for the salvation of Sicily, to put a stop to the evils that are now present, receiving honors for themselves and for their tribe both in the time to come and now, then on these terms, just as has also been said before, call in ambassadors whom they would be willing to make sovereign authorities over the reconciliations—from here, from outside, or both, as many

356d as they should agree on. When they come, let them first set down laws and the sort of regime in which it is consonant for kings to come to be sovereign authorities over sacred things and over however many other things are fitting for those who were once benefactors. But let them create guardians of the laws,[13] thirty-five in number, as rulers of war and peace together with both demos and council.[14] Let there be other lawcourts for other things, but let the thirty-five initiate cases involving penalties of death and exile. Besides these, let the judges always be

356e selected from among the rulers of the previous year, one from each ruling office—he who seems to be best and most just. For the following year, let these judge cases involving penalties of death, imprisonment,

---

12. I.e., the power of the Spartan kings, Laconia being the name of the region in which Sparta lay. The authority of Sparta's dual-kingship decreased steadily over time. The Spartan kings retained their military roles as generals as well as certain priestly religious functions, but their political power, even over matters of war and peace, was quite limited by the time of this letter.

13. "Guardians of the laws" (*nomophulakas*) is the title Plato's Athenian Stranger gives to one of the highest offices he creates for the city discussed in the *Laws*, though there they number thirty-seven instead of thirty-five; see especially book 6 of the *Laws* for the description of that office.

14. The demos of a Greek polis was comprised of the totality of its citizenry, what might later have been called "the commons." In a democracy, the demos expressed its political will in the "assembly" (*ekklēsia*). Even in democracies, however—and also in other regimes—it was common to have a separate institution known as a *boulē* ("council" or "senate"), formed of a more manageable subset of citizens, empowered to deal with daily administrative affairs.

and removal of the citizens;[15] but let it not be possible for a king to come
357a to be a judge in cases involving these sorts of just penalties, since he, like a priest, is to be pure of murder, imprisonment, and exile.

"These things I intended to come to be for you while I lived, and I intend them now; and once I, together with you, had prevailed over our enemies, then, had guest-friend Furies[16] not prevented me, I would have set things up in the very way I intended, and after these things, had deeds followed upon thought, I would have recolonized the rest of Sicily, taking from the barbarians—so many as did not carry on the
357b war against the tyranny on behalf of the common freedom—what they now have, and recolonizing, with the previous inhabitants, the Greek places in the ancient and patrimonial habitations. I counsel everyone in common even now to intend and to do these same things and to call everyone toward these actions, and to hold that he who is not willing is a common adversary.

"And these things are not impossible. For he who judges to be impossible such things as happen to be in two souls, and which come readily
357c to those who try to find what is best by calculating, can hardly mean well. The two souls of which I speak are those of Hipparinus, the son of Dionysius, and of my own son; for I suppose that, if these two were to agree, all these things will also be so resolved by all the other Syracusans who are solicitous for the city. But, having given honors, together with prayers, to all gods, and to as many others for whom, together with gods, it is fitting, do not leave off persuading and making proposals to friends and those with whom you are in conflict, softly and in every way, until
357d you shall have achieved the completion of the things that have now been said by us, like divine dreams standing before ones who are awake, clear, and fortunate."[17]

---

15. For the difference between "exile" and "removal" from the city, see n. 84 to Letter Seven.

16. The Furies were ancient goddesses believed to wreak divine vengeance upon human beings who had committed great offenses, especially those involving the failure to uphold solemn duties or obligations. As the phrase "guest-friend Furies" implies (*xenikai erinues*), these included the obligations of *xenia*, guest-friendship; see n. 12 to Letter Three.

17. The last word of this letter, which I here translate "fortunate," is the adjective *eutuchē*. It is a form of the same word that also ends Letters Four, Five, and Eleven, the imperative verb *eutuchei*, which I translate "Good luck!"

Letter Nine

Plato to Archytas the Tarentine:[1] Do well!

357e Those close to Archippus and Philonides[2] arrived at our place both bearing the letter which you gave them and reporting the things from you. They accomplished the matters concerning the city without difficulty—for it was not altogether laborious—and they went through for us thoroughly the things from you, saying that you are restless because you are not capable of being released from the lack of leisure connected with the common things. That the most pleasant thing in 358a life is to do one's own thing, especially if someone should choose to do things of such a sort as you too have chosen, is clear to nearly everyone; but you need to take the following to heart as well: that it is not only for oneself that each of us has been born, but one's fatherland gets a certain portion of our birth,[3] one's parents another, and the rest of one's friends another, and many things are given also to the propitious moments that overtake our life. When the fatherland itself calls one to the common

1. On Archytas, see n. 86 to Letter Seven.

2. Two Pythagorean philosophers belonging to Archytas's philosophic circle at Tarentum; they are included in Iamblichus's list of Pythagoreans from Tarentum (*De vita Pythagorica liber* 267).

3. Lit. "of our coming-into-being" (*tēs geneseōs hēmōn*).

358b things, perhaps it is strange not to hearken; for that turns out at the same time also to leave a space for paltry human beings, who do not proceed from the best[4] to the common things.

Enough, now, about these things. But we have a care also now for Echecrates, and will do so in the time to come, because of you, and because of his father, Phrynion, and because of the youth himself.[5]

---

4. It is usually assumed that this means "from the best motive," but no noun is given in the text. The Greek could also be construed as meaning broadly "from the best place," or perhaps "from the best thing," i.e., affair or occupation, in contrast to "the common things."

5. Echecrates is the name of the man to whom Phaedo narrates the conversation that took place on the day of Socrates's death in Plato's *Phaedo*. This man, known as Echecrates of Phlius, was "a Pythagorean and a pupil of Philolaus and Eurytus, who in their later life taught at Tarentum" (Morrow 1962, 259n3). However, Nails (2002, 139) argues that Echecrates of Phlius could hardly have been a "youth" at the time of the writing of Letter Nine. There was another Echecrates, perhaps related to the first, who, like Archippus and Philonides (above), is mentioned by Iamblichus in his list of Pythagoreans from Tarentum (*De vita Pythagorica liber* 267).

Letter Ten

Plato to Aristodorus: Do well!

358c I hear from Dion that you are now, and have come to be through everything, a special comrade of his, exhibiting a character that is the wisest one with a view to philosophy;[1] for it is the steadfast, and faithful, and healthy[2] that I myself claim is the true philosophy, and as for the other wisdoms and clevernesses, which extend to other things, I suppose that I name them correctly by calling them "niceties."[3] But be strong and remain in the very character traits in which you now remain.

---

1. The first two words of this sentence seem to read "I hear from Dion" (*akouō Diōnos*). However, the whole sentence could also be read "I hear that you are now, and have come to be through everything, a special comrade of Dion's."

2. Or "sound" (*hugies*).

3. Plato here employs an unusual noun, *kompsotētas*. Isocrates uses the word to refer to refined or ornate literary and rhetorical style (*Panathenaicus* 12.1). The word is formed from the adjective *kompsos*, for which LSJ suggests "nice," "refined," "subtle," "clever," etc., and which appears twice in the *Letters* (318b6, 361a4).

Letter Eleven

358d Plato to Laodamas:[1] Do well!

I sent a letter to you before as well, saying that it makes a great difference, with respect to all the things you say, for you to come to Athens yourself; but since you claim that it is impossible, second after this would have been if it were possible for me or Socrates[2] to come—just 358e as you said in the letter you sent. But right now, Socrates is ill with strangury;[3] and as for me, it would be indecorous if, having arrived there, I should not accomplish the very things for the purpose of which you are calling upon me. But I do not have much hope that these things would come to be—as for the reasons why, there would be need of a long, other letter, which would go through everything thoroughly—and at the same

1. Nothing else is known of this Laodamas.

2. Since Plato, who was in his twenties when Socrates died, makes excuse of his advanced age in this letter (358e5–6), it is generally thought that this reference must be to the "Younger Socrates" of Plato's *Theaetetus*, *Sophist*, and *Statesman*. If so, this is the only extant reference to him by any contemporary outside of those dialogues, with one exception: Aristotle refers to (and rejects) a philosophical position the "Younger Socrates" used to hold at *Metaphysics* 1036b25 (see Granger 2000, 415n1). It has only rarely been considered that this may be a sort of joking—and consciously anachronistic—reference to Socrates himself; see Wohl 1998, 63–65.

3. As Nails explains, "Strangury (*stranguria*: strangled urine) is a condition in which an obstruction causes urine to be discharged spasmodically and painfully, drop by drop" (2002, 269). Cf. Aristophanes, *Thesmophoriazusae* 617.

time, I, because of my age, am not in a sufficient bodily condition to be wandering and undergoing dangers of the sort that occur by land and by sea; and now everything pertaining to journeys[4] is full of dangers.

359a However, I can give counsel both to you and to the colonists, which, "after I have said it," says Hesiod, "might seem to be paltry, but it is hard to think."[5] For if they suppose[6] that, by the giving of any laws whatsoever, a city would[7] ever be well established without the existence of some sovereign authority caring for the daily regimen[8] of both slaves and free in the city, so that it might be both moderate and manly, they do not understand[9] correctly. Now moreover, if there are already men worthy 359b of this ruling office, this [sovereign authority] might come to be; but if there is need of someone to educate them, you will have neither he who will educate nor they who will be educated, as I suppose; but what remains is for you to pray to the gods.

And in fact the earlier cities too were established in nearly this way and were well managed thereafter, under the coming-to-be of conjunctions of great affairs, both in war and in the other actions—whenever, at the propitious moments, a man both noble and good[10] came about 359c having great power; one ought and is compelled to be eager for them[11] beforehand, but to understand them as I say and not to be mindless by supposing something will be readily accomplished. Good luck.

---

4. Or "everything in the traveling routes" (*panta . . . en tais poreiais*).

5. This line does not appear in Hesiod's extant works, and, as Morrow observes ad loc., "its meaning [is] uncertain." "Paltry" (*phaulon*) could also be rendered "simple" here. The final phrase, "is difficult to think" (*chalepon noēsai*), has been reasonably given by various translators as "is difficult to understand" (Post), "is hard to take" (Morrow), and "was difficult to think of" (Harward).

6. The reading "they suppose" (*oiontai*) appears in several of the later manuscripts. The earliest and generally best have instead *oion te*, which leaves the sentence grammatically difficult. Translators have universally adopted the former reading.

7. In both of the best manuscripts, marginal emendations suggest that "a city would" (*polin an*) is a textual corruption from "a regime" (*politeian*). The alternative reading would be "For if they suppose that, by the giving of any laws whatsoever, a regime was ever well established."

8. Or "way of living," or also, possibly, "arbitration" (*diaitēs*).

9. "Understand," both here and in the last line of this letter, translates a form of *dianoeō*, for which I have generally used the English word "intend." See n. 5 to Letter Three.

10. On the formula "both noble and good" (*kalos te kai agathos*), see n. 21 to Letter Seven.

11. The only grammatically valid antecedent of this "them" (*auta*) would seem to be the "great affairs" mentioned above.

Letter Twelve

Plato to Archytas the Tarentine: Do well!

We received the reminders[1] that have come from you with amazing 359d gladness and we admire the one who wrote them as extraordinary; the man seemed to us to be worthy of his ancient ancestors, for indeed these men are said to be Myrians[2]—they were among those expelled[3] from Troy

1. "Reminders" translates the word *hupomnēmata*, a word that often refers to texts written for the purpose of preserving a record of something—what we might call "memoranda." Frede has made the use of this word in this letter a key point of his argument against the letter's authenticity (Burnyeat and Frede 2015, 20, 24–25), and has in turn made the alleged inauthenticity of this letter a key point in his argument against the authenticity of the whole *Letters* (23–24). His argument hinges upon the claim that "the meaning or use of this term [viz. *hupomnēmata*] is rather difficult to determine and to explain. One thing which is clear is that it excludes dialogues and speeches," a claim that he bases on a line in Diogenes Laertius. But this supposition is mistaken. As noted by Pappas (2017, 40–41), Plato evidently suggests that his dialogues may have the purpose of being such "reminders" at *Phaedrus* 276d3; consider also 278a1. The same word appears three other times in the *Letters*: once just below at 359d6, and also in Letters Seven (344d9) and Thirteen (363e4). The instance in Letter Seven especially should be compared with the passages of the *Phaedrus* cited.

2. It is not known who these Myrians were. It is possible that the Greek word here is not the demonym "Myrians," but the adjective of identical spelling, *murioi*, literally meaning "ten thousand," and figuratively something like "countless" (as the English "myriad"). It would be no clearer to us, however, who these "myriad" ancestors were than if the correct reading were "Myrians." See Harward 1932, 230n2; Burnyeat and Frede 2015, 19.

3. Or, possibly, "those who emigrated" (*exanastantōn*).

in the time of Laomedon[4]—good men, as the myth that has been handed down makes clear. But the reminders from me, about which you sent a letter, are not yet in sufficient condition, but I have dispatched them 359e to you in whatever condition they happen to be in; and concerning the guarding,[5] the both of us are in accord, so that there is no need for encouraging.

---

4. As Frede explains, "Laomedon is obviously the king of Troy, father of Priam, repeatedly referred to in the *Iliad*, but also for instance in Apollodorus's *Biblotheca*. . . . [He] hired Apollon and Poseidon to build the walls of Troy, but once they had finished the task he refused to pay them; whereupon Poseidon sent a terrible sea monster which could only be appeased by being offered Laomedon's daughter Hesione. Heracles agrees to kill the sea monster, and thus to save Hesione, if Laomedon gives him his horses. Heracles kills the monster, but Laomedon refuses to give him the promised horses; Heracles with an army captures Troy. In the aftermath of this Priam becomes king of Troy. So there are two falls of Troy: the one under Laomedon and the other under Priam. So the *Μύριοι* are obviously people who leave Troy in the events which lead up to the first fall of Troy or after this fall" (Burnyeat and Frede 2015, 19–20).

5. On "the guarding" (*tēs phulakēs*), see Harward's note ad loc.: "φυλακῆς has been explained as a reference to Plato's guardians in the *Republic*. It is more likely that the word simply means the custody of the notes. We may suppose that Plato and Archytas were agreed that notes on important philosophical questions ought not to be allowed to fall into the hands of such a person as Dionysios."

Letter Thirteen

It is denied that this is by Plato.[1]

1. This sentence appears in almost all the manuscripts as though it were the final sentence of Letter Twelve. However, as Hackforth correctly acknowledged, "There seems to be no means of deciding whether the note . . . belongs to xii or xiii" (1913, 163). That is, the manner in which early copies of the *Letters* were transcribed would have made it difficult for copyists to discern where the line belonged, so that the text of even our oldest manuscripts is more likely to reflect the best guesses of some earlier editors than anything else. For his part, Hackforth notes his agreement with Burnet that the line should be appended to the end of Letter Twelve, "because it is very much more natural to suspect xii to be spurious than xiii" (163). But this judgment is fundamentally debatable. Ficino (1484), Cudworth (1678), and Bentley (1838, 409–13), though they differed on the question of authenticity, all took the line as referring to Letter Thirteen. In any case, while this note is at least as old as the ninth century, it must be stressed that we have no way of knowing precisely when it was added to the manuscripts. We cannot say whether the doubt, to which this note attests, regarding the authenticity of Letter Twelve or Thirteen arose among Plato's near contemporaries or more than a thousand years later (see, e.g., Burnyeat and Frede 2015, 6).

Vastly underconsidered, however, is the possibility that this line is itself an *authentic* part of the original *Letters*. If we are to entertain the hypothesis that the *Letters* is a unitary work of Platonic political philosophy—one that bears as a motif an "obsessive concern with [its] own authenticity" (Wohl 1998, 84), and more than once enigmatically seems to deny the genuine Platonic authorship of Plato's writings—we should recognize that it would not be out of place for its author to have set this riddling line at the head of Letter Thirteen in particular: of all the letters in this collection, Letter Thirteen is the most explicitly concerned with its own genuineness (360a3ff., 363b1–6). In any case, there is every bit as much reason to believe the note may attach to Letter Thirteen as to Letter Twelve, regardless of one's position on the status of the *Letters* in the Platonic corpus. I have placed it here in accordance with my own best guess.

360a Plato to Dionysius, Tyrant of Syracuse: Do well!

Let the beginning of this letter be at the same time also a token[2] to you that it is from me. Once, when you were hosting a feast for the Locrian youths,[3] you, who had been reclining at a distance from me, rose, came over to me, and, being in a friendly way, spoke some phrase 360b that was well put (as it seemed to me at least) to the one reclining next to me—and he was one of the beauties—who then said, "In many ways, to be sure, Dionysius, you are benefited in wisdom by Plato." And you said, "And in many other things, since even from the moment of his very summons, because of the very fact that I sent for him, straightaway I was benefited." This, then, must be preserved in such a way that the benefit to us from one another may always increase.

And I, so as to produce this very effect, am now sending you both some of the Pythagorean things[4] and some of the divisions[5]—as well as 360c a man, just as was resolved by us then, of whom you and Archytas, if

---

2. The word "token" translates *sumbolon*—the origin of the English "symbol"—a word that appears here, at 363b1 below, and nowhere else in the *Letters* (but cf. n. 31 below). *Sumbola* were originally used as a means of confirming the identity of two contracting parties or their representatives. Upon their agreement, the parties would break an item in two and each take one piece as a *sumbolon*, which could thereafter be presented, say by a messenger or representative, to prove that the message in fact came from the other party. The word thereafter came to refer also to other means of proving authenticity (such as wax seals and certain kinds of identity tokens), and could sometimes refer to a prearranged "secret signal" or "password." One should consider especially Plato's use of the word at 363b1 below.

3. Locris was a Greek city on the Italian mainland with several points of connection to Plato and the Syracusan story of the *Letters*. Dionysius the Younger's mother, Doris, was from Locris (Plutarch, *Dion* 3, 6), as was the physician Philistion apparently referred to in Letter Two above (314e3; see n. 57 to Letter Two)—this Philistion, moreover, was among the teachers of Eudoxus, mentioned just below, who also studied with Archytas and eventually, as it seems, with Plato at the Academy (see n. 9 below). It should also be noted that the Platonic character Timaeus, of the *Timaeus* and *Critias*, is said to be from Locris (*Timaeus* 20a1–3; cf. *Laws* 638a7–b3).

4. Presumably these "things" are texts; but Plato's vagueness here is of a piece with a pattern throughout the *Letters* according to which he often uses an unspecified neuter plural to refer to doctrines, ideas, or other intellectual products of a school of thought, both his own and others'. See n. 44 to Letter Two.

5. This is the only explicit reference to Pythagoras in the *Letters*; implicitly, however, Pythagoreanism has been present in the *Letters* in the figure of Archytas, who is well known to have fostered a Pythagorean philosophic circle in Tarentum (see n. 86 to Letter Seven). Since the nineteenth century if not earlier, it has been speculated that the "Pythagorean things" to which Plato refers here would include Plato's *Timaeus* and that the "divisions" (*diaireseōn*) would include Platonic dialogues such as the *Sophist* and *Statesman*, wherein the Eleatic Stranger—a follower of Parmenides, who stood at the head of the *other* great Italian philosophic school in this day—demonstrates his technique of discovering definitions by dividing the whole through "dichotomies." See the notes of Souilhé, Harward, and Morrow ad loc.

indeed Archytas has come to you, would be capable of making use.[6] His name is Helicon,[7] his family[8] is from Cyzicus, he is a student of Eudoxus[9] and very adept[10] concerning the latter's things;[11] moreover, he associated with one of the students of Isocrates,[12] and with Polyxenus,[13] one of Bryson's[14] comrades. But, what is rare in addition to these things, he is neither ungraceful to encounter nor is he like someone of bad character, but rather he would seem to be easygoing and of good character.[15]

360d And I say these things in trepidation, because I am bringing to light an opinion concerning a human being—not a paltry animal, but one easily changeable, excepting some very few and with respect to few things. Since I was fearful and distrustful about him too, I myself was both examining him, when I encountered him, and inquiring of his fellow citizens, and no one said anything nasty about the man. But examine him yourself also and beware. Most of all, now, if you should in any

---

6. On Archytas, see n. 86 to Letter Seven.

7. The only other extant reference to this Helicon is in Plutarch's *Life of Dion* (19.4). There he is said to have been a man close to Plato (a *sunēthēs*) who so impressed Dionysius the Younger by predicting a solar eclipse that the tyrant awarded him a talent of silver.

8. Or "his tribe" (*genos*); see n. 8 to Letter Seven.

9. Eudoxus has been described as "the greatest of the classical Greek mathematicians and second only to Archimedes in all antiquity" (Kline 1972, 48). For discussions of his breakthroughs in geometry, astronomy, and medicine, see van der Waerden 1961, 179–89; on his moral philosophy, see also Aristotle, *Nicomachean Ethics* 1172b9–35. He is said to have been taught by Archytas (see n. 86 to Letter Seven) and Philistion (see n. 57 to Letter Two), and to have been a student and companion of Plato (Diogenes Laertius 8.8.86; Strabo 17.29; Proclus, *On Euclid* 67.2–3), and he was renowned for giving laws for his native Cnidus (Diogenes Laertius 8.8.88; Plutarch, *Adversus Colotem* 32).

10. Lit. "altogether graceful" (*panu charientōs echōn*).

11. I.e., his teachings, doctrines, or philosophy; see n. 4 above and n. 44 to Letter Two.

12. Isocrates (436–338 BCE), a contemporary of Plato, was an enormously famous and successful Athenian teacher who wrote and published an unusual variety of political philosophic texts. In Plato's *Phaedrus*, the young Isocrates is said to be a companion of Socrates, who has high praise for him (278e4–279b3). The resemblance of Plato's Letter Seven to Isocrates's *Antidosis*—both being autobiographical and apologetic works, employing elaborate literary framing devices, and written toward the end of their authors' lives—has been noted and should be considered (Post 1925, 58–61; Morrow 1962, 50–52; Harward 1932, 197).

13. On Polyxenus, see n. 5 to Letter Two.

14. Little is known of Bryson of Heraclea. He is criticized a few times by Aristotle for his "eristic" attempt to solve the geometric problem of squaring the circle (*Posterior Analytics* 75b40–76a3; *Sophistical Refutations* 171b16–172a7) and for his argument that there is no such thing as the use of foul language (*Rhetoric* 1405b6–16).

15. "Of bad character" and "of good character" are here literal translations of the antonyms *kakoēthēs* and *euēthēs*. The words have further connotations that should be considered. The former may mean especially "malicious," and the latter often carries the negative meaning "naive" or "simpleminded." Likewise, *elaphros*, literally "lightweight" and here rendered "easygoing," can also mean "simpleminded," but could also be translated "lighthearted" or "cheerful." The word appeared in Letter Two above, where it was translated "easy" (314e5).

60e way whatsoever have leisure, learn from him and also philosophize with respect to the other things; otherwise, have someone thoroughly taught by him, so that, learning when there is leisure, you might come to be better and might be well reputed, in such a way that your being benefited because of me will not let up. So much, then, for these things.

61a Concerning the things that you sent a letter telling me to send to you, I had the Apollo made, and Leptines is bringing it to you.[16] It is of a young and good craftsman; his name is Leochares.[17] Another work of his was very nice as it seemed to me, so I bought it, wishing to give it to your wife, because she cared for me, both when I was healthy and when I was ailing, in a manner worthy of both me and you. Give it to her then, unless something else should seem good to you. I also send twelve jars 61b of sweet wine for your children, and two of honey. But we came after the season for storing figs, and the myrtle-berries that had been stowed away rotted; but we will take better care hereafter.[18] Leptines will tell you about the plants.[19]

I got the money for these things—for both these things and certain taxes for the city—from Leptines, saying what seemed to me to be most decorous for us as well as being true: that what we spent on the Leucadian ship[20] was our own, nearly sixteen minae;[21] so I got this, and having 61c got it, I both used it myself and sent you [pl] these things.

---

16. This Leptines (who is not to be confused with his father of the same name, brother to Dionysius the Elder), though mentioned in none of Plato's other letters, is evidently the one who is to convey this letter—or, at least, the gifts mentioned in this letter—to Dionysius, and it seems throughout this letter that both Plato and Dionysius consider him a trustworthy associate; in this respect, he performs the function here in Letter Thirteen that Archedemus did in Letter Two (see n. 1 to Letter Two). It has often been presumed, with reasonable cause, that this is the same man mentioned by Iamblichus as a Pythagorean from Syracuse (*Vita Pythagorica* 267). Certainly, this would seem to be the same Leptines who Diodorus Siculus says ruled Syracuse together with Dion's murderer Callippus (16.45.9), and who Plutarch claims later assassinated Callippus (*Dion* 57.6).

17. Leochares, who would indeed still have been a "young craftsman" at the time of this letter, "became a sculptor of scarcely less celebrity than his contemporaries, Scopas [his teacher] and Praxiteles" (Harward 1932, 235n10). Some Roman sculptures thought to be copies of his work, most notably the *Apollo Belvedere*, have been distinguished with the highest reputation among classical works of art.

18. Attic figs were renowned; see Athenaeus, *Deipnosophistae* 14.67.

19. The word for "plant," *phuton*, has the same root as the philosophically important word for "nature," *phusis*. This is the last occurrence of any word related to *phusis* in the *Letters*.

20. Harward notes the suggestion of Ritter that "Leucadia" may rather have been the name of the ship (1932, 235n12).

21. A decent sum of money, roughly two and a half years' worth of wages for a skilled laborer such as a carpenter (Engen 2004); see n. 143 to Letter Seven, noting that there were sixty minae to a talent.

Next after this, hear about how things stand concerning your money, both yours at Athens and mine. I will use your money, as I was then saying to you, just as that of my other associates: I use as little as I can for as many things as seem, both to me and to him from whom I get it, to be necessary or just or decorous. The following sort of thing, then, has now 361d fallen out for me. My nieces (the ones who died that time when I did not put on the wreath, though you directed me to)[22] have left four daughters: one is now marriageable, another is eight years old, another is a little beyond three years old, another is not yet one year old.[23] Of these, it falls to me and my associates to give away in marriage[24] those whose marriages I live to see; as for the others, let them farewell.[25] Now, it does not fall to me to give away in marriage those whose fathers should come to be richer than me; but at the moment, I am the most well-off of 361e them, and I, together with others and with Dion, gave away their mothers. Now, one of them will marry Speusippus, since she is his sister's daughter. There is need in her case of no more than thirty minae; for we consider this a measured gift. Furthermore, if my mother should meet her end, there would be need in turn of no more than ten minae for the building of her tomb.[26] And concerning these things, these are pretty nearly my necessities at the moment; but if some other private or public expense should come to be because of my arrival at your court, just as I was saying then, I need to fight to make it so that the expense should 362a come to be as little as possible; but insofar as I am not capable, the cost is yours.

Next after these things, concerning the expenditure of your money at Athens, I say that, first, if there should be some need for me to spend

---

22. It is not possible clearly to make out the event to which Plato is referring here. Evidently, some of Plato's nieces died while he was in Syracuse. It is possible that Dionysius "provided Plato with a funeral banquet and pressed him, perhaps unceremoniously, to adhere to all the details of Athenian custom," including the wearing of a wreath (Harward 1932, 235n13). But it is equally possible that Plato here refers to some occasion that merely coincided with, or bore some other relation to, the death of his nieces.

23. This sentence dates the letter fairly precisely. If this youngest of Plato's grandnieces is less than one year old, but her mother's death occurred while Plato was in Syracuse with Dionysius, then this must have been written considerably less than a year following Plato's return to Athens.

24. The word for "must be given away in marriage" is *ekdoteon*, which in this context implies above all the need to provide a dowry. This word appears twice more in the next sentence, where the connection to Plato's finances is made perfectly clear.

25. The third-person plural imperative form of the valediction I have translated "farewell" elsewhere in the *Letters* (*chairontōn*); cf. n. 1 to Letter Three.

26. On the value of a mina, see n. 21 above.

for a chorus or some such thing,[27] there is no guest-friend of yours who will give it, as we were supposing;[28] and next, if it should make a great difference to you in some case, in that it will profit you for the money to be spent immediately (whereas if it is not spent, but rather delayed until someone should come from you, it will harm you), such a thing, aside from being hard, would also be shameful for you. For indeed, I tested these things, at least, by sending Erastus to Andromedes the Aeginetan,[29] your [pl] guest-friend, from whom you directed me to get anything I should need, since I was wishing also for other greater things which you sent a letter telling me to send to you. But he said, appropriately and humanely,[30] that when previously he spent money for your father he only barely recovered it, and that he would now give a small amount but not more. So, instead, I got the money from Leptines; and in this, at least, Leptines is worth praising, not because he gave, but because he did so eagerly; and in both saying and doing the other things concerning you, it was manifest that he was able to be of service. For I ought to report, both with respect to such things as these and their opposites, of what sort each person appears to me to be in relation to you.

362b

362c

So, then, I will be frank with you concerning money; for it is just, and, at the same time, I would speak as one who has experience of those around you. Each time those who report to you suppose they are bringing report of an expense, they are not willing to report this, on the grounds that they will be incurring hatred; habituate and compel them, therefore, to explain these things, as well as the others; for you need both to know everything within your power and to be a judge, and not to flee from knowing. For of all things, this will be best for you with respect to your rule; for you too would say, and you will say, that it is good, both with respect to the other things and with respect to the acquisition of money itself, that the expenses be correctly spent and correctly returned. Therefore, let not those who assert that they are solicitous for you

362d

27. In Athens, wealthy residents were regularly called upon to pay for "liturgies" (*litourgiai*), i.e., to provide the funding for major public works. These included military expenditures, such as the outfitting of triremes, as well as cultural or artistic ones, such as paying for choruses to prepare and perform musical productions at dramatic festivals.

28. Apparently, Dionysius and Plato had hoped that someone wealthy, who shared ties of *xenia* with Dionysius and lived in or near Athens, might agree to loan funds to Plato, to be repaid by Dionysius, in case of urgent need.

29. On Erastus, see n. 1 to Letter Six. Andromedes is otherwise unknown.

30. Or "in a human way," (*anthrōpina*), in the sense of "as any person would."

slander you to human beings; for it is neither good nor noble for your reputation to seem to be hard to do business with.[31]

362e Next after these things I should speak about Dion. I cannot yet speak about the other things, until the letters come from you, as you claimed they would; however, concerning those things which you were not allowing me to bring up to him, I neither brought them up nor conversed about them, but I attempted to find out whether he would bear the things that are coming to be hard or easily, and it seemed to me that he would be aggravated, and not without commotion, if it should come to be.[32] But with respect to the other things concerning you, Dion seems to me to be measured, both in speech and in deed.

363a To Cratinus, Timotheus's brother and my comrade,[33] let us give a hoplite corselet, one of the soft[34] ones for infantrymen, and to Cebes's daughters, three chitons seven cubits in length,[35] not the expensive Amorgian ones but the Sicilian linen ones. You probably recognize Cebes's name, for he is the one who was written about in the Socratic speeches, conversing, together with Simmias, with Socrates in the speech about soul, a man who is both an intimate of, and bears good-will toward, us all.[36]

363b But now, concerning the token that pertains to the letters—all those letters I would send in seriousness and those I would not—I suppose that you remember it. But nevertheless, think about it and turn your mind very much toward it; for there are many directing me to write

---

31. The manuscripts here are corrupt, and it is impossible to know for certain what was written. "[H]ard to do business with" translates *dussumbolon*, which was the suggestion of Schneider and stands as the most likely guess. In any case, it should be noted that *some* word related to *sumbolon*, translated "token" elsewhere in this letter (see n. 2 above), appears here. Because the *sumbolon* was used between two contracting parties, the word could also refer to the contract itself, and hence *dussumbolon* means something like "hard-bargaining" or "hard to do business with."

32. According to Plutarch (*Dion* 21), the matter at issue here is Dionysius's desire to give Dion's wife away in marriage to another man, his friend Timocrates.

33. Of Cratinus, nothing else is known. His brother Timotheus (fl. c. 375–360 BCE), however, was an eminent Athenian general, and a friend and pupil of Isocrates (see *Antidosis* 101–39, and the letter *To Timotheus*).

34. Both of the best manuscripts include notes in a second hand claiming that the correct reading is *mala kalōn*, "very beautiful" or "very noble," rather than *malakōn*, "soft."

35. The chiton was a typical ancient Greek tunic. The Greek version of the "cubit," or length of a forearm, was the *pēchus*, measuring roughly 18 inches.

36. Cebes and Simmias were two Theban companions of Socrates, and his main interlocutors, in Plato's *Phaedo*. See also Xenophon, *Memorabilia* 1.2.48, 3.11.17; and on Simmias, Plato, *Phaedrus* 242b.

whom it is not easy to refuse openly. For a god begins the serious letter, gods the less.[37]

The ambassadors,[38] too, begged me to send you a letter, and appropriately; for they are very eagerly extolling you and me everywhere, and 363c not least Philagrus, whose hand was then ailing. And when Philaedes had come from the Great King,[39] he was speaking about you; did it not require a very long letter, I would have written what he said, but as it is, inquire of Leptines.

If you should send the corselet or anything else of the things about which I am sending this letter, give them to anyone you yourself might wish, or else to Terillus; he is one of those who is always sailing, an associate of ours and adept[40] both in other things and in philosophy. (He is related by marriage to Tison, who was *polianomos*[41] when we sailed away.)

---

37. See n. 2 above for a discussion of the important word *sumbolon*, translated "token" in this paragraph. In this context, it would not be out of place to use the translation "secret sign" or "password." Bentley has provided what probably remains the most insightful suggestion concerning this cryptic passage: "The *symbol* [Plato] here speaks of made no part of the letters, nor began the first paragraph of them; for here's neither θέος nor θέοι in that manner in any one of the thirteen. 'Twas extrinsic (if I mistake not) to the letter, and was a mark at the top of it in these words, σὺν θεῷ ["with a god"] if it was a serious one; otherwise, σὺν θεοῖς ["with gods"]. These two were the common forms in the beginning of writings or any discourse of importance: and in their usage were equivalent and indifferent; philosophers, as Xenophon and others, having it sometimes σὺν θεοῖς; and poets, as Euripides and Aristophanes, σὺν θεῷ. So that Plato could not have chosen a symbol fitter for his turn, being in neither way liable to any suspicion, nor any inference to be drawn from it to discover his real opinion" (1838, 412). It is unmistakable that Plato's choice of password suggests some inclination toward monotheism; Bentley's purpose in discussing it is to refute Cudworth's argument that this marks Letter Thirteen as the work of a Christian forger. According to Harward's note ad loc., this contention of Cudworth's began the controversy surrounding the genuineness of the letter. On a close variant of the expression *sun theōi* in the *Letters*, see n. 20 to Letter Two.

38. There are no extant external sources that illuminate anything of significance about the details of these paragraphs. Nothing is known of these ambassadors or their mission, nor about either Philagrus or Philaedes, to whom Plato refers next, nor about Terillus or Tison, to whom he refers in the following paragraph.

39. The typical designation for the king of Persia, who would have been Artaxerxes II at this time.

40. Lit. "graceful" (*charieis*); on this usage, see Harward's note ad loc.

41. The office of *polianomos* is known from inscriptions to have existed in a certain Tarentine colony in southern Italy; there was no such office at Athens. There is almost no evidence from which to deduce much about the rank or duties belonging to the title, but it seems it would have denoted a magistrate of considerable political status.

363d Be strong, and philosophize, and urge on[42] the other youths, and offer fond greetings to your fellow-spherists[43] on my behalf, and command both the others and especially Aristocritus,[44] that if any speech or letter should go from me to you, to take care that you perceive it as quickly as possible, and to remind you so that you take care of what is said in the letters that have been sent. And now, do not fail to take care of the returning of the money to Leptines and return it as quickly as possible, in order that the others, too, in seeing him, might be more eager to be of service to us.

363e Iatrocles, the one who was then, together with Myronides, set free by me, is sailing now with the things[45] sent from me;[46] so set him up in your hire somewhere, then, as he has goodwill toward you, and if you should wish, make use of him in any matter. And this letter, either itself or a reminder of it, save; and be the same.

---

42. The word for "urge on" is *protrepou*, which means more literally "to turn someone or something toward some object or goal." This same word is sometimes used in connection with exhortation toward philosophy, as it is thematically in Plato's *Cleitophon* (see, e.g., 410e5–8).

43. "Fellow-spherists" translates *susphairistas*, a word that in some contexts would suggest "one who plays at ball with another" (LSJ, s.v.). This may be the meaning here, as is implied for example by Harward's translation ad loc., "Give my greetings to your tennis-club" (see also Bury and Post, ad loc.). But Morrow prefers the other evident possibility, translating "Give my greetings to your fellow students of the spheres," which, as he explains in a footnote, would refer to the study of astronomy (see also Post 1925, 140–41n16). One should not overlook the theme of Pythagoreanism in this letter, and in the *Letters* generally, in interpreting this strange phrase.

44. Nothing is known of this Aristocritus.

45. It is equally possible that this could mean "the men sent from me."

46. Nothing is known of either Iatrocles or Myronides.

Interpretive Essay

The Political Challenges of the Philosophic Life

Plato's *Letters* does little to dissuade the reader from concluding that the whole affair of Plato's dealings with the Syracusans was a disaster. Twice Plato accepted the invitation to return to Syracuse to serve as tutor to the young tyrant, and twice he wound up imprisoned there with his life in danger. If the reason for all this was some hope for the establishment of philosopher-kingship, that hope turns out to have been unreasonable, and acting upon it imprudent. Dionysius never lived up to the philosophic promise others claimed he had (330a2–b7, 340b1ff.); and as for Dion, for whose sake Plato seems to have risked so much for so long, in the end it seems that, for all his nobility, he lacked the shrewdness and discernment to survive and prosper in the cutthroat political struggle he initiated when he overthrew the Syracusan tyranny (333d7–334a6, 334d6–335c1, 351c6–e2; see also 321b5–c1). At best, it seems Plato has been a poor judge of character. At worst, the affair stands as an indictment of Plato's doctrine of philosopher-kingship altogether. Can Plato be respected as a political philosopher if his one great attempt to put his philosophic claims to the test resulted in catastrophe? The gravity of what is at stake in the *Letters* is underlined by Plato's confession in Letter Seven regarding his role in Syracuse's recent history. Plato admits that, though it was never his intention, the whole Syracusan disaster—culminating in the civil war, which at the time he writes is still roiling, with all its destruction and slaughter—came to pass on account of him (327a1–5 with 327d3–328b1; cf. 353c8–e5, but see also 326e1–3, 350d6–7).

But all of this is rather more in the way of a first impression than anything clear enough to justify us in rendering judgments about either Plato's practical wisdom or his culpability in Syracuse. To begin with, it is helpful to recognize that the characterization of Plato's political activities we have just given reflects above all the narrative of Letter Seven. The more we compare the account of Letter Seven to what we find in the other letters, however, the more we are reminded that Letter Seven is only one such account, and one that belongs to a specific context—Plato's reply to the late Dion's followers' request for help in waging the war against tyranny in Syracuse. When Plato wrote to Dionysius himself, or to other Greek rulers and statesmen in other circumstances, he spoke somewhat differently on all of Letter Seven's major themes, such as political counsel, philosophic education, and Plato's own political motives. If indeed Plato has prepared the *Letters* as a coherent work of political philosophy, he has done so in such a way that we, the readers, are invited to observe him in a variety of attitudes, each suited to a particular permutation of addressee and occasion. It is our job then to draw our inferences about Plato's genuine thought and understanding from a careful comparison of the manners in which he approaches these various situations. Ultimately, it is only by taking up an exploration of the whole *Letters*, in a spirit of openness to whatever may be the lesson Plato meant it to convey, that we can arrive at justifiable conclusions regarding the questions we have already begun to raise on the basis of our first impressions. What is the connection between Plato's intention in going to Syracuse and his doctrine of philosopher-kingship? What explains his evidently poor judgment over the course of the whole affair? And why would he write about it all in a way that can so easily be seen as spotlighting his failures in thought and action?

Our inquiry will proceed in three phases. First, we will attempt to extract from the *Letters* what seems at first to be its most promising and intriguing content: the character and substance of Plato's direct and concrete political counsel to actual rulers or aspirants to rule. As we will see, however, one cannot isolate this theme—the character of Plato's narrowly *political* counsel in the *Letters*—from his overriding concern for the defense and promotion of philosophy. With a view to this higher priority of Plato's we will be led to a second pass at the *Letters*, in which we will seek to ascertain what it can teach us about the way in which Plato presented philosophy to the world and to his students. Only after these two major and distinct but connected themes—Plato's political counsel on one hand and his presentation of philosophy on the other—have been explored will we be prepared to examine with sufficient perspicuity the disaster that unfolded for Plato in Sicily, and to offer some suggestions as to its underlying causes and implications.

Part One

Political Counsel in Plato's *Letters*

It is natural for avid readers of Plato's dialogues to approach the *Letters* with the following keen anticipation. Whereas in the dialogues Plato writes only in the voices of his characters and never in his own, we will now be hearing, for the first time, Plato speaking for himself. And since Letter Seven is famous for sections such as the Platonic autobiography and the philosophic digression, we seem to have here the promise of revelatory candor on the part of the great philosopher on a wide variety of interesting subjects. Yet a first reading of the *Letters* is apt to leave us with a sense of disappointment, as if some part of what we had hoped to find was strangely absent.

The missing element comes into focus when we consider the *Letters*' strange treatment of Socrates. For Plato has given us his Socrates as the hero of the Platonic dialogues, as the peak of human virtue, and as setting the standard to which human intellect and character must be held. As students of those dialogues, we naturally come to the *Letters* hoping to see that when Plato at last emerges from behind the scenes, he is revealed to be the preeminent student of Socrates, who came to share his teacher's peak virtues by doggedly following the course of Socratic education to its ultimate conclusion. What we find, however, is that the *Letters* not only highlights Plato's catastrophic and all-too-human *failure* to serve the cause of philosophy in Sicily, but moreover that the great figure of Socrates is stunningly absent from the text (or nearly so). Plato appears to be no Socrates, and Socrates all but disappears. We are inclined to explain this by Plato's famous claim in Letter Two that the writings attributed to him are not truly his, but are rather "of a Socrates become beautiful and new (*kalou kai neou*)" (314c1-4). By this, we are given to understand that the historical Socrates was less impressive, less dazzling than the Platonic reimagining of him as the star of the dialogues. Accordingly, it is only with puzzling brevity, in Letter Seven, that Plato ever mentions the role Socrates played in the story of his life, and there Plato speaks only of "a man who was my friend, the elderly Socrates" (324d8-e1)—in notable contrast to the description of the "new" or "young" (*neos*) Socrates of the dialogues. Moreover, while Plato lauds the "elderly" Socrates's justice and piety, he makes no mention of his wisdom, or his philosophy, or his philosophic teaching. And this is to say nothing of the bizarrely banal passage in Letter Eleven, where it is said that Socrates (who in fact must be long dead) cannot travel to help in the founding of a colony because he is ill with strangury, a painful urinary infection (358d3-e1).

Thinking about Plato's strange treatment of Socrates in the *Letters* thus helps us to clarify the sense that something important is disappointingly absent from the text. For we might well have hoped, in turning to the *Letters*, to gain assurance from Plato that the power of Socratic wisdom is as uncannily effective in guiding political action as it is in guiding the Platonic Socrates to dialectical victory in his refutations. Instead, the distance Plato puts between himself and his Socrates in the *Letters* provokes us to wonder whether Plato has misled us in the dialogues by giving to his Socrates an aura of infallibility, by exaggerating the power and sufficiency of Socratic philosophy to guide one's life aright. If not by the light of Socratic wisdom, how did Plato think it best to approach and to manage practical and political affairs? Now, as our exploration of the text will reveal, the unifying theme of the *Letters* is the way in which Plato's fame as a political philosopher brought with it some responsibility, and many opportunities, to provide political counsel to famous and powerful men across the Greek world of his day. Whatever disappointment the *Letters* may leave us with as regards Plato's relation to Socrates and to Socratic education, we must welcome the prospect of learning how Plato brought his own wisdom to bear on actual political affairs. Let us begin, then, by asking: What kind of advice was Plato wont to give in his capacity as a political adviser?

Especially if we allow Letter Seven to loom over the *Letters* as we are led to do by its stature, one answer stands out as our clear starting point: Plato counsels the institution of philosophic rule, the capstone of the utopian regime made famous from his *Republic*. This is a highly consequential suggestion for our understanding of Platonic political philosophy. It implies that Plato wrote his *Republic* not merely as a thought experiment, nor as a defense of philosophy against its violent opponents, but as a vehicle for the promotion of his genuine political vision, for which he strove in his own lifetime, that philosophers might somewhere come to power as political rulers. By no means will this be our last word on what the *Letters* reveals about Plato's promotion of philosophic rule. But before we can assess the suggestion that he seriously wished to establish such a regime, we must examine the manner in which this suggestion comes to light from a reading of Letter Seven, and especially of that letter's first major section.

The Origin of the Idea of Philosophic Rule and the Intention of Dion

Letter Seven is addressed "to the intimates and comrades of Dion" in Syracuse; it belongs to the time following Dion's assassination, and it is Plato's response to a request from Dion's posthumous supporters. The Dionean party in Syracuse is now mired in a bloody civil war without the vision and guidance of its illustrious leader, and its representatives have apparently appealed to Plato to provide help for their cause, "in deed and in speech" (324a1). The sense of this appeal is indicated by the fact that, in Plato's restatement of their request, they have insisted that they are carrying on with the same "intention" (*dianoian*) that had animated Dion. Plato shows that he understands the significance of this claim: he strongly asserts that he knows precisely what Dion's "intention and desire" had been, since it had been during the time of their first meeting—when Plato, at forty, first visited Syracuse and met a twenty-year-old Dion—that Dion "took hold" of the "opinion" that he "continued holding to the end." It is only if Dion's intimates and comrades prove to share Dion's "opinion and desire," says Plato, that he will grant their request for his partnership. Plato, for whom opinion or thought is primary, here acknowledges that Dion's guiding opinion was formed as a result of his association with Plato. This, then, is the thrust of Dion's followers' request for help: it was Plato who inspired Dion with the dream he was pursuing; is it not incumbent on him, then, now that Dion lies dead, to help Dion's supporters bring this dream to fulfillment?

The foundational and lifelong opinion Plato says Dion acquired during their first meeting was "that the Syracusans should be free, dwelling under the best laws" (324b1–2). It was a patriotic opinion, in the sense that it expressed Dion's wish for the greatest well-being of his fatherland. Dion then apparently learned from Plato that civic well-being, or what makes life good for the citizens of a regime, consists of these two related components: freedom and good laws. That is, Dion learned to hold a certain high-minded political opinion, which we find expressed frequently in the history of political philosophy—namely, that genuine liberty is not equivalent to mere license or freedom from constraint. This view holds that human beings, in the absence of proper legal and customary constraints, naturally pursue ease and pleasure, shirk labor or responsibility, and, as a result, slump into a life devoid of the higher fulfillment available only to those who have cultivated good moral habits (see 334d5–335c2). Such a dissolute life could hardly be called "free," since no one with a clear view of it would freely choose it; rather, those mired in it lack the moral and intellectual means to escape, and even the awareness needed to wish to escape (see 326b5–d6). Paradoxically, then, genuine liberty is achieved only through a specific kind of restraint imposed, in the best case, by law. The restraint cultivated by wise laws teaches the citizen by inculcating habits of serious devotion to one's community, and thus prepares the citizen for profound fulfillment through just and virtuous activity (see 354d1–355c7).

The whole opening of Letter Seven, then, gives the strong impression that Plato and Dion shared this view of freedom or liberty, the view Plato has insisted Dion's comrades must also hold as the condition of his coming to their aid. That impression is strengthened by a puzzling feature of the letter's structure, which comes to sight in the following way. In this same opening section, Plato says it would be "in no way amazing if some one of the gods should" instill this same opinion of Dion's in the mind of Dion's successor, Hipparinus, who is now just at the same age Dion was when he met Plato. Thus we learn that Dion's patriotic opinion, in Plato's view, shares some kinship with those opinions reported by human beings as the content of divine revelation. It is of interest, then, that Plato next proposes to recount "the way of [Dion's opinion's] coming to be"—and yet what *actually* follows is a brief and famous section of Platonic *auto*biography, culminating in Plato's development of the doctrine of philosophic rule. We learn that it was in the wake of that development that Plato first met Dion, and so we are given to understand that Dion's patriotic opinion is somehow a reflection of his belief, learned from Plato, that the best regime would be the regime governed by philosophers. That is, Dion's political career is presented as having been continuous with Plato's own political philosophic project.

We gain greater clarity on the relationship between Plato's political philosophy and Dion's political agenda through observation of a few details from the famous autobiographical section itself. That section of Letter Seven begins, "When I was young, I underwent the same thing as many do: I supposed that, as soon as I should become my own master, I would engage straightaway in the common affairs of the city" (324b8–c1). What follows is the explanation of what came to dampen, even to extinguish, that youthful enthusiasm. This explanation features the only discussion in the *Letters* of Plato's friendship with Socrates; but despite the fact that the transformation Plato describes culminates in his "praise of philosophy" in the form of the doctrine of philosophic rule, Plato nowhere describes Socrates as a *teacher*, either of Plato or of anyone else—or, for that matter, as a philosopher (cf. 325c1–2 with *Apology of Socrates* 24b6–c1). Instead, Plato's account of his turn away from politics prominently features two famous instances of Socrates's persecution by the Athenian regime. The first is the story of the Thirty Tyrants attempting to force Socrates "to carry off one of the citizens [Leon of Salamis] by force to be put to death, in order that [Socrates] should participate in their affairs whether he should wish to or not" (324e1–325a2; cf. *Apology of Socrates* 32c3–e1). The second is the trial and execution of Socrates, which was perpetrated by the restored Athenian democracy—to which, as Plato casts it, Socrates had been loyal in refusing to arrest the democrat Leon of Salamis.

It was in examining these things, as well as "the human beings who were doing the political things, and also the laws and customs," that Plato became altogether disillusioned with the possibility of achieving anything in politics. In brief, Plato came to see that the corrupt condition of real cities, of their laws and customs, made them so profoundly resistant to genuine improvement that they were all but "incurable." Only "friends and faithful comrades," of a quality not easily to be found, working together in concert and employing "some amazing artifice," could ever have any hope of success—and even then, the realization of their hope would be dependent on "fortune" (325c5–326a5). But this despair regarding political *action* did not stop Plato from continuing *to examine* (*skopein*) questions of better and worse with respect to laws and customs, "and moreover concerning the whole regime." And now, at last, the theme of philosophy is introduced into Letter Seven:

> And I was compelled to say, praising correct philosophy, that on the basis of this it is possible to see distinctly both the just political things and all in private matters; therefore the human tribes will not cease from evils until either the tribe of those philosophizing (correctly and truly, that is) should come into the positions of political rule, or that of those who are in power in the cities should, by some divine fate, really philosophize. (326a5–b4)

Thus do we have it that Plato's story, not only of his abandonment of his own political aspirations, but of his abandonment of any hope of political efficacy anywhere, culminates with his praise of philosophy by way of his famous doctrine of philosophic rule. That is, this story proves to be the story of how Plato came to conceive of the crucial political-philosophic idea around which his *Republic* revolves.

Having articulated this "praise of philosophy," Plato ambiguously says that it was with "this intention" in mind that he sailed over to Sicily for the first time. Plato devotes his account of the first portion of his arrival (before he entered Syracuse) to an impassioned denouncement of the hedonism he encountered among the Sicilian Greeks. No one raised among such customs, Plato insists, could ever become prudent, moderate, or virtuous in any way; nor could any city steeped in such customs ever be at peace "under any laws whatsoever," but would instead cycle endlessly between tyranny, oligarchy, and democracy, as its rulers "won't put up with hearing the name of a regime of justice and equality under the law" (*isonomou*; 326b6–d6). And it was in turn with all *this* in mind, in addition to the intention with which he began, that Plato says he entered Syracuse and met, for the first time, a young Dion, to whom he "reveal[ed] . . . through speeches the things that seemed to [Plato] to be best for human beings and counsel[ed] him to do them" (327a2–4). We can easily imagine how these revelations would have reflected Plato's disapproval of the way of life of the Sicilian Greeks and how this critique would have led naturally to the patriotic opinion of which Dion then took hold. It is constraint by good and wise laws—precisely what is absent in the permissive culture of the Siceliotes—that inculcates the daily habits conducive to virtue, excellence, and happiness. Hence, Dion came to see the libertinism of his own culture as inimical to true liberty and came to long for a life of justice and virtue as a devoted member of a just and virtuous community.

Plato recounts that Dion thereafter wished "to live the rest of his life in a manner differing from the many Italiotes and Siceliotes, having come to cherish virtue more than pleasure and the rest of luxury; from which point he led his life until the event of Dionysius [the Elder's] death in a manner that was rather aggravating to those living according to what is lawful convention in a tyranny" (327b1–6). Zealously devoted to Plato's lofty political philosophy, holding the decadent lifestyle of his contemporaries in contempt, and sententiously insisting on his own (that is, Platonic) high moral principles, Dion understandably became unpopular and tiresome to the pleasure-loving Syracusan courtiers. This was the effect of Platonic philosophy, as taught by Plato himself—specifically, as we are invited to surmise, of the teaching of the *Republic* regarding philosophy's power to resolve humanity's deepest political problems—on a "good learner" who "hearkened keenly and intently such as none of the young [Plato had] ever met" (327a6–b1). Indeed, as Plato stresses, this was not the only effect, for Dion's Platonic education turned out much later to be the cause of Dion's deposing of Dionysius, and hence of the whole ongoing tragedy of the Syracusan civil war.

That Dion had learned from Plato to long for a regime of philosophic rule is evident from the terms in which he solicited Plato's return upon the death of Dionysius the Elder. He sought Plato's help in bringing the newly crowned Dionysius the Younger to the same "desire for the noblest and best life" to which Dion himself had been brought by Plato, in "great hopes of establishing, without slaughters, deaths, and the evils that have now come to be, a happy and true life throughout the whole land." He considered the opportunity at hand to be the gift of "some divine fortune," and told Plato that, "now if ever, there was every hope of bringing to completion the outcome that philosophers and rulers of great cities would be the same" (327d1–328b1). It is unambiguous that Dion, at least, had philosophic rule over Syracuse in mind as a serious possibility. Did Plato? He did, after all, accept Dion's invitation. And the connection he has drawn in this letter between his claim about philosophic rule and his second venture to Sicily is plain to see. Moreover, when Plato recounts his inner deliberations about whether or not to accept Dion's invitation, he reports resolving that, "if ever someone was going to undertake to bring these intentions concerning both laws and regime [or *Laws* and *Regime*] to completion, it must be attempted also now; for if I should sufficiently persuade just one, I would be achieving all good things," and hence explains, "I set out from home . . . ashamed of myself in the highest degree lest I should ever seem to myself to be altogether, solely, and artlessly a certain speech, voluntarily taking hold of not one deed ever" (328b8–c7).

Whatever its purpose, there is no denying that the whole undertaking in Syracuse appears to have been a debacle. It would reflect poorly on Plato's prudence, political wisdom, and foresight if his earnest hope in going was to bring the rule of philosophy, and with it the "cessation of evils" for humanity, at last into existence. But in fairness to Plato, there is ample evidence that he despaired from the start of any real success. Indeed, the statements just quoted in which Plato appears to indicate his intention to try for the rule of philosophy in Syracuse are directly interwoven with indications of other, less fanciful concerns and goals. Consideration of these other concerns will lead us toward a more grounded view of Plato's political activity and ultimately to the concrete Platonic political counsel we are seeking. But in order to appreciate Plato's articulations of these latter concerns in their context, we must first come to see why they sit directly alongside the other, misleading indications we have been reviewing. Specifically, we must gain some appreciation of why Plato allows himself to seem so similar to Dion in his opinion, desire, and intention throughout Letter Seven. For Dion, as we have seen, was keen to try for philosophic rule in Syracuse; the key to recognizing that Plato was not is to come to see the difference between the two men.

For this it becomes important to consider the literary character of the *Letters*. Plato speaks to us only indirectly in this work. Just as, in his dialogues, Plato allows us to observe his Socrates in a variety of specific circumstances, which give crucial context to whatever Socrates says, so in each letter we must consider the person or people to whom Plato addresses himself, and the circumstances that have called for his writing (see 363b4–5). It is not a coincidence that the only overt references to the doctrine of philosopher-kingship in the whole *Letters* occur in Letter Seven. The circumstances of this letter require that Plato eulogize Dion. He is writing to Dion's "intimates and comrades" to discuss the legacy of their late, beloved leader, who has given his life, nobly, for his patriotic political dream (see 334d6–335c1, 351c6–e2; cf. 321b5–c1). If Plato had an unfavorable view of Dion or of his understanding of Platonic philosophy, he could hardly spotlight it in this letter.

As has been clear to many readers, however, Letter Seven has purposes beyond its officially stated one, just as it is addressed to audiences beyond the one identified in its opening salutation (cf. 323d7, 324b5–6, 330c3–8, 334c3–4, 338a2, 341e1–342a1, 344d3–4). Plato, we may surmise, thought of us, too, as prospective readers. What is more, if Letter Seven was *never* really intended as a letter to be sent to Dion's friends and associates, if Plato wrote it as the centerpiece of this political philosophic *book*, then we are, in a sense, its *primary* intended readers. Yet we are to understand that Plato's didactic method here is to let us see *how he would* have had to speak and write to the heirs of Dion's political legacy. And because this letter is effectively an "open letter," in that it is addressed indiscriminately to a somewhat ill-defined group of people, it is in fact in this letter above all that Plato demonstrates for us how he wrote to a broad audience *in general*. Viewing the letter in this light, then, we might even go so far as to interpret Plato's choice of addressees for Letter Seven as indicating that whenever Plato wrote for broad publication and general consumption (see 314c1), he kept in mind the effect his writing would have on those whose impression of Platonic philosophy was akin to the one held and reproduced by Dion—on those "akin" to Dion (*tois oikeiois*; cf. 313c7–d3). But since, as we have said, these are not Plato's *only* readers, he has found ways to indicate his true judgment of Dion in the same writings.

We must, therefore, examine the *Letters* with some care in order to grasp the crucial difference between Plato and Dion, so that we can better distinguish Plato's motivation for going to Syracuse from Dion's motivation for inviting him. We can begin to illuminate this difference by further considering what we have dubbed Dion's "patriotic opinion," which Plato said was the lifelong, abiding opinion by which Dion's political aspirations were guided, and which Plato suggests Dion learned directly from him. The opinion, to restate it, was "that the Syracusans should be free, dwelling under the best laws," and it reflected the noble equation of freedom and the yoke of law. Now, while Plato's explicit articulation of this opinion occurs in the opening of Letter Seven, the same opinion is implicitly at the heart of Letter Eight, the companion to Seven. It is therefore worthwhile at this point to turn to a fuller examination of Letter Eight.

The Relationship of Freedom to Law in Letter Eight

Like Letter Seven, Letter Eight is addressed "to the intimates and comrades of Dion," and purports to answer their request for Plato's help. Unlike in Letter Seven, however, Plato here gets immediately to the matter at hand: after his characteristic salutation, "Do well!" he expresses his intention to "go through . . . as much as is in [his] power" what intentions the Syracusans should adopt in order "most of all really [to] 'do well'" (352b4–5). The brevity of Letter Eight as compared with Letter Seven is further proof that Letter Seven has people and purposes in mind beyond Plato's response to the request for help from Dion's followers, since it is plain from Letter Eight that Plato is capable of responding to that request without anything so elaborate and complex as Letter Seven. Letter Eight, then, would appear to be the place in the *Letters* where Plato most directly provides what we are now seeking: his practical political counsel to real people in a real situation. And our expectation or hope for what this counsel will contain is only heightened by the fact that Plato indicates his intention to clarify the meaning of his characteristic salutation. For one might well think that to know what is required for one "really to do well" is to know the human good.

It turns out, however, that Letter Eight does not so clearly contain the practically useful advice it appears to promise. For Plato admits that the difficulty of fulfilling this promise, of providing genuinely good and usable counsel to one faction embroiled in a civil war, is nearly insurmountable. The difficulty is that it is not enough to counsel what seems "to the many" to be necessary, namely, whatever will produce "as many evils as possible for their adversaries in war and as many goods as possible for their friends," because "it is in no way easy for one doing many evils to others not also to suffer many further evils himself" (352c8–d5). What is needed, then, is counsel that points to what is "either advantageous for all, both enemies and friends, or as little evil as possible for both" (352e3–4). But how likely is such a thing to be possible in the context of a civil war? Circumstances must dictate to a considerable extent how far it is possible for a given person genuinely to prosper or to "do well." The more one is in a position to abstain from harming others, to avoid having enemies, the fewer the obstacles (consider *Republic* 335b2–336a8; Xenophon, *Memorabilia* 4.4.10–12). But in the case of Dion's followers in Syracuse, real prosperity is almost certainly out of reach; Plato's proposal in Letter Eight to counsel what is really advantageous for the Sicilians amounts to a promise to advise a course of action that will be almost impossible to follow. As Plato himself says in concluding his introductory remarks, "Such counsel and undertaking of speech resembles a prayer. Let it be altogether, then, a certain prayer—for one ought always to speak and think, in all things, beginning from the gods" (352e5–353a2). The plan Plato will here propose will depend on divine help for which one can only pray.

There is another important clue to the character of this "prayer," which we discover in considering the structure of Letter Eight. About halfway through the letter, Plato makes a significant change. Saying that what he has so far laid out has been "natural," Plato bids "the friends of Dion to explain" it "to all Syracusans," calling it the "common counsel" of himself and Dion. That foregoing counsel is thus set apart from what is to follow, which Plato introduces by announcing that he will now "interpret" what Dion would say *himself* "if he were [still] breathing and capable of speaking" (355a1-7). This switch in authorship of the counsel is the primary reason for our present examination of Letter Eight: Letter Eight provides a rare opportunity to compare and contrast Plato's and Dion's ideas of sound political counsel. To be sure, we do not have here quite so direct a comparison and contrast as we might wish, since we are not contrasting the counsel that Plato says Dion would give by himself to the counsel that Plato says *he* would give by *him*self, but rather to their "common counsel"—a phrase that seems to indicate that the first half of the letter represents counsel that is given by Plato and Dion *in partnership*. It is perhaps best to imagine this joint counsel as exemplifying that strain of Platonic exhortation and counsel that most of all charmed and captivated Dion and animated his political activity. The very fact that this joint counsel is acknowledged to be a prayer, however, shows Plato qualifying the practicality of the joint counsel—by contrast, Plato's qualifying influence is notably absent from the second half of the letter. To oversimplify slightly, we can say that the first half of the letter gives us the nuanced view Plato presented to Dion, winning his endorsement, while the second half shows the partial and therefore distorted version of that view Dion himself took away from Plato's presentation and proceeded himself to proselytize. Consider, for instance, that the "common counsel," which more fully reflects Plato's own thought, begins with the imperative "think" (*noēsate*), as he bids his readers to think about what he might mean (352c4). Plato even says, toward the end of this section of his counsel, that he will "converse" as an "arbiter" with each of the two parties, namely, "those who tyrannized and those who were tyrannized," as though each party were a single individual (354a3-5). Plato thus effectively acknowledges that the counsel he is providing is better suited to dialogue with one or two interlocutors than to the persuasion of a multitude. By contrast, Dion's counsel is presented as an oratorical address to the Syracusans, and, in parallel to Plato's imperative "think," begins with the direction to "accept" (*dexasthe*) such laws as he prescribes for them (355a8).

Letter Eight is therefore immensely valuable to our understanding of the relation in which Dion stands to his teacher, and we will have more than one occasion to revisit it for that reason. Lest the present digression lose track of its purpose, however, we will focus now only on the element of this letter that illuminates the difference between Plato and Dion regarding Dion's patriotic opinion, and specifically regarding his understanding of freedom. In the latter half of the letter, wherein Plato "interprets" Dion's would-be advice to the Syracusans, Dion insists above all that the city's inhabitants must accept laws that "make the virtue of the soul most honored" (355b3–4). Those living properly under such laws, says Dion, will achieve their full and completed potential as "really happy" human beings (355c2). This will amount, it seems, to "freedom under kingly rule" for the subjects and "accountable" "kingly rule" for the rulers, "with laws as masters both of the other citizens and of the kings themselves in case they should do anything illegal" (355d8–e3). That is, Plato here has Dion affirm the view that the citizens' life of subjection to genuinely good laws is a life of happiness and freedom—even if Dion is somewhat loose in his application of the word "freedom": he also speaks of himself, his father, and the young Hipparinus, each in his time, as having "freed" the Syracusans from the oppression of barbarians or tyrants, though without having established the rule of law he continues to extol (355e6–356a7, 357a7–b1). All of this must be compared to Plato's usage when speaking, not for Dion, but in his own name (or that of his and Dion's "common counsel"). Plato appears willing to agree that the deposition or circumvention of a tyrannical power amounts to an act of liberation or "freeing" (see 333b4, 334a2, 336a3, 7; cf. 329b4). But neither here in Letter Eight nor anywhere else in the *Letters* does Plato himself ever assert that lawfulness is equivalent to, or even compatible with, freedom. Precisely to the contrary, Plato is consistent—in both Letters Seven and Eight—in characterizing the subjection to law needed by the Syracusans as a form of *slavery* (334c6–7, 337a2–8, 354c3–6). Plato's Dion comes closest to this, as we have seen, when he speaks of "laws as *masters* both of the other citizens and of the kings" (emphasis added), but this comes in the same breath as his speaking of "freedom under kingly rule." Nowhere does Dion speak so frankly as Plato does of *enslavement* to laws and even to "kingly laws."

In fact, at the center of Letter Eight, just before Plato transitions from his and Dion's "common counsel" to his interpretation of Dion's own counsel, Plato directly addresses the opposition of slavery and freedom in one of the richest and most intriguing formulations in the *Letters*. First, he criticizes the bygone Syracusans who lived in the democracy preceding the rule of Dionysius the Elder. Plato says that they suffered from a "disease" "because of the excessive anarchy, making use of an unmeasured passionate love (*erōti*) of freedom"; the Syracusans of his own day, says Plato, must beware of this disease, lest they contract it "out of insatiability for a certain unpropitious freedom" (354d2–5). For it was in the throes of that love of freedom that the Syracusan democrats illegally executed their ruling generals, "in order that they should in no way be enslaved with either justice or law as a master, but be altogether free in every way; hence did the tyrannies over them come to be" (354d8–e3). Passionate or "erotic" love of freedom, which makes slavery to "justice or law" seem as repugnant as slavery to a tyrant, is disastrous and must be warded off like a disease—needless to say, the *Letters* nowhere indicates that Dion ever acknowledged such a limitation on the goodness of freedom. (Where Dion speaks of *eros* in this letter, it is in reference to the tyrannical party's passionate desire to rule [355d5].)

It is here that Plato makes his rich and cryptic pronouncement "For slavery and freedom are each, if excessive, altogether bad, but if [each] is in measure, altogether good; and slavery to a god is measured, to human beings unmeasured; and law is a god to moderate human beings, pleasure [a god] to the imprudent" (354e–355a). Imagining again that this proclamation belongs to the presentation of his political philosophy by which Plato won Dion over, we can easily understand how Dion would have heard it, or rather misheard it. That is, one can briefly articulate the superficial and edifying *gist* of the statement, without attending to its nuanced complexity, as follows. To mistake the unobstructed and unmitigated pursuit of pleasure for true freedom is imprudent and altogether bad; it is no better in fact than slavery. What is genuinely good for human beings requires moderation, which in turn points to faithful obedience to the law. To the truly wise, happiness, the good, all human fulfillment, are seen clearly to lie along the path of moderation, piety, and lawfulness. But this path can only be open in a regime of laws: tyranny must be replaced with something like kingship so that slavery to human beings can be replaced by fulfillment, and true freedom, through obedient lawfulness.

But a close and unprejudiced reading of the passage does not so clearly articulate this view and may in fact raise more questions than it provides answers. Most obviously, there is the following paradox. Plato says that slavery "in measure" is "altogether good" and that slavery to a god is measured—slavery to human beings, of course, is "unmeasured," and presumably, therefore, "altogether bad." But in what he says next, Plato does not contrast slavery under divine masters to slavery under human masters. He identifies instead two different gods to whom one might be enslaved: law, god of the moderate or sound-minded (*sōphrosi*); and pleasure, god of the imprudent or mindless (*aphrosi*). A stubbornly literal reading would force us to conclude that, for the mindless, slavery to pleasure is altogether good. The strangeness of this proposal prompts us to correct our reading by inferring that the mindless, as such, worship a *false* god, and that only the *sound*-minded know the true god, law. But even with this correction, Plato's statement is not as clear-cut as we might think. For Plato has spoken of the total badness of slavery under human beings, but has said nothing of slavery to false gods. He has, in fact, given no explicit assessment of slavery to pleasure; we may only infer what may be implied by saying that it is slavery to the god of the foolish. Moreover, even what he says about being a slave to the law is problematic. Does his claim (that the moderate or sound-minded have law as a god) mean that this is the *only* or *ultimate* god to whom the wise bow? Even, say, if there is a conflict between the law of the city and what the gods demand, such as we know from, for example, Sophocles's *Antigone*? But as almost any sensible person knows, the law as one finds it in one's political community is liable to be seriously defective precisely because it is not of divine origin, is not "a god," but human (consider *Statesman* 293e7ff. and Xenophon, *Memorabilia* 1.2.40–46 and 4.4.7–25).

What, then, can Plato mean by saying that the moderate are measured in enslaving themselves to their god, Law? Either he means by "law" only such law as the wise would obey, in which case the "moderate" do not enslave themselves to any set of real, existing laws, but evaluate the laws under which they find themselves and obey them only insofar as they are in accordance with what we might call the "true" law (as in the regime of Plato's *Laws*); or Plato here means by "moderate" something narrowly political or otherwise qualified, so that in speaking of "the moderate," he does not designate simply "the wise"—but in that case, a question arises as to how much more the god of the "moderate" is to be revered than that of the imprudent, and we are left to wonder to what extent the god of the wise may align in the end with pleasure just as well as law. Or, indeed, perhaps Plato is quite serious in saying that moderation indicates the necessity of enslaving oneself to the law as one finds it in one's political community and of avoiding the enthralling power of pleasure, and yet does not mean that this is the *whole* of what guides the wise person's activity. For what one might easily miss in this complex Platonic pronouncement is that, though he begins by saying that both slavery *and* freedom are altogether good only when they are in measure, he goes on to identify only the measured and unmeasured versions of *slavery*. This provokes the question, in what does measured freedom consist for the moderate and wise? Consider that, at the beginning of Letter Two, Plato claims that he himself is "great" because he makes himself "a follower," not of the law, nor indeed of pleasure, but of his "own reason"; in the same moment, he bemoans the truth of Dionysius's allegation that Dion, who is in the process of raising an army to march on Syracuse, is not likewise ruled by Plato's reason (310c1–6). Dion and Plato do not take their bearings alike, in political action at least.

We may summarize the upshot of our consideration of Letter Eight as follows: Dion's opinion that freedom was simply compatible with obedience to the law constituted a misunderstanding of Plato, one that reflected Dion's own native hopes and prejudices. Plato himself speaks only of *slavery* to the law and is more careful than Dion was in his use of the word "freedom." Apart from his references to the liberation of a city from the yoke of tyranny, then, in what manner does Plato himself, in contrast to Dion, employ the word "freedom"?

Plato's View of Freedom and Dion's View of Philosophy

There is one place in Letter Seven where Plato rather plainly criticizes Dion, though not harshly, and it is in this same place that he indicates his own understanding of what constitutes genuine liberty. Dion's assassination, says Plato, was facilitated and partly perpetrated by a pair of Athenian brothers in whom Dion had imprudently placed his trust. The mistake in Dion's judgment stemmed from the fact that he trusted in a kind of "promiscuous comradeship belonging to most friends, which they work out through hosting someone as a guest-friend (*xenizein*) or through initiation into the lesser and greater mysteries," as distinguished from such bonds as are formed "from philosophy" (333e1–4). In defense of the reputation of Athens and its citizens, whose virtue and trustworthiness might seem to have been tarnished by the actions of the Athenian brothers who betrayed Dion, Plato points out that he, an Athenian himself, remained true to Dion despite all he might have gained from doing otherwise, attributing this to the fact that his own bond with Dion came to be "not through vulgar friendship, but through partnership *in liberal education.*" "*In this alone,*" he concludes, "ought one who possesses mind to trust, more than in kinship of souls and of bodies" (334b3–7; emphasis added). Plato thus juxtaposes Dion's catastrophic error in judgment with what is rare in the *Letters*, a statement about liberty made in Plato's own name—indeed, a statement that identifies a form of liberty worth exalting above all else. It is the liberty of "liberal education" (*eleutheras paideias*), that is, such education as befits a truly free human being, or rather, and more to the point, such education as can *make* one truly free. Freedom means above all freedom of the mind. This explains why and how it can be said that a soul cannot be free if it lacks the habits of moral virtue and self-restraint—since it will be unable to *recognize* and thus to choose a life worth having; and also why Plato cannot fully endorse the idea of freedom under the law, even under good laws that would inculcate those virtuous habits—for genuine freedom of the mind cannot rest satisfied with the authoritative and peremptory manner in which even the best code of laws necessarily articulates and insists on its vision of virtue and the human good. Philosophy's demand for unfettered questioning—"measured" freedom in the view of the wise—puts philosophy in tension with the spirit of law as such (cf. *Republic* 537e1–541b5).

There is a paradox, however, in what Plato implies about his relationship with Dion here. For Plato claims he was loyal to Dion on account of their "partnership in liberal education"; but was that loyalty not to some extent misplaced, given that Dion himself erred so badly in his own judgment by trusting those who became his assassins? More to the point, can the supreme trustworthiness of friendship through liberal education or philosophy really be maintained if that education does not itself impart or include firm knowledge of the very fact that, and the reason why, other so-called friendships cannot be trusted—that is, precisely the knowledge Dion lacked? In short, what good is Plato's "trustworthy" friendship with Dion based on liberal education, if Dion cannot be trusted to be prudent in his *own* choice of friends? The resolution to this paradox is to be found by taking account of the decorum Plato observes in his writing, and particularly in this letter, in his critique of Dion's judgment. In criticizing Dion's failure to recognize the untrustworthiness of "vulgar friendship," Plato shows us a glimmer of the truth amid the eulogistically exaggerated terms in which he otherwise describes the strength of his own friendship with Dion. In other words, Dion must not have obtained so complete and transformative a "liberal education" as Plato tactfully implies that he did in writing to the late Dion's distraught and grief-stricken followers. Yet to say that Plato judged Dion to have been deficient in his pursuit of education is itself paradoxical in view of the general impression given by the *Letters*. Was Dion not a zealous devotee of Platonic philosophy? Was he not persuaded that philosophy provided the best life for a human being? Was his own plan in taking over the rule of Syracuse from Dionysius not to lead the city as a philosopher-king?

It is the last of these questions that first opens our eyes to the unexpectedly limited character of Dion's relationship to philosophy. Over the course of his counsel to Dion's followers in Letter Seven (334c3–337e2), Plato makes it clear that the plan he and Dion jointly had for the education of Dionysius was distinct from the plans that both he and Dion developed in the wake of that first plan's ultimate failure. Dionysius's failure as a ruler, says Plato, was due to his "having been in no way willing to make use of justice throughout his whole rule" or "empire"; but, "had philosophy and power really come to be" in the same ruler of that empire, Plato continues, the "true opinion" regarding the key to political and individual happiness, "shining out among all human beings, both Greek and barbarian," would consequently have been "sufficiently set down in everyone." That is, it would have meant the "cessation of evils" for humanity, and it is in this sense that Dionysius, in his failure, "inflicted the greatest harms," not only on Plato, but "on all other human beings" (335c4–e1). These goals, says Plato, "common goods for all," were sought "first"; what Dion undertook, together with Plato, "meaning well toward the Syracusans" (but not necessarily "for all"), was "second" (337d5–8). Had Dion secured his rule over Syracuse, says Plato, he would have made the city "free," "adorned the citizens with the proper and best laws," and then "striven eagerly . . . to recolonize all Sicily and make it free from the barbarians, casting some out and subduing others" (335e3–336a8); the goods achieved by this "Plan B," as we may call it, do not extend to the barbarians, as did "Plan A," involving Dionysius himself. We cannot help but think of the relation between these two plans as at least parallel to that of the regime of the *Republic* (the best imaginable city, in which justice is secured by the absolute rule of benevolent philosophers) to the regime of the *Laws* (the best practicable city, from which philosophy is generally absent, but wisely given and carefully guarded laws ensure a just political order).

We may summarize our conclusions regarding Dion's relationship to philosophy as follows. Dion had hoped above all for Plato to educate Dionysius toward philosophy, believing that the manifest, perfect justice of genuine philosophic rule would shine as a beacon to the rest of the world and herald a new age of happiness for humanity; when this failed, Dion attempted (coordinating to some extent with Plato—see *sumpraxai* at 337d6; but cf. 321a5–b5) to conquer Syracuse in order both to free it and to establish a rule of new, wise laws throughout Sicily. But this was not to be the rule of philosophy, as indeed Dion never thought of *himself* as a potential philosopher-ruler. The closest that Plato ever comes to suggesting that Dion was involved with the activity of philosophy is in this same section of Letter Seven: imagining a scenario in which Dion's plan had been successful, Plato extrapolates, "And had these things in turn come to pass through a man who was just and courageous, moderate, and philosophic, then the very same opinion concerning virtue would have come to be *among the many* that, if Dionysius had been persuaded, would have come to be among, so to speak, *all human beings* and saved them" (336a8–b4; emphasis added). The grammar of this sentence makes it ambiguous whether Plato is affirming that Dion himself would have been such a man or not. But in the context of Letter Seven, addressed as it is to the followers of Dion still mourning his loss, this ambiguity comes awfully close to damning with faint praise. Likewise, by replacing the cardinal Platonic virtue of being "wise" with being "philosophic" in this enumeration, Plato implies that Dion lacked wisdom. Had Dion succeeded in giving good laws to the Syracusans, his *reputation* of being associated with philosophy, more than any ability to govern wisely himself, would have benefited the reputation of philosophy in turn.

Indeed, it seems Dion was widely known for his *connection* to Platonic philosophy. But when we attempt to reconstruct, from the *Letters*, the real substance of his involvement in philosophy, we find, in confirmation of the impression we have just now been forming, that it was shallow in some critical respects. Dion certainly admired Platonic philosophy for what he believed to be the clarity with which Plato had revealed to him the true aspect and requirements of human happiness. Above all, he was powerfully impressed by Plato's identification of moral virtue as a sine qua non of such happiness, both for the individual and for the political community. Dion therefore loved and exalted philosophy *as a means* for identifying and pursuing the requirements of a good life, which he saw as characterized above all by the virtuous self-restraint and devotion to a higher cause that give justice, courage, and moderation their essential nobility. The promotion of moral virtue was therefore, to Dion, the real *purpose* of philosophy, and the establishment of the perfectly just political order its highest and ultimate task. But it seems he believed in the possibility of all this on trust, thanks to the persuasive power of Plato's speeches. For nowhere is it ever suggested that Dion himself pursued philosophy as an activity.

Much of the *Letters* may be said to abstract from the genuine activity of philosophy, from the philosophic life. This is partly because the *Letters* is a book Plato wrote to be published, and Letter Seven shows us that when Plato wrote so as to be widely read he minimized the profound difference between himself and Dion as much as the subject matter would allow. Neither the Academy nor Plato's activity as a teacher in it is ever mentioned in the *Letters*. The opening words of the whole text refer to the inordinate time Plato spent, or wasted, in the Syracusan court: "After I had been occupied for such a long time with you" (*diatripsas egō par' humin chronon tosouton*). He refers exceedingly rarely to his *own* "not indecorous" occupations (*tas emautou diatribas ousas ouk aschēmonas*), which he left behind in Athens during that time (329b1–2). But the *Letters* is not entirely without reference to the content of genuine philosophic thinking, thanks to the fact that not Dion but Dionysius appears to have pursued the study of philosophy somewhat seriously for some period of time. The two parallel passages in which Dionysius's involvement with philosophy is most directly treated help to bring out by contrast the emptiness of Dion's involvement with philosophy. Letter Two contains the only passage in the Platonic corpus in which Plato himself explicitly undertakes to teach someone the highest principles of his philosophy: he explains to Dionysius, albeit through all but impenetrable "riddles" in case the letter should fall into the wrong hands, his view of what he calls the "nature of the first." In Letter Seven, in response to the rumor that Dionysius has written a handbook purporting to explain the principles of Platonic philosophy, Plato gives an account of the nature of knowledge and of reality that explains why no one with a correct grasp of these things would ever attempt to put this into writing (and therefore why any such attempt on Dionysius's part would only reveal his ignorance of Platonic philosophy as well as his lack of self-knowledge).

Without ever becoming perfectly explicit about Plato's thought, then, these two passages nonetheless indicate the subject matter treated by Plato's most "serious" philosophic activity. "The nature of the first," and "the highest and first things concerning nature," suggest questions of cosmology, ontology, metaphysics, and epistemology. It is true, Plato indicates that these same subjects are connected somehow to his moral and political philosophy. But nowhere in the *Letters* is there the slightest indication that Dion, for his part, ever showed any interest, ever spent any time, in the pursuit of these more theoretical philosophic questions. Perhaps the greatest proof of this is given by the shortest letter in the collection, Letter Ten. In this letter, written to a comrade of Dion whom Plato has not met—but who, Plato hears, is the most highly reputed for wisdom of all Dion's friends—Plato says that "it is the steadfast, and faithful, and healthy" that Plato himself claims "is the true philosophy," dismissing all "the other wisdoms and clevernesses, which extend to other things" as mere "niceties" (358c3–6). Not only does Plato thus abstract completely from any suggestion that philosophy is an inquiry into nature, he denies that philosophy is an activity *at all*. This means that, as far as Plato is concerned, anyone who, like this Aristodorus, has come to learn about philosophy through Dion must think that philosophy is above all a tool for bringing about political harmony through justice and virtue, or that philosophy is nothing but the soil upon which civic friendship and patriotic loyalty can flourish—and Plato is perfectly happy to leave such a person with such a distorted view.

Plato, then, is not being candid when he says that he shared with Dion the firm, supremely trustworthy friendship that can only be founded on liberal education and philosophy, because Dion did not really understand what philosophy means for Plato. Perhaps this is indicated above all in Letter Six. In this letter, Plato attempts to forge a new friendship between his three addressees: Hermias, the monarchical ruler of Atarneus in Asia Minor, and Erastus and Coriscus, two men who had spent considerable time studying with Plato in Athens. The steadfastness of this friendship is to be assured by the trio's communal practice of philosophy. But here, Plato is blunt in disclosing the fact that the two Platonists—they who have spent their time acquiring "this beautiful wisdom of the Forms"—are completely inept when it comes to practical political affairs. It is they who need to take shelter under Hermias's "defensive power," under his "wisdom that guards against the wicked and unjust," since they themselves are "inexperienced" on account of having lived so long with Plato and his companions. They require safety provided by one who knows how to fend off political dangers, "lest they be compelled to be careless of the true wisdom in order to take care over the human and compulsory [wisdom] more than they need to" (322d4–e5). Whatever the reason, then, that two philosophers may trust each other so much more surely than those whose friendships are founded on other bases, this steadfastness is *not* essentially useful when it comes to the challenges of political action. Letter Six thus reveals that philosophy is not—contrary to the primary impression that Plato gives—the solution it seems to be to the problems that turned Plato away from politics in his youth (see 325d1–2).

In Letter Seven, Plato gives us some help in understanding the nature of Dion's deep misunderstanding of the meaning and import of Platonic philosophy. Twice in that letter's philosophic digression, Plato discusses ways in which his readers or pupils might misunderstand his teaching; both times, Plato seems to include a veiled pointer to Dion. First, when Plato explains how he himself would undertake to communicate the content of his most serious philosophic thought, he says that his account would fill some "with a lofty and empty hope as though they had learned some august things" (341e5–6); and when he later considers the reasons why someone, having been exposed to Platonic philosophy, might not continue to pursue it, he says that his hearer might consider the things he heard "beyond him" or "not on his level" (*ou kath' hauton*), as "greater" than him; and Plato indicates that such a person might doubt his own ability to live "while taking care of practical wisdom and virtue," but would see the great themes of Platonic philosophy as "worthy with a view to the education of a free soul" and would honor his teacher on that account (345b3–c2). Of Dion it may be said that he revered Plato and his philosophy, that he believed the Platonic claim that philosophy is the key to the resolution of humanity's political woes; but he could not claim to understand how exactly that is true because he considered the actual practice of philosophy "beyond him," and so did not really grasp what philosophy entails.

Plato's Concern for the Reputation of Philosophy

Dion was wrong ever to believe that Plato's description of philosophic rule in the *Republic* was a blueprint for political action. He never seems to have considered, for example, Plato's indications both that philosophers will not wish to rule (*Republic* 499a11–c5, 519c4–521b6; cf. *Letters* 357e4–358a2) and, compounding the problem significantly, that the people will be profoundly resistant to being ruled by philosophers (*Republic* 487e1–489c9, 501c4–502a4). In saying this about the *Republic*, of course, we risk plunging ourselves into the weeds of a very old debate, which we could hardly hope to resolve to the satisfaction of all. Simpler than tackling the whole meaning of the *Republic* is to point out that

Dion was wildly optimistic to think he could ever bring about philosophic rule *in Syracuse.* Plato's excoriation of the Syracusan regime in Letter Seven, in which he says precisely that its licentiousness and lawlessness are such that no good regime could ever take root there, disqualifies it as a candidate for becoming the regime of the *Republic,* which can only arise in a city where a vanishingly rare attachment to virtue has been carefully cultivated by its lawgiver (*Republic* 497b1–d2). Otherwise, it seems the philosophers would have to begin by exiling every citizen over the age of ten (540d1–541b5), whereas Dion believed that a life of "indomitable bliss" for *all* the Syracusans could be achieved without bloodshed (*Letters* 327b6–d7). By the same token, Dion's overestimation of Dionysius's philosophic potential was itself likely a necessary result of Dion's failure properly to understand the substance, and hence the requirements, of philosophy. With respect to the possibility of rulers coming to philosophize, Plato says there would be need of "some divine fate" (326b3–4; see also 326a5), whereas Dion appears to have thought that all the requisite divine help had already been proffered by the time he invited Plato to Syracuse (327e4–5).

The remaining difficulty for our view—that only Dion's misunderstanding of Platonic philosophy could have led him to believe in the possibility of anything like the regime of the *Republic* in Syracuse—is Plato's own apparent endorsement of philosophic rule in Letter Seven itself. But here, if we attend carefully to the text, we will find not only that Plato never claims to have hoped for success in Syracuse, but that he never even claims to think that philosophic rule is possible. What he says is that, in light of his observations of the treatment of Socrates and of other political matters, he was compelled *to say* something in praise of philosophy—namely, that human beings would not be free from evils until philosophy and political power should coincide. But it is perfectly possible to understand Plato as saying that he was compelled to promote a certain *portrayal* of philosophy, to bolster its reputation by praising it—we may even grant that he thinks it would be a great common good for human beings *if* philosophic rule could ever emerge—without insisting that he believed in that regime's possibility.

There is substantial evidence, then, that Plato must have considered the idea of philosophic rule in Syracuse a nonstarter. Thus we have come to recognize a significant gulf separating Plato's and Dion's understandings of the meaning of the doctrine of philosopher-kingship. The effect of this recognition, however, is to intensify the basic question as to why Plato accepted Dion's invitation at all. What did he hope to accomplish in Syracuse that was worth taking such grave risks as were evidently involved? This question is put into particularly stark relief when we consider Letter Eleven, in which Plato is responding to a man named Laodamas, who has invited Plato to come lend his expertise in the founding of a new colony. Plato declines the invitation with the following rationale: "It would be indecorous (*aschēmon*) if, having arrived there, I should not accomplish the very things for the purpose of which you are calling upon me. But I do not have much hope that these things would come to be . . . and at the same time, I, because of my age, am not in a sufficient bodily condition to be wandering and undergoing dangers" (358e2–6). But *all* of this could just as well have been said in response to *Dion*'s invitation—indeed, all the more so with respect to Plato's third and final visit, from which Plato indeed says he tried to beg off by making pretext of his old age (317c5–8, 338c3–5). The question of why Plato went back to Syracuse for the second and third times, the journeys on which he tried to provide Dionysius with an education in philosophy, represents the major puzzle of the *Letters*' whole drama. Indeed, even those letters that do not deal with Plato's activity in Syracuse, nay, *especially* those letters (Five, Six, and Eleven) intensify that puzzle.

We come back at last, then, to Plato's account in Letter Seven of his private deliberations about whether to accept Dion's first invitation to return to Sicily. Now, there are some parts of this passage in which Plato seems to indicate he was serious about *some* kind of political undertaking. For example, he says that he would have been ashamed to have to see himself as being, so to speak, "all talk and no action" on account of never having voluntarily undertaken any serious deed (328c4–8). In the same breath, however, he gives another pair of important considerations. First, he insists on the religious duty he had toward Dion under the Greek custom of *xenia*, guest-friendship: having been a *xenos*, a guest, of Dion, Plato had received favors from him—on his first visit to Syracuse and perhaps over the following two decades—the repayment of which was now Plato's religious obligation (328c7–d1; see also 329b1–2). Of course, we must recognize that a shadow is cast on this argument by Plato's later denigration, which we have already discussed, of friendships founded on *xenia*.

But the *reason* for which Plato says his loyalty to Dion had become an urgent matter takes us, in an unexpected way, to the second reason for his departure. The urgency of Plato's need to help Dion is indicated by Plato's saying that Dion "had really come to be in no small dangers" (328d1–2). In Plato's preceding description of Dion's invitation itself, by contrast, all had been excitement and enthusiasm. Nowhere did we get any sense that Dion himself recognized he was in grave danger. This would seem to be of a piece with the unpopular haughtiness Dion assumed after his first encounter with Plato; his zeal for Plato's hypermoral philosophy, his hopeful faith in the promise of philosophic rule, all brings with it a certain obtuseness regarding the impression he must make on those around him who remain unpersuaded of his vision. Indeed, Letter Four, the only letter addressed directly to Dion himself, concludes with this warning from Plato: "Take to heart . . . that you seem to some to be rather lacking in the proper courtesy. Let it not escape your notice that it is through being agreeable to human beings that it is possible to act, but stubbornness dwells with loneliness" (321b5–c1). Dion never understood or cared about the animosity he aroused in Syracuse with his rigid, moralistic preaching about philosophy. Plato, for his part, makes the angry popular resistance to philosopher-rulers a major theme of the *Republic* (see 473e6–474a4ff., 487b1–d5ff., 499d8–502a4),

So Plato saw, as Dion did not, that Dion was getting himself into serious trouble. And in deliberating about whether to accept Dion's invitation, the decisive consideration appears to have come out of Plato's thinking through what would happen if he should decline the invitation, and Dion, without the benefit of Plato's awareness and counsel, should be sent into exile. Plato imagines the exiled Dion arriving at his doorstep in Athens with the following accusation: the harm suffered by Dion is a minor thing compared with what Plato, by his inaction, has done to "philosophy, which," as Plato's imagined Dion puts it, "you always extol and which you claim is held in dishonor by the rest of human beings—how has it not been betrayed at this point, together with me, insofar as a part of what has come to pass was up to you?" (328e3–5). "If these things had been said," Plato concludes, "what decorous answer would I have to them? There isn't [one]" (329a5–7). Thus, when in summary Plato describes his departure for Syracuse, he says, "In going, I both acquitted myself in relation to Zeus Xenios and rendered the philosopher's part unimpeachable—it would have come to be a matter of reproach had I participated in shamefulness and vice by in any way becoming soft and being cowardly" (329b3–7). From all this it is clear that Plato's concern for the reputation of philosophy was the preeminent reason for his agreeing to go to Syracuse to become the philosophic tutor of Dionysius the Younger (see also 347e6–7).

This conclusion is corroborated by an important statement in Letter Two, the only place in the *Letters* where Plato provides a simple, concise answer to the question of why he went to Syracuse to meet Dionysius the Younger. He says there, addressing himself directly to Dionysius, "I myself came to Sicily with a reputation of being quite distinguished among those in philosophy; and I wished, by coming to Syracuse, to get you as a fellow-witness in order that, through me, philosophy would be honored even among the multitude" (311e5–312a2). Now this is not identical to what he says in Letter Seven. The statement in Letter Two identifies the positive goal of establishing a good reputation for philosophy by winning over the young tyrant; the indications in Letter Seven point to the damage that philosophy's reputation would sustain if Plato declined Dion's invitation. But there is an obvious consistency between the two accounts, in that they both stress the reputation of philosophy as Plato's primary concern. And when we consider the interpretive suggestion we have already advanced, that the whole doctrine of philosopher-kingship, and in this sense the whole *Republic*, were conceived out of a necessity Plato felt to praise philosophy in light of his observations of political life, we begin to see that Plato's journeys to Syracuse, too, fit into the great motif that plays through virtually every one of Plato's writings: the tension between philosophy and the city as represented by the Athenians' persecution of the quintessential philosopher, Socrates. This is not the place to dilate further on that important theme. But we are now in a position to see that the *Letters* points us toward an interpretation of the whole doctrine of philosopher-kingship as primarily intended to bolster the public image of philosophy.

This in turn means that Dion's misunderstanding of philosophy and of the doctrine of philosophic rule was not unintended by Plato. Dion was a member, albeit of special importance and impressive character, of the "multitude" that Plato sought to win over toward a gentler disposition to philosophy. And so in Dion's zealous love of Platonic philosophy as the truest foundation of justice and virtue, we see something of what Plato *hoped* people would think and say about philosophy on the basis of his work. Recall that Plato never even tried to determine whether Aristodorus, to whom Letter Ten is addressed, may have had a more sensitive awareness of the genuine character of philosophy than Dion himself. When dealing with the "comrades of Dion," Plato promotes the view of philosophy as the instrument of utopian politics: "true philosophy" as "the steadfast, faithful, and healthy."

Plato's Reticence to Provide Political Counsel

We began by asking what kind of advice Plato was wont to give in his capacity as a political adviser. The first possibility we had to consider was that Plato counseled the establishment of a regime ruled by philosophers, since his account in Letter Seven gives the impression that he and Dion shared this goal for Syracuse. We have now arrived at the conclusion that Plato's purpose in Syracuse was to do with the public defense and promotion of philosophy and was not a serious attempt to bring about a cessation of evils for humanity by establishing a regime of philosophic rule. But this should not be the end of our investigation of Plato's practical political counsel. The *Letters* portrays Plato engaged in political activity, and so it is here more than anywhere else in the Platonic corpus that we may hope to find Plato showing how his political-philosophic wisdom may actually illuminate the political world and usefully direct the actions of someone seeking to navigate it. Yet such lessons are surprisingly difficult to find in the *Letters*. We might be tempted to say that Plato's purpose in the *Letters* is to dispel the notion that he possessed any practically useful political knowledge. In order to give the proper context and qualification to such political counsel as Plato does give in the *Letters*, then, we must first show how Plato's reticence to reveal it actually forms the unifying impression of the text as a whole.

To begin with, it seems that whatever political acumen Plato may possess does not issue in any clear or immediate way from his philosophy per se. For whenever Plato discusses or presents philosophy in the *Letters* with any semblance of its true proportions and concerns, it appears to stand at some remove from politics. In the "philosophical" passages in Letters Two and Seven, political philosophy is mostly left behind in favor of what seem like abstruse cosmological and epistemological subjects; in Letter Six, Plato associates "this beautiful wisdom of the Forms" with total ineptitude in practical affairs and separates "the true wisdom" from "the human and compulsory" wisdom; and this separation accords with Plato's claim in Letter Two that "by nature, practical wisdom and great power come together in the same place, and they always pursue and seek each other and come to be together" (310e5–6)—for this obviously does not mean that rulers naturally become philosophers or vice versa, but rather that wisdom and power seek each other out because, as Plato's list of examples suggests (311a1–b4), each lacks something it hopes the other can provide. Plato repeatedly indicates a disjunction between the study of Platonic philosophy, on one hand, and the development of insight and ability useful for the pursuit of political goals, on the other. Yet as the *Letters* makes clear, Plato was frequently sought out for his political wisdom, perhaps especially because of his reputation as author of the *Republic*.

So we continue to press the question: What does Plato say, what does he do, when called upon to give political counsel?

In general, it seems that Plato responds to requests for counsel by declining to provide any advice at all. When Plato digresses from the narrative account of his Sicilian engagements in Letter Seven to address Dion's associates' request for help—the first of Letter Seven's two major excursuses—he begins by stating the principled reason for his policy of turning away so many who come seeking his guidance. He begins by laying out the prerequisite conditions of his willingness to provide anyone with personal or political counsel, using the analogy of a doctor who is called upon to counsel someone living a life of unhealthy habits. Plato says that the courageous way to respond to such a request is to make certain that the patient is willing to reform his way of life, and otherwise to refuse to give any counsel at all. That is, the patient must pledge to obey the doctor's orders, which will be directed not only at curing the painful symptoms, but at developing a new, healthy, holistic daily regimen. Likewise, then, if someone with power in a city comes to Plato to ask for counsel, but the city is "deviating altogether from the correct regime and in no way willing to go in its tracks," and if moreover Plato is warned that, as a counselor, he is to let the regime remain as it is on penalty of death, then the courageous thing for him to do is to walk away and deny them any counsel (330e2–331a5). Plato will only counsel individuals or cities who request his help if they agree to cede him the ultimate authority over any decisions bearing on their adherence to the way of the "correct" regimen or regime.

Plato's application of this principle is on display in Letter Three. Letter Three contains Plato's twofold defense against what he claims are slanderous accusations, some of them being propagated by Dionysius himself, regarding the influence Plato exerted as a political adviser at Syracuse. In response to the allegation that Plato prevented Dionysius from pursuing his ambitious vision for a Sicilian empire, Plato clarifies that he *did* support the tyrant's plan to recolonize the island's Greek cities, but *not until* Dionysius had been educated (319a2–c4). Admittedly, this was a point of some confusion for Dionysius—who responded to the effect of, "Educated in what? Geometry?!"—which response, however, may be said to give credence to our sense that education in Platonic philosophy points elsewhere than toward expertise in practical political affairs. In any case, Plato here was apparently true to his word, in that he would not counsel political action until the advisee had first completed the necessary transformation.

Likewise in Letter Eleven, Plato declines the invitation from Laodamas to participate in the founding of a new colony, explaining that he does not believe his contribution would be likely to assure the success of the undertaking. But the advice he gives to Laodamas in place of his partnership goes even further in emphasizing Plato's pessimism regarding the efficacy of wisdom as a guide to political action. No act of lawgiving, Plato warns, can be sufficient to establish a city well unless someone is present who can oversee the daily regimen of all the inhabitants as a "sovereign authority," so as to ensure that they are being instilled appropriately with moderation and courage. If no one present is up to that task, says Plato, then the situation is irremediable: for there will be no one present capable of educating anyone to become such a "sovereign authority," nor will there be anyone capable of learning what must be taught (359a2–b3). "What remains" in that case, says Plato, is "to pray to the gods." In the absence of anyone willing and able to serve as a wise sovereign, the success of the regime—even if the lawgiver was wise—will depend on such strokes of fortune as could only be controlled by divine power. Plato thus denies that *any* political counsel is sufficient for the guidance of a city lacking the means to establish and to maintain virtuous habits or the appropriate combination of moderation and courage among the inhabitants. In what we are compelled to suggest is the vast majority of cases, even the most elevated and developed prudence is inadequate on its own to ensure the success of major political undertakings. Divine assistance or fortune, for which one can only pray, is needed as a supplement to ensure that the political health of the city is sustained.

But Plato's policy regarding political counsel is still *more* restrictive than we have recognized so far. For in Letter Seven's first digression, Plato explains that, unless he is asked directly, he will not even consider providing personal advice, on his own initiative, to any individual, nor would he ever use force to compel anyone to take counsel they do not wish to accept. Even if the individual in question should be his own son, says Plato, he would let the matter lie rather than use force—and if it should be his own mother or father, the use of force would be downright impious "unless they are out of their senses due to illness" (331b4–c2). From this solemn injunction against compelling one's mother or father, Plato at last extrapolates to conclude that one must be wary, too, of offering *political* counsel even to one's father*land*: "If [one's city] does not appear to him to be nobly governed," "he should speak" only "if he is neither going to be talking in vain nor put to death for speaking; but he should not bring force against a fatherland to produce a change of regime when it is not possible for it to come to be best without exile and slaughter of men; rather, *he should keep quiet and pray* for the good things for both himself and his city" (331c7–d5; emphasis added). Unless one can transform one's political community into *the best* regime—however that ambiguous phrase is to be understood—and without recourse to exile or killing, one should not offer counsel at all, but "keep quiet and pray."

As it happens, Plato has occasion in the *Letters* to explain how he applied this principle in his own life at Athens. At the end of Letter Five, Plato imagines and addresses the following accusation against himself, reminiscent of the *Apology of Socrates*: "Plato, it is likely, pretends to know what things are advantageous to a democracy, but when it was possible to speak in the demos and to counsel the things best for it, he never went up to utter a sound" (322a4–7; cf. *Apology* 31c6ff.). The answer Plato wishes to promote is as follows:

> Plato was born late in [the life of] the fatherland and came upon the demos already elderly and habituated by those who came before to do many things unlike to his own counsel—since, of all things, it would be most pleasant for him to give it counsel as to a father, if he didn't suppose that he would be taking risks in vain and doing nothing more. (322a8–b4)

Again, the *Letters* indicates that Plato lived his life true to the principle he lays out in Letter Seven; he never brought his political counsel to bear on the affairs of his fellow Athenians, as they were not in a condition to accept it. The letter closes with an implication that the Athenians were in "an incurable state" (322b5–c1). By avoiding participation in political deliberation that could only have served to endanger him, Plato chose the artful and manly course.

But we must also put this statement from Letter Five in its proper context: this Platonic apologia occurs because Letter Five is one place in the *Letters* where Plato actually claims to possess, and offers to share, some useful political knowledge. He writes to a young Perdiccas, ruler of Macedon, to say that he is sending along an associate of his, a man named Euphraeus, to serve as Perdiccas's political adviser. Euphraeus will be useful, says Plato, because he possesses a certain rare understanding especially helpful to a young ruler. Plato says that each type of regime—democracy, oligarchy, and monarchy are the ones he names—has a distinctive "voice," like an animal. Regimes flourish if they use their proper voice in addressing themselves "both to gods and to human beings," and if their actions accord with their voices; but those regimes that try to imitate the voice of another are ruined. Euphraeus, says Plato, can help Perdiccas "in finding out the speeches befitting monarchy" (321d2–322a2). It is because he has thus revealed his own possession of this knowledge that Plato feels compelled to conclude the letter, as we have just seen, by defending his failure to employ that knowledge for the benefit of the democracy of his own Athenian fatherland. Thus Plato at least clarifies what he *would have* counseled to the Athenians had he encountered them at a more propitious time—and, presumably, what he would counsel to any city with ears to hear him. Of course, what this counsel really urges—that each regime must be sure to speak only in its own voice—is quite consistent with Plato's caution *against* trying to bring about a change of regime in one's own community. In fact, Plato's insistence that a regime strive to remain what it is must strike any would-be reformers as stiflingly conservative. It seems, for example, that Plato would never counsel a monarchy to turn itself into a democracy: for either the monarchy is healthy (or willing to become healthy), in which case one should help it become the best monarchy it can be with no admixture of democracy, or else it is stubbornly unhealthy, in which case Plato offers no counsel but to pray for good fortune. His answer to the important question whether he would support the transition from a tyranny to a kingship is obscured by his choice of words in Letter Five.

Plato's Reluctant and Qualified Proposal of Oligarchy and the Problem of Foundings

It seems Plato's considered view is that, in most cases, more will be lost in the attempt at significant political reform than one can reasonably expect to gain, especially given the part that chance must play. Yet we would wish to hear what Plato had to say in more difficult, more pressing circumstances, in which some positive course of action must be chosen. What about a case in which it is patently obvious that the status quo, or the likely outcome of inaction, is unlivable (see 358b1–3; *Republic* 347a10–c5)? What if there is a genuine crisis, a situation in which the city must either change or perish? In such a situation, there would be no question of aiming at "the best" regime—certainly not the best imaginable regime or the rule of philosophy, nor even the best regime one could reasonably hope to attain by incremental improvement if the city were basically sound. If Plato were compelled to provide counsel in such circumstances, he would have to bend from his habitual insistence on aiming at the ideal by instead pointing to what he saw as the best available, pursuable course of action—however low that bar might prove to be. But since Plato says that *all* the cities in his time were "governed [so] badly" as to be "nearly incurable" (326a3–4), his counsel in a situation like this would shed some light on a vast region of ordinary political reality regarding which he tends not to offer any advice.

Of course, it is precisely such a situation that hangs over Letters Seven and Eight, and therefore over the whole *Letters*, giving to the work its urgency and dramatic tension. For the context of these two letters, both addressed "to the intimates and comrades of Dion" in the wake of Dion's assassination, is the ongoing civil war between those in Syracuse seeking to reinstate the monarchy and the addressees, who wish to overthrow the tyrants in the name of freedom. The city is in need of some means of escape from its terrible and bloody civil strife—for which, we must not forget, Plato has admitted some responsibility: it was Plato's initial influence on Dion decades ago that set the Sicilian tragedy in motion; so it falls upon Plato now to offer some guidance to the Syracusans as to their best available course of action. It is at the end of the first digression in Letter Seven, after he has elaborately detailed his policy regarding requests for counsel and the manner in which he has followed this policy at Syracuse so far, that Plato at last relents in his resistance to providing counsel and suggests what he thinks should be done—as opposed to his advice in Letter Eight, which, as we have seen, was merely a "prayer."

Plato leaves no doubt that the rule of philosophers is not an option for the Syracusans in their present circumstances. Even the hopes that Dion himself had cherished of establishing philosophic rule in his city had depended upon the philosophic education of Dionysius, the attempt at which, Plato stresses, has been a failure (335c2–e1). Plato goes on to suggest that, had *Dion* in turn succeeded in his own campaign to take over the city and to reform it, he would have implemented a somewhat different, *second*-best regime (337d4–6)—a suggestion that accords with our assessment that Dion himself did not partake in the activity of philosophy. Dion, Plato reiterates, intended to make Syracuse a city of freedom, adorned by the best laws (335e3–336b4). He counsels Dion's followers to continue to emulate their fallen leader, making patriotism and temperance the touchstones of their daily lives and attempting to build a Sicilian empire of equality under the laws (336c2–d7). And yet,

Plato finally concedes, "if it should be that these counsels have come too late, since the many and varied conflicts naturally growing each day among the factions are pressing upon you," there must be recourse to some other strategy (336d7–e2). The dreams of Dion must be set aside, and something must be done to end the terrible hostility between the parties. A *third*-best and more practicable option—some "Plan C"—must be pursued.

What follows is therefore Plato's counsel for those who live in a regime riven and convulsed by the worst kind of factional strife. The principle underlying this counsel is that there will be no cessation of these evils until both factions put aside their grudges (336e2–337b3). As we know from Letter Eight, it is the refusal of either faction to settle for less than total victory that endlessly prolongs the conflict: one party may gain the upper hand for a time, but eventually the tides will turn, and the recently oppressed will seek to exact vengeance on their oppressors (353c8–354a3). Letter Seven accords with Letter Eight in stressing the need for the Syracusans to escape this deadly cycle and, moreover, in advising that this is to be accomplished by the institution of a new set of laws, which, crucially, must apply equally to all who live under them. Thus Plato here advises members of the victorious party to impress their superiority upon the defeated precisely by demonstrating that they are "more willing and capable of being slaves to the laws" (337a6–8).

But here in Letter Seven, in contrast to Letter Eight, Plato takes up explicitly and in detail the question of where this new and impartial legislation is to come from. Plato says the victorious party must call in a great council of legislators, dozens of men from all over Greece who meet the following qualifications: they must be old, they must be patriarchs of great families of well-known and respected lineage, and they must be relatively wealthy. The Syracusans are to beg these eminent Greeks to come by promising them the greatest possible honors in the city, in exchange for which the legislators must swear oaths to favor neither the victors nor the vanquished in their lawgiving (337b3–c7). Apart from this, Plato gives no prescription as to the content of the law or the form of the regime; Plato himself in no way offers to take up the task of lawgiving. He leaves this entirely to the respectable gentlemen who will be called in to rewrite the Syracusan constitution.

What form of regime is likely to emerge from the adoption of Plato's proposals? Though Plato provides no specific guidance as to the structure or appointment of political offices, one arrangement is suggested more than any other by the details of his counsel. By urging the Syracusans to reserve the city's highest honors for the legislators (337c2–3), Plato intimates that these legislators should be invited to occupy the ruling offices themselves. Moreover, the suggestion that Plato is thinking of the legislators as a potential ruling class is corroborated by his strange specification that "as a number, fifty such are sufficient for a city of ten thousand men" (337c1–2). Plato thus indicates that the number of legislators should be *proportionate* to the size of the city. But why would a larger city require more legislators? Will not the increase in quantity likely dilute the quality? It seems rather that Plato is arranging for the members of this constitutional convention to transition easily to becoming a new class of citizen rulers—at least for a time (cf. *Laws* 681c7–d5).

Thus, in this particular situation, Plato invites the establishment of an elevated kind of oligarchy at least as much, and probably more, than any other form of government: the law will be laid down by, and the highest honors reserved for, a group of elderly, prestigious, and wealthy gentlemen representing about half of 1 percent of the citizen population. We are reluctant to call the regime an aristocracy, since Plato in his *Republic* reserves that term for the ideal version of rule of the few, literally the rule of "the best" (445d3–6; cf. 544c1–3, 545b3–7). Plato gives the Syracusans no direction as to how they might vet their legislators for any particular traits of *character*: not only will they not be philosophers, Plato has explicitly included neither wisdom, nor justice, nor *any* moral or intellectual virtue among their necessary qualifications. To be sure, the Syracusans would do best to choose the most virtuous and competent legislators they can get, and Plato has done what he can to direct the Syracusans toward well-qualified candidates by describing the social class or station from which the legislators should be sought. We can say that Plato aims for the type of regime that, in the best case, comes to be *called* "aristocracy," and comes to be viewed as worthy of approbation by its citizens and posterity. Even the best real aristocracies are, after all, oligarchic in some measure at least: in practice, aristocracy is the rule of the few and rich, who, over generations, are vulnerable to being led astray from their political responsibilities by concern for their own wealth (cf. Aristotle, *Politics* 5.7). But in the best case, at which Plato is aiming, wherein the rulers are governed by a concern to preserve the honor belonging to their offices and their lineages, there is reasonable hope for decent, equitable rule.

We may go so far as to speculate that Plato's recommendation of this elevated oligarchy, this realistic form of aristocracy, as a third-best but *achievable* option has a certain resonance with his presentation of the devolution of regimes presented in book 8 of the *Republic*. Let us presume that the golden regime, the rule of philosophy, is but "a prayer"; consider then that the silver regime, for which Plato must invent the name "timarchy," which is after all a "middle" between the imaginary "golden" regime from which it emerges and the oligarchy that will follow (547c6–7), is in any case only possible in the rarest of circumstances—only Lycurgus's founding of Sparta might be said to fit the bill; then oligarchy itself, the bronze regime, is, in the best case, the highest regime for which one might realistically aim or for which there is any encouraging precedent. However that may be, it seems that this form of rule, not by philosophers or wise men but merely those of good repute among the Greeks, is what Plato considers the best realistic solution to the Syracusans' need for a new regime to restore peace and order to their city.

It would hardly be surprising for a student of Platonic political philosophy to register a sense of disappointment at this conclusion. When finally pressed, the great champion of philosophic utopia counsels the adoption of an imperfect and mundane form of government. It is therefore worthwhile to conclude our exploration of this theme by returning to Letter Eight. For Letter Eight as a whole, as we have seen, purports to do again precisely the same thing that we have been discussing Plato doing at the very center of the *Letters*, that is, at the end of Letter Seven's first digression: to provide practical political counsel to the Syracusans in the midst of their mortal dilemma. But as we have also seen, Plato does not make the move in Letter Eight, which he does in Letter Seven, of counseling on the presumption that circumstances have foreclosed the possibility of truly following in Dion's footsteps. On the contrary, the counsel of Letter Eight is suffused with the spirit of Dion, the first half presenting the "common counsel" of both him and Plato, and the second half presenting Plato's "interpretation" of what Dion himself would counsel if he were still alive. By carefully comparing the political counsel of Letter Eight, then, with his advising toward oligarchy in Letter Seven, we can appreciate more fully why Plato considered the loftier Dionean alternative to be basically misguided, and hence why he found it necessary to promote a more mundane course of political action when circumstances finally required real, practical advice.

Letter Eight is consistent in directing the Syracusans to transform their regime into a kingship. Kingship here must be distinguished from monarchy: Plato's Dion ultimately recommends a system of three kings so as to satisfy the varied existing claims to political honor and power in Syracuse (356a7ff.). We begin by noting, however, that Plato himself leaves quite unclear whether the transformation of Syracusan tyranny into a kingship is even possible—a fact that bears some relevance to his characterization of the counsel contained in the letter as a "prayer." When Plato first proposes this transformation into a kingship, he adds the qualification "if it should be possible" (354a7–b1). Now, although he proceeds to affirm that "it *is* possible, as Lycurgus," "a wise and good man," "showed by deed" (354b1–2; emphasis added), his subsequent explanation of this proof of concept is problematic. For one thing, his story of Lycurgus being provoked by the degradation of Argos and Messene occurs nowhere else in extant accounts—including Plato's *Laws*, in which the case of Sparta is compared with those two cities, but the history presented is altogether different (690d1–692b1). More importantly, however, the example Plato cites does not prove his point: Lycurgus *preserved* a kingship in danger of devolving into tyranny as the kingships of Argos and Messene had done. But Plato here asks the Syracusans to *transform* their tyranny—which has been a tyranny since the regime's inception (353b3–4)—into a kingship.

If the Lycurgus example does not prove that such a transformation is possible, then we are left without resolution to the doubt Plato initially casts on its possibility. We may characterize the difficulty in the following way. "Kingly rule" is here explained as rule in which "law [is] a sovereign king over human beings," and "human beings [are not] tyrants over laws" (354b8–c2). Now Lycurgus is thought to have preserved the kingship of Sparta by establishing two new political institutions to counterbalance the kingly power and thus to *maintain* the rule of law. But in Syracuse there is no living history of lawful or kingly rule—even the democratic regime preceding the tyranny of Dionysius the Elder and Hipparinus was "anarchic," the people ruling "luxuriously" over their rulers, judging their superiors "in no way . . . according to law, in order that they should in no way be enslaved with either justice or law as a master." This indeed, says Plato, was the source of the tyranny (354d4–e3). There is no doubt but that—to say nothing of the difficulty of changing the "form" of regime in a city (*eidos* at 354c5; see 321d4–e6)—a new act of lawgiving will be required if a kingship is to be established.

Plato, for his part, gives no sign that he ever held out hope for a legislator to refound Syracuse as a kingship. It is clear that, in Plato's view, the establishment of an excellent legal order is a matter not only of tremendous difficulty but also of chance—indeed, this was the specific and explicit conclusion of the series of observations that led Plato to withdraw from politics according to Letter Seven (326a1-5). But Plato makes it equally clear that Dion, for his part, failed to appreciate the monumental difficulty of bringing about "freedom under kingly rule" (355d8-e1). Accordingly, in Letter Four (which belongs to the critical time following Dion's initial triumph over Dionysius), Plato advises Dion that he must be prepared to *outdo* even Lycurgus and Cyrus (320d5-8)—a task to which, as it would turn out, Dion was not equal. We must recognize that, in attempting to provide useful advice to the Syracusans—that is, in Letter Seven, which proves to be a franker and more practicable version than Letter Eight—Plato's primary concern was to contrive some means for generating new laws for the Syracusans: laws devised and laid down not by lawgivers who are rare paragons of wisdom or virtue, but by lawgivers who are conventionally respectable and therefore practically obtainable Greek gentlemen. One cannot produce a Lycurgus at will, but one may hope to construct a stable and benign oligarchy (consider *Laws* 710e5-7), which will be vastly preferable to the ravages of civil war.

Plato's counsel to Dion's comrades thus expresses a kind of political realism not usually associated with Platonic political philosophy. This strain of Platonic realism helps us to identify, by contrast, the major defect in Dion's own political idealism. The counsel Plato offers the Syracusans in Letter Seven is focused almost exclusively on the need to find a legislative mechanism by which to obtain a new and stable Syracusan constitution. The Platonically reanimated Dion of Letter Eight, however, is singularly insensitive to the need for such a mechanism. This imagined Dion begins his address to the Syracusans with the injunction that they must accept the right kind of laws—laws that accurately reflect the Platonic denigration of pleasure and money, and the Platonic exaltation of care for the soul (355a8-c6). This beginning is crucially flawed: Dion here gives no explanation of where these laws will come from. Moreover, he concludes this initial injunction by insisting thus: "That these things I encourage are true, you will recognize by deed if you shall taste the things now being said concerning laws, which seems to come to be the truest test concerning all things" (355c5-8). Does not the metaphor of taste suggest that the Syracusans must *experience* life under such laws as Dion describes? In other words, the Syracusans cannot be persuaded to accept Dion's recommendation until they have already accepted it and "tasted" its fruit firsthand. To his credit, Dion does at least seem aware that the Syracusans are not likely to be persuaded as he himself was by the force of Plato's persuasive rhetoric alone. But he seems to overlook the fact that, if the Gordian knot he has unwittingly described is to be split, the Syracusans must be *forced* to "taste" the laws they will ultimately learn to love. It is no use merely to direct them to "accept" such laws in speech.

Dion is perfectly clear that it is *after* their "having accepted such laws" (355c8) that he would have the Syracusans attend to the form of the regime. It is at this moment that he reckons with the "danger" that "has taken hold of Sicily," and thereby recognizes the need to accommodate both of its rival factions under the new regime and its laws—to "cut down the middle," as he puts it, by establishing three kings, including representatives of both factions. That is, it is only after the Syracusans' acceptance of the initial laws, of unexplained provenance, that Dion will deal with those exigent circumstances that in Plato's view called for the abandonment of the Dionean course altogether. Plato saw that it would be extremely difficult to get the dominant faction at any given time to prefer compromise to the hope of annihilating the enemy; and then, in the unlikely case that one faction should choose compromise, Plato knows that the only hope of obtaining legislation that will be viewed as impartial is to invite lawgivers from outside the city—and even then the vanquished party must be cowed into submission "by means of a pair of compulsions, awe and fear" (337a3–5). Dion is stunningly inattentive to this whole cluster of obstacles and concerns. It is as if he hopes or expects that the new laws, to be accepted spontaneously by all the Syracusans in common, are to arrive via some deus ex machina.

Dion's whole counsel proves to be pervaded by this same grave difficulty. The first order of business for the three kings, who are to be established only *after* the Syracusans have accepted good laws, will be to "set down laws and the sort of regime in which it is consonant for kings to come to be sovereign authorities," and so on (356c8–d2). The circularity of this procedure is a result of the key failing of Dion's political thought: he has not given sufficient attention to the difficult problem of political foundings. It seems he recoils instinctively from the ugly business of "laying down the law" for a new regime. It is in the nature of such a task that it take place in a context of political and legal flux, and, as Machiavelli's intensive treatment of the theme infamously makes clear, even the noblest political undertakings require some not altogether noble beginning. Plato's counsel to bring in respectable Greeks to found the new Syracusan regime would seem merely to point to the gentlest possible version of such a beginning.

Even more than in Letter Seven, Plato shows his awareness of the true dimensions of the problem of political founding in Letter Eleven, where he responds to a request for his help in the founding of a new colony. Plato warns that the colonists' attempt at founding will fail without a properly educated sovereign to oversee the daily life of the city's inhabitants—in the absence of such a sovereign, nothing would remain for the colonists to do but "to pray to the gods" (359b3). But, Plato continues, "the earlier cities too were established in nearly this way and were well managed thereafter, under the coming-to-be of conjunctions of great affairs, both in war and in the other actions—whenever, at the propitious moments, a man both noble and good came about having great power" (359b4–8). There is an ambiguity here: Does Plato intend for his account of the origin of "the earlier cities" to lend support to his paradigm of a colony overseen by a wise sovereign authority? Or is this account rather supposed to encourage Laodamas and the colonists, to make them more hopeful, in the event they find themselves lacking such a sovereign authority and forced to resort to prayer? That is, is the "noble and good" man who exercises his "great power" for the sake of the city meant as a model of the educated sovereign? Or is his appearance, together with the "conjunctions of great affairs," an example of the alternative to such a sovereign, which benevolent gods might provide?

On one hand, Plato concludes by stressing to Laodamas the necessity of remaining eager and thoughtfully prepared for the emergence of the right opportunity, whether "in war" or "in the other actions," and ends the letter with the word *eutuchei*, "good luck" (359b8–c3)—the same word with which he ends all of the letters (or portions of letters; see 337e1) most fully devoted to providing political counsel (321c1, 322c1, 357d2). Plato evidently counsels Laodamas, then, to be ready to intervene as a "noble and good man" himself, should the opportune moment arise. On the other hand, it is unlikely that Plato considers Laodamas a candidate to be the sovereign overseer described earlier in the letter—otherwise, there would have been no need for Plato to raise the question whether anyone qualified for the office existed among the colonists. It seems, then, that we must distinguish the case of the wise sovereign who actively upholds the courageous and moderate ways of life in the city from the case of the noble and good man who seizes power at a critical moment. For the latter case, which Plato claims has generally obtained in successfully established cities, Plato indicates a need both for divine providence—it is a case for which the colonists should pray—and for vigilance and decisive action on the part of the founder, combined with "good luck."

There is a difficulty, however, in which Plato becomes involved by offering counsel to the prospective founder: the good fortune for which Laodamas and the colonists should pray, and the propitious moment that the founder must seize, is a moment of grave crisis for the city, a "conjunction of great affairs, both in war and the other actions." His phrase here is reminiscent of a passage in the *Laws*, where the Athenian Stranger claims that the great innovations or revolutions in laws and regimes are always prompted by "chances and misfortunes of every sort," such as "war," "harsh poverty," "plagues," and prolonged periods of inhospitable weather. The Stranger takes this as evidence that "no mortal ever legislates anything," since "almost all human matters belong to chance," before adding that the same thing may just as well be said thus: "In all things a god—and together with a god, chance and a propitious moment—pilots all the human things" (709a1–b8). The Stranger's equivocation as to whether human affairs are determined providentially or purely accidentally has a parallel in Plato's telling Laodamas both that he must resign himself to prayer and that he must prepare himself to seize decisively upon a moment of "good luck" when it arises. There are, however, the following differences. The Stranger, who has decided to devote a great deal of energy to helping his interlocutors in the founding of their new colony, is quite explicit in his enumeration of the varieties of catastrophe that decide the course of human affairs. Plato, who leaves Laodamas on his own in the founding of his colony, providing only so much advice as can fit into a very brief letter, speaks vaguely about the "propitious moments" for which Laodamas must be prepared. By referring to Laodamas's model as a gentleman, a "noble and good man" (*kalos te kai agathos*), Plato emphasizes the difficult but noble end at which the founder aims; he directs the reader's gaze as much as possible away from the observation that the insight about the "propitious moments" for the founding of cities could equally be exploited by an aspiring tyrant. Machiavelli, by contrast, is much less cautious in his counsel to princes. This difference in degree of cautiousness is reflected also by the fact that Plato declines in this context to make the Machiavellian suggestion that human virtue might substitute for fortune or divine favor (cf. 353b4–7). Plato is much less willing than Machiavelli to encourage the prospective founder to discard his belief in divine providence as a determining factor in political affairs.

Does the *Letters* suggest in any consistent manner that Platonic *philosophy* issues in concrete political guidance? More than anything else, the *Letters* suggests that political affairs belong too much to the realm of flux and chance to be mastered or that great political undertakings require more good fortune than one can reasonably hope for. The possibility that the vicissitudes of fortune may be subject to the wills of providential deities does little to alter this dim evaluation of human efficacy: prayer, as anyone can observe, offers no guarantee of good fortune (*Second Alcibiades* 138a7–b4). But our portrait of Plato, resigned to the indomitability of political affairs and thus reluctant to provide political counsel, remains woefully incomplete without the identification of the alternative to political striving that he would direct us to choose in its place. We have already recognized that the whole Platonic Syracusan project was driven to a great extent by concern for the reputation of philosophy. It is devotion to philosophy that appears to hold the highest place in Plato's economy of concerns, higher certainly than political activity in itself, and it seems to be *only* this end that can draw him into political activities to which he would otherwise be totally averse. To go to such great lengths for such a cause, however, indeed to risk the kind of danger and destruction that were consequent to Plato's dealings in Syracuse, calls for some explanation. What is the character and import of this philosophic activity, for the sake of which Plato was willing to go so far and at such a great cost?

Part Two

The Presentation and Substance of Platonic Philosophy

Plato has two distinct ways of presenting or discussing philosophy in the *Letters*. In reference to the ideal of a regime of philosopher rulers, Plato presents philosophy as the key to humanity's political salvation, and therefore as a means to a political end. At other times, however, Plato discusses the activity of philosophy as a quest for clarity and understanding, and thus for individual fulfillment, without reference to its political utility. It is helpful to recognize, moreover, that these two aspects of Platonic philosophy as presented in the *Letters* roughly correspond to Plato's relationships with Dion and Dionysius, respectively. In our exploration of Plato's political counsel in the *Letters* (which focused naturally on Plato's relationship with Dion), we encountered the first, more political of his presentations of philosophy as reflective of some part of Dion's political hopes; but we have not yet seen much of Plato's alternative presentation of philosophy, in which the teaching, learning, practice, and life of philosophy receive more attention, and which generally arises in reference to Plato's relationship with his erstwhile pupil, Dionysius. As we turn now to a study of the theme of philosophy in the *Letters*, we must attend to both of its facets, and above all to the relationship between those facets. What compels Plato, in his mission to defend and promote the reputation of philosophy among the Greeks, to alternate between these two different—sometimes even incompatible—portraits? What does the *Letters* contribute to Plato's pursuit of that mission? And which of his two portraits of philosophy more closely resembles the truth in Plato's view?

For the sake of arriving at comprehensive answers to these questions, we will chart the following two-part course through four of the five Platonic letters in which philosophy is explicitly discussed. First, we must briefly revisit the version of Platonic philosophy we have already encountered—the version that Dion especially came to cherish as the key to political happiness—by reconsidering a handful of passages we have touched upon above: the famous autobiographical section of Letter Seven, as well as Letters Ten and Six. This time, however, we will give greater attention to what these passages tell us about Plato's strategy for promoting philosophy than about his strategy for offering political counsel. Specifically, we will seek to elucidate the sense of Plato's claim in the *Letters* that philosophy should be hailed as the solution to our political ills. Having made this beginning, we will quickly see that Letter Six is of particular importance to our understanding of Plato's presentation of philosophy in the *Letters*, since it is in Letter Six that Plato most seems to straddle the divide between his two versions of philosophy—and thus shows the contradiction between them. In Letter Six, philosophy is presented as the ideal source of stability and prosperity for a political ruler, but also as a theoretical activity lacking political applicability, to be pursued for its own intrinsic benefits. The first portion of our exploration of the theme of philosophy in the *Letters*, then, will conclude by showing how Letter Six allegorically represents the dilemma Plato faces in choosing how to portray Platonic philosophy.

From there, we will move on to the second and much longer portion of our study of philosophy in the *Letters*: a close examination of two passages in which Plato, in discussing his education of Dionysius, most elaborately describes the course of study and subject matter involved in the pursuit of Platonic philosophy (as opposed to its political utility). These passages are, first, his notoriously enigmatic account of "the nature of the first" in Letter Two, and second, the famous "philosophic digression" of Letter Seven. In addition to the basic interpretive task of deciphering what each of these passages teaches about Platonic philosophy, we will especially seek to clarify the connection between the two passages, which is most evident in their parallel treatments of a common theme: in both passages, Plato discusses the difficulties involved in the practice of philosophy, which compel him to write about philosophy only in surprisingly guarded and even dissembling ways. Thus our exploration of the theme of philosophy in the *Letters* will help us in understanding why Plato has written about philosophy in such a confusing and paradoxical manner.

I

Philosophy as Solution to the Challenge of Politics

The autobiographical section of Letter Seven describes the extinguishing of Plato's youthful political ambitions and aspirations. This change in Plato is said to have been the result of his examination of politics, which was itself prompted by Athens' repeated mistreatment of Socrates. Plato's acknowledgment of the grave difficulty involved in "manag[ing] the political things correctly" came initially with the observation that "one is not able to act without men who are friends and faithful comrades." But since one cannot hope to find such men where venerable laws and customs are being corrupted, and since he finally concluded that "all of the cities" of his time were "being governed badly," Plato determined that to cure actual regimes of the pathologies that beset them is beyond the reach of human action (325c5–326a5). We also saw that Plato's resignation regarding the political efficacy of human endeavor gave rise to his praise of philosophy. Plato took to declaring that only the ascension of philosophers to stations of political rule or the turning of those who rule to philosophy—the latter requiring providential help—can put an end to the evils suffered by humanity by putting the clear apprehension of justice to use in politics (326a5–b4). The lack of trustworthy friendships is the problem that undermines the prospect of effective political action; the rule of philosophers is apparently the solution. But how is the rule of philosophy, even granting philosophy's exclusive access to the form of justice, to overcome this *particular* political problem? That is, how can philosophy supply these vanishingly rare friendships, which alone are trustworthy enough to be reliable in the midst of the treachery, slander, and deceit that beset the powerful or ambitious political actor?

Of the two versions of philosophy we find in the *Letters*, it is the more political version, which Plato consistently presents in connection with his relationship to Dion, that he employs in order to address these questions. We see this exemplified most completely by Letter Ten: Plato tells Dion's comrade that "the true philosophy" is nothing other than "the steadfast, and faithful, and healthy," and Plato disparages all other "wisdoms and clevernesses" as forms of refinement or sophistication that miss the mark of philosophy properly understood. Plato presents philosophy as consisting in sound moral character. When we put Letter Ten together with the autobiographical section of Letter Seven, then, we see the implication that friendship as fostered among those who share in philosophy has the strength and stability to withstand the stresses and strains suffered by any bond exposed to the violent flux of political life. Indeed, in Letter Seven we learn that the necessity of acquiring "faithful friends and comrades" was the moral of the great political lesson Plato and Dion were jointly attempting to impart to Dionysius: those (Darius, the Athenians) who acquire such friends build magnificent empires; those who do not (Dionysius the Elder) remain "paltry" by contrast and survive only "with difficulty" (331d6–332c7). Plato even blames Dion's own downfall on his failure to make philosophy the exclusive foundation of his political partnerships, and on his trusting instead in the protection promised by religious authorities in exchange for pious observance. In this respect, philosophy is presented as offering what even religion only pretends to offer. But if the problem of the trust needed for success in political action is solved by the supreme faithfulness of friendships grounded in philosophy, why is it that the definition of philosophy as "the steadfast, and faithful, and healthy" does not appear in Letter Seven itself, where this problem is articulated?

The presentation of philosophy is a puzzle without a clean solution; Plato cannot display all of its pieces at once without falling into manifest contradiction. The literary form and structure of the *Letters*, as a collection of letters addressing disparate people and circumstances, is singularly useful in this regard: it allows Plato to present different pieces, or combinations of pieces, of the puzzle concerning the presentation of philosophy in different places. Letter Six is particularly valuable for our understanding of this feature of the *Letters*. In order properly to appreciate Letter Six, however, we must appreciate its relationship to the rest of the *Letters*, beginning with the recognition that Letters Five and Six form a pair that must be considered in their juxtaposition. Even their position within the *Letters* makes them stand out together, as they constitute a digression from the great narrative arc flowing from Letter One through at least Letter Eight. That is, whereas Letters One through Eight otherwise proceed in chronological order and deal exclusively with the Dion-Dionysius affair, Letters Five and Six are unrelated to the politics of the Italian and Sicilian cities and are not clearly located on the timeline of Plato's Syracusan entanglements. In each one of these two letters, moreover, Plato is in correspondence with the ruler of a Greek city—with Perdiccas of Macedon in Letter Five, and with Hermias of Atarneus in Letter Six—and in both cases, Plato is involved in an exchange of favors: he offers counsel and the services of his associates to the ruler with a view toward benefits the ruler can provide to those same associates in return. (As a point of historical interest at least, we may note that Plato's greatest student, Aristotle, would benefit from friendly relations with both of these regimes.)

In examining these letters as a pair, we cannot fail to be struck by the following contradiction between them. In Letter Five, Plato sends Euphraeus to help the young Macedonian ruler hold fast to the monarchical "voice" belonging to his regime; Plato thus speaks emphatically as if political expertise belongs to him and to his students. In Letter Six, however, Plato characterizes his students, Erastus and Coriscus, as being virtually devoid of political judgment or expertise on account of their attention in proper measure to Platonic philosophy or, as he puts it, the "beautiful wisdom of the Forms." As regards this contradiction between Letters Five and Six, it is evident which of the two contrary portraits is the more truthful one: the insinuation of political naivete in Letter Six notwithstanding, Plato's claim to possess political wisdom and his ability to impart such wisdom to his students are indisputably on display in Letter Five. So why in Letter Six does Plato so emphatically deny such wisdom in his otherwise laudatory description of his two students? The contradiction is best explained by reference to the fact that philosophy goes unmentioned in Letter Five but is thematic in Letter Six. This shows that Plato is willing to highlight his possession and teaching of practical insight into politics, but not in the context of discussion of his teaching of philosophy. The only exception to this principle would be that most memorable and famous Platonic point of contact between philosophy and politics, the doctrine of philosophic rule.

In Letter Six, however, the idea that Plato might be discussing or suggesting philosophic rule is utterly implausible. For how could the ideal political rulers be men as politically inept as Erastus and Coriscus are said to be? In this respect, the presentation of philosophy in Letter Six conflicts with that of Letter Seven (as the only Platonic letter in which the subject of philosopher rulers is explicitly broached): by suggesting that Platonic philosophers lack the ability to perceive and respond to political dangers, Plato undermines the persuasiveness of his claim that philosophers would make ideal rulers. Yet there is also a point of *agreement* between the presentation of philosophy in Letter Six and the claim in Letter Seven that philosophers are uniquely suited to overcome the perennial obstacles to political action. For what makes Erastus and Coriscus politically inept is also what renders them not only harmless but singularly useful to the ruler Hermias. Unlike Perdiccas, who is in need of guidance on account of his youth (321d2–4), Hermias appears to have the rule of Atarneus well in hand. Plato indicates that he is well supplied in arms, allies, and money, and what is more, Plato judges him to have "acquired . . . both by nature and, through experience, by art" "a certain defensive power" that would allow him to make prudent use of these assets (322e1–323a1). The respect in which Hermias lacks power, according to Plato, is that he is in need of "friends who are steadfast and who have healthy character" (322d3–4). Erastus and Coriscus can provide such friendship for the same reason that allows them to benefit from it in turn. Plato vouches for the trustworthiness of Erastus and Coriscus in overwhelmingly strong terms on the basis of the fact that they have been "occupied with us, who are measured and not bad, for a long part of their life" (322e2–3, 323a2–3). But this same, lifelong occupation is also responsible for their being "inexperienced," and for their resultant need for "wisdom that guards against the wicked and unjust" (322d6–e1). Their time spent in an activity we are left to assume was the study of philosophy in Plato's Academy has rendered them perfectly upright but desperately vulnerable; by attending for so long to the attainment of "true wisdom," they have failed sufficiently to acquire "the human and compulsory" wisdom that would allow them to fend off the "wicked and unjust." Their trustworthiness makes them ideal friends for Hermias, while their naivete leaves them in need of Hermias's "defensive power." This much is in accord with the presentation of philosophy as "the steadfast, and faithful, and healthy" in Letter Ten—which in turn agrees, as we have seen, with Letter Seven's indication that only philosophy can solve the problem of political action posed by the unavailability of "men who are friends and faithful comrades."

Thus we can say that the presentation of philosophy in Letter Six in part supports and in part contradicts the "Dionean" view of philosophy in evidence in Letters Seven and Ten. On one hand, Letter Six supports the idea that philosophy is the solution to the problem of trust in political activity; on the other hand, it can do this only at the expense of making philosophers appear politically inept, thereby undermining the appeal or plausibility of philosophic rule. The reasons for Plato's reluctance to make claims of political wisdom on behalf of philosophy are seen especially by the comparison with Letter Five. Plato may be able to sell the percipient Euphraeus as adviser to the young and inexperienced Perdiccas, but to the seasoned and prosperous Hermias, such a prospective associate would likely appear not only useless but suspicious. Anyone shrewd enough to be a competent adviser could pose a threat if unconstrained by loyalty to the regime or its ruler, and is all the more dangerous if "courageous," as Euphraeus is said to be (321e7; cf. Xenophon, *Hiero* 5.1). The fact that Plato feels he must defend himself at the end of Letter Five for possessing political wisdom he never brought to light for the benefit of the Athenians is a reminder that political wisdom is likely to be as much an object of suspicion in a democracy as in a monarchy.

Taken together, Letters Five and Six help us to recognize Plato's principle of separating discussions of his teaching of true philosophy from his offering of political counsel. Yet our very articulation of this principle makes us aware of its inadequacy as an explanation of Plato's political philosophic writing in general. For Platonic political philosophy is most famous for its manner of *combining* philosophy and politics, not least of all in Letter Seven. Precisely the fact that Letter Six undermines the doctrine of philosophic rule (by denying that philosophers are politically savvy) puts us in mind of Letter Seven's promotion of philosophic rule, which by extension thus affirms what Letter Six denies. How does Plato get away with the doctrine of philosophic rule, given the precariousness of making claims to political wisdom on behalf of philosophy?

The clue to the answer to this question lies in an observation we have already made regarding the definition of philosophy as "the steadfast, and faithful, and healthy" in Letter Ten. What makes that definition so strange is that philosophy is thus described as a collection of *character traits*, to the exclusion of any acknowledgment that philosophy is rather a kind of *activity*. Now, one might wish to respond to this concern about the inadequacy of Letter Ten's definition of philosophy by reference to the famous Socratic thesis that "virtue is knowledge." The ostensible meaning of this paradoxical dictum is as follows. If indeed moral excellence, or virtue (*aretē*), is, as we intuit it to be, the perfection of the human soul (*Republic* 444d13–445c2), then—since everyone surely desires the greatest good for her or his own soul (see *Republic* 438a3–4; *Philebus* 20d1–10)—acts of viciousness, as harmful to the soul of the actor, must signify that the actor is ignorant or confused as to what would truly be beneficial (*Apology of Socrates* 25c5–26a8, 29d1–30b4; *Protagoras* 352a1–360d8; *Meno* 87c11–89d6; *Gorgias* 476a7–479e9). A virtuous person is one who correctly understands that the greatest good can be obtained only through virtue; a vicious person is one who mistakenly chooses some other, lesser good (such as pleasure) at the expense of virtue, and therefore at the expense of what is genuinely the greater good. Perhaps, then, it may be reasonable to say what Plato says about philosophy in Letter Ten. For if philosophy, by revealing the truth about moral character, illuminates the path all human beings would wish to travel whether they know it or not—namely, the virtuous path toward happiness or fulfillment—then perhaps there is sense in claiming that the ultimate or most important result of philosophy for the philosopher is the perfection of the soul through the attainment of moral virtue. Indeed, something like this claim is crucial to the doctrine of philosophic rule, since it affirms that the philosopher, as an essentially moral or virtuous human being, can be trusted with political power (see *Republic* 484d5ff.; *Letters* 326a5–7).

But even to say that philosophy is such knowledge of the virtues as is, rightly understood, identical to the possession of those virtues is to fail to portray philosophy as the *quest* for that knowledge (consider *Symposium* 204b4–5). It is precisely the unfinished character of that quest, the uncertain nature of virtue, that makes philosophy what it is in the context of the political community: a restless seeking for understanding that necessarily calls the community's traditional or doctrinal teachings about virtue before the cold and unwavering tribunal of reason. Indeed, Plato's Socrates himself readily acknowledges that his equation of virtue with knowledge may be "nobly spoken," but cannot be taken as gospel (see *Meno* 89d3ff.; *Protagoras* 360e6ff.). In order to present philosophy as a potential political panacea, however—what we have called the "Dionean" version of Platonic philosophy—Plato must soften and obscure its volatile or potentially subversive dimension, which goes with its being a dynamic, questioning, seeking activity. Note in this connection that Plato's presentation of the trial of Socrates in Letter Seven—which belongs to the introduction or explanation of his statement on the need for philosophic rule—mentions the charge of impiety but not that of corrupting the young (325c1–2). Socrates is made innocuous in this portrayal in accordance with the portrayal of philosophy as simple, common decency: Socrates is not said to have been a teacher of philosophy, because philosophy, in this view, is not really something one teaches; Plato says Socrates was pious and just—it would be redundant to add that he was a philosopher. Likewise, to say that the evils plaguing humanity cannot be dispelled until the philosophers and the rulers are one and the same is merely to say what is totally uncontroversial: the best rule would be the rule of the perfectly wise and perfectly just. This indeed is the point of the Platonic doctrine of philosophic rule, and this is why Plato says that belief in the truth of this doctrine is equivalent to the belief of those who have been "justly reared and educated in the ways of pious ruling men" (335d6–e1).

The doctrine of philosophic rule, violating as it does the Platonic principle of separating discussions of philosophy from those of politics, is possible only if philosophy is presented in a drastically truncated form. The "Dionean" understanding of Platonic political philosophy involves a *distortion* of Platonic philosophy, because it fails to recognize philosophy as an ongoing *activity* of critical inquiry and questioning. Letter Six is a bridge between this drastically truncated presentation of philosophy and the correction of that distortion. While Letter Six upholds the notion of philosophy as the basis of trustworthy friendship, it also acknowledges, as we will now see, its essentially dynamic and transpolitical character. And it is especially when Plato presents philosophy in its distinctive activity as a quest for coherent knowledge that he must hold it at a distance from political activity and politically active understanding.

We have said that the definition of philosophy as "the steadfast, and faithful, and healthy" in Letter Ten indicates the manner in which philosophy can be presented as the solution to the political problem identified in the autobiographical section of Letter Seven: the need for friends one can trust in politics. Yet as we have also stressed, Plato does not present that solution in Letter Seven. Even if he there implies that trustworthy friendships must be grounded in philosophy (333e7–334b7), he gives no indication of how philosophy brings about such friendships. For to do this would be to discuss something of the meaning of philosophy or of what it is to philosophize, and Plato is evidently averse to entering on such a discussion in the vicinity of his claims that the philosopher possesses significant political wisdom. It is rather in Letter Six, where it is implied that philosophers are oblivious to political affairs, that Plato appears to indicate how philosophy can produce genuinely trustworthy bonds of friendship.

The first mention of philosophy in Letter Six is in reference to Plato's goal of forging a mutually beneficial friendship between, on one hand, his longtime pupils Erastus and Coriscus, who now live in faraway Ionia, and, on the other hand, Hermias, who rules the Ionian city of Atarneus. Plato urges the three of them to "hold fast" to one another so as to bind themselves in "a single braid of friendship" (323a5–b1). Referring to his whole account of the "friendship and community" to be initiated by this letter as an oracular pronouncement, Plato claims that his prophecy of good things to come from his proposed arrangement will be fulfilled, "whenever we all—both we and you—shall philosophize insofar as we are capable and as is appropriate to each of us" (323c1–3)—"if," he finally adds, "a god should be willing" (323c5). The religious cast Plato gives to philosophy here—for neither the first nor the last time in the *Letters*—comes to define the letter's closing lines, in which he indicates the nature of the wisdom to be gained through philosophy. He concludes by assuring his addressees that if all of them "really philosophize," they will all come to know, "as clearly as is within the power of happy human beings," "the god who is leader of all the things that are and the things that will be, sovereign father of the leader and cause" (323d2–6).

Plato portrays philosophy here as the activity that illuminates the divine origin of and rule over the entirety of existence, revealing, to the extent it can be revealed to human beings, the great god after whom we naturally seek: a paternal ruler attentive to our relationships to other human beings, including our oaths—for Plato enjoins his addressees to swear oaths by this god in their consultation of this letter as a "compact and sovereign law" governing their friendship (323c8–d4). The revelation thus available to us through philosophy fulfills us in the sense that it makes us into "happy human beings"—presumably because it assures us of our place as spiritual beings within the vast cosmic order in which we find ourselves. Indeed, Plato presents himself not only as having obtained this rare and powerful wisdom, but as having gained access through it to a source of further, divinely revealed, oracular or prophetic revelations—note that he opens the letter with the words "To me some one of the gods appears" (*Emoi phainetai theōn tis*; 322c4). Moreover, it would seem that the attainment of direct knowledge of the divine through philosophy brings us into communion with others who have done likewise. It is in this way—by being grounded on shared knowledge of and reverence for the true cosmic divinity—that the joint activity of philosophy has the capacity to forge powerful and thus dependable friendships strong enough to remedy the lack of steadfastness that is otherwise endemic in human nature.

Having seen these astounding promises that Plato makes on behalf of philosophy, we may now intensify our scrutiny of his undertaking in Letter Six. For, although Plato insists on delivering only "good prophecy," passing over in silence what might turn out if the parties do not philosophize adequately, he nevertheless spends a good portion of the letter detailing the procedure to be followed if one member of the triumvirate determines "to dissolve" their "single braid of friendship" (323b2–c1). Indeed, the danger posed by this possibility must be great: the lack of steadfastness in all that is human is to be counteracted by the parties' philosophizing; but *until* they have sufficiently philosophized, the danger of human inconstancy looms over the undertaking. What assurance can there be that the previously unphilosophic ruler Hermias in particular will hold to the required regimen of philosophizing? Note, furthermore, that Plato first allows that his prophecy will be realized if each of them philosophizes "insofar as [they] are capable and as is appropriate to each"; but the apprehension of the cosmic deity, which seems to hold the key to philosophy's ability to bind these men together, will only be attained if they "*really* philosophize" (emphasis added). We may recall here that, in Plato's major statement on his doctrine of philosophic rule in Letter Seven, he refers to the possibility that "those who are in power in the cities [might], *by some divine fate, really* philosophize" (326b2–4; emphasis added). Hermias's limited capacity for philosophy may prove a critical hindrance to the effectiveness of the plan Plato proposes in Letter Six.

Protecting the Philosophers

The procedures Plato puts in place to deal with possible threats to the friendship between his students and Hermias in Letter Six make manifest his basic strategy: Plato will try to manage their joint affairs himself, directly and indirectly, as much as possible. The centerpiece of this strategy is Plato's injunction that his three addressees collectively "use" or "consult" this very letter "as a compact and sovereign law, which is just" (323c6–d1). In the event of a prospective breach of the friendship, Plato directs the offended parties to send a "letter of accusation" to him and his associates in Athens; in response, Plato will send "speeches" that he claims will be able to restore the damaged partnership "by justice and by awe"—unless, that is, "the dissolution happens to have been great" (323b2–c1). As lawgiver for this community of three, then, Plato intends to be, if not quite present, at least available to his subjects as an arbitrator for the settling of disputes.

Consider how different this is from the Platonic Dion's attempt, in Letter Eight, to set up a ruling triumvirate in Syracuse: Dion there failed to recognize the importance of the lawgiver who would establish the regime, and gave the task of establishing the triple-kingship to the very Syracusans over whom the kings would subsequently rule. Moreover, Dion's nominations to the kingship were the leaders of parties at present engaged in fierce and open hostilities. Plato, in attempting to bring together three men much less hatefully disposed to one another, still finds it crucially necessary not only to establish protocols for preventing or repairing rifts between the parties, but even to remain himself active as the overseeing and adjudicating legislator. As Plato says in Letter Eleven, a founder is gravely mistaken who supposes that, "by the giving of any laws whatsoever, a city would ever be well established without the existence of some sovereign authority caring for the daily regimen" or "arbitration" (*diatēs*) in the city (359a2–7). Even the description of the cosmic deity with which Letter Six concludes seems to reflect this necessity. For that god is said not only to be the "leader of all the things that are and the things that will be," but also "*sovereign father of* the leader and cause" (323d2–4; emphasis added). The perfect legislator must not only set down the established order and set its activity in motion, but must also remain as a sovereign authority or "lord" (*kurion*) over the order he has created.

The parallel between the attempt to legislate the triple-friendship in Letter Six and the proposal of a triple-kingship in Letter Eight is compelling. But we must stress yet again that the arrangement of Letter Six is not presented as a proposal for political rule. Plato never suggests that the bond to be formed here will provide Hermias with any specifically political advantage, despite Plato's claim that friendship with Erastus and Coriscus will provide him with the greatest available increase in power "in all things." We are impelled to guess that this "power" will consist in or derive from the apprehension through philosophy of the cosmic deity. Unlike the complementary suggestions of Letters Seven (that firm friendship is the key to political achievement) and Ten (that philosophy is nothing but the firmness of character requisite for such friendship), Letter Six indicates that the friendship produced by communal philosophizing produces its own, nonpolitical, mystical-philosophic benefits. And this, of course, accords with the depiction of Erastus and Coriscus as artless theoreticians, lost in their arcane "wisdom of the Forms," and hence defenseless against the "wicked and unjust" of the world. Indeed, if the benefit to Hermias of this arrangement is left rather vague, Plato specifies the good he is seeking for Erastus and Coriscus with notable clarity: his goal is to find a safe haven for his longtime pupils, where they can attend to "the true wisdom" in proper measure, without being hectored by "the wicked and unjust" into spending inordinate time cultivating "the human and compulsory" wisdom.

This feature of Letter Six—the *preference* of Erastus and Coriscus to spend their time in contemplation—casts Letter Five in a new and different light. In Letter Five (where philosophy was not mentioned) the only justifications given for Plato's failure to serve as political adviser to the Athenians were the incapacity of the demos to recognize and to heed sage counsel and its propensity to mistreat the counselor. Without for a moment gainsaying the probable truth of that circumstance, we see in Letter Six (where philosophy *is* mentioned) an alternative or additional explanation: on account of his dedication to transpolitical, cosmic, and divine studies, the philosopher does not *wish* to spend time in, or even think about, the practical requirements of political activity. Now, the content of Letter Five itself—its affirmation that students of Platonic philosophy may be useful political counselors—suggests that the ineptitude of Erastus and Coriscus in Letter Six may be overstated. Letter Six would then not so much deviate from Letter Five as complement it: it is not that Plato and his pupils *cannot* serve as political counselors; it is that they would *rather* not. And we may now add that there are some indications in Letter Six, too, to that effect. The concern is not that Erastus and Coriscus should be compelled to attend to the "human and compulsory" wisdom *at all*, but only "more than they *need* to" (emphasis added). This implies that there has been *some* need for them to seek this wisdom already. Moreover, Plato's own recognition in this letter that "the human is not altogether steadfast" involves some glimmer, at least, of "human wisdom." And it is this insight into human nature that impels Plato to an act of lawgiving—in that he calls on his addressees to treat this letter as a "sovereign law"—perhaps the highest political activity, or at least the political activity requiring the most extensive and profound grasp of "human wisdom."

Obviously, Letter Six does not constitute a "real" act of lawgiving, and not only because the letter as a whole is likely a fiction. To have access to this letter's real significance as a piece of Platonic writing, we must appreciate its allegorical character. Plato here pretends to attempt, by an act of lawgiving, to form an alliance between political power (Hermias) and philosophy (Plato's two students). Plato's purpose in so doing is to safeguard philosophy, which is by nature beset by political dangers, and so in need of political protection. The arrangement hoped for in Letter Six is something like the philosopher's ideal situation: the friendship and protection of a powerful ruler under which the philosophers can be free to pursue lives of contemplation. Letter Six speaks allegorically of a regime in which the lawgiver has encouraged religious reverence for philosophy, and in which the rulers are by divine law and oaths bound to friendship with the philosophers.

The real lesson of the letter, however, is the demonstration of the practical infeasibility of this ideal arrangement. Let us begin by recalling why Plato's "legislation" of this friendship was required in the first place. If Plato cannot offer his associates as political counselors for the reasons we have outlined, his offer to Hermias must be based on the great benefit Plato promises is available in philosophy itself. But Hermias's capacity for philosophy is likely to be extremely limited, and therefore the friendship Plato wishes to set up will be necessarily and dangerously unstable. Now, Plato asserts that he will personally oversee the relationship's stability by hearing and adjudicating any case brought by one member against another. Here, however, the trouble intensifies. Most obviously, Plato's great distance from Atarneus will impede his ability to respond nimbly and effectively to problems on the ground. He must remain at a distance because his real business is at Athens: his journeys to Syracuse are the exception in the *Letters*; as a rule, he declines invitations to travel for political purposes. The philosopher-legislator is, to say the least, unlikely to be present to oversee the regime he has founded.

Perhaps this explains why Plato delegates responsibility for interpreting his legislation to his trio of subjects. In instructing them to consult the letter as their law, Plato tells the three of them that they must read this letter, "most of all as a group, but otherwise in twos—in common as often as, within [their] power, [they] are able . . ., swearing with seriousness that is not unmusical, and at the same time, with the playfulness that is a sister of seriousness" (323c6–d1). This encouragement to playful musicality in swearing to make use of Letter Six as a "just" and "sovereign law," this liberation from and caution against unqualified "seriousness" or rigidity, indicates that Plato's letter—which he claims to have written with divine inspiration—is to be approached rather as one would approach a poem, a product of the Muses. Yet the procedure mandated by this "legislation" includes a critical safeguard against harmful misinterpretation: the exceedingly small community founded by this compact, the tiny readership to which Plato intends to restrict this piece of writing, is one in which the philosophers outnumber the nonphilosophers. Thus Plato's insistence that the letter be read "most of all as a group, but otherwise in twos" ensures that the "sovereign law" is always interpreted in the presence of at least one of the philosophers. Erastus and Coriscus may read the letter in the absence of Hermias, but Hermias is never to read it without at least one of those two present.

It is significant that there is no question of Hermias being *overpowered* by the philosophers on account of their greater numbers. The arrangement of Letter Six does nothing to change the fact that, as far as might is concerned, the philosopher must be at the mercy of the ruler. Even the legislator Plato is bound by this necessity. His plan to induce an offending party to fall in line "by justice and by awe" is reminiscent of his counsel to the Syracusans in Letter Seven to compel the intransigent "to be subject to the laws by a means of a pair of compulsions, awe and fear" (337a3–5). But Plato cannot compel by means of fear because he can muster no threat of force against the powerful Hermias. The philosopher must operate through persuasion, and Plato tries to take advantage of the philosophers' majority in this community to keep Hermias persuaded of an appropriate interpretation of Letter Six. This will be all the more important given the likelihood that Hermias will encounter frustration with the pursuit of philosophy to which he is being directed, an eventuality that Plato explicitly refuses to discuss (323c2–3). But when we consider the broader meaning of Letter Six, we must realize that its solution to the philosopher's need for protection is inappropriate in any real circumstances, since the philosophers must always constitute a tiny minority of the political community.

Letter Six thus indicates the inadequacy of its own strategy for defending philosophy. In doing so, however, it brings our attention to the key difficulties to which Plato's actual strategy must attend. To see this, we must first expand our view of Letter Six's relationship to the other letters, in which Plato is compelled to speak more seriously to the issue he treats only allegorically in Letter Six. Letter Six is the first in the *Letters* to be addressed to more than one recipient, a feature it shares only with its immediate sequels, Letters Seven and Eight. But whereas Letter Six restricts its readership to a small community unnaturally populated by a majority of philosophers, Letter Seven is effectively an "open" letter. And as we have already seen, Plato's activity in Syracuse generally, and above all his promotion of the doctrine of philosophic rule, was largely in service of the reputation of philosophy for the sake of his philosophic friends (consider 347e6–7). The fact that Letter Six sketches a strategy for defending philosophy that is both generally impracticable and incompatible with the doctrine of philosophic rule (because it reflects the disinclination of philosophers to be involved in politics), helps us to see how some of that doctrine's features are necessary responses (as well as pointers) to the real circumstances in which philosophy finds itself.

For example, Plato avoids arousing Hermias's suspicion of Erastus and Coriscus by presenting them as virtually devoid of political acuity, but this means that Plato can offer nothing more to the ruler than an unlikely promise of philosophic enlightenment. Such a strategy might be viable if there could always be a philosopher on hand to attend personally to the concerns and frustrations that will develop over the course of the ruler's studies, to assuage any doubts or fears that the promised philosophic enlightenment may never be achieved. In practice, however, Plato cannot get away with presenting the philosopher as useless to the political community as such. The doctrine of philosophic rule solves this problem by presenting the philosopher as the possessor of transformative political wisdom, albeit at the cost of distorting the real subject matter with which philosophy, as an ongoing critical activity, is essentially concerned. But then, how is Plato to absolve the philosopher of the charge he brings up in Letter Five, that the philosopher fails to discharge the obligation he has to employ his political wisdom in and for his fatherland (cf. 358a2–4)? Letter Six stresses that philosophers, unable to defend themselves by force (or "fear"), must instead make their defense in terms of justice—compulsion "by justice and by awe" rather than "awe and fear." The success of the doctrine of philosophic rule depends on Plato's ability to establish the philosopher's perfect justice and to inspire awe or reverence for philosophy.

The presentation of philosophy in Letter Six, then, serves a number of purposes. As a piece of writing addressed to multiple recipients, including philosophers and rulers, seeking protection for philosophy by bringing these readers into a harmonious partnership, this letter serves as an introduction to the central political challenge of Plato's political-philosophic writings. It allows us to see why the doctrine of philosophic rule must distort the nature of philosophy by giving it a truncated presentation. Put another way, Letter Six helps us begin to see why the doctrine of philosophic rule is necessarily mythical. For Letter Six indicates that true philosophic friendship emerges from the shared possession of wisdom concerning the "cause" and "leader of all the things that are and the things that will be," a kind of sharing and hence friendship that do not help to solve the political problem concerning the need for trust that turned Plato away from politics in the first place. Once we recognize, on the basis of Letter Six, the reasons for the inadequacy of philosophic friendship to this purpose, we can better see, even in Letter Seven, how Plato calls into question the political efficacy of philosophy. Recall that Plato gave Darius's and the Athenians' building of their respective empires as examples to persuade Dionysius that the success of political undertakings depends on one's possession of faithful friends, concluding that "there is no greater sign of virtue and vice than this, whether one is bereft of such men or not" (332c4–6). Yet, when we consider these empires and their origins, it comes to seem rather doubtful whether their histories give us reason to think that *philosophy* must be the ground of politically useful friendships.

But if Letter Six gets us closer to an undistorted view of philosophy, it takes only the first steps in that direction. This is not only because Plato here dresses up philosophy in mystical and religious garb—as a matter of fact, the further we get from the "Dionean" distortion of philosophy in Letter Seven with its denial that philosophy is a distinctive activity of critical questioning, the more Plato stresses such garb. The presentation of philosophy in Letter Six is especially problematic in that it conceals how enormously difficult an activity genuine philosophizing is. From Letter Six, one might infer that one need only give philosophy one's best effort in order to enjoy its fruits. The two most famous and elaborate presentations of philosophy in the *Letters*, to which we will turn next, make clear that this is far from the case.

II

The Philosophic Riddles of Letter Two

Though one might well argue that the theme of philosophy permeates the *Letters* from its opening words, the first explicit reference to and discussion of philosophy occurs in Letter Two. It is noteworthy that the first appearance of the word comes in an expression of Plato's concern for the reputation of philosophy, together with a defense of its piety; indeed, once he has concluded his discussion of how he and Dionysius can together best serve the pious *cause* of philosophy, Plato leaves off using the word "philosophy" altogether until the end of Letter Six. And yet it is just *after* the midway point of Letter Two, at which the word "philosophy" abruptly disappears from the text, that Plato presents a tantalizingly enigmatic discussion of the highest themes of his philosophic education. We begin, then, with that enigmatic discussion, as we turn next to our exploration of the actively critical and theoretical dimension of philosophy as presented in Plato's *Letters*.

The second half of Letter Two begins with an abrupt change of subject. Plato turns from the question of whether or under what general terms he and Dionysius should carry on their philosophic course of study as teacher and student to a rather specific question that has arisen for Dionysius in his studies: "The little sphere is not in the correct condition," Plato suddenly and mysteriously declares; "Archedemus will clarify this for you when he comes" (312d2–3). This is the first indication in the *Letters* of what Plato's education of the tyrant Dionysius may have contained. We are here given to understand that the instruction included some geometrical or astronomical subject, an instruction that continues with the help of their go-between, Archedemus. That an education of this kind might be valuable to a ruler is certainly conceivable; the example of Anaxagoras and Pericles, listed among many others earlier in the letter (311a5–6), provides a useful starting point for our thinking about the reciprocal benefits that such an education might bring. By the brief mention of the "little sphere," then, we are made to think of an education in the mathematical necessities underlying reality as we know it, which has the power of liberating the student from superstition by suggesting the possibility of a comprehensive causal account of the cosmos that is naturalistic or does not have recourse to suprarational divinities or other supernatural elements.

We immediately learn, however, that, whatever the subject of the "little sphere," it is not the matter to which Plato accords the highest rank. He turns next to a matter still "more honored and more divine," in which it seems that the go-between Archedemus is also well versed. Plato refers to this more honored and divine subject matter as "the nature of the first," and reveals now that Dionysius had been prompted to send Archedemus to Plato in the first place because Dionysius was perplexed and seeking greater clarity on this point (312d3–7). It is Plato's response—the only place in any extant writing in which Plato endeavors directly to explain to his reader the meaning of his philosophy—that makes Letter Two so important for us in our attempt to find a correction to the distorted presentation of Platonic philosophy seized upon by Dion and those like him. But Plato refuses to clarify the matter openly in this letter. He says that he must "explain" his answer "through enigmas" or "riddles" (*ainigmōn*) so that any unintended reader of the letter will not be able to understand its contents (312d7–e1). Hence, we as readers are lifted momentarily out of the drama of the letter—or rather, we become a part of it—by the realization that we ourselves are just such unintended recipients as Plato describes. His presentation here of "the nature of the first" has been conveyed in such a way as to prevent precisely us from understanding it. Inevitably, and perhaps by design, the very fact that Plato says he is hiding his meaning only heightens the reader's curiosity; eager Platonists have hardly been discouraged from seeking here some communication, some clarification that comes directly from the mouth of Plato and not through his mouthpieces, which might confirm their various interpretations of the philosophic riddles of the dialogues. Indeed, Platonic interpreters over the millennia have espoused such a great variety of unprovable hypotheses regarding the identity of Plato's "king of all things" as should make us wary of offering yet another attempt at deciphering the enigmas. We will do best to stick closely to what is clear from the text and not to presume the possibility of matching the account here in Letter Two to anything else known or supposed about Plato's thought.

Plato's enigmatic account of "the nature of the first" refers to "the king of all things," "a second," and "a third" as comprising what seems to be a three-part hierarchical cosmic ordering structure (312e1–4). All that is said about the latter two principles is that the "second things are around a second, and the third things around a third." While there is a suggestion, then, of a tripartition of all existing beings, the cleanness of that partition is undermined by Plato's saying that "*all* things," not just the "first" ones, "are around the king of all things" (312e1–2; emphasis added). Whatever the essential character and place of the second and third in this account, they are certainly subordinate in existence and power to the "king." What is more, "all things are for the sake of him," and that is "responsible for" or the "cause of" "all the noble things." In this account, then, the totality of the cosmic whole in which we find ourselves (i.e., "all things") is oriented by or toward a universal ruler; by describing this ruler as a "king," Plato invites Dionysius, as well as us, to understand that "all things" are governed by a wise and beneficent ruler, by a king as opposed to a tyrant. Most important of all is the single reference Plato makes to any particular class of beings: the "noble" or "beautiful" things are explicitly said to have been caused by the highest and "first" entity in the cosmos. This portrayal of the cosmos, then, is one in which the entity to which every other being owes its existence or its purpose—either directly or, as it seems, mediately, through the "second" and "third"—is distinguished above all by its special, causal relationship to the beautiful or noble things. It is a cosmos in which the wellspring of beauty, that element of human experience that most powerfully announces the existence of a spiritual depth in the world to which our own souls are attuned, is to be found at the most exalted level of a natural, universal hierarchy of principles or causes. Beauty, in this account, is not in the eye of the beholder, but has objective reality beyond any merely human vantage point; beauty is no epiphenomenal outgrowth of a fundamentally material or subhuman organic process, but belongs to the fundamental dimension of reality. In short, Plato here describes a world in which our most profound longing to be at home in the whole is fundamentally satisfied.

Up to this point, the presentation of philosophy in Letter Two accords rather well with what we have seen in Letter Six. The implicit promise in this cryptic statement on "the nature of the first" is akin to what Plato suggests to Hermias in saying that, by philosophizing, he can come to know god, a "sovereign father of the leader and cause," insofar as this knowledge is within the grasp of "happy human beings." But there is a question as to the precise extent of the "riddles" or "enigmas" here presented concerning "the nature of the first." It is perhaps likely to be the reader's first impression, and at any rate it is least troubling to assume or to conclude, that the enigmas consist only in the terse, Delphic statements on the "king," "second," and "third" we have already discussed. Perhaps, however, those statements serve only to provide the setting for the more substantial—though occasionally just as cryptic—discussion that follows, of the human soul's quest to learn about the triumvirate of governing principles Plato has just described. Plato's teaching on "the nature of the first" would then refer to, or rest upon, or at least include, a fundamental understanding of *human* nature, of the soul's characteristic hopes and longings regarding the whole of which it is a part. It may be noted that every other use of a word related to *phusis* ("nature") in Letter Two refers in one manner or another to specifically *human* nature. "Human wisdom," wisdom about the human, plays a greater role in Platonic philosophy than is suggested in Letter Six.

Plato's description of the human quest to learn about the governing or ordering cosmic principles he has so cryptically described, while hardly straightforward, is nonetheless dramatic and poignant. The human soul seeks this understanding not in any dispassionate or disinterested way, but rather "reaches out" or "yearns" to learn about these cosmic principles by "looking to the things akin to itself" (312e3–5). This amounts to a claim about the natural starting point or disposition of the human soul in its quest for wisdom about the first principles of the order in which it finds itself. The soul yearns to see *itself* reflected in some way at the highest or deepest level of reality; it wishes to confirm that the world the human soul experiences is in fact the world as such; the human soul needs to know that its own highest concerns and ideas are, or at least *can* be, *the* concerns and ideas as recognized by the highest cosmic power. Somehow, however, the human soul determines that nothing akin to it could ever be "sufficient" to occupy this highest place in the cosmic order (312e5–313a1). Perhaps the difficulty lies in the attempt to attribute to a fundamentally caused being, such as the human soul, the ultimate or first cause of reality as we know it. In any case, the problem quickly deepens after this, for Plato immediately and enigmatically adds, "Indeed, about the king and the things of which I spoke, there is no such thing" (313a1–2). The status of the hospitable cosmos Plato has only just sketched is suddenly thrown into uncertainty. Is there a known cosmic king or not? Is the first cause of the whole we know identifiable, or in our searching for it do we merely gaze into unfathomable depths?

Plato says that the soul comes next to a questioning as to what indeed, if it is not the humanoid cosmic king, is the character of the originating or ordering principle of the whole as we know it: "Well then, but what sort of thing?" (313a3). Plato gives pointed emphasis to this question by here referring to Dionysius as "child of Dionysius and Doris" in explaining that one can never hit upon the truth if one has not been relieved of "the labor pains coming to be in the soul" about it—pains that he says are "responsible for all evils" (313a3–6). It seems likely, then, that it is in one way or another this question, or the "labor pains" regarding it—the painful challenge of deducing and affirming, from one's own observations and premises, a difficult truth—with which Dionysius is now struggling and on account of which he has reached out to Plato for philosophic guidance. But, as we now learn, this crisis has developed as something of a delayed reaction to what was Plato's original discussion with Dionysius about these matters. That first discussion, which had taken place while Plato was in Syracuse, had left the tyrant underwhelmed. He had claimed to have already "thought of this" and that it was his own "discovery." It has evidently been only since then that Dionysius has come to be troubled by what Plato had said to him about "the nature of the first" (313a6–b1).

Plato's description of the manner in which Dionysius's initial reaction gave way to subsequent doubt provides some clarification of what exactly it was that Dionysius claimed already to have discovered. Wrongly supposing that he had "firmly" grasped the "demonstrations" or "proofs" regarding "the nature of the first," Dionysius failed to "tie them down," so that now, as Plato explains, they "dart about . . . around the imagined thing, but there is no such thing" (313b6–c1). Plato's need to repeat the phrase "there is no such thing" points to Dionysius's mistake: his thinking is still guided by his hopes concerning the character of the cosmic "king," which he believes he sees or "imagines" giving order to the whole. He had initially been underwhelmed with Plato's description of a first cause, but only more recently has come to feel the sting of doubt or uncertainty as to its essence or fathomability. Dionysius has written to Plato because he now sees—after having entertained some rival accounts, theories, or modes of inquiry (312c3)—that no one but Plato points in the direction of worthy answers to the most urgent fundamental questions. Plato's offer to help Dionysius through his difficulty is grounded in his insistence that the tyrant is only going through the same experience that *everyone* has upon beginning his studies with Plato (313c1–5). And so it is with an apparent promise to relieve Dionysius of his confusion and dismay through education that Plato claims he can at last answer conclusively the question that prompted Dionysius to write to him in the first place: the question of how the two men should be disposed toward one another (313c5–7).

This is the third and final time in Letter Two that Plato refers to the reason Dionysius wrote him the letter to which Letter Two is a response. This third indication is similar to the first, though not identical. In both cases, Plato speaks of how the two men are to deal with one another; in the first case, one could think it was a question of how each one would act most prudently toward the other (312b2–3); in the last, Plato appears to speak in terms of a necessity or obligation that governs the two of them as a pair. Accordingly: in the first case, Plato left it open whether Dionysius would or should pursue his education under him, and advanced considerations regarding the manner in which each of them would be benefited or harmed by honors conferred or withheld on each side; now, by contrast, he points the way unambiguously toward Dionysius's prospective advancement along the path toward initiation into the truths of Platonic philosophy. We can say that this shift is explained by the intervention of the second reference to the reason for Dionysius's writing (312d3–7), in which we learn that what prompted Dionysius was at once his concern for how the two of them must be disposed toward one another *and* his perplexity regarding "the nature of the first." If this letter should inspire Dionysius to believe that Plato can help him resolve his philosophic problem, Plato will be in a better position to dictate the future terms of their relationship and thereby to manage the problems he identified in the letter's first half.

In this, too, Letter Two corroborates what we had gathered from Letter Six. Philosophy—that is, *true* philosophy, Platonic philosophy as opposed to the alternatives in which Dionysius has been dabbling—can transform a relationship based merely on contingent exchange of benefits into one in which the parties genuinely share some stable common ground. It is to participation in a bond of this latter kind that Plato invites Dionysius. If, Plato proposes, Dionysius should continue his process of "testing" and "comparing" the various accounts to which he has been and continues to be exposed, then, "if the test is true," Plato's teaching will take root in him and naturally grow, making Dionysius "an intimate" both to the teachings and to Plato's unspecified "us" (313c7–d3). The Platonic education is thus presented as the true education, as the education by nature. Those who partake of this education gain an intimate familiarity with one another, a bond of kinship, rooted in their shared experience of fulfillment through the development of true understanding within themselves, which derives its stability from the stability of the fixed natural necessity revealed and grasped through common investigation.

Unlike the account in Letter Six, however, it is clear from what Plato says in this letter that there are considerable obstacles to joining in such a bond. The philosophic activity of investigation into the first principles of nature, as it turns out, is necessarily a painful one on account of its requirement that one challenge one's most stubborn hopes and beliefs. Moreover, as opposed to the promise of Letter Six that Hermias and the others would, by devoting themselves to philosophy, come to know the great, providential cosmic deity, Plato here leaves it much less clear whether such a being exists. The path he urges Dionysius to follow in the passage succeeding the enigmas is therefore a long and uncertain one, and Plato must do what he can to make it seem less daunting. He recommends that the two of them continue to discuss Dionysius's perplexities (*aporiai*) through letters ferried back and forth by Archedemus. After "two or three" such exchanges, Plato suggests, *if* Dionysius can "test" Plato's writings adequately, the matters perplexing him should begin to change their aspect substantially (313d4–e2). Plato further heightens Dionysius's anticipation of immanently achieving resolution and clarity by saying that the "cargo" being transported by Archedemus is "nobler and dearer to the gods" than anything he will ever carry (313e3–314a1).

Clearly, however, there is no guarantee that Dionysius will in fact succeed in achieving this resolution in the "two or three" exchanges Plato proposes as a kind of minimum. *Everyone*, Plato has already said, encounters such problems as Dionysius is now facing when embarking on an education in Platonic philosophy; "almost no one has few" problems (313c2–5). It is apparently not common, without considerable training at least, to be able to "test" Plato's correspondences in the requisite way. As Plato explains, some have been hearing such things from him for as many as *thirty years*—people who, by any ordinary measure, are intelligent, discerning students—who only now, at their advanced age, are experiencing the shift in perspective Plato unrealistically proposed might come to Dionysius on the basis of "two or three" more letters (314a8–b5). It seems we must acknowledge the significant possibility that, if Dionysius decides to continue as a student of Plato in the manner Plato recommends—including by making a public display of honoring Plato and his philosophy (312b6–d1)—he may well remain in a kind of intellectual limbo of partial understanding for the rest of his life. A great deal hinges upon the enigmatic process of "testing," which Plato has set out as the means, or obstacle, to Dionysius's enlightenment.

The Question of Philosophic Writing in Letter Two

The ambiguity regarding the length and difficulty of the Platonic education standing between Dionysius and the clarity he seeks is an instance of one of Letter Two's most puzzling themes: the letter is highly paradoxical regarding Plato's pedagogical approach in general. The most glaring example of this paradox concerns the question whether Letter Two actually contains Plato's understanding of "the nature of the first" at all. On one hand, Plato has explicitly said that he has written the letter in such a way that its contents would be indecipherable without the oral key, or explanation, to be supplied by its original carrier, Archedemus (312d4–e1). On the other hand, once he has gone through his enigmatic account and directed Dionysius as to how they should proceed, he counsels the tyrant to "beware . . . lest these things ever be exposed to uneducated human beings" (314a1–2), and again, to "beware in examining these things lest you come someday to regret their having been unworthily exposed now" (314b5–7). Dramatically, Plato at last tells Dionysius that he should read the letter "many times" and then "burn it up" (314c5–6). But what could be the great danger in "exposing" the contents of this letter to others if it has intentionally been written in such a way as to make it indecipherable to anyone but Dionysius (with Archedemus's help)?

We may begin our approach to this question by taking note of the various curious effects of Plato's injunction to burn the letter. Most immediately, it draws our attention again to the fact that the letter is now in *our* possession, which tells us that Plato's directive must have gone unheeded. Indeed, it is unsurprising that Dionysius would have wanted to keep a copy. The very fact that Plato ostensibly wants the letter burned intensifies the reader's curiosity—a curiosity that has already been stoked by Plato's indication that it is "precious cargo" to be carefully protected, that it is "dear to the gods" and thus promises something approaching divine revelation. Perhaps, then, Plato had no expectation that the letter would be burned; perhaps his telling Dionysius to do so was only the first step in a long-term strategy to intrigue him, arouse his hopes, and draw him into the decades-long challenge of contemplating the Platonic mysteries. All of this points cohesively and neatly to the suggestion that Letter Two *does not* contain a genuine attempt on Plato's part to communicate his understanding of "the nature of the first." His expressions of concern about the guarding of the letter would then be only lures intended to pique Dionysius's interest. Let us state this as a provisional interpretive hypothesis about Letter Two: Plato's apparent attempt to educate Dionysius in this letter is merely apparent, not a true example of Platonic pedagogy but rather of the Platonic rhetoric by means of which Plato attracts potential long-term students and followers.

This hypothesis receives support from what Plato says more generally about writing in Letter Two. In warning Dionysius to "beware in examining these things" of "exposing" them to others in a way he might later consider unworthy, he advises that it is better "to learn by heart" than to write things down, "for it is *not possible* for things written not to be exposed" (314b7–c1; emphasis added). Plato's earlier poetic flourish, then, in which he explained that his account of "the nature of the first" must be written in riddles *in case* something should happen to the letter "in the folds of sea or earth" (312d8), understated his evaluation of the likelihood of that possibility. Plato *always* assumed his writings would be exposed to people apart from his intended readers; he would therefore never commit anything to writing if he earnestly wished to keep it a secret. The urgency of Plato's desire for this letter to be burned, then, is certainly feigned. But this implies that Plato deliberately writes Letter Two in such a way as to deceive Dionysius. For if the letter only *pretends* to contain the wisdom and understanding Dionysius seeks, why write it at all? Why not just send Archedemus to serve as Platonic tutor to the tyrant? Moreover, if Plato is willing to be deceptive regarding his willingness to convey his teaching on these matters, how are we to know whether it was *ever* his intention to educate Dionysius?

Indeed, it is not only Plato's attempt to educate Dionysius through his writings that comes into question here; what Plato says about writing in Letter Two has implications that reach far beyond Letter Two itself: "I have never written anything at all about these things," Plato famously declares, apparently referring to "the nature of the first," "nor are there written works of Plato, nor will there be any at all, but those now spoken of are of a Socrates become beautiful and new" (314c1–4). Plato indeed claims that *none* of the writings he has produced—he leaves us no room to exclude either the *Letters* in general or Letter Two in particular from this claim—contain genuine expressions of his own thought on the highest philosophic questions. Letter Two thus comes to sight as a model of Plato's manner of writing in general. Plato's writings, which he intended for broad dissemination and hence for many readers besides those to whom he was keenest to communicate, must have been composed in such a way as to be indecipherable on their own. The correct interpretation of Plato's writings requires the guided instruction of someone like Archedemus, who already understands Plato's meaning. Moreover, the statements of the Platonic Socrates must above all not be mistaken for Plato's own thoughts.

Surely Plato must have known that the majority of his readers would assume the contrary of all this: that the Platonic Socrates was merely a mouthpiece for Plato himself, and that the Platonic dialogues contain a full education in Platonic philosophy. Just as Plato deliberately deceives Dionysius by feigning willingness to educate the tyrant, then, he also deliberately misrepresents himself through his dialogues, misleading his readers into believing that he means to convey to them his genuine understanding. Indeed, the dialogues contain equally misleading portrayals of *Socrates*; Plato has effectively admitted that the Socrates of the dialogues, to whom those dialogues "belong," is in some significant part a Platonic fiction. In light of Plato's statements on writing in Letter Two, then, we have been led to a dramatic broadening of our provisional interpretive hypothesis: Plato's feigned willingness to educate Dionysius in that letter is only one instance of a deceptive appearance belonging to *all* his writings. The perplexity we encountered as to why Plato would have bothered to write and send Letter Two to Dionysius is therefore only a special case of a much broader perplexity to which these passages have given rise. For we must now consider the question, Why did Plato write the *dialogues* at all? Why devote his whole literary career, the greater part of his life, to the creation and elevation of this fictive "Socrates," based on a historical Socrates who was so manifestly important to Plato himself, and yet a fictive character from whom Plato now distances himself most surprisingly? For Plato's attribution of the dialogues to his beautified Socrates is also his denial that those same works are "of Plato."

If we are to make sense of Plato's immense dedication to the production of his literary oeuvre and to its hero, the Platonic Socrates, we will have to refine our provisional hypothesis that Plato's writings are not genuinely meant as didactic guides to his true thought on the greatest matters. Let us continue to take Letter Two as our model. Plato makes it clear in this letter that he does not want to "expose" his thought regarding "the nature of the first" indiscriminately. But why not? Plato follows his warning to Dionysius against exposing the contents of the letter by explaining the impression his written teachings make on two distinct audiences: for "the many," there are "almost no more ridiculous things to be heard than these," whereas for "those of good natures," there are none "more amazing and more inspired" (314a2–5). The majority of people will be derisive of the Platonic account contained in this letter. Is it against this derision, then, that Plato wishes to guard? That cannot be quite right: since Plato believes that it is impossible for things written not to be exposed (and therefore wrote about "the nature of the first" in Letter Two only in "riddles" or "enigmas"), we can be sure that he *expected* this letter to be read and received with precisely the kind of derision he describes. This helps to clarify for us that it is not Plato's *actual* view of "the nature of the first" that will incur the ridicule of the many, but the *riddle* he poses about "the nature of the first" in this letter.

Our analysis deepens when we recognize that the other group of readers Plato mentions, "those of good natures," themselves face a considerable interpretive challenge in studying Plato's writings. For they, like the many, will not be presented straightforwardly with Plato's view—Plato never stated that view frankly in writing—but with his riddle concerning that view. To say that the readers with good natures are "amazed" and "inspired" by these passages is not yet to say that they have correctly understood them—in fact, it would seem that *both* "the many" *and* "the good-natured" belong to the "uneducated" readers with whom Plato's warning to Dionysius not to expose the contents of the letter is concerned. Plato has already said that everyone, upon first hearing him, is in the same state of perplexity as Dionysius, "and though one has more problems and another has fewer, they are rid of them only with difficulty—and almost no one has few" (313c2–5). The path that lies ahead *even* for those with "good natures" (whoever they are) is very long. "Being spoken often and for many years," says Plato, these Platonic speeches "are with difficulty, like gold, purified with much diligent activity" (314a5-7). Plato's written presentation of his philosophic view is designed to be relatively opaque to most readers; its enigmatic contents will strike most as ridiculous and others as awesome. But this is not to say that they must *remain* opaque. Contained within these riddles somehow is the "gold" of Plato's true view. The misleading impressions with which that truth is mixed must be cleared away by reflecting upon Plato's formulations diligently over a long period of time.

That Dionysius was originally among "the many" in his reaction to Platonic philosophy is clear from the dismissive manner in which he first responded to it (313a6-b1). But Plato continues to invite him to the prolonged study that could ultimately produce genuine understanding in the tyrant. Plato does not insist, then, that it is only "those of good natures" who will succeed in being educated by him in the long run. At any rate, there is something suspect about those "old" human beings, of whom there are "plenty," who have just now begun fundamentally to change their views after more than three decades of listening to Plato. For Plato does not quite say that these have come to see the truth or that they are philosophers, and their being so numerous speaks against the likelihood of their being genuinely wise. For that matter, it must be said in fairness that not even Erastus and Coriscus in Letter Six are called philosophers by Plato. Our attention is drawn, rather, to an extremely small group that Plato nearly passes over altogether. "*Almost* no one has few" problems in following through the Platonic education; but this means that there are some who, although their problems are great and their "labor pains" surely intense, nonetheless move through the key developments of the Platonic education in a relatively short time—fewer, we may imagine, than thirty years.

We have now a reasonable resolution to the paradox concerning Platonic education and writing in Letter Two. The urgency with which Plato warns Dionysius against exposing the contents of this letter contains a kind of comical irony. For he *knows* his writing will be exposed, and has taken measures to ensure that what he wishes to conceal from the many about his genuine view is not visible on the page. He has written in such a way as to seem ridiculous to some and inspired to others, but he will be transparent to no one. This does not mean, however, that this writing does not contain a genuine Platonic education at all. It must be considered carefully and at great length, but a certain very few readers may eventually come to see what within it constitutes real Platonic wisdom.

There is every reason to think, then, that this is true also of the dialogues featuring the Platonic Socrates, for it is even clearer in their case than in the *Letters* that Plato intended for them to be published and broadly distributed. What Letter Two helps us to see is that Plato may have been most interested in educating a small contingent of readers other than the ones to whom his writings are obviously addressed.

As for Dionysius, we have already noted how the whole conceit of this letter communicates to us his failure to heed Plato's caution: the letter has not been burned. As it turns out, however, we have evidence of a further transgression to this effect on Dionysius's part. For the sister passage to the one we have been considering, the philosophic digression of Letter Seven, is motivated by Plato's need to respond to rumors that Dionysius has himself produced a text that he claims contains the full Platonic understanding of philosophy. The philosophic digression of Letter Seven, then, responds to the failure of Letter Two to contain or to control Dionysius's influence on the manner in which Platonic philosophy is promulgated. Taken together, these two most elaborate discussions of philosophy in the *Letters* provide a thorough treatment of the question Plato faced in presenting his philosophy to the world and to Dionysius in particular: How to handle the proliferation of misinterpretations of Platonic philosophy, which Plato not only knew would arise but even intended to stimulate?

As much as the discussions of philosophy in Letters Two and Seven are linked by their common purpose in dealing with the dangers of Plato's attempt to educate Dionysius, however, these passages will ultimately be found to complement each other even more profoundly in regard to their substantive teaching on the nature of Platonic philosophy itself. While the digression in Letter Seven appears to clarify some central problems of Platonic metaphysics much more fully than anything Plato says in Letter Two, it is only in Letter Two that Plato provides an honest acknowledgment of the "labor pains" brought about by the deepest philosophic questioning. Between Letter Two's indication of the *psychological* obstacles to the pursuit of Platonic philosophy and Letter Seven's discussion of the *technical* challenges of that same pursuit, we have as rich and full a discussion of the central problems of Platonic philosophy as Plato ever wrote. But we are still far from establishing the complementarity of these two passages, which might after all be taken to be incompatible or even contradictory. Let us prepare our examination of Letter Seven's philosophic digression, then, by examining its clearest echo of the philosophic passage in Letter Two—namely, Plato's statement in Letter Seven on the problem of philosophic writing. Having considered this clearest point of connection between Letters Two and Seven, we will be better positioned to take up a full interpretive analysis of Letter Seven's philosophic digression and to understand how that passage fits together with what we have just learned from Letter Two.

The Problem of Writing in Letter Seven

Letter Seven's philosophic digression comes about in the following way. Having concluded his "counsel to the intimates and comrades close to Dion," Plato opens the second half of the letter (and thus of the *Letters*) by addressing those readers who are "repeatedly asking" about why he went *yet again* to Syracuse—his third and final journey—and especially those who wonder whether the journey "came to pass at once appropriately and harmoniously" (330c6–7, 337e4–338a2). The story of Dionysius's renewed invitations and Plato's eventual decision to return is driven by the fact that, according to accounts reaching Plato from several sources, Dionysius was said at last to have come around to a genuine and ardent interest in philosophy (338b5–7, 339b2–4; d1–4). When eventually he arrived back in Syracuse, Plato's goal was to test the veracity of the reports that claimed Dionysius had "been kindled by philosophy as by a fire" (340b1–4). His means of ascertaining this, as he explains, was one particularly "fitting for tyrants, especially those filled with misunderstandings," as Dionysius was (340b4–7). The test is administered by laying out "the whole problem" of philosophy and all the "toil" it requires: the many difficult subjects of learning to be mastered, all the puzzles to be solved, and all of the discipline that is required to remain sharp in the pursuit of understanding. If the hearer "should really be a philosopher," he will turn his whole life toward this challenge; Dionysius, by contrast, dealt with his inability to follow the path of philosophy by pretending already to have mastered "the greatest things" through "hearsay from others" (340b7–341b3).

This test is well suited to tyrants because the hearer cannot blame the teacher for his own inability or unwillingness to strain himself along the path the speaker has laid out (341a3–7). Yet Plato's examination of Dionysius was not without further consequence. For Plato now reports—and here the philosophic digression really begins—that Dionysius is said to have later produced his own writing, based upon what he heard from Plato on that occasion, but presented it "as though it were his own," without attribution to Plato (341b3–5). It is to counteract the effect of such writings—whether the rumors about Dionysius's publication are true or false, Plato notes that "others have written about these same things" (341b5–6)—that Plato will now enter into a discussion of his philosophic views. For anyone who writes of the things Plato "takes seriously" and claims to know about them, he contends, are lacking in knowledge both of themselves and of "the problem" at issue (341b6–c4). Plato thus sets out to explain why *any* writing claiming to expound Plato's thought regarding the most serious philosophic questions must be dismissed as the writing of someone who has necessarily misunderstood Platonic philosophy.

Here we have the overarching interpretive puzzle of this whole portion of text. For it is surely strange that this so-called philosophic digression, which has garnered more attention than any other passage in the *Letters* on account of its unusually clear presentation of Platonic metaphysics and epistemology, should be introduced as an explanation of the reasons for which Plato would *never* attempt to clarify the deepest points of his philosophy in writing. If the discussion that follows here is not an attempt to clarify Plato's view of these matters, what is it?

The problem is helpfully illuminated by comparing the present passage to the parallel sections of Letter Two. There is here in Letter Seven an echo of Plato's statement from Letter Two to the effect that "there are no written works of Plato." But the restatement in this context moves in a slightly different direction. In Letter Two, Plato flattered Dionysius by insisting that this writing was for his eyes only and must not be "unworthily exposed" to "uneducated human beings." In Letter Seven, Plato's claim that there is not, "nor will there ever come to be," any writing about the things he "takes seriously" leads him instead to emphasize the total impossibility of communicating his knowledge of these things through speech of any kind: "It is in no way speakable as are the other subjects of learning, but rather, from the coming to be of much intercourse concerning the problem itself and living together, suddenly, as from a jumping fire, a light is kindled, and, having come to be in the soul, it straightaway nourishes itself" (341c5–d2). Could there ever have been any real hope for Dionysius, then, to come to an understanding of "the nature of the first" through any amount of correspondence with Plato? The presentation here makes it seem rather that philosophy is not so much *taught* as it is transmitted, somewhat mysteriously and even mystically, from one philosopher to the next through a process that can be encouraged by the arrangement of favorable circumstances but not totally controlled. In any case, there is little in this passage to suggest any hope that the "spark" of philosophy might have leapt from Plato to Dionysius across the Ionian Sea. Were it possible to communicate his understanding in this way, Plato suggests, he could have done nothing "nobler" than to produce the "great benefit for human beings" of "lead[ing] nature forth into the light for all" (314d6–e1).

The apparent difference between the statements in Letters Two and Seven, then, is as follows. Despite his paradoxical pleas for Dionysius to burn the letter lest it be exposed to the unworthy, Plato says in Letter Two that the "speeches" (including his writings) containing his ultimate teaching can only be understood by means of a long process of "purification," whereby the "gold" of his true meaning can be extracted. In Letter Seven, he explicitly claims that the most important things *cannot* be communicated through writing. But there are reasons to think that the statements in Letter Two are more to be believed. To begin with, Plato's denial of ever having written anything concerning the matters in question in Letter Two (314c1–4) contains a qualification not present in Letter Seven (341c4–5): the admission that there are writings *said* to be "of Plato" but belonging in truth to "a Socrates become beautiful and new." Admittedly, this qualification hardly amounts to more than a puzzle, which we have already identified and to which we will yet return more than once: if not simply to communicate his understanding of philosophy, why *did* Plato write the Socratic dialogues? But there is also a more straightforward piece of evidence in Letter Seven itself. Plato concludes the introduction to the philosophic digression by saying that he holds the attempt to communicate the things about which he is most serious not to be "good for human beings *unless for some few*—however many are themselves capable of finding them out through a small indication" (341e1–3; emphasis added). That is to say, there *is* a way of writing about the highest questions regarding nature—including, presumably, "the nature of the first"—but such a writing will only communicate its message successfully to supremely astute readers, who are extraordinarily rare and need only small, if crucial, help.

But the publication of such writings would not be good, according to Plato, for the vast majority of readers. These writings "would fill some" of them, "in no way harmoniously, with incorrect disdain, and others with a lofty and empty hope as though they had learned some august things" (341e3–342a1). To be sure, this is presented here as Plato's rationale for *refusing* to publish such writings as he is describing—and this, despite the facts that, as Plato boasts, "in being written or said by [Plato], these things would be said best" and that, "if they were written badly, it would pain [him] not least" (341d2–4). But the two reactions Plato says would be produced by erroneous interpretations of his writings intended for the few sharpest readers—the "incorrect disdain" and the "lofty and empty hope"—bear a striking resemblance to the two reactions of the "uneducated," which he described in Letter Two, to the speeches containing the hidden "gold" of his genuine teaching: "the many," he said, would find the writings "ridiculous," and "the good-natured" would find them "amazing" and "inspired." Viewed in the light of Letter Two, then, Plato's protestations in Letter Seven, to the effect that he could not and therefore did not attempt to write about the things he took "seriously," become an explanation of just how he *did* write about those very things. His writings are intended to convey their deepest meaning by "small indications" to those readers capable of profiting from such, despite the problematic effects these writings may have on the two types of readers bound to misunderstand.

The Argument against Writing from the Structure of Being

It is with this insight into the character of Platonic writing that we turn to the next section of the digression, in which Plato proposes "to speak at still greater length" about the things he takes seriously so that they might "be clearer once they have been stated" (342a1–3). He says he will present "a certain true speech," which "has often been said by [him] before," and which "opposes him who has dared to write of such things at all" (342a3–5). It must be said that this is not a promise to explain what Plato thinks about the things he takes seriously. Plato has said that no one possessing a full understanding of his thought—which would include, crucially, both self-knowledge and knowledge of "the problem" here in question—would attempt to present that thought in writing. What follows is to be *a* true argument against such writing, but he does not say it is *the* argument articulating the full Platonic understanding. Yet he has also promised that the latter might be "clearer" on the basis of what follows. We must be ready for that clarity to be available only on the basis of "a small indication."

The account Plato unfolds here is presented as a complete ontology—a scheme that purports to describe the correct classification and structure of all the beings or types of being that together make up existence—but gives special emphasis to the status and grounds of scientific knowledge (*epistēmē*). For "each of the beings" (342a7), says Plato, there are five things that can be said to be "of" it, that is, to pertain or belong to it. The first three are grouped together as the three things "through which," in the case of any given being, scientific knowledge about it comes to be: (1) name, (2) *logos* (i.e., "definition" or some other "account" given in rational speech), and (3) image—as we shall learn, an "image" of a given "being" is an instance of it, which we apprehend by means of sense perception and, crucially, which is subject to generation and corruption in the manner of all material beings (342b1–3, c1–2). Speaking generally, then, scientific knowledge of a being comes about through sense perception, as each of "the three" is essentially located "in sounds" (i.e., the words that make up the names and *logoi*) or "bodies" (342c6). Scientific knowledge itself is the *fourth* thing that may be said to be "of" any of the beings. Finally, Plato adds that "there is need to set down as fifth the very thing that is knowable and is truly a being" (342a8–b1). Altogether, then, we have the thing itself ("the fifth"), scientific knowledge of it ("the fourth"), and the three things through which that knowledge comes to be. The distinction between the first three (which make up the whole of the material, perceptible world) and "the fifth" is critical and characteristically Platonic: it is the thing that is "knowable," not the perceptible "images" of it, that "is truly a being." The apple one holds in one's hand is not "truly a being"; it is merely, at best, an image of a true being, through which image, in part, one can come to scientific knowledge of the true being. The knowable is more real than the perceptible—the Platonic ontology is hierarchical in the sense that it contains gradations of "being."

For all that "the fifth" occupies the highest rank in this Platonic ontology, however, it is posited with a note of reservation. Plato says that one "needs" to set this down as fifth, whereas he did not speak in that way of any of the other four. The existence of name, rational account, image, and scientific knowledge is immediately manifest in our basic experience of the world; the same cannot be said of "the fifth." To see what is meant by the "need" to posit "the fifth," let us consider the example Plato uses, on the basis of which we are to "think . . . about all things": the circle (342b3–4). It is from our experience with its name (and synonyms), its *logos*, and instances of circles "drawn and erased," "turned on a lathe and destroyed," that we come to possess scientific knowledge of the circle. Now, it is obvious that the *logos* Plato provides, "that which is everywhere equally distant from the extremes to the middle," will never precisely apply to any image of a circle; such geometrical exactness does not exist in material bodies (343a5–9). But this means that the knowledge obtained through "the three," though it must be knowledge *of* something, is *of* something never actually perceived. To begin with, then, there is something like a *grammatical* necessity to posit the circle itself as fifth, the "knowable" thing, since there is nothing else for our knowledge to be "of." But this grammatical necessity, while indicative, is relatively superficial, as we can see by considering what it would mean *not* to posit the circle itself as truly being. One might wish, for example, to entertain a materialist hypothesis, according to which *only* the perceptible "are truly beings." But if "the fifth," the circle itself, is not a being, then it will be meaningless to say that any shape "drawn" or "turned on a lathe" is an image *of* a circle, for this would be to say that it is an image of something that does not exist. We would thus be hindered from saying what seems immediately obvious. For the reality of "the fifth" as its own being is what makes it possible to say that the objects of our experience belong objectively and really to species or classes.

We must consider this in more cases than just that of the circle, as Plato has instructed us to carry our thinking from the case of the circle to "all things," including, for example, "every animal" (342b4, d7). If there is no "dog" itself, no "fifth" pertaining to dogs, then can we ever hope meaningfully to make the claim that this and that object of our experience *are* both dogs, speaking objectively of what is independent of human perception and cognition? Moreover, Plato says the same account will hold for "every body" including those "having come to be according to nature (fire, water, and all such things)" (342d6–7). But this amounts to a far-reaching critique of any thoroughgoing materialism. For if "the fifth" does not exist for any of the beings, then we are also prevented from identifying physical elements—whether fire and water, or carbon and oxygen, or photon and electron—on the basis of which to attempt a reductionist explanatory system of what we experience. Indeed, could we even say that this and that were both "bodies" in the first place? At most, we might hope to say that one experience reminds us of another. But this is to leave ourselves well short of what we surely wish to be able to say, which is that there *is* a kinship between these two things in fact—they are both bodies, both fires, both good people, or whatever—and that this kinship has some reality independent of the impressions they make on our conscious perception. Thus Plato indicates that scientific knowledge as such is *of* "the fifth" (342d8–e2). For such knowledge does not refer especially to *particular* bodies or phenomena, but rather to the categories to which we believe the bodies belong. If those categories are not objectively real—if the phenomena are not "images" *of* the things themselves, as Plato puts it, and if our definitions are not *of* beings that truly are—then we cannot have scientific knowledge that pertains to the objects of our experience. For there will then be no grounds upon which to assert any special connection between our impressions of our experiences—of the relationships we speculate may exist between them—and their underlying truth.

When Plato speaks of the "need" to posit the existence of "the fifth," then, he may be referring to a sine qua non, not only of any scientific knowledge, but for even our most basic impression of the phenomenal world to be anything more than a fiction produced (in part, at least) by the perceiving human consciousness. Our problems in this regard, however, are not simply solved even by the positing of "the fifth" as what truly is. The puzzle we encounter here is one well known to beset the Platonic doctrine of the Forms or Ideas and related passages: How are we to understand the relationship between the perceptible, changeable "three" and the fundamentally "different," imperceptible but knowable "fifth," which "suffers nothing" (342c2–4)? To say that a perceptible object is an "image" of something imperceptible hardly does more than beg the question. Now, Plato is famous for giving "participation" as the solution to this problem: "If something other than the beautiful itself [or "the noble itself"] is beautiful, it is beautiful on account of not a single thing other than because it *participates* in that beautiful [i.e., in the beautiful itself]" (*Phaedo* 100c4–6; emphasis added). But participation cannot amount to any useful answer here, as the following considerations make clear. First, as much as Platonists through history may have relied on participation to clarify the doctrine of the Ideas, Plato's own work does not consistently stress this solution. Aside from the passage in the *Phaedo* to which we have just referred, no other Platonic presentation of the Ideas makes use of it (see, e.g., *Republic* 509b2–10, 509d1–510b1). The exception to this might seem to be the *Parmenides*, where a young Socrates presents the theory of the Forms, with participation as a critical feature, as his solution to the paradoxes of Zeno and thus as an alternative to the philosophy of Zeno's teacher, Parmenides (128e6–131a2). But the *Parmenides* is a dialogue about what is *wrong* with the theory of the Forms in general and of the doctrine of participation in particular. Parmenides there advances a number of trenchant critiques that Plato never attempts to refute in any of his writings (cf. *Timaeus* 51a1–52d1; see also Aristotle, *Metaphysics* A.9). And the problem upon which we have focused, that of the interaction or relationship between the perceptible phenomena and the imperceptible, knowable true beings, is stressed by the Platonic Parmenides as jeopardizing the possibility of philosophy as such (*Parmenides* 133b4–135c5).

Plato knew, then, that, while positing "the fifth" as that which "is truly a being" may suffice to address some epistemological and ontological challenges, it opens up a set of new ones at least as difficult and as numerous. But here in the philosophic digression of Letter Seven, it is apparently not his concern to articulate or to address those challenges. The only mention of "participation" in this passage points us, in fact, to a related but different problem. Plato concludes that "someone who did not somehow or other get hold of the four will never completely *be a participant* in scientific knowledge of the fifth" (342d8–e2; emphasis added). This brings to our attention the fact that it is not only the relationship between the first three and "the fifth" that is in need of explanation, but also *our own* relationship to "the fifth." By what human capacity or part of human nature does it become possible for a human being to recognize the kinship between an object of sensory experience and an independently existent, imperceptible being of which the object is an image? We could again look elsewhere in the Platonic corpus for help—to the Platonic notion of "recollection," for instance (see, e.g., *Phaedrus* 247c3ff.)—but again we must appreciate Plato's singular unwillingness in Letter Seven to advance any such doctrine or myth. He leaves the problem unsolved.

We should, however, take up the further puzzle present in the passage just quoted regarding the participation of human beings "in scientific knowledge of the fifth." For what can Plato mean by saying that participation "in scientific knowledge of the fifth" is impossible unless one should "get hold of the four"? Was scientific knowledge itself not "the fourth?" How can this be anything but the incoherent or circular claim that attainment of some scientific knowledge is a prerequisite to attainment of that same scientific knowledge? The only available answer lies in the fact that Plato has by this point expanded the category of "the fourth": "scientific knowledge and mind and true opinion" are "set down . . . as one, being not in sounds, nor in shapes of bodies, but within souls, by which it is clear that it is different from both the nature of the circle and from the three" (342c4–d1). It seems Plato's initial statement, that scientific knowledge is obtained through names, *logoi*, and images, has been amended to say that scientific knowledge is obtained through those three together with some combination or subset of true opinion, mind, and such forms of intellectual apprehension as exist essentially in souls. Hence, "scientific knowledge" would seem to have been elevated as the highest *version* of intellectual achievement with respect to a given being, possible only by way of other, lower forms, such as true opinion.

Yet among the constituent elements of "the fourth," Plato most of all extols not scientific knowledge but mind: "Of these, mind has approached most nearly in kinship and similarity to the fifth, while the others are more distant" (342d1–3). In the question of how the human being "participates" in "scientific knowledge of the fifth," or generally of the connection between human being and imperceptible "fifth," mind occupies a place of central importance—to be sure, at any rate, there can be no scientific knowledge without mind. For, as Plato here indicates, it is the human mind that seems to have the capacity to reflect or to grasp "the fifth," to recognize imperceptible beings of which the names, *logoi*, and objects of sensory experience properly belong. And, as he seems to say, a mind that is actively holding some being steadily in its focus, a being that is in that moment nothing perceptible or material, is the closest thing in our experience to what "the fifth" itself would have to be—a pure concept, without any perceptible or material qualities. What is more, it is mind that brings us to the necessity of positing "the fifth" in the first place because of the manner in which the mind experiences perceptible objects (including artificial objects, 342d5) as members of classes. Or rather, it is our need to explain how it is that the world as experienced by the human mind exists independently of the human mind that brings us to the necessity of positing "the fifth." Without an understanding of the nature of mind, then, and of its relationship to the rest of existence, we can never answer the question whether our sense of the articulation of the whole and of the nature of the beings that make it up has validity beyond or prior to our conscious human awareness. More specifically, we cannot insist upon "the fifth" being that which truly is until we can speak clearly on the metaphysical status of mind. We would need to determine whether human minds are only instances of their own "fifth," of which the nature is such that mind is the apprehender of the true beings, including itself.

But the acquisition of such an understanding represents a profound difficulty because the mind cannot be known in the same manner as the other beings of which scientific knowledge is possible. Plato's list of things that are like the circle does not include anything listed under the heading of "the fourth." Nothing about mind is perceived with the senses; it is known to us as the inner matrix of our perceptions, opinions, and thoughts. All this makes it very unclear, however, how we could ever ascertain whether a mind belongs to a "fifth" of its own. If Plato's account describes our acquisition of scientific knowledge of "each of the beings," what can it mean that mind does not appear on the list of genera covered by his account? Is mind, then, not a being? This line of inquiry leads us to the third and perhaps most glaring omission from the philosophic digression. Just as this passage is without discussion of participation or recollection, it also lacks any reference to a cosmic mind or deity, knowledge of which is made out to be the goal of philosophy in Letters Two and Six. Scientific knowledge of such an entity could do much to assuage our epistemological concerns. Among other reasons, it would confirm the existence in the cosmos, even the primacy therein, not only of immaterial being as such (which in itself is a lot), but of immaterial mind specifically, of which the nature includes apprehension of the world as composed of distinct physical and spiritual entities and processes, each characterized by kinship to immaterial classes or categories. It is only a small step to see that, when we consider the category of the noble things in particular (342d4–5), the preceding considerations greatly illuminate Plato's account of the soul's search for "the first" in Letter Two.

Having surveyed the problems raised by this passage in this way, and having noted Plato's consistent silence regarding the various solutions he proposes in other places, we can now try to characterize the sense and aim of the passage as a whole. The purpose is evidently not to provide a complete, explanatory, metaphysical account of the whole of existence and our relationship thereto. For Plato nowhere here answers the great questions (of which we know him to have been aware) that beset the account he articulates. Rather, Plato here indicates the basic features—and some of their implications—of our intuitive belief that we know, or can come to know through sense perception together with mind, about the beings that make up the whole. We have attempted to put our finger on the points in this presentation where some further metaphysical apparatus would be needed to make up a complete explanatory picture. We may therefore speculate that the passages to which we have referred in passing—for example, in the *Republic* and *Phaedrus*—are (in addition to whatever else they may be) Platonic intimations of what a fully elaborated scheme would have to look like in order sufficiently to address the basic requirements and problems indicated here in the philosophic digression of Letter Seven—tailored, of course, to the specific purposes they are designed to serve in their respective dramatic contexts.

The Limit of Human Knowledge

We should be careful not to lose sight of the stated purpose of this passage: to argue against anyone who would "dare to write" of the things Plato takes seriously (342a3–6). It is on this note that Plato concludes the section we have just finished discussing (343a1–3). In the course of that conclusion, however, Plato introduces a new argument, different from the one he has been sketching so far. He now submits that all things other than "the fifth" "undertake to make clear the 'of what sort' about each thing no less than the being of each, because of the weakness of the speeches" (342e2–343a1). It is only with the addition of this rather opaque proclamation that Plato concludes by at last reaffirming what it was to be the purpose of this section to demonstrate: that no one who understood Platonic philosophy would "dare" to try to communicate that philosophy through speech, and especially in "something unchangeable . . . which indeed happens with what has been written in engraved writing" (343a3–4).

The next section of the philosophic digression begins as a further clarification of this concluding point, which, Plato says, "one needs to learn again" (343a4–5). In this renewed attempt, the problem of the "of what sort" and the "what," which Plato has just introduced, is said to be only one—albeit the "greatest"—of the myriad arguments that may be adduced to show that "each of the four . . . is unclear" (343b6–8). Of this myriad, two other such arguments are specified, each making use once more of the example of the circle. The first is that every material image "is full of the opposite of the fifth," just as an image of a circle "everywhere touches the straight" (343a5–7); the second is that names (and therefore *logoi*, which are composed of names) are "unstable," since "there is nothing to prevent the things now called round from being called straight," and so on (343a8–b6). These arguments, then, are aimed at denigrating the first three by showing why none of them can attain to the purity of "the fifth" to which they refer—they are indicative of it, but cannot be identical to it. In this way, these arguments are meant to establish the incommunicability of the truth concerning the true beings. Yet it must be said that they accomplish this only partially, at best. Plato has already said that scientific knowledge of "the fifth" is to be obtained through the first three (together, perhaps, with opinion and mind). Why would a capable teacher not at least attempt to instruct his pupil or reader by means of "the three," simply stressing in addition the merely illustrative character or lack of exactness of his geometrical diagrams or images, as well as the need to take care over the precise intended meanings of his words (especially for non-Greek readers or Greek readers in the distant future)? Would this attempt not be worthwhile, whatever obstacles to correct understanding might remain for the student? In short, how do these arguments establish that no one "with a mind" would "dare" to commit his thoughts to the "unchangeable" characters of written text?

But maybe it is unfair to press Plato on these "lesser" arguments against the "unclarity" of "the three," when he has himself identified what he claims to be the "greatest" argument of this kind. This argument takes aim at the "unclarity" not just of the first three but, as we have noted, of each of the first four. Whenever any soul seeks the "what" or the "being" of something, says Plato, "each of the four" instead "hold[s] out to the soul," whether in "speech" or in "deed," merely the "of what sort" (343b7–c4). That is, whereas "the fifth" contains only what belongs purely and essentially to a given being without reference to the material "images" of it that pass into and out of existence, each one of "the four" communicates about it by reference to the accidental qualities of just those material images. An image of a flower—whether we mean by this a single, particular flower, or, for example, a painting of a flower—is of, so to speak, a *specific* flower, of such and such color, and shape, and proportion, none of which is essential to the imperceptible "flower" in itself. If one tries to articulate that by which one knows a flower upon perceiving it—namely, that which all those objects of our experience share that happen to be flowers—one will inevitably describe the *qualities* shared by flowers as such. Yet if we reduce the meaning of "flower" to a set of perceptible qualities, we are again saying no more than that two or more objects of our experience reminded us of one another by the manner in which they struck our perceiving minds. Moreover, since any two flowers, however similar, also differ in many aspects, it becomes a question whether the classification unifying some of them as members, say, of some one species, or all of them as flowers, truly possesses greater objective validity, or is truly less arbitrary, than some alternative classification that would separate, say, the largest from the smaller instances of a given species, or those of most vibrant color from the paler. The definition can do no more than to separate off from a larger class or genus some species or subset by reference to some distinctive qualities or attributes: a circle is a sort of shape, a flower is a sort of plant, a virtue is a sort of character in souls, and so forth. To give only the "of what sort," the *poion ti*, of a being, then, as opposed to its "being" or "what," its *on* or *ti*, is to be mired in the world of images and instances known through sense perception, and thus to fail to capture the trans-sensory, metaphysical being, which, by somehow inhabiting each instance, gives it its membership in the objective category to which it belongs.

We cannot fail at this point to be struck by Plato's sudden demotion of "the fourth." At first, it seemed that scientific knowledge, originally identified as "fourth," would be the central focus of this passage; "the fifth," by contrast, was added almost as an afterthought. The category of "the fourth," soon expanded to include true opinion and mind, was favorably distinguished from the first three by its immateriality, and mind in particular was singled out as the closest approach to "the fifth" of which we are capable. With the argument about the "what" and "of what sort," however, "the fourth" is lumped together with the sensible objects and speeches from which it is derived, and all are denigrated equally for their failure to provide that which the soul is really seeking in its quest for knowledge. While Plato at first appeared to hold out some hope that the human mind, in possession of scientific knowledge, could extricate itself from the shadowy, imperfect, material world known to us through the senses, it now seems that all of our intellectual experience, including scientific knowledge, is confined to that imperfect sensible world. Even without being explicitly discussed, the problem of participation rears its head. The true beings and their alleged images are separated by an unbridgeable chasm, and our knowledge of the beings, grounded as it is in the sensible, is stuck on the wrong side of the divide. Plato leaves us here at a total impasse. He has indicated no avenue along which we might still hope to find access to the "what" of the beings, to any direct grasp of "the fifth" itself. Nor in any of what follows is there any resuscitation of the hope that human beings might somehow come into contact with "the fifth." But this must prompt to us to consider how well we have understood the Platonic prohibition against writing, which this whole passage is meant to support. Plato had given the impression that speech and writing are too subject to the weakness and flux of the sensible world to be able to capture the eternally fixed truths contained in his wisdom of "the fifth." At this point, however, it is completely unclear in what such wisdom would consist, or in what way Plato could claim to have any direct grasp of "the fifth."

Yet the digression does build from this point to a major statement on the understanding available at "the utmost extent of human power" (344b7–c1). The movement that culminates in that conclusion begins with Plato's otherwise unexpected turn to a discussion of refutation. At first, Plato distinguishes two ways in which "the four," on account of their natural weakness, can be refuted. The difference between the two ways hinges on whether the questioner, with regard to the matter at hand, has been "habituated" by the proper rearing "to seek the truth." If the questioner has not been so habituated, then, though the questioner may yet be perfectly capable of "tossing around and refuting the four," nonetheless those being questioned do not "become ridiculous . . . to the questioners," since neither party imagines anything that would be more satisfactory than the images being refuted (343c5–d2). Plato here puts us in mind of a kind of playful, eristic activity, in which the questioner's willingness to refute any imaginable claim is grounded in and reflects the view that no claims at all are solid or true (see *Philebus* 15d4–16a3; *Euthydemus* 275e4–6, 276e5, 303d6–e4). If, on the other hand, the questioner knows to "compel" the questioned party "to answer and to clarify the fifth," that is, the "what" as opposed to the "of what sort," he is able to "confute" his interlocutor, and thus to make him seem ignorant "of the things about which he is undertaking to write or speak" (343d3–6). Seen in contrast to the previous type of refutation, this one could easily make us think of the refutations of the Platonic Socrates, which are framed around "What is?" questions, and in which the interlocutor is frequently tripped up by Socrates's insistence that he identify that which gives to all instances their common character (e.g., *Theaetetus* 146c7–147c6; *Greater Hippias* 289a8–e6; *Euthyphro* 6d1–e7). Yet Plato adds about this type of refutation that, though those who hear it may be unaware of it, it is not in fact "the soul of him who has written or spoken that is refuted, but the nature of each of the four, being naturally poor" (343d6–e1). It might well change our understanding of the Socratic refutations if this were meant as a description of them (cf. *Alcibiades* 112c10–113c4; *Theaetetus* 154c7–d7; *Republic* 349a6–3, 350e1–9; *Protagoras* 359c5–d1).

It transpires, however, that Plato ascends one rung further to describe a third and highest form of refutation, albeit only in passing. We are able to say that it is the highest version because it is described as an element in what appears to be Plato's description of the greatest attainment of knowledge possible for human beings (343e1–344c1). What is totally unexpected about this description, however, which also makes us think even more of the Platonic Socrates's characteristic refutations, is that Plato suddenly narrows his focus from the acquisition of scientific knowledge generally to the knowledge of virtue specifically. This knowledge, which Plato first describes as "scientific knowledge of the good-natured," is available only to those who are, by nature and rearing, "akin to the matter" of the scientific knowledge being sought, in that they possess the uncorrupted elements of a "good nature" themselves (342e2–344a2). Plato indicates that this kinship does not refer to the intellectual virtues—"goodness at learning" and a good memory—though these too are necessary to a student's success. Rather, being "akin" to the matter means possession of appropriate traits of moral "character." These latter, however, are identified not as the moral virtues themselves, but rather as "kinship" with "the just things" and everything else "noble" (344a2–8). This is in keeping with the Socratic thesis that virtue is knowledge, in the sense that the *seeker* after knowledge of virtue cannot yet be said to *possess* that virtue. In other words, the philosopher, whose love of knowledge indicates that the knowledge in question remains unattained (cf. *Symposium* 204b4–5 with *Republic* 485a10–b3), is as such not yet in possession of virtue but seeking it—the philosopher should rather be said to possess a "kinship" with the virtues (cf. *Republic* 487a4–5).

Recalling the Socratic thesis positing the identity of virtue and knowledge is crucial also for resolving the following paradox. Plato says kinship with the noble things is necessary for a student who will obtain this "scientific knowledge of the good-natured," "for it does not come to be to begin with in dispositions alien to" the matter sought (344a4). Yet he appears to specify the content of this knowledge as "the truth of virtue" *and* "of vice," "to the extent" that these can be learned; to gain knowledge of one is to gain knowledge of the other along with it, "for it is necessary to learn them simultaneously" (344b1). Now, if this refers simply to the fact that, when one learns anything true one also learns that everything contradicting it is false, one might think on this basis that it could be equally possible for one whose soul bears a kinship to *vice* to learn first of vice and thereby necessarily also of *virtue*—sneaking in, as it were, through the back door. But since virtue is knowledge and vice is ignorance, a kinship to vice points not in the direction of learning but of complacency or worse. One must long to perfect one's soul through virtue, and thus to have some original sense or divination of that for which one longs and is in need, in order to set out and remain on the path toward knowledge of that perfection (cf. 340c1–6). Knowledge of this perfect or perfecting virtue naturally brings with it, as a corollary or counterpart, knowledge of the associated imperfection, which is to say knowledge of vice, or knowledge of ignorance. Moreover, since it is necessarily the good-natured soul that obtains knowledge of the good-natured, this knowledge is necessarily self-knowledge.

There is a critical ambiguity, however, in the scope Plato gives to this knowledge. For just after saying that one must learn of virtue and vice "simultaneously" (to the extent it is possible to do so), he adds, "and the false and true of the whole of being simultaneously" (344b2). The ambiguity lies in the following detail. In each case, "simultaneously" (*hama*) would seem to refer to the fact that one learns the two contraries at once. But it is difficult not to see a reading of the common "*hama* . . . *hama* . . ." construction as indicating that learning the truth of virtue and vice *brings with it*, "simultaneously," knowledge of "the false and true of the whole of being." Would the apparent correspondence of "false" with "virtue" and "true" with "vice" then indicate that the "whole of being" is characterized more truly by the imperfection of what is bad than the perfection of what is good? The implausibility of these readings almost requires that we reject them. And yet one cannot deny that little if anything has prepared us for the narrowing of Plato's focus from beings generally to virtue in particular, nor that it is only with this turn that Plato gives us anything like a portrait of the culmination of the quest for knowledge.

That portrait has something like the following features. If one possesses such a nature and rearing as Plato has described, there is a "way leading through all" of "the four," "shifting up and down to each one," which "does with difficulty give birth" to scientific knowledge of virtue (343e1–e3). The difficulty of this process, the fact that it requires "total occupation and a great deal of time" (343b2–3), combined with the rare concatenation of character traits the student must possess, necessarily makes the acquisition of this knowledge extremely uncommon. The "occupation" (*tribēs*) required of the student proceeds by a "rub[bing] (*tribomena*) against one another" of the "names and definitions, sights and perceptions," that is, of "the three," as well as by "kindly refutations" in which "questions and answers" are employed "without envy" (344b3–6). Plato thus describes a kind of dialectical examination, proceeding through a process of refutation, of the "images" of virtue of which we have experience and to which our speech refers. The image of rubbing these together recalls the passage in Plato's *Republic* where Socrates clarifies the procedure by which he will seek knowledge of justice with his interlocutors:

> We supposed that if we undertook to contemplate [justice] in some bigger thing of those that have justice, we would more easily catch sight of what it is like in one human being. And this bigger

> thing seemed to us to be a city, and we founded the best one we could, knowing well that [justice] would be in the good [city], at least. What appeared to us there, let us now carry up to the individual, and if they agree, it holds nobly; but if something else should appear in the individual, we will go back up to the city and test it, and perhaps by examining and rubbing them against one another, we would make justice shine out as from a fire; and when it has become manifest, we will confirm among ourselves that it is stable (*bebaiōsometha*). (434d6–435a3)

To obtain the Platonic "scientific knowledge of the good-natured," then, or to "learn the truth of virtue to the extent possible" and "of vice," one must clarify and compare the various opinions as to the meanings of justice and of the rest of the virtues with a view to ascertaining what the virtues themselves must be. Justice, for example, comes to sight as the ordering principle of a political community, to which each member must submit, subordinating and even sacrificing individual happiness to the common good; but justice also comes to sight as the moral excellence of soul that perfects and even makes happy the individual human being. How is this contradiction in common opinion to be resolved or overcome? One must submit oneself to refutation in order to clarify and bring into coherence one's own opinions, or to become aware of the reason for their incoherence and its implications.

Plato's focus on justice in particular, and on virtue in general, makes us aware that the question of the "what" and the "of what sort" has a dimension—when what is sought is virtue—that we have not yet considered. For instance, in the *Republic*, Plato's Socrates draws attention to the problematic tendency to attempt to say whether justice is something good, that is, to say what *sort* of thing it is—whether it is a virtue or a vice, a kind of wisdom or a kind of ignorance, and whether it is good or bad for human beings—before determining *what* it is (354a13–c3). The reason, however, for thus losing sight of the quest for the "being" of justice does not seem to be especially that "the nature of each of the four" is "poor." Rather, the reason is the initial belief of the seekers in the great inherent value of what is being sought, and the strength of their hope to find that justice is of such great value, that most appears to direct (or misdirect) their efforts (336e7–9, 347d8–348a6). Where justice and the rest of virtue are concerned, we are not such dispassionate investigators as we are in the case of the circle. Yet we must also remind ourselves of the fact that Plato holds out, as the culmination of the good-natured student's quest for truth, nothing more than "scientific knowledge." That is, Plato says nothing about the fact that this knowledge, as an instance of "the fourth," must itself be "naturally poor" and therefore inadequate for providing the "what," the "being," "the fifth" of virtue. He does not explain how it will release us from "every perplexity and unclarity" of which, he has said, "the four" "fills every man" (343c4–5). Still, this is not to say that the acquisition of this knowledge is worthless. It produces "practical wisdom . . . as well as mind, straining to the utmost extent of human power" (344b8–c1). On one hand, then, one gains, not wisdom as such, that is, theoretical wisdom (*sophia*), but "practical wisdom" or "prudence" (*phronēsis*) concerning the virtues, which is of no small importance or worth. And, on the other hand, one gains "mind" or "intelligence" (*nous*), which Plato has said is the closest approach a human being can make to "the fifth." This, as he says, is as far as human nature can reach in its quest for justice and virtue, and indeed for the "false and true of the whole of being."

Platonic Philosophy and Platonic Writing

As we must continue to remind ourselves, Plato is compelled to provide the philosophic digression of Letter Seven in order to prove that if indeed "either Dionysius or someone lesser or greater wrote something of the highest and first things concerning nature, he had in no way heard or learned soundly the things of which he wrote" (344d4–6). Plato himself refers to this section of the letter as a "tale" or "myth" and a "wandering" (344d3). To reiterate, then, it must not be taken for a straightforward exposition of the "highest and first things concerning nature," much as it may seem to be such a thing. It may perhaps teach about such things "through a small indication," as myths sometimes do. But the myth is largely misleading in the following way. Plato gives the impression that he has access to "the fifth," and that it is in this that his wisdom regarding the "highest and first things concerning nature" consists. Yet his explanation of why this cannot be set down in writing effectively indicates that human beings *cannot* truly access "the fifth." Indeed, the matter of its genuine existence must for that reason remain a question. Paradoxically, then, the "wandering" digression through which Plato has just led us may after all convey as solid a conclusion as can be conveyed about the "true beings."

By the end of the passage, however—and therefore, in that part of the passage that directly produces and explains his final denouncement of writing—Plato is no longer speaking of "the fifth" at all. He has returned at this point to a vignette of teacher and student that recalls his account of the transmission of Platonic philosophy at the beginning of the digression. In that earlier account, Plato claimed that what he "takes seriously" is "in no way speakable," but is rather like a "light . . . kindled" in the student "as from a jumping fire" after "much intercourse" between teacher and student "concerning the problem itself" and a period of "living together." Now, in the later passage, some details are filled in. The "intercourse" of teacher and student proceeds by "making use of questions and answers . . . without envy." The "light" that is kindled is "practical wisdom" and "mind," and it is produced by the dialectical examination, the "rubbing together," of accounts and images of justice and the other noble things. Writing cannot provide the most far-reaching education because the writer will not be present with the reader to spend time in refutation through questions and answers (see *Phaedrus* 275c5–276a9).

Refutation as a requirement of education—as opposed to refutation's other manifestations and uses, which Plato has also mentioned—appears in this account only once justice and the rest of virtue have become the focus (as opposed, say, to the example of the circle). This suggests that the deficiency of writing is made most acute by the challenge inherent in the investigation of those subjects in particular. It is not in Letter Seven, however, but in Letter Two that Plato most vividly describes the nature of the challenge inherent in investigating the ontological status of the noble things. Dionysius's perplexity and urgent need for Plato's help are likened there to labor pains, which Plato says are "responsible for all evils." And it seems that this pain must be connected to the fact that the investigation into "the nature of the first" raises questions as to the character and even the existence of the divine principle underlying existence in general and, especially, the existence of the noble or beautiful things. Indeed, Plato has suggested that it is by submitting one's opinions about the noble things, or about "virtue and vice," to refutation that one might ultimately settle the vexing questions concerning "the whole of being" with which Dionysius is concerned in Letter Two. At any rate, when Plato bids us to learn about "all things" by considering the example of the circle, he obscures the profound difference between this geometric example and the cases of the noble, the good, and the just. Not that we should doubt that the question of "the fifth" as it pertains to geometry would be of considerable interest to Plato; but as it turns out, it is not an immediately illuminating case regarding the reasons why he chose not to write about that which he took "most seriously." It is difficult to see why anyone would forgo writing a geometrical treatise out of concern that what is here and now called "round" may in some other time or place be called "straight." It is more easily imaginable how variations in the meaning of the word "justice" could cause a problem for the political philosopher.

Unlike the philosophic digression's introductory section, Plato's last words about his abstention from writing about "the serious beings" do not mention the impossibility of such writing. Rather, he speaks of his refusal to "cast them down amid the envy and perplexity of human beings" (344c2–3) or to "cast them out into dissonance and unseemliness" (344d8–9). There is a doubt or "perplexity" (*aporia*) involved in philosophy that is generally ill suited to the human constitution. It results from the chasm, which we cannot traverse, between the natural poverty of "the three," and hence of "the fourth" that emerges from them—the highest form of understanding to which the human mind can attain—and the purity and perfection of "the fifth," which exists nowhere in our experience, but which is needed for our initial understanding of science and of "the whole of being" to cohere. It is the juxtaposition of the passages in Letters Two and Seven, which Plato clearly invites, that directs us to the question of what this great disjunction means for us as beings concerned with "the nature of the first."

What, then, are we to make of the writings that Plato *did* "cast out" among human beings? The Socratic dialogues contain refutations, but not of the highest kind described here. That is, they never portray Socrates engaged over time with a good-natured pupil who comes to "learn the truth of virtue" and "of vice," and "the false and true of the whole of being." But this means that, if we are to deduce from the Socratic dialogues what would be of the highest importance for our own Platonic education, we must infer from the dialogues conclusions and implications that go beyond those emphasized by the Platonic Socrates himself. The Socratic refutations can help us to recognize the natural poverty of "the four," which results in each thing being such and such in one sense but not in another, and in the difficulty of tracing the lines that separate the objects of our experience into natural classes—which would allow us "to carve up" the world "by forms, by joints where they are naturally" (*Phaedrus* 265e1–2). They can help us to see, with respect to the good, the noble, and the just, the speeches and images that must be set against one another in dialectical examination. But they leave to us the task of determining the import of those insights for the opinions and aspirations with which we first set out on our investigation.

Plato concludes that "every man who is serious about the serious beings" will necessarily refrain from producing writings about these things (344c1-3). If there has been any lawgiver who was also "serious," then the laws he wrote "were not the most serious things" to him (344c4-7). The only alternative is that the writer had been driven out of his senses during the time of his writing, perhaps by a desire for honor (344e1-2)—Plato knows that the Homeric heroes were wrong to attribute such madness to the gods (344d1-2). Strictly speaking, then, there are three possible explanations for the Platonic writings, including the *Letters*. The first is that, as Plato maintains, they do not contain his thought about the things he took most seriously. The second is that at least some of the writings *do* contain his thoughts on these matters, but that he was not altogether in his senses when he wrote them. The third is that he is not a "serious man." Now, Plato himself dedicated no small time and attention to at least one extensive piece of writing that largely takes the form of legislation and which, of course, is called the *Laws*. Plato appears to tell us here that we should not take that work so seriously, for he, at any rate, did not. He also claims to engage in an act of lawgiving in the *Letters* itself, namely, in Letter Six, the whole of which he bids his addressees to treat as a "sovereign law, which is just." He also, however, instructs those addressees to swear by the letter, or law, "with seriousness that is not unmusical, and at the same time, with the playfulness that is a sister of seriousness." The question of how "seriously" we are to take Plato's writings on laws and regimes would seem to be bound up with the question of the proper relationship between seriousness and playfulness. For if, in Plato's considered philosophic judgment, even the most solemnly serious matters deserve after all to be treated with a measure of playfulness, then perhaps we do not denigrate his political works so much by suggesting that those works—and even Plato himself—are less than fully "serious." We should at least be wary of becoming enthralled by the mistaken view belonging to those of Plato's "good-natured" readers and followers who, like Dion, swell "with a lofty and empty hope as though they had learned some august things."

PART THREE

Plato in Syracuse

The core story of the *Letters*, the center of its drama and the unifying narrative thread running through its winding literary structure, is that of Plato's failed attempt to carry out Dion's plan of educating Dionysius to philosophy. This failure is what renders Plato's fateful decision to involve himself in the political affairs of the Syracusan tyranny so questionable in retrospect. How did Plato think that the reputation of Platonic philosophy would benefit from this fraught and risky venture, as he evidently did? We have learned from our examinations of the themes of Plato's political counsel and Plato's presentation of philosophy throughout the *Letters* that he never believed in Dion's vision for a regime of philosophic rule in Syracuse and that he could never have been sanguine about Dionysius's prospects as a student of Platonic philosophy. What precisely were the benefits—for himself, his friends, his school, and his project of promoting philosophy—at which Plato aimed in fostering a relationship with Dionysius?

Plato does not present his answer to this question simply or directly anywhere in the *Letters*. Instead, he slowly and methodically develops a complex portrait of his puzzling, tension-ridden relationships with both Dion and Dionysius over the course of the entire *Letters*, from its first page to its last. In order to arrive at an accurate understanding of Plato's motives and intentions in pursuing and maintaining these relationships, then, we must try to follow his presentation of his dealings with these men as he unfolds it. What we find in adopting this approach, however, is that we cannot separate our questions about the story Plato tells *in* the *Letters* from questions Plato compels us to raise regarding his composition *of* the *Letters*. That is, Plato indicates in the *Letters* that his conception and composition of this astoundingly intricate and innovative text were themselves a response to the growing repercussions of his activities in Syracuse. We will not obtain a full picture of Plato's strategy and plan in the Syracusan affair if we fail to include the writing and publication of the *Letters* itself as part of the story.

In what follows, then, we will seek to shed light on what it was Plato sought to accomplish in and through his dealings with Dionysius and Dion, and also how those relationships ultimately gave rise to Plato's conception and composition of the *Letters*. We will begin with the opening cluster of letters, in which Plato indicates that his composition of the *Letters* became necessary as a response to the proliferation of harmful rumors about his associations with Dionysius and Dion. After we have gained some insight into Plato's struggle to control the public perception of these relationships, we will be better prepared to seek out a properly nuanced view of the truth about those relationships, especially as regards the substance, and the reason for the failure, of Plato's attempt to educate the Syracusan tyrant. By comparing and contrasting the divergent accounts of Letters Two, Three, and Seven, we can piece together an account of the Platonic education Dionysius received, giving particular attention to that education's most sensitive subjects: theology and tyranny. For it was Dionysius's failure to appreciate the nuances of Plato's teachings on these subjects that produced the most serious problems for Plato and for his reputation.

Having clarified the details of Plato's failure to educate Dionysius, we will have to take up one of the most puzzling features of Plato's whole Syracusan saga. Why, after things had gone so poorly in his first attempt with Dionysius, did Plato agree to go for his *third* visit, to revive his failed project of educating the tyrant? We will find the answer by attending to one of the more intriguing and even mysterious characters in the *Letters*: Archytas, the philosophic and powerful Tarentine statesman and addressee of Letters Nine and Twelve. In considering the role Plato's friendship with Archytas played in Plato's Syracusan activities, we seem at first to round out our understanding of Plato's motivations in going to Syracuse and associating with Dionysius—but Plato has a final twist in store for us. The *Letters* ends with Letter Thirteen, which suddenly brings to our attention, among other things, the financial benefits made available to Plato and his friends through Plato's connection to Dionysius. We will conclude our study of the *Letters* by considering how the revelations in Letter Thirteen change our understanding of Plato's Syracusan adventure.

The Opening Drama of the *Letters* and the Problem of Slander

Over the course of the first three letters, all of which are addressed to Dionysius, we find Plato referring repeatedly to the slanderous rumors that have plagued his undertakings in Syracuse since he and Dionysius first met, and that continue to follow and disturb him still. The opening of the *Letters* thus conveys to the reader that the fallout of Plato's undertakings in Sicily, the problem to which he is still attending even after having concluded his third and final Sicilian visit, concerns the public perception of his activities and involvement with the Syracusan tyranny. In our investigation of Plato's failed dealings with Dion and Dionysius and of his subsequent decision to write the *Letters*, then, we are naturally drawn to focus on the details of this opening trilogy—and indeed of its sequel, Letter Four, addressed to Dion himself. Before delving into those details, however, let us take a broad overview of these opening letters, noting the content and tone of each, so as to understand how they fit together and what impression they, as a group, convey to the reader about the character of the *Letters* as a whole.

Letter One is a portrait of Plato slamming the door shut behind him on his way out of Syracuse. Of course, he has retreated to a safe distance before penning this sententious reprimand of his erstwhile Sicilian host. By the time he writes, he has returned safely to Athens; he haughtily sends back the money Dionysius had given him for a travel allowance, as if to be sure not to owe him anything (in addition to which, the sum provided wasn't even enough) (309b8–d1). Letter One, then, is full of Plato's high-handed censure of the way Dionysius treated him while he was at the tyrant's court—which is why we may be surprised to find in Letter Two that the embers of their relationship are not altogether extinguished. And it is not only because of Dionysius's newly aroused interest in Plato's teaching about "the nature of the first" that the lines of communication have been reopened at the time of Letter Two. What is really motivating Plato in this letter is the problem of rumor or slander (*diabolē*), which hangs over the *Letters'* opening trilogy. We may say that the writing of the *Letters* became necessary—what seems in Letter One to be the *end* of the story must in fact be only the beginning—because the problem of slander against Plato that is raised in Letter One proves not to have been resolved.

Let us be more specific about this "problem of slander" as it arises in these letters. In Letter One, Plato bemoans the "vexatious" or "disgusting" slanders he endured during the time he spent managing Dionysius's political affairs while Dionysius himself was "receiving the benefits" and was apparently unscathed by these onerous rumors (309a1–4). Plato indicates that he was willing to suffer this unjust state of affairs because he knew that the truth would ultimately prevail: witnesses to the events in question, "those taking part in the regime" together with Dionysius, for whose sake Plato had apparently stood up or had taken risks himself on previous occasions, would confirm that "the more brutal things" that took place under the tyrant's reign could not possibly have received Plato's sanction (309a4–b2). Plato's quick dismissal of this matter notwithstanding, the reader is inclined to feel a measure of alarm on Plato's behalf. Of what has he been accused, and how can he be so sure he will be acquitted?

Plato reopens his correspondence with Dionysius in Letter Two on account of *additional* troublesome rumors that are circulating and have now been relayed to Plato himself. Rumor has it ("they say") that two men named Cratistolus and Polyxenus have brought damaging reports to Dionysius: one of them claimed to have overheard some of Plato's entourage at Olympia "accusing" Dionysius, which has prompted Dionysius to express the opinion both that Plato "ought to keep quiet" concerning him, and that Plato's "associates"—Dion excepted, for some reason—"ought to keep from doing or saying anything nasty" toward him (310b4–6, c7–d2). Plato, for his part, denies any awareness of his companions' having said what Cratistolus or Polyxenus claims to have heard them say (310d2–3). The crisscrossing channels of communication through which this gossip has been conveyed, amplified, and distorted are characteristically difficult to sort out. What is clear is that the business has become enough of a problem for Plato that he is now writing to Syracuse to address it. These rumors, then, seem to be more troubling to Plato than those to which he referred in Letter One.

The map of the *Letters* provided to us by way of Letter Seven helps us greatly in putting flesh on the bones of this little story in Letter Two, thus allowing us to appreciate the story's true but somewhat hidden significance. Letter Seven reveals that the meeting at Olympia referred to in Letter Two is Plato's meeting with Dion at the Olympic games, when the philosopher was en route for the third and final time from Syracuse back to Athens. At this meeting, the exiled Dion solemnly swore to Plato that he would at long last return to Sicily to take revenge on Dionsyius (350b6–3). This tyrannicidal resolve of Dion's appears to have been formed at least partly in response to hearing Plato's account of what had most lately transpired for the philosopher in Syracuse. So in truth Plato *was*, then, "accusing" Dionysius in Olympia; and what is more, while Plato himself claims in Letter Seven to have refused, out of gratitude to Dionysius, to endorse or to join in Dion's tyrannicidal undertaking, Plato also says that he explicitly invited Dion "to call upon [Plato's] friends if they were willing" (350c3–4). We understand now that Plato is being quite disingenuous in his pretension to ignorance of what is troubling Dionysius in Letter Two: Dionysius's warning that Plato's associates must not say *or do* anything "nasty" to him refers, as Plato must well know, to Dion's imminent return aiming to overthrow and to kill Dionysius. The details provided in Letter Seven also help us better to understand, in the opening lines of Letter Two, the strange exemption Dionysius is said to have granted to Dion among all Plato's associates: at issue there for Dionysius is not exactly Dion's hostility or his alarming preparations—Dionysius likely understands the grounds, and may even acknowledge the justice, of Dion's grievance and thus of the need for war between them to settle their differences. What concerns Dionysius is Plato's acquiescence to Dion's recruitment of Platonic associates to the cause of the violent overthrow of Dionysius's regime.

Plato's response to Dionysius's concern and warning in Letter Two points us to the broader significance of the grave situation at hand. Dionysius's recognition that it would be too much to ask Plato to restrain Dion himself is an indication, Plato says, that Plato does not "rule [his] associates." "For if I were thus ruling the others, and you, and Dion," he continues, "then would there be more good things for us and all the other Greeks, as I claim" (310c1–5). If Plato cannot even control Dion, one of the most ardent Platonic disciples there ever was (327a5–b1), what hope could there be for his institution of such philosophic rule as would fulfill the Platonic promise of uplifting and enlightening the Greeks? Plato thus acknowledges that the power he has to direct the actions and affairs of others through speech or reason is extremely limited; whatever part he may have played in precipitating the events now unfolding, he is no longer in a position to direct the course of those events. Now, it is true that the passage in Letter Seven describing Plato's meeting with Dion at Olympia leaves some ambiguity as to just how much power Plato *could* have exercised over Dion at the critical moment (350d7–351a1). But what Letter Two itself stresses more emphatically is that, at the moment to which this letter belongs, Plato's immediate challenge regards how he might yet hope to control the *rumors* about his involvement in Dion's coup.

We understand better now, then, why the need to address the problem of these rumors has prompted Plato to reopen the lines of communication with Dionysius—despite the fact that earlier rumors about his involvement in Dionysius's tyranny (alluded to in Letter One) did not stop him from deciding to cut off ties in the first place. For the disaster of Dion's failure will reflect particularly badly on Plato and on Platonic philosophy if Plato is believed, as he might easily be, to have been a co-conspirator in, or even the mastermind behind, the campaign to oust Dionysius. The problem of slander or rumor to which Plato must attend is precisely the difficulty of altering the manner in which he is perceived now that the gossip has begun to spread. The whole first half of Letter Two is taken up with the question of how Plato and Dionysius are going to "correct" the manner in which their association will be spoken of in the future—with a view, ultimately, to protecting the reputation of philosophy (311d8–e4). It is not enough for Plato to cut ties and wash his hands of the whole Sicilian affair; he must attend to the rippling effects upon his reputation of having involved himself so openly in an ordeal that is becoming increasingly messy.

Plato's approach to this weighty challenge in Letter Two suggests that he hopes to work in concert with Dionysius to ensure that their relationship is publicly seen and discussed in a favorable light. By the time of Letter Three, that hope has evidently run out. The simplest explanation for this is that the relationship between the two former associates has soured on account of Dion's campaign against Syracuse, which at this point can no longer be denied or disguised. Plato responds in Letter Three to allegations being spread by Dionysius himself, which suggest that Plato has long been plotting against him and is now at last attempting to realize his audacious scheme of usurpation. Specifically, Dionysius claims that Plato long ago prevented him from carrying out a two-part political program: "to colonize the Greek cities in Sicily," that is, to reclaim and repopulate the towns desolated by the Carthaginians in their wars against Dionysius the Elder, and to "unburden the Syracusans by replacing the rule of tyranny with kingship." Dionysius, that is, had ambitions–stymied by Plato, as he claims–to succeed where his father had failed by making Sicily a flourishing home for free Greeks. And now he is alleging that Plato's intention is to "teach Dion to do these very things," so that Plato and Dion, "by means of [Dionysius's] own intentions, are taking [his] rule away from [him]" (315c8–e1). Evidently, Plato's attempts in Letter Two to smother the nascent rumors of his involvement in Dion's plot against Syracuse have utterly failed. Dionysius himself is now actively fueling the most damaging version of those rumors, making Plato out to be the puppet master behind Dion and his campaign.

Plato's immediate response is a counter-allegation: "You do injustice to me by saying the opposite of the things that happened" (315e2–3). His next move is more surprising. Plato complains that Dionysius's slander is particularly unwelcome on account of the copious slanders Plato has *already* endured, which allege that Plato had acted as puppet master over Dionysius himself while he was still in Syracuse, and that he was therefore responsible for "any error" or "transgression" (*hamartēma*) committed by the tyrant during that time (315e3–7). In other words, Plato decides to respond in Letter Three to the problematic slander he was already addressing in Letter Two by bringing up in addition the separate slanders to which he referred in Letter One. Hence, he sets out to deliver "a defense speech (*apologia*) against both the slander that occurred before and that which is now naturally growing greater and more vehement after it" (316b1–2). Plato surely means for us to think here of his *Apology of Socrates*, in which Socrates takes up the formal accusation against him–against which he, too, begins with a counter-accusation to the effect that his accuser has accused him falsely (24c4–8)–only after introducing and responding to older "slanderous accusations" against him, which he claims have long circulated the false rumor that he studied and taught natural science and sophistic rhetoric.

If this was a strange procedure for Socrates to adopt at his trial (cf. Isocrates, *Busiris* 5), it is even stranger for Plato here. What is the point of making a "defense speech" here at all, where there is no trial and no jury (315d5)? The futility of making this defense to Dionysius in a private letter is what makes Letter Three one of the more obvious cases of an "open letter" in the collection; the epistolary form would seem, that is, to be no more than a literary device. Plato's Letter Three can easily be seen as having been written with the apologetic purpose of counteracting the damaging slander that has arisen as a result of his activities and influence in Syracuse. But when we consider that the need for such a defense was precisely what Plato described in Letter Two, that the problem of slander or rumor runs continuously through these first three letters, that Letter Three itself calls our attention to the literary elements of the epistolary form by beginning with a reflection on the salutation with which every other letter in the collection begins, and that the massive centerpiece of the *Letters*, Letter Seven, is itself obviously an open letter with the same apologetic purpose we are now clarifying, we are met with the compelling suggestion that not just Letters Three and Seven but the whole *Letters* has been written as a defense of Plato's political activity in Syracuse. We must yet consider how similar the activity Plato defends (insofar as it arises from or involves *philosophy*) is to the activity his Socrates defends in the apologia to which Letter Three implicitly alludes.

Letter Four as Satyr Play

Before returning to examine the details of Plato's opening letters to Dionysius more closely, we should pause to consider the helpful light shed on those letters by their sequel, Letter Four. Over the course of Letters One through Three, we see Plato's desire to bid good riddance to his Sicilian misadventures sadly thwarted by the necessity of dealing with his perceived connection to the approaching civil war. Letter Four is set at the moment of Dion's initial triumph in that war; it promises to reveal the truth of Plato's connection to the Dionean coup d'état, which connection Dionysius has alleged and Plato denied in their correspondence contained in the preceding letters. Letter Four, then, both belongs together with the opening trilogy of letters and is clearly set apart from it. This alone may bring to mind the format in which the Greek tragedians presented their plays at festivals: each trilogy is followed by a "satyr play," a kind of semicomic relief featuring a chorus of the eponymous, ribald, bestial minions of Dionysus. This interpretive suggestion is supported, to begin with, by the tragic motifs in the first three letters. Indeed, Plato quotes the tragedians three or four times in the brief and moralistic Letter One, all for the sake of chastening Dionysius: his tyrannical greed has cost him Plato's friendship, which will prove in time to have been worth far more than the riches Dionysius pursued at Plato's expense (309b7–8, 309d1–310a10). Moreover, Plato's desire to inaugurate the *Letters* under the auspices of the god of tragedy is indicated by the name of the letter carrier, an otherwise unknown (and so quite possibly invented) man named Bacchius (309c1), that is, "the Bacchic one," an epithet of Dionysus (aka Bacchus) himself.

The tragic tone of the *Letters* is struck at the outset with the emphatic reference to Dionysius's tyrannical hubris: we are made to lament the clouding of his judgment that led him to abuse his would-be philosophic benefactor, ruining the hopes of a fruitful partnership between the two of them and thus dooming himself to the fate prescribed to tyrants by "the majority of the . . . tragedians" (309d5–6). True to tragic form, moreover, the fallout from the tragic figure's blind hubris consumes not just the transgressor, but everyone in the drama. Plato, having been so undeservingly dishonored by the tyrant, says that he "will henceforth deliberate in a less humane way concerning [him]self" (310b6–7). Plato intimates that he has left Syracuse more cynical, more jaded, than he was when he arrived. His experience with Dionysius has disabused him of his former naive optimism, has taught him, so to speak, that the poets are right in their unqualified condemnation of tyranny. In this way, Dionysius has been responsible for a great disappointment of whatever the hopes were with which Plato began. It seems to be in retaliation for the pain of this bitter disappointment that Plato is venting his spleen against Dionysius in Letter One.

The scope of the tragedy broadens as the *Letters* continues. The partnership that Dionysius has spoiled promised to shine out far beyond the Syracusan court, "for if [Plato] were . . . ruling" Dionysius, there would "be more good things" not just for them, but also for "all the other Greeks" (310c2–4). By the time we reach Letter Three the disaster for Plato—and for the reputation of philosophy, with which his own reputation is inextricably bound (311d8–e6)—has become markedly more severe. For all of Plato's sanctimoniousness in Letter One, some uncertainty has now arisen, among the public at least, as to whether Plato may not be guiltier of injustice than Dionysius. The letter ends with the question of which of the two men must submit to just punishment, Plato calling upon Dionysius to acknowledge the wisdom of the hubristic poet Stesichorus and to imitate his "palinode" by recanting the lies he has told about Plato (319e2–5). Letter Three—the only Platonic letter to refer to hubris—thus ends by reaffirming Plato's prediction that Dionysius will suffer divine retribution for his misdeeds, but now with significantly less confidence than he evinced in Letter One, even opening the possibility that divine forgiveness may yet be available to the tyrant.

Letter Three gives a clear and consistent answer to the question why Plato would ever have allowed himself (and philosophy) to become embroiled in such a mess. Everything he did, from the moment of his arrival to his final departure, was out of belief in and loyalty to *Dion*, and especially for the sake of putting a stop to Dionysius's unjust persecution of Dion (316c4–d5, 317a5–318a5). It is in the immediate wake of Letter Three, and under the impression that letter has given us, that we come to Letter Four, the only letter in the collection addressed to Dion himself. We turn to this letter, then, in anticipation of something more uplifting than the tragedy that has preceded it, a glimpse of the friendship that *was* worthy of Plato's devotion all these years. The manner in which this anticipation is disappointed and deflated is precisely what gives this "satyr play" its tragicomic dimensions. It might seem at first blush that things have turned out well and that justice has been served after all: Dion and his collaborators have evidently deposed the tyrant (320e2). But Plato cautions that "the greatest contest concerns things yet to come" (320b3–4). Dion has distinguished himself as a general, but now he must prove himself as a lawgiver, and therefore must demonstrate his possession of virtues distinct from, and much rarer than, the ones that have carried him to this point (320b4–c3). Dionysius the Younger was a relatively paltry rival; Dion's competition now is with the likes of the glorious Lycurgus and Cyrus. And the understanding between Plato and Dion—some parts of which Plato guards with notable secrecy (320c5)—is evidently that the regime Dion will now attempt to found will surpass any that has ever existed, that even Lycurgus and Cyrus themselves will come to seem "ancient" or "outdated" in light of Dion's innovations (320d6–7).

The poignant humor in this letter arises from the enormous disproportion between the ambitions Plato and Dion have apparently fostered together and the actual scope of what is possible under Dion's leadership. In fact, we have already had occasion to note, in our study of Letter Eight, Dion's failure to grasp the hard problems faced by the founding lawgiver. Moreover, Plato's insinuations here point to Dion's belief (not shared by Plato) that he is to bring about, in some form or other, the rule of Platonic wisdom in Syracuse, and this under the eager scrutiny of "people from every inhabited region" (320d3–5). We may recall that in the letter following this one, Plato counsels the monarch Perdiccas with the political wisdom that one must never attempt to change the form of one's regime (321e3-6). Indeed, it seems that the observing public is rather down on Dion's chances of success. The expectation is that Dion will be unable to work together with the likes of Heraclides and Theodotes—friends of Dion's for whom Plato stuck his own neck out according to a story that was just recounted in Letter Three (318c1-d1)—and that the struggle for preeminence among them will be the end of Dion (320d8-e4). Poor Plato must now look helplessly on as the reputation and legacy of his political philosophy hang in the balance of Dion's quixotic mission.

But why is Plato so helpless? Can he not at least hope to direct Dion toward the path of least calamity? Perhaps we should have considered ourselves warned when Plato told us in Letter Two that he does not rule Dion. For what is more fully revealed in this letter than anywhere else is that, whatever Plato has claimed about his relationship to Dion in other places, Dion is not looking to Plato for guidance in this moment. Plato pleadingly calls upon him toward the end of this letter to write back; Theodotes and Heraclides are in communication with people back in Greece, but Plato and his associates have heard nothing from Dion's camp (321a6-5-b). Thus Plato appears in this letter not exactly on the tragic stage, but rather in the audience: he likens himself to a child in the theater, "shout[ing] [his] encouragements in seriousness and with goodwill" in hopes of spurring Dion toward a happy result (321a2-5). Surely, the image will sooner put us in mind of a farce than of the gravity of a tragedy—Plato acknowledges that it may well "appear ridiculous" (321a1-2). The dark humor here comes not from the Bacchic satyr's frenzied lust, but from the solemn Dion's equally fervent, equally uncontrollable desire for much loftier ends and the immortal honor attached to them.

Specifically, Plato's encouragements urge Dion to control the competition for this honor between himself, Heraclides, and Theodotes. He tells Dion to make a show of providing "a doctor's treatment" if the competition ever threatens to rend the friends asunder and thus to ruin their endeavor (320e4-321a1). Plato directs them to compete rather as actors in a troupe—seeking individual honors only in such a way as will serve and elevate their common effort—and to write to Plato personally "if there is need of anything" (321a5-7). We are reminded of the other triumvirates in the *Letters*: the trinity of divine causes in Letter Two, the trio of addressees in Letter Six, and the Platonic Dion's ill-conceived triple-kingship in Letter Eight. One can hardly deny that the ideal among these is the one most clearly organized into a hierarchy, that is, the one that is effectively a monarchy. Dion's regime in Letter Eight helps us most clearly to see why Dion will fail: he does not appreciate the need for a singular leader to serve as the founding lawgiver (cf. 359b7–8). The comedy of the situation comes out most clearly in the comparison to Letter Six. For here in Letter Four, Plato has no chance of maintaining any control over this triumvirate through the regular correspondence he requests; there is a ridiculous disproportion between what Plato purports to be attempting with Dion and what is actually possible.

The problem in Letter Six was that of establishing a stable, trustworthy friendship. It is the same problem that Plato told us, in Letter Seven, turned him away from political action altogether (325d1–2). In various ways throughout the *Letters*, philosophy is proposed as the answer to this problem; but Plato tells us, also in Letter Seven, that Dion failed to appreciate the indispensability of philosophy in grounding stable, trustworthy friendships (333d7–334a6). Here, at the very end of Letter Four, Plato leaves Dion with a final piece of counsel. "Take to heart," Plato advises, "that you seem to some to be rather lacking in the proper courtesy. Let it not escape your notice that it is through being agreeable to human beings that it is possible to act, but stubbornness dwells with loneliness" (321b5–c1). Needless to say, this was prescient advice, though naturally ineffective. Dion's Platonic idealization of politics abstracts from the practical political need to appease real, flesh-and-blood human beings, with irremediable flaws, to whose preferences and desires Dion would have to pander in order to have success. It was not un-Platonic of him to disdain the idea of such pandering, but it was un-Platonic of him to fail to recognize how far away from political life that disdain should properly have carried him.

Letter Two on the Common Good between Philosopher and Tyrant

The first three letters highlight the disastrous consequences for Plato's reputation resulting from his involvement with Dionysius; Letter Four, by revealing Dion's ineptitude, must leave us wondering anew how Plato ever could have thought it was a good idea to accept Dion's invitation in the first place. We may cast the puzzle in terms of the problem of trust Plato stresses in Letter Seven: Is it not strange that Plato took on his Syracusan project *without* the kind of trustworthy friend and partner that is, according to Plato himself, a prerequisite to any political success?

That a lack of *pistis*, trust, was at the core of Plato's failure with Dionysius is indicated from the opening line of the *Letters*: Plato begins Letter One by recalling that he had once been the man "most trusted" by Dionysius in his court (309a2); the thrust of Plato's reproach is that Dionysius has turned away such a trustworthy friend, something far more valuable than "shining gold" and the other trappings of tyrannical excess (cf. 322d1–4). The critical problem of Plato's relationship with Dionysius was precisely the problem we encountered in Letter Six: for there to be stable trust between philosopher and ruler, the ruler must "really philosophize"; but this means that the trust in question cannot be counted on during the dangerous period of education *toward* genuine philosophy, during which it is quite unclear how the ruler will be persuaded to remain friendly. When Plato gives his own succinct statement on "the cause" of his failure in Syracuse, he says that Dionysius "came to light as not much trusting" him, and that this distrust concerned the question of what Plato's "business" (*pragma*) was (312a3–6). As Plato puts it in Letter Three, the relationship between them was merely a "wolf-friendship" (318e4–5).

And yet, given that "the character of Dion's soul . . . was by nature weighty," that is, unlikely to be moved or changed, and "had already reached its middle age" (328b5–6), any hope Plato had for success in Syracuse must have relied on winning over the relatively young Dionysius. What is clear enough is that Plato's attempt to gain Dionysius's trust was, if not the sole purpose, at least a major goal of the program of education he offered to the tyrant. The most massive and pressing questions about that education, however, remain unanswered. For we have yet to clarify sufficiently how this relationship between Plato and Dionysius was meant to work. What benefit did Plato think he could plausibly offer to Dionysius that could entice him toward the pursuit of an education in Platonic philosophy? And what, ultimately, was the benefit Plato himself was seeking in return?

We begin our investigation of these questions with Letter Two, since Letter Two presents the height of Plato's attempt to salvage his deteriorating relationship with Dionysius, to reestablish the tyrant's belief in a common good between them. We have already examined the second half of the letter, in which Plato tries to entice Dionysius to embark on a very long journey of study under Plato's guidance—it is itself an attempt to solve the problem of trust between philosopher and non- or pre-philosophic ruler. But we have not yet looked closely at what Plato does in the first half of the letter, before the theme of philosophy is explicitly introduced. There, by way of disclosing frankly to the tyrant "how things happen to stand" between the two men (310d5–7), Plato presents a kind of education drawn from his understanding of human nature—an education that differs starkly from, but stands obviously in parallel with, the education regarding "the nature of the first" in the letter's second half. After observing that the nearly universal renown of both Plato and Dionysius among the Greeks has made their intercourse the subject of widespread discussion and gossip, Plato undertakes a lengthy explanation, "starting from the top," of the grounds of his emphatic prediction that this public discussion is bound to continue "in the time to come" (310d6–e2). And this explanation begins with the claim that, "by nature, practical wisdom (*phronēsis*) and great power come together in the same place, and they always pursue and seek each other and come to be together" (310e5–6). Plato thus proposes to explain his relationship with Dionysius as an instance of an established pattern of human nature.

Plato's focus in what follows, however, is not the natural relationship of *phronēsis* and *dunamis*, but rather the character and extent of the accounts that are generated and promulgated among human beings when great exemplars of these qualities meet and form partnerships (310e7–311a1). And this observation is not presented as a deduction from Plato's understanding of human nature, but rather as supported inductively by extensive evidence: Plato lists eight or nine cases of well-known affiliations between wisdom and power, altogether comprising twenty figures well known from history and mythology, meant to illustrate the lasting notoriety that inevitably attaches to partnerships of this type (311a1–b7). The lesson Plato means to impart to Dionysius, then, is the following one: "When we meet our end, the speeches about us will not be passed over in silence either, so care ought to be taken over them" (311c1–3). The common ground to which Plato seeks to appeal to Dionysius here is the two men's concern for their own reputations—especially their posthumous reputations. And yet, Plato's list of historical and mythological *phronēsis-dunamis* partnerships *does* after all provide us a valuable starting point in thinking about what Plato may have thought he had to offer, and to gain, in trying to educate Dionysius. For, while its ostensible purpose is to demonstrate the lasting fame or infamy of all such relationships, this list also contains a rich source of possible motives for both parties, from which we may take our bearings.

Let us therefore turn to a close examination of Plato's list of paradigmatic partnerships between practical wisdom and political power, so that we may then consider which if any of these models might correspond to the partnership Plato hoped to create with Dionysius. For example, Plato's list begins with the provocative case of Hiero and Simonides. Hiero, like Dionysius, was the tyrant of Syracuse in his time; how closely did Plato's intentions in approaching Dionysius match those of Simonides in going to the Syracusan tyrant's court? Simonides is the only "wise man" among those listed by Plato who is mentioned in connection with *two* "powerful" ones. In this context, then, he stands out for his promiscuity: whatever it is he sought, he was apparently as happy to seek it from a Sicilian tyrant as from a Spartan general. From what is known of Simonides independently of this letter, we might speculate that he sought wealth and comfort above all: tradition has preserved Simonides's reputation for covetousness and a gourmand's appetite. But the image of Simonides "at the doors of the wealthy" is incongruous with the contempt for riches Plato expresses in all of these opening letters (cf. also *Republic* 489b6–8).

Perhaps Plato is more like his next paragon of *phronēsis*, Thales, of whom he has made use in his dialogues to represent the theoretical philosopher's total disinterest, and resulting laughable ineptitude, in practical affairs (*Theaetetus* 174a3–b1; *Greater Hippias* 281c3–8). But Plato did not remain aloof from politics as did Thales—of whom, incidentally, no attestation of any relationship to Periander has come down to us. Was the relationship between Dionysius and Plato, then, rather in the mold of Pericles and Anaxagoras? In the *Phaedrus*, Plato's Socrates tells us that Anaxagoras helped Pericles to become a more skillful orator by teaching him about the things aloft and the nature of mind and mindless things, whence Pericles derived crucial lessons, necessary to the art of rhetoric, concerning the soul (*Phaedrus* 269e1ff., and cf. 270a4–5 with *Apology of Socrates* 23d5); in the *Apology of Socrates* Anaxagoras is the prime representative of the notorious impiety of natural philosophers, and hence of their imperiled position within the political community (26d1–6). At a crucial moment, it appears that Pericles was able to help Anaxagoras survive the pious Athenian backlash against his naturalistic doctrine. The case of Anaxagoras reminds us that Plato, as a philosopher, is prone to being suspected of impiety, which alone might explain his desire to befriend a politically powerful man such as Dionysius.

We come next to Croesus, Solon, and Cyrus. Here, for the first time, Plato reverses his ordering of the pairs: the exemplars of wisdom precede the exemplar of power. Plato highlights this by referring to Croesus and Solon as "wise" (*sophous*, not *phronimous*), which he must stress or specify since both Croesus and Solon were also powerful statesmen. The reversal of the two categories makes us aware of the special case of the founding lawgiver, Solon: he represents the synthesis of power and practical wisdom; his political power protected him during his lifetime, and the influence he exerts through his legislation does much to protect his posthumous reputation. In all three cases where Plato reverses the exemplars of *dunamis* and *phronēsis*, we find lawgivers, and in each case we can see that the lawgiver is more self-sufficient, less concerned to "pursue and seek" his counterpart, than the exemplars of practical wisdom who are not lawgivers: the wise Solon never even met the powerful Cyrus; Zeus's "prudent" partner Prometheus was mostly a thorn in his side; and as for the legendary Minos, while he may be thought to have depended on Polyidus for his art of divination in some matters, these matters would not have encompassed his crowning act of lawgiving, which was said to have been inspired directly by Zeus, the god of law himself.

In suggesting a parallel between the acts of lawgiving of Solon and Minos, however, we have blurred the line Plato has drawn between the two sections of his list: the first section, Plato says, lists people about whom "human beings enjoy conversing" among themselves, whom we know from prose works of history and philosophy, while in the second section Plato proceeds to the "imitations" thereof produced by the poets, which refer to ancient, mythical characters. And there is a critical shift in the meaning of *phronēsis* when we cross over to the poets' presentations. The education Thales and Anaxagoras may have made available to powerful statesmen, and even the teaching of Simonides, a poet himself but famously portrayed by a philosopher and historian, are hardly identical to the divine wisdom of Tiresias and Polyidus, the "prudent" counterparts of Creon and Minos, respectively, who possess their wisdom through divine revelation or the art of divination. The "prudence" or "practical wisdom" of these latter exemplars as they are portrayed by the poets is compatible with, because it is dictated by, their piety; and their usefulness as political advisers lies in their ability to communicate what the gods want or intend. The juxtaposition of these seers to Thales and Anaxagoras points to a great and abiding question of political philosophy: Is the highest wisdom, and therefore the ultimate guide for human action, accessible to reason and the senses unaided by revelation, or is divine revelation necessary for the most prudent human life and therefore for the best possible regime and laws (cf. *Meno* 99b1–d5)?

The question is pertinent here with respect to Plato. Is the prudence or practical wisdom that Plato would have offered to Dionysius on the basis of his political philosophy, whatever he may have hoped to receive in exchange, more akin in the crucial respect to the prudent counsel Anaxagoras gave to Pericles or to that which Tiresias gave to Creon? What, in Plato's view, is the place of piety in counsel to a tyrant? Plato's speculation, at the end of his list, that "the first human beings brought together Prometheus and Zeus in the same way" as the poets brought together their own sets of exemplars, does not settle the matter (311b2–4). For we have already seen from later letters, and from later in this letter, that Plato can uphold the importance or appearance of piety without relying on traditional beliefs in the Olympian gods.

The list we have been examining offers not only a source of suggestions as to Plato's modus operandi in dealing with Dionysius, but also a variety of possible modes in which he may hope or wish to *portray* the relationship in retrospect. The explicit purpose of this portion of the letter to Dionysius is for him to come to see that "care must be taken over" what will be said about the two of them after they have died (311b7–c3). But we know from the *Letters* itself that Plato never succeeded in recruiting Dionysius to this "care" or task. We must recognize, then, that the *Letters* itself *is* Plato's way of "taking care over" what will be said about the two of them after they have died. Now, Plato concluded his list of exemplars by noting that the postures of these famous figures with respect to one another varies in the various accounts, "some coming into conflict with each other, others into friendship, and still others into friendship at one time and into conflict at another, being like-minded about some things and conflicting about others" (311b4–7). This refers especially to the pairs of examples presented by the poets, though we might note, with respect to the first half of the list, the tendency of Xenophon (in his pseudo-historical *Hiero* and *Education of Cyrus*, to which Plato implicitly refers) to bridge the conflicts between *phronēsis* and *dunamis* by means of the sharing of wisdom. The poets, for their part, appear from the evidence of Plato's list to have been especially fond of portraying the baneful dissolution of partnership between potentate and seer.

The depiction of the place of wisdom in the political realm is a matter of no little importance to those poets and prose writers who have generally been responsible for the depiction—and this is certainly the case also for Plato. The *Letters* extends and belongs to the project of refining or reinventing this depiction, to which Plato's writings may be said to be generally devoted. This would explain the otherwise baffling implication later in Letter Two that each of these letters, and the *Letters* as a whole, as instances of Platonic writing, "are of a Socrates become beautiful and new" (i.e., the Socrates of the dialogues, as opposed to the Socrates of the *Letters* itself). Plato certainly presents the relationship between himself and Dionysius throughout the *Letters* as "friendship at one time," "conflict at another," but according to a complex and novel literary pattern.

Greetings and Salutations

We have gathered from Letter Two that the *Letters* is Plato's "correction" to the widespread rumors about his relationship with Dionysius. But Plato does not suggest that this "correction" is equivalent to his presenting the *truth* of the matter. Plato's concern was rather that he and Dionysius come to be "better spoken of" with respect to anything that "has not been nobly done" in the course of their association, his highest end being service to the reputation of philosophy (311d6–e4). A full account of the relationship between Plato and Dionysius, which accurately describes not only the original intention of that relationship but also its ultimate failure, must surely include some reference to the things that were "not nobly done" between them and which might have otherwise reflected poorly on Platonic philosophy. And yet these will be precisely the details that Plato would have needed to present in a delicate or guarded way, and which called for Plato to explain himself to his readers by means of such an unusual and puzzling text as the *Letters*. We turn next to Letter Three, then, with a view to understanding what elements of Plato's relationship with Dionysius called for the greatest sensitivity in Plato's composition of the *Letters*.

Dionysius's and Plato's postures of accusation, defense, and counter-accusation in Letter Three speak to the failure of Plato's attempt in Letter Two to work *with* Dionysius to "correct" public perception of their mutual affairs. Letter Three is the flagship of Plato's mission in the *Letters* to defend his activities in Syracuse. With this in mind, we find that its introductory section is particularly intriguing. For here Plato comments on the meaning of the special Platonic salutation that begins every other letter in the collection: "Do well!" This opening of Letter Three shows us that the care with which the *Letters* has been written, which was indicated by Plato's treatment of the theme of writing in Letter Two, extends even to the apparently minor matter of the salutation. Moreover, this passage turns out to provide a key to understanding the major difficulties involved in Plato's education of Dionysius, and thus reveals something critical about what has made the *Letters* necessary.

Plato opens Letter Three by asking whether it would not be more appropriate for him to greet Dionysius with the conventional "rejoice" (*chairein*) than with Plato's customary and idiosyncratic "do well" (*eu prattein*). He claims to have been led to this question by the manner in which Dionysius addressed Apollo in a written inquiry he sent to the oracle at Delphi. According to his envoys on that occasion, Dionysius addressed the god, "Rejoice and preserve a tyrant's life of having pleasure!" (316b6). Of course, Plato is quick to condemn Dionysius's addressing a god in this shocking way. But his condemnation may not only be for the sake of correcting Dionysius's behavior; it may also be an instance of Plato's attempt to "correct" the public perception of his relationship with Dionysius. For Dionysius's attitude toward the gods might well be thought to be a reflection of the education he received from Plato. Has he not sought Plato's instruction regarding "the nature of the first"? Have we not gathered that his soul was in the throes of labor pains on account of his doubt concerning the character of the first cause connected to the noble things? What is to prevent people from surmising on the basis of Dionysius's flagrant immorality and impiety that his relationship to Plato resembles Pericles's to Anaxagoras more than Creon's to Tiresias?

To be sure, the *Letters* provides good support to Plato's defense against these insinuations. Plato wrote to Dionysius in Letter Two of honorable behavior, pious devotion (to philosophy), and of a cosmos ordered by a divine *king* as opposed to a tyrant. Indeed, it is just the point of the *Letters* that it should document Plato speaking and acting in such a way as to contradict the most dangerous rumors that might arise. Since the *Letters* contains no explicit indication that it is anything but a somewhat disorganized sheaf of letters, and especially because Plato makes such a fuss in Letter Two (and elsewhere; 359e1–2, 363b1–6) about the contents being a matter of secrecy, the reader of the *Letters* will get the impression that these are private and candid communications from Plato to his associates. Our exploration of the *Letters* has revealed, however, that Plato is merely adopting a *posture* of candor in this text. One is tempted to say that Plato speaks in the *Letters* as a man who has arranged for his own telephone to be wiretapped without letting on to the eavesdroppers that he knows they are listening. A man who publicly defends himself in writing against slander and rumor will be suspected of distorting the facts in his own favor. He stands a better chance of winning the trust and favor of his judges if his *private* correspondence concerning the very matters in which he requires a defense appears to exonerate him. In this way, Plato has created the *Letters* as an authorized source of biographical material without giving the impression of having significantly edited or redacted any details. Of course, the *Letters* differs in a crucial respect from the decoy conversation of a man who knows he is being spied on: for Plato not only writes "in character" to the addressees but also, in some cases, will give a small indication to the eavesdroppers themselves regarding the circumstances that brought him to be in need of a device such as the *Letters*, and the manner in which he tried to handle them.

To return to Plato's condemnation of Dionysius's greeting to Apollo, we find that Plato's need to defend himself as the erstwhile tutor of Dionysius is driven especially by the tyrant's regrettable lack of prudence or practical wisdom. The impious or hubristic manner in which Dionysius addressed Apollo at Delphi explains much about Plato's efforts in Letter Two. We can see better now why he tried so hard to persuade Dionysius to take care to be reputed for piety and decency. What is more, we get yet another indication as to why Plato was so concerned to have Dionysius refrain from *writing*. For Dionysius's manner of greeting Apollo might not have caused Plato any trouble had the tyrant not sent his inquiry, introduced by his impious and unseemly salutation, in a written letter, which was, predictably, read and exposed by his messengers. Nor is this the only important reference to writing in Letter Three. Before taking up the task of his "double apology," Plato makes note of a rumor he has heard: it has been said that Dionysius, "or someone else" from his circle, has been *adding* to Plato's "preludes to the laws," which had been the object of Plato's diligent work for a time in Syracuse. Plato responds dismissively, evincing confidence that "it will be clear which [parts are which] to those capable of discerning my style" (316a4–6). A discerning reader will be able to tell the difference between an authentic work of Plato and a forgery.

More to the point may be the alternative reading, made possible by Plato's pregnant ambiguity: *tois to emon ēthos dunamenois krinein* may equally mean "to those capable of judging my character." Plato's moral character (*ēthos*) is to be distinguished from Dionysius's. The danger represented by interpolation or addition to Plato's text is therefore the danger of having Plato's moral character besmirched, his reputation contaminated. It is precisely the danger of which we have been speaking—namely, that of Plato getting caught up in Dionysius's reputation for immorality and impiety. Plato thus indicates to us the importance of coming to understand precisely what the difference was between him and Dionysius. And *that* is what makes Plato's commentary on the salutation at the beginning of Letter Three so important. For Plato explains that he would never bid a human being, and certainly not a god, to do as Dionysius has bid Apollo: "a god, because I would be commanding against nature, for the divine lies far away from pleasure and pain," "a human being, because pleasure and pain engender much harm, the pair of them begetting badness at learning, forgetfulness, imprudence, and hubris in the soul" (315c2–6). Thus Plato distinguishes himself from Dionysius in two ways: by his understanding of human things and by his understanding of divine things.

Regarding the human things, Plato distinguishes himself not only from Dionysius but from the general run of human beings. For it is common practice among human beings to greet each other with the word "rejoice" (*Charmides* 164d6–e5), and yet Plato thinks that with this greeting people fail to bid each other to obtain what is best for them. Pleasure is not simply the good, nor is pain simply the bad (though it is bad). Each must be evaluated according to its utility in fostering *intellectual* virtue, and both pleasure and pain are found to be positively harmful when measured by this standard. But it does not seem as though the intellectual virtues to which Plato points—aptitude for learning, a good memory, prudence, and either moderation or piety depending on how we understand "hubris"—can by themselves constitute the human good. They are mainly means to doing or learning other things well. Surely the human good cannot be indifferent to what things are learned or done by means of intellectual virtue (consider *Republic* 504a4–506a7).

But if Dionysius's view of the good is implicitly reflected, as the many's view of the good may be thought to be reflected, in the use of the greeting "rejoice" (see *Republic* 357b6–8a7, 586a1–b6; *Protagoras*

352b2–357e8), Plato's alternative greeting does little to clarify his own considered opinion. *Eu prattein* is deliberately ambiguous: does it mean "do well" or "do good"? Is the ambiguity a sign of Plato's humility in the face of the difficulty of the question of the human good (cf. *Second Alcibiades* 142e1–143a5)? Or does it rather direct us toward a consideration of the *relationship* between the two readings: prosperity and fulfillment on one hand, and selfless dedication to the demands of moral virtue on the other (*Alcibiades* 116b2–d6)? At any rate, the only sense in which Plato's customary greeting can be said to prompt us to employ our intellectual virtue toward any particular end is that the greeting itself poses a riddle that demands our careful thought and attention (cf. *Apology of Socrates* 21d4–6 with *Symposium* 204d8–e7).

What is surprising about the terms in which Plato condemns Dionysius's greeting to Apollo, however, is that, while Plato's denigration of pleasure seems to entail a fortiori a rejection of "a tyrant's life of having pleasure," he makes no explicit reference to, does not explicitly condemn, tyranny itself. If the goodness of pleasure and pain must be considered only in relation to the good of the soul, must not tyranny, on its own terms, be measured by the same standard (cf. *Republic* 586e6–587b10 with *Symposium* 204a8–b4, 205d1–8)? This same observation is relevant to the manner in which Plato distinguishes himself from Dionysius with regard to his understanding of divine things. Dionysius's greeting to Apollo was ambiguous: one might suppose that the he was asking the god to preserve the life of pleasure for *human* tyrants such as himself; but Plato draws our attention to the other reading—namely, that Dionysius bids Apollo *himself* to continue living a tyrant's life. The grounds on which Plato criticizes greeting a god in this way imply that he possesses some substantial theological knowledge. Not only is he able to say with confidence that "the divine lies far away from pleasure and pain," but he claims that for a god to partake in pleasure would be "against nature." According to Plato, gods are constrained by nature; knowledge of nature can indicate to us such limitations as may exist on the power of the gods. Plato's silence on Dionysius's reference to tyranny, then, is all the more striking when it comes to what Plato has to say about the divine. Is it against nature that a god should be a tyrant? Again, if the tyrant's life is *necessarily* a life of pleasure, then it is a fortiori against nature for a god to be a tyrant in Plato's account. Plato's theological knowledge cannot be complete without some knowledge of what characterizes tyranny—that is, without some political knowledge or political science.

What can Dionysius himself have had in mind by suggesting that Apollo either might endorse or partake in tyranny? In the *Charmides*, Critias, a future tyrant, claims that the famous Delphic inscription "Know thyself"—which effectively means nothing other than "be moderate" according to Critias's definition of moderation—is a *greeting* rather than a counsel, and implies that it would be incorrect for Apollo to greet those entering the temple by exhorting them to "rejoice" rather than to "be moderate." "Thus, the god," Critias says, "greets those entering the temple somewhat differently than [do] the human beings" (164e3–4). Dionysius, an actual tyrant, greets Apollo as though he were a human being, bidding him, not to be moderate, but to endorse tyrannical excess. This is not to say that Dionysius does not believe in the existence or divinity of Apollo. The fact that he sent a delegation to Delphi indicates his belief that he has something to gain therefrom. Indeed, this belief is connected to his manner of addressing the god. For it is not at all clear whether the Platonic god who partakes neither of pleasure nor of pain will have cause or power to be moved by prayer and sacrifice or that he will be concerned in the slightest with honor. Dionysius appears to believe that a god who can be propitiated, whose providence can be won, must share the disposition and outlook of a human tyrant. Plato no longer seems particularly hopeful that he can educate Dionysius (315c5–7).

The comparison of Plato's and Dionysius's modes of address at the beginning of Letter Three has shed some helpful light on the subject of Plato's education of Dionysius. We can now see more clearly that there are some subjects of education that the *Letters* must treat with particular sensitivity: it is critical that Plato not be seen as having been responsible for Dionysius's troubling attitudes toward the gods and toward the tyrannical life. Hence, we must next strive to clarify what influence Plato had on Dionysius's thinking regarding, on one hand, theology, and on the other hand, tyranny.

Plato, Dionysius, and the Gods

Insofar as Letter Three reminds us of Plato's *Apology of Socrates*, we are led to consider the danger that Plato might himself be charged with the capital crimes with which Socrates was charged—impiety and the corruption of young students, to put them briefly. We recall that, in referring to Socrates's trial in Letter Seven, Plato refers only to the former charge (325c1–2). We will begin, then, with that: Is Plato guilty of having educated Dionysius to impiety? We have seen from the anecdote that appears at the beginning of Letter Three that Dionysius must have held some quite unconventional views of the Olympian gods.

Plato, for his part, will hardly be suspected of being an orthodox believer in the Olympian gods. One need only read his Socrates's critique of the poets' depictions of the gods in book 2 of the *Republic*, and subsequent description of the true god, to recognize that Plato was at least open to questioning theological views common among the Greeks. The *Letters* does nothing to contradict that impression. Plato presents himself as a believer in divinity, but one whose idea of the divine does not hew closely to Greek religion typically understood—we have gathered this much from his opining that the story of Zeus and Prometheus was concocted by "the first human beings" (311b2–4). The *Letters* contains only one oath sworn in direct discourse; it is Plato's totally unspecific oath, "by the gods" (349b6; cf. 350b7–8). Plato's indications (in Letters Two and Six) that philosophy reveals the great, sovereign god of the cosmos do not specifically preclude the possibility that this god is, say, Zeus, but neither does Plato invite that interpretation in any way. The *Letters* consistently suggests that *true* (i.e., Platonic) philosophy is equivalent to true piety because it discloses true knowledge of the divine, which is not necessarily compatible with the stories of Homer and Hesiod.

To be thorough, we should note the three places where Plato invokes Zeus by name in some way. All are in Letter Seven, the letter that is most explicitly composed as an "open" letter. In the first instance, Plato says that by agreeing to go to Syracuse after Dionysius took the throne, he "both liberated" or "acquitted [him]self in relation to Zeus Xenios and rendered the philosopher's part unimpeachable" (329b3–5). In this case, Plato's relationship with Zeus is effectively adversarial; Zeus represents a danger or threat, which Plato seeks to escape. Plato forestalls any possible charge of having failed in his pious duty of *xenia* toward Dion, and it is precisely in doing this that he serves the reputation of philosophy. We may note conditionally that, if service to philosophy is Plato's highest end, then "liberation" from Zeus Xenios could refer to the establishment of the philosopher's reputation for piety among pious human beings, rather than the evasion of divine punishment. In any case, Plato's concern with Zeus here pertains only to the possibility of suffering retribution; he does not suggest that pious service to Zeus is a form of moral virtue that perfects the soul.

Plato's final invocation of Zeus in Letter Seven also points to the question of the goodness of piety. It comes as an expression of incredulity at the notion that Dionysius might have come to a genuine understanding of Platonic philosophy from their "single intercourse": "how that ever came to be, 'Zeus knows,' as the Theban says" (345a2–3). The only other appearance of this Theban phrase is in Plato's *Phaedo*, where Socrates's Theban companion, Cebes, utters it with a laugh in response to Socrates's paradox concerning piety: If it is better for some to be dead than alive, then why in such cases would piety forbid suicide (62a1–9)? Can it be that piety requires one to do what reason teaches is imprudent and bad for oneself? Plato cannot dispose of the possibility that Dionysius was granted an understanding of Platonic philosophy through some act of divine providence; but if such gods exist, their concern with human beings is instrumental to their own ends and not for the sake of human fulfillment or prosperity as an end in itself (see *Phaedo* 62b1–9).

It is Plato's second invocation of Zeus that pertains directly to Plato's actual education of Dionysius. In Letter Seven's first digression, Plato repeatedly compares his present counsel to the comrades and intimates of Dion to the past counsel he and Dion had jointly been giving to Dionysius (331d6–7, 332c6–7, 333a5–7, 334c3–4). Plato says that his advice in this letter makes the third time he is giving "the same counsel and the same speech," which culminates in the conclusion that those who unscrupulously pursue political gain are "the small and illiberal characters among souls," who know "nothing of the good and just things, both divine and human, in the future and the present propitious moment" (334c4–d5). Plato says that he "undertook first to persuade Dion [of these things], second Dionysius, and third now" his addressees, begging these last to "be persuaded . . . for the sake of Zeus Third Savior" (334d5–7). This is, then, a very traditional, even somewhat superstitious invocation of Zeus: the third time is the charm, and may Zeus Savior rescue the Syracusans from their plight. Of course, the intervention of Zeus is said here to depend on Dion's comrades' obedience to Plato (cf. 340a3–b1, 353b4–7).

That of which they must be persuaded is, then, the moral-political principle in which Dion strongly believed. In Dion's view, philosophy means the acquisition of knowledge of "the good and just things, both divine and human," and it teaches us how to behave in politics, at every moment and with a view to the future. Specifically, it teaches that it is the great, liberal, just soul, never the avaricious lover of pleasure, money, and vengeance, who procures the good for himself and for his community. Dion, of course, was persuaded by and obedient to Plato and his teaching on these points, while Dionysius never was (334d8–e9, 335c2). But even in writing to Dion's followers, Plato must explain himself further if he is to succeed in promoting the point of view adopted by Dion. For one might well ask how Dion's observance of these purportedly Platonic principles has benefited Dion and his city when Dion's actions have brought about the horrors of civil war in Syracuse and led to his assassination, while Dionysius still lives in the hope of regaining his throne.

Plato therefore elaborates upon the correctness of the path chosen and followed by Dion and eschewed by Dionysius. Dion, he says, has died nobly, since he "aim[ed] at the noblest things, for both [him]self and [his] city," while Dionysius "lives but not nobly" (334d8–e3). Plato implies that not even the badness of death can outweigh the importance and choice-worthiness of the noble. The corollary of this, which Plato states, is that eternal life would not by itself make us happy—contrary, as he says, to the opinion of "the many" (334e4–5). The position represented by the tyrant Dionysius is thus associated with the common opinion of the many: that death is the ultimate evil and pleasure the ultimate good. But by what rational argument does Plato profess to be able to defend the Dionean alternative against the tyrannical view shared by Dionysius and the many? Given Dion's manifest failure to bring prosperity to himself or to Syracuse during his life, it seems Plato must demonstrate that the soul persists after death, "for no bad or good worthy of account belongs to the soulless, but this will turn out to belong to each soul, either while it is with a body or after it has been separated" (334e5–335a2).

In fact, Plato fails to offer any rational argument to support the idea that Dion is better off in death than Dionysius is in life. Instead, Plato's attempt to persuade the intimates and comrades of Dion to follow their leader's example despite his recent, grisly demise now turns to an appeal to religious authority: "One really always ought to be persuaded by the ancient and sacred speeches" (335a2–4). These speeches, as Plato explains at length, "reveal to us" not only that our souls are immortal, but that they are judged and punished according to the sins we have committed in life, "wherefore ought one to believe that it is a smaller evil to suffer even the great sins and injustices than to do them" (335a5–7). It is helpful to recognize that this, according to Plato, *is* a part of the teaching with which he persuaded Dion. Dionysius, for his part, did not buy it. And while Plato indicates that the tyrant is worse off for having failed to be persuaded on this score, since "one really always ought to be" so persuaded, Dionysius's resistance to accepting what can only be known through hearsay speaks in his favor, intellectually. After all, Plato's lesson here is hardly unproblematic: the old religious dogmas that teach "that the soul is deathless" stand in need of some reconciliation with Plato's own claim that no one is "naturally deathless."

The last piece of evidence for us to consider regarding Plato's education of Dionysius regarding piety comes in Letter Two, where Plato *does* offer something that sounds more like a reasoned argument for the immortality of the soul. Plato is concerned to show that the exemplars of *phronēsis* and *dunamis* he has cited "would very seriously strive to be better spoken of than they are now," if only they could (311d3–5), in order to persuade Dionysius that "it is necessary, as is likely, for [Plato and Dionysius] to care about the time to come" (311c3–4). Plato explains this necessity by reference to "a certain nature," according to which "the most servile" human beings neglect the matter of their posthumous reputations, "while the most decent do everything in such a way that, in the time to come, they will hear" people speaking well of them. From this, Plato dares to draw the inference "that those who have died have some perception of the things here; for the best souls divine that these things are so, while the most depraved ones don't say so, but the divinations of the divine men are more authoritative than those of the men who aren't" (311c3–d3). Plato's principle, then, is to imitate "the most decent" (*epieikestatoi*), to whom he also refers as "the best souls," and "the divine men." That is, Plato speaks as if it were evident that the correct models of prudent behavior, that is, "the best souls," are the most decent ones, and moreover that their behavior is indicative of some crucial revealed wisdom without which we could not hope to guide our lives aright.

It would seem, then, that in the wake of his impious implication concerning the origin of knowledge about Zeus and Prometheus in Letter Two, Plato puts himself in the camp of Polyidus as opposed to Thales and counsels Dionysius accordingly. Or at least, this might be our conclusion but for one important detail: Plato does not claim to receive the divinations himself. He claims only to interpret the behavior and utterances of others, evaluating them as "evidence" (*tekmērion*). His interpretation indicates that he has made some important observations about the relationship between decency and piety. He has noticed that the most decent, whose concern to protect their posthumous reputations suggests that they anticipate being able to be benefit from their present labors after they are dead, are also the ones who profess to have divined that they will indeed still be able to learn of the state of their reputation after death. Plato's interpretation of the evidence suggests that the most decent, perhaps not always consciously but consistently, act on the basis of revealed knowledge about the fate of the human soul, and that *this* is the well-grounded and well-calculated justification for the sacrifices they are willing to make to ensure their posthumous glory.

This is not the only conceivable interpretation of the evidence Plato examines. But it is the interpretation Plato presents in this context, advancing it as evidence for sensation—or at least hearing—after death, in order to support his plea for Dionysius to concern himself with what will be said about him in the distant future. Plato does not present himself as a Polyidus or a Tiresias, then, since he possesses no special access to divine revelation. But neither is he a debunking Anaxagoras—at least that is our impression from the counsel he now gives. Plato has taken the position that moral decency is the surest way to a happy afterlife on account of the good repute one earns thereby. It is at this moment, at the spiritual and moral high point of his self-presentation so far, that Plato introduces to the *Letters* two central themes that will remain closely linked throughout: philosophy and piety. Assuring Dionysius that, "to speak with god," they can yet "correct" anything that has occurred ignobly between them, Plato finally clarifies what seems to be his guiding principle: "I myself say that opinion and speech about the true philosophy will be better if we are decent, but if we are petty, the opposite. And in fact, about this thing, we could act no more piously than to take care, nor more impiously than to be careless" (311d8–e4).

The importance Plato accords to the matter of his own reputation, and thereby to his own afterlife, here becomes somewhat unclear by the suggestion that he is, and is attempting to make Dionysius into, a pious apostle of philosophy. That is, Plato's concern to promote good "opinion and speech about the true philosophy" now appears to be the determining factor in his adherence to the principles of decency. The best souls or divine men are decent because they sense that their reputations will determine the quality of their afterlives, but the *most* pious course of action adheres to decency for a more selfless reason: dedication to the reputation of Philosophy. There is some reason to think that the phrase "to speak with god" in this passage is a Platonic euphemism indicating his doubt that what he proposes is likely to turn out. Apart from this instance, the phrase appears twice more in the *Letters*, both in the short Letter Four to Dion (320b3, c7), where it is clear that the hopes Plato expresses are in vain. But Plato's double use of the phrase in his letter to Dion, compared with his single use in the longer letter to Dionysius, is a reminder that Plato's education of Dion, and their subsequent relationship, took a very different course than his education of Dionysius.

We are left, at any rate, with the impression that Dionysius presented stouter resistance against the portions of Plato's moral education calling for religious leaps of faith. That Plato had a heterodox religious teaching is obvious—if one means that he was impious in this sense, one may have the point. But it seems likely that Plato never presented Dionysius with any atheistic teaching, or with any teaching that explicitly opposed decent moral behavior (cf. *Apology of Socrates* 26b8ff.). It is conceivable, however, that the process of considering and attending to Plato's theological teaching served to hone Dionysius's awareness of some critical difficulties in moral philosophy. That his concern about these difficulties may have deepened with time, even after Plato's departure, is suggested by the second half of Letter Two.

Plato, Dionysius, and Politics

Connected to the question whether Plato taught Dionysius to challenge Greek religious dogmas is the question whether he corrupted his view of morality. More specifically, as we have already seen in regard to Dionysius's greeting to Apollo at Delphi in Letter Three, the question is whether Plato encouraged Dionysius toward a greater embrace of tyranny. This proves to be a delicate matter. To begin with, we took note earlier of the curious fact that—in stark contrast to the thrust of Letter One—Plato's firm rejection of Dionysius's greeting to Apollo in Letter Three makes no reference at all to its implications about tyranny. The significance of this detail grows as the letter continues. Plato proceeds to lay out the latest slanderous accusations against him, which allege that he had prevented Dionysius from "coloniz[ing] the Greek cities in Sicily and . . . replacing the rule of tyranny with kingship" (315d1–3). Now, his "defense" against these slanders consists in a story, in which he and Dionysius discussed before two witnesses the reasons for which Plato had told him to *delay* in recolonizing the Greek cities—Plato had insisted that this must not be done before Dionysius had been educated (319a2–c3). Yet there is no reference in this defense to the matter of tyranny and kingship. In fact, neither tyranny nor kingship is mentioned anywhere in the letter after the initial statement of Dionysius's accusation, until the charge is repeated, and once again decried as slanderous, in Plato's closing statements (319c7–d2).

Thus does it turn out that the *earlier* slanders, which Plato himself brings in, are crucial with regard to the issue of tyranny. For those slanders alleged that Plato was responsible for certain unpopular political decisions made under Dionysius's reign, referred to here as "errors" and in Letter One as "the more brutal things" (315e6, 309a4). But Plato's defense against this charge in Letter Three mostly skirts the issue. For Plato rebuts these earlier slanders by telling the story of how he came to Dionysius's court in the first place, stressing that his allegiance was always to Dion, that he always distrusted Dionysius, and that, once Dion was sent into exile, it was all Plato could do to "bid farewell to the political things" and "to attempt to make [Dionysius and Dion] friends with each other as much as possible" (316c3–e4ff.). But this means that the beginning of Plato's account of events comes *after* the critical period in which he was actually *involved* in "the political things" at Syracuse. After all, he went as far in Letter One as to *begin* by saying that he had at some point "become most trusted of all in managing [Dionysius's] rule" (309a1–2), and that he "often kept guard over [his] city as a ruler with full powers" (309b2–3). His retelling in Letter Three would seem to have cut out these crucial periods.

In fact, however, Plato does speak briefly to the time prior to Dion's exile in the passage that *precedes* his "double apology" against the two sets of slanders: "I was voluntarily engaging in a few of the political things in common with you at the beginning, when I supposed I could do something more; I was taking seriously, in a measured way, some other, minor things and the preludes to the laws" (315e7–316a2). Although we cannot know in what "few political things" Plato was taking part with the tyrant, we must give some attention to the one thing he indicates more clearly: his work on "the preludes to the laws." This refers to an important idea presented by the Athenian Stranger in Plato's *Laws*. In book 4, the Stranger suggests an innovation in lawgiving: the laws themselves should be preceded by "preludes" that will help render whoever is to be commanded by the laws "more tamely and favorably disposed," to make him "more favorable and a better learner," so that "the order, which indeed is the law, be received more favorably by the one to whom the lawgiver speaks the law, and, because of this favorableness, more in the manner of a good learner" (718d2–7, 723a4–7). This is said to add an element of persuasion to the violence or compulsion ordinarily employed as the law's chief mechanism (718b2–4, 722b4–c2). The preludes to the laws are meant to usher the would-be citizen or subject by persuasion into a broad horizon of opinion concerning every matter of practical importance to human life in such a way as to prepare him willingly to take on the yoke of the new laws, with confidence that obedience to them will result in his greatest happiness (see 715e7–734e2)

It is in this same context that the Athenian Stranger makes one of his more shocking statements, and one that is directly relevant to the *Letters*. Just before explaining his idea of preludes for the laws, the Stranger asks his interlocutors to consider what someone who possesses the perfect art of legislation, a "lawgiver who has hold of the truth," would pray to receive from the god for the sake of founding a city, namely, that which, "if it were present to him through fortune, he would need only the art" (709c5–d3). To Cleinias's dismay, the Stranger reveals that the lawgiver would pray for "a tyrannized city," since in "tracing out, by his own acting, everything" the subjects ought to do and not to do, "praising and honoring some things, laying censure upon others, and dishonoring the one who disobeys," the tyrant can produce the quickest and easiest changes to the habits of those he rules; it is in a tyranny that the wise lawgiver can institute the necessary changes most quickly and easily (709e6, 711b4–d4).

Is it possible, then, that Plato had in mind to be a new legislator for Syracuse, with Dionysius as the partner through whom to implement the tyrannical but necessary political measures? Let it be said by way of clarification, if not quite in defense, of such a project, that, according to the Stranger in the *Laws*, tyranny is here *merely* a means and never itself the end. Thus the Stranger says that if the right tyrant should have the "good fortune" that there "come to be in his time a lawgiver worthy of praise, and that some fortune lead them to the same place . . . then nearly everything will have been achieved by the god, which [he does] whenever he should wish for a certain city to do surpassingly well" (710c7–d5). The end is a regime in which it is least possible for those occupying the ruling offices to rule in their own interest at the expense of the ruled, calling their own advantage "justice"; it is a regime in which the ruling offices will be filled by "servants of the laws," so that the law "is master of the rulers and the rulers are slaves of the law"; the regime will in this way avoid the "ruin" that awaits any city in which the law is itself "ruled over" and thus "lacks sovereign authority" (713e3–715d6). The harshness of tyrannical government, it seems, is to serve as a means to the production of genuinely virtuous political ends.

The Stranger's account of how this paradox may be resolved, however, casts new doubt on whether Plato's misadventures in Syracuse could ever fit the bill of the ideal founding conditions described in the *Laws*. For it is not just any tyrant who is suitable for this purpose. Aside from having the good luck to fall in with the "lawgiver worthy of praise," the tyrant will ideally be "young, having a good memory, a good learner, courageous, and magnificent by nature," as well as possessing moderation in the sense of self-restraint (709d10–e8). And what is more, it will also be necessary that "a divine *eros* for moderate and just practices should come to be in" the ruler with whom the legislator is to collaborate, which the Stranger suggests will be particularly unlikely (711d6–7). Now, perhaps Plato believed that he could help to inspire this "divine *eros*" in Dionysius: "It is nothing amazing," he says, "for a young human being, hearing about affairs worthy of account, if he is a good learner, to come to a passionate desire (*erōta*) for the best life" (*Letters* 339e3–5). If so, Dionysius's reported greeting to the god at Delphi serves as evidence enough that Plato never succeeded in his task. But how should we evaluate Plato's decision even to make the attempt, given how unlikely his prospects of success were sure to be? He has said that Dionysius was "very unknown" to him before he sailed to Syracuse (316d1). Could he reasonably have hoped for him to possess all the extraordinary virtues the young tyrant of the *Laws* must exemplify?

Even the account of the partnership between wise lawgiver and young tyrant in the *Laws*, then, casts doubt on the suggestion that such a partnership was Plato's purpose in writing his "preludes to the laws" in the acropolis. That suggestion faces even greater difficulties once we begin to examine it in the light of other relevant passages from the *Letters*. What, for example, of Plato's claim in Letter Seven that the "laws of a lawgiver" can never have been "the most serious things" to him, "if indeed he himself was serious" (344c4–7)? It is not impossible for this statement to accord with Plato's saying in Letter Three that he was "taking seriously, in a measured way, . . . the preludes to the laws" (316a2–3), for perhaps this "measure" is exactly appropriate for a man for whom certain other things are "most serious." Yet what this comparison brings to our attention is the failure of Letter Three to indicate what it was that Plato *was* most serious about.

Let us make this point by reference to the contrast between Letters Two and Three. Letter Two introduces the theme of philosophy to the

Letters, and contains one of the most significant portraits of philosophic education in all of Plato's writings; Letter Three scrupulously avoids mentioning philosophy at all (consider 319c4). This contrast—which makes the pair Two-Three akin to the pairs Five-Six and Ten-Eleven—is particularly significant when we recognize that Letter Three contains the fullest account of Plato's activities in Syracuse outside of Letter Seven. How has Plato managed to narrate an account of his projects in Syracuse without reference to philosophy? Consider especially the relevant statement from Letter Two: "I myself came to Sicily with a reputation of being quite distinguished among those in philosophy; and I wished, by coming to Syracuse, to get you as a fellow-witness in order that, through me, philosophy would be honored even among the multitude" (311e5–312a2). Moreover, in Letter Seven, of course, Plato says that he took his *first* visit to Sicily (during the reign of Dionysius the Elder), with his doctrine of philosophic rule in mind (326a7–b5). The account of Letter Three, in which the whole of Plato's activity in Syracuse is said to have been for the sake of his loyalty to Dion, is at the very least misleading. We cannot have a full picture of his political activities there without understanding the place of philosophy in his intentions. And yet, the evidence continues to mount that Plato makes a point of keeping his discussions of his philosophizing separate from his discussions of his involvement in political action.

A couple of passages help to clarify the difficulty we face in determining Plato's political influence on Dionysius's regime. In the first digression of Letter Seven, Plato describes the counsel that he and Dion jointly gave to Dionysius (331d6–7, 332c6–7). This, then, is the only place in the *Letters* where Plato describes the critical time before Dion's exile (apart from his saying in Letter Three that he was involved in some political things and was writing the preludes to the laws). Moreover, the fact that Dion and Plato in this vignette *jointly* counsel Dionysius reminds of Letter Eight, in which Plato describes his and Dion's common counsel to the friends of Dion in Syracuse (355a3). But as we saw in Letter Eight, this means that Plato's own thoughts and intentions are blurred in their mixture with Dion's less coherent understanding. The joint counsel to Dionysius described in Letter Seven, then, accords more or less with the story in Letter Three: Plato and Dion counseled Dionysius to take up an education in virtue before undertaking any serious political activity, promising that, if he did, he could succeed where his father had failed, recolonizing the Greek cities of Sicily (332c2–333a5). What stands out in this account to Dion's followers in Letter Seven, as opposed to the account written to Dionysius himself in Letter Three, is Plato's indication that he and Dion were "speaking in riddles," "for it was not safe" to speak clearly about the tyrant's need to acquire virtue (332d5–7; cf. 319c4–6): the hope they held out to him about recolonizing the Greek cities of Sicily was something of a ruse (332d7–e4). In other words, the account in Letter Seven gives some credence to Dionysius's accusation in Letter Three: Dion and Plato *were* misleading him, and this may explain why he was so confused about the education he was supposed to receive (in "geometry," for example) before actualizing his political vision (319b7–c2).

It is possible that Dionysius's confusion was, in its own way, a further product of the complication involved for Plato in having to work and counsel jointly with Dion, whose hopes for the power of Platonic philosophy were always exorbitant. Dion envisioned the realization of philosophic rule in Syracuse (327e3–328b1), while Plato must have been deeply skeptical (326b6–d6). Perhaps it was at Plato's urging that he and Dion agreed to avoid broadcasting this vision—there is evidence throughout the *Letters* that Plato was hesitant to speak openly during Dion's life about what Dion had in mind for Dionysius (cf. 320c5 with 319c4–6, 332d5–7)—since Plato knew better than Dion that the hyperbolic flights of fancy to be found in the Platonic writings contain much besides the solid core of his understanding, and are likely to arouse derision more than anything else (314a2–7, 327b4–6, 328d1–2). There is a place in the *Letters*, however, where we are made privy to more mundane examples of political counsel offered by Plato to Dionysius—Dion, in this case, not being involved. The final section of Letter Two is something like a postscript: it comes *after* he bids Dionysius to "be strong" (*erroso*)—the same valedictory phrase with which he closes Letters One and Ten (310b1, 358c7)—and to burn the letter after reading it many times (314c4–6). In this final section or postscript, then, which comes to serve as a kind of connective tissue between the philosophic Letter Two and the political Letter Three, Plato advises Dionysius on a motley host of issues.

The strangeness of this section of Letter Two is not so well described by saying that the matters in it are prosaic as that they are discussed perfunctorily and without context, so that their import is somewhat difficult to ascertain. And yet, this brief and difficult passage does provide some important information. We can begin by breaking it down into four sections. First, Plato discusses a group of men, naming Polyxenus and Lycophron in particular—intellectuals it seems, sophists perhaps—whom he has sent to spend time at the court of Dionysius (314c7–d7). Plato flatters the tyrant by assuring him that he "altogether surpass[es] them, both in nature and in method concerning speeches"; he approvingly acknowledges the gifts Dionysius has given them; and he finally suggests that Dionysius should not pay them too much mind. Second, Plato takes up an issue concerning a man named Philistion—known to us from much later texts as a physician influential in the history of ancient medicine—whose return to Athens Plato requests on behalf of Speusippus (314e1–4). This matter is touchier than the first; Plato must vouch for Philistion, assuring Dionysius that the doctor will not simply flee if allowed to leave. We here catch a glint of the genuinely tyrannical character of Dionysius's reign. We catch another in the third section (314e4–315a2). Plato commends Dionysius for releasing an unnamed man from confinement; he seems to acquiesce, however, to the necessity of treating more severely some other characters in the case. To judge him harshly, we could say that Plato thus condones brutal tyrannical measures; more charitably, we would say that he is doing his best to influence Dionysius to rule with as much justice and humanity as possible. In any case, Plato is here involved in life-or-death matters of individual subjects accused of injustice, such as every regime must deal with prolifically. Finally, Plato singles out one man for special commendation (315a2–5). Someone named Lysiclides is deserving of favor and recognition for continuously speaking in the best possible terms of the relationship between Plato and Dionysius. Here the main concern of the letter reappears.

What we get from this section, then, is a snapshot of the relationship between the two men with emphasis on two features, or rather, on the manner in which these two features are intertwined. The first feature of their relationship stressed here is the traffic back and forth between them of Platonic companions. The gifts some of them have received from Dionysius remind us of the benefits available to such men in such circumstances. And the reference to Speusippus reminds us, much more directly than we are used to in the *Letters*, of the Academy back in Athens and of the weight of Plato's responsibility to care for his friends and students there. The second feature stressed, however, is the danger, in which Plato is constantly involved, of dealing with a tyrant. At least one man important to Plato and Speusippus, namely, Philistion, seems to be trapped in Syracuse—much as Plato himself had been, and more than once (329d1–330a2, 347c6–348a4). Plato tries to extricate him from the tyrant's clutches; the gravity of the situation is highlighted by the discussions of the rock quarries (used as prisons) and of the unfortunate Hegesippus. Inevitably, not only counsel must be provided to the tyrant, but also flattery. And all the while, it is critically important that the public perception of Plato's relationship with Dionysius remain consistent with the image of Platonic philosophy Plato wants to promote. Long after any dream of philosophic rule in Syracuse has dissipated for even the most hopeful observer, Plato persists in fostering Dionysius's interest in philosophy (cf. 330b4–6). It is all for the sake of his own philosophic companions and associates, who stand to gain from an open invitation to live and work under the tyrant's patronage.

But does this final section of Letter Two not also suggest that there were significant dangers involved for Plato's friends who went to Syracuse? What would have been the appeal for a Platonic associate to leave life in democratic Athens for the perils of the tyrant's court? In answer to these questions, we may at least begin by adducing the fate of Socrates as evidence enough that the Athenians were no guarantors of safety for philosophers in Plato's time. The focus of the final sections of our exploration of the *Letters*, then, will be Plato's attempts to foster a stable and stimulating environment for intellectual life under Dionysius's reign. As we will now see, the character in the *Letters* whose relationship to Plato is most of all connected to Plato's hope to nurture the life of philosophy in Syracuse is Archytas of Tarentum.

Archytas and the Meaning of Plato's Third Visit

The character of Archytas is introduced just after the midway point of Letter Seven, which is to say the midway point of the entire *Letters*. It is the point at which Letter Seven's first digression, which contains Plato's counsel to Dion's followers, ends and gives way to the continued narration of Plato's history with Dionysius the Younger. It is significant for our thinking about Archytas that Plato indicates a shift in the audience for whom he is writing at this point in Letter Seven. The first digression, which ends here, has resulted from Plato's insistence that his counsel to Dion's followers not be put off as a peripheral matter. *Before* beginning that digression, however, Plato promised that, once he was done providing his counsel to the Syracusans, he would return to "go through thoroughly" "how many things [Plato] did," and why he did them, on his *final* journey to Syracuse, to show "that they were appropriate and just," and that he would do all this "for the sake of those repeatedly asking what indeed [he] was wishing when [he] went" (330c3–7). Thus Plato has told us that the whole second half of Letter Seven, which he begins by addressing anyone "who cares" that "the later journey and sailing came to pass at once appropriately and harmoniously" (337e4–6), is written for a different audience from the first half. This second audience "asks repeatedly" about the justice and appropriateness of Plato's final journey (cf. *Republic* 519d8–9); they are not so interested in Plato's political counsel regarding the contemporary situation in Syracuse as they are perplexed by Plato's decision to return *yet again* to the tyrant's court. Comparing the second digression to the first, we might say that the second audience is more interested in philosophy than politics. In Letter Seven, it is only the second digression that presents philosophy as an activity of critical questioning.

The second half of Letter Seven begins with the story of Plato's being urged, from many quarters, to return to Syracuse. This story is a good example of the contrast between Plato's narratives in Letters Three and Seven, as the version in Letter Three is full of holes on account of that letter's abstention from any mention of philosophy. In Letter Three, we hear that Plato, a year after declining an initial invitation to return, began receiving heaps of letters from Italy and Sicily encouraging him to change his mind and accept, and that Dion himself, and many others, added their voices to that chorus. In this version, the only explanation Plato offers for their zeal is to say that Dionysius had vaguely threatened to confiscate all of Dion's property—and this indeed is what Plato claims swayed him in the end (317a5–e1). In Letter Seven, however, we learn what was really behind the great push for Plato to return to Syracuse when he tells us that "word from Sicily was spreading far that Dionysius had at present returned amazingly to a desire for philosophy" (338b5–7). Here Plato reveals that his reticence to accept Dionysius's initial invitation was not truly in protest of the terms of the invitation being unfavorable to Dion (cf. 317a5–8); nor was it that Plato dismissed the reports about Dionysius and philosophy as obviously or necessarily false, since he "had surely known many such things to come to pass for the young with respect to philosophy." Rather, Plato says in Letter Seven that it "seemed to [him] safer . . . to bid a great farewell to both Dion and Dionysius" (338b8–c3). In this telling, then, Plato's loyalty to Dion was not a determining factor in his decision-making at this point; he simply did not believe anything worthwhile could be achieved in going back to Syracuse (cf. 322b5–c1).

In the sequence of events reported in Letter Three, Plato's rebuffing of the initial invitation is followed immediately by his receipt of a letter from Dionysius one year later with a threat against Dion's property. That same letter is indeed described and even quoted in Letter Seven (with the salutation discreetly redacted; cf. 339c1–2 with 315b4–6, 327b5). But in Letter Seven, there is a substantial passage that intervenes between his initial rejection of Dionysius's invitation and his receipt of the letter a year later. In this intervening passage, Plato describes a crucial event that took place in Syracuse during that year, an event not mentioned in Letter Three: the arrival in Syracuse of Archytas, a famed statesman and Pythagorean philosopher and mathematician, whose guest-friendship with Dionysius had been arranged by Plato prior to his previous departure (338c5–d1). Archytas's arrival coincided with an explosion of interest in philosophy in the city. And while much of the philosophic discussion with which the city was abuzz was confused or misguided because it built upon older misunderstandings spread by Dion (338d1–4), it was nonetheless this cultural development in Syracuse that brought Dionysius to desire to be honored for his privileged relationship to the great master himself. It was that concern for honor on Dionysius's part, in Plato's estimation, that genuinely sparked the tyrant's desire to have Plato return (338d4–339a3).

When Plato describes his decision at last to relent from his refusal to go back to Syracuse in Letter Seven, he gives the following account of his reasoning: "Yet again the same speech was coming, that there was a need [for me] not to betray Dion, nor my guest-friends and comrades in Tarentum; and lurking beneath this for me was that it is nothing amazing for a young human being, hearing about affairs worthy of account, if he is a good learner, to come to a passionate desire for the best life" (339e1–5). Of the three considerations presented here, the first and third—loyalty to Dion and the possibility of a change in Dionysius—were said explicitly to have been insufficient to move him the previous year. The only thing that has changed is the addition of consideration for Archytas. The letters from Italy and Sicily of which we heard in Letter Three are revealed in Letter Seven to have been "from Archytas and those in Tarentum," who warned that, if Plato "did not go now, [he] would be altogether rending apart their friendship with Dionysius, which . . . was no small matter with respect to the political things" (339d1–5). For Plato to cut ties with Dionysius would be to undermine whatever grounds he had given the tyrant for believing that the relationship with Archytas was worthwhile. Archytas and his friends, Pythagorean philosophers, had found a home at the Syracusan court and were successfully cultivating active interest in philosophy there. It was to avoid jeopardizing them and their work that Plato once more "veiled" himself (340a2) and set out from home "for the third time into the strait by Scylla" and "destructive Charybdis" (345d8–e2).

Our thesis about the centrality of Archytas in Plato's decision to make his third and final journey to Syracuse is confirmed by the presence of Letters Nine and Twelve, each addressed to "Archytas the Tarentine." In this alone, Archytas is already doubly distinguished among addressees in the *Letters*: he is the only named recipient apart from Dionysius himself to have more than one letter dedicated to him, and he is the only one apart from Dion, to this point in the book, to have his demonym included as part of his address. His being likened both to Dion and to Dionysius, even if only in these superficial ways, is appropriate, as we learn immediately in Letter Nine. For Archytas is both an eminent statesman devoted to his fatherland and a man with aptitude and affinity for philosophy. Archytas is the closest thing we find in the *Letters* to a philosopher-ruler.

Letter Nine, however, demonstrates with great clarity how far below the ideal this reality lies. The occasion for this letter is the successful completion of some unspecified business between Plato and Archytas in Athens, at least part of which was political in nature: "the matters concerning the city," Plato reports, were taken care of "without difficulty—for it was not altogether laborious" (357e2–3). The political affairs in which Archytas is involved are presented, in this respect, as not particularly challenging. It is not Archytas himself, however, who came to Athens for this purpose—otherwise there should have been no letter at all—but his proxies, some men affiliated with Archippus and Philonides, two men whom we may suppose, on the basis of much later accounts, to have been Pythagorean philosophers close to Archytas. The reason for Archytas's sending proxies rather than coming to Plato in person is evident from what Plato says he has heard about Archytas's situation—namely, that Archytas suffers from "the lack of leisure" that comes with attending always to "the common things," that is, the affairs of the community (357e4–5). The political things may not always be challenging, but they are constantly demanding. Plato expresses his sympathy on this point; in contrast to "the common things," Plato identifies the doing of "one's own thing" as "the most pleasant thing in life," "especially," he specifies, "if someone should choose to do things of such a sort" as Archytas has (357e6–358a1). The political life is mainly tedium, especially for the philosopher.

Plato offers some words of consolation and encouragement to Archytas in the form of a twofold argument against giving up his office. The first is, so to speak, a moral argument: "it is not only for oneself that each of us has been born," Plato reminds his friend, but also for one's fatherland, one's parents, one's friends, and the other "propitious moments that overtake our life" (358a2–6). Without the individuals and communities who give birth to us and sustain us, who provide us with access to daily necessities, who protect us and allow our lives to contain more than mere life, we could not exist. Plato speaks to the debt of obligation we seem to ourselves to incur by our reliance on these other human beings, and encourages Archytas to remember that one can claim no right to live life for oneself alone. His second point, however, is less deontological and more consequentialist: "When the fatherland itself calls one to the common things, perhaps it is strange not to hearken; for that . . . leave[s] a space for paltry human beings, who do not proceed from the best [motive] to the common things" (358a6–b3; cf. *Republic* 347a10–c5).

Some light is shed here on Plato's own political activities. Plato's attainment to a position of fame and influence as a philosopher has brought him to a position of unique opportunity to help and protect his own community, including the community of philosophic friends he has fostered in Athens (cf. 311e5–312a2, 347e6–7). To let pass this opportunity for the sake of doing his "own thing," much as this would have been safer and more pleasant, would have been to allow a need felt by Plato and his friends to go unmet. Moreover, Plato would thus have left to others the tasks of demonstrating and of reporting, to the world and to posterity, what happens when one attempts to bring together philosophy and political power according to the vision of his *Republic* (see *Letters* 328b8–c2). Plato's presentation of his own political undertakings in the *Letters*, even when, through its mixture of tragedy and farce, the *Letters* may portray him as imprudent or bumbling, is, from Plato's own point of view, the best possible version of such a presentation (see 341d2–4). The first letter to Archytas admits that the suspension of philosophic activity for the sake of political activity may present itself in some cases as a necessary evil. This theme quietly pervades the *Letters* from its very first words: the opening phrase to Dionysius, "after I had been occupied for such a long time with you," brings to our attention the strangeness of Plato leaving behind his own "occupations, which were not indecorous, [to go live] under a tyranny that didn't seem to be fitting with respect to [his] things or to [him]" (309a1, 329b1–3).

The second letter to Archytas, Letter Twelve, is an understated reminder of that for the sake of which all this has been done. Plato refers to texts, which he calls "reminders" (cf. *Phaedrus* 276d3, 278a1), that he and his associates have been delighted to receive from Archytas (*Letters* 359c6–d1). Their admiration for the author of these texts—possibly Archytas himself, though we cannot be sure of this from what Plato says in the letter—has led them to declare him a worthy heir to the legacy of his ancient ancestors, "good men" who were said to have been expelled from Troy in connection with the gross and hubristic impiety of the king Laomedon against Zeus and Poseidon (359d1–6). Plato also responds to Archytas's inquiry concerning Plato's own "reminders." Plato says that they are "not yet in sufficient condition," but has sent them anyway in their unfinished state (359d6–7). There is nothing here of Plato's concern that "it is not possible for things written not to be exposed," and Plato makes no request that Archytas burn this letter or his unfinished drafts (314c1–6). The reason for his confidence is clear: "Concerning the guarding, the both of us are in accord, so that there is no need for encouraging" (359e1–2). Plato and Archytas share an understanding of the need for discretion. As opposed to the lengthy Letter Two, which is presented in full despite Plato's instruction to burn after reading, Letter Twelve survives only as this tiny, enigmatic note. Plato's unfinished drafts referred to in this letter were never exposed.

Plato's Surprise Twist Ending

There is a remarkable parallel between the postscript to Letter Two and the whole of Letter Thirteen. To state this formulaically, we could say that the final section of Letter Two is to that letter as Letter Thirteen is to the entire *Letters*. The postscript of Letter Two is preceded by Plato's bizarre disavowal of authorship for all the supposed Platonic writings, not excluding the very letter in which that disavowal is expressed; Letter Thirteen is headed by a bizarre note disclaiming Plato's authorship of that letter in particular. The postscript of Letter Two stands in jarring contrast to the letter to which it is appended, moving suddenly from lofty philosophic subjects to a hodgepodge of quotidian matters; Letter

Thirteen is teeming with statements and implications about the transaction of Plato's business with Dionysius that clash scandalously with impressions left by the preceding letters. These are also the only two places in the *Letters* where we find mention of Speusippus.

It is not difficult, then, to imagine reasons why the note "It is denied that this is by Plato" would have been appended to the beginning of this letter (359e3). The shocks begin even in the salutation: Plato addresses Dionysius, for the only time, as "tyrant of Syracuse," bidding him, as usual, to "do well," without a whiff of condemnation (360a1–2). This is only the beginning of the dissonance between Letter Thirteen and Letter One, which of course was marked by strident denunciation of tyranny in general and Dionysius's tyranny in particular. To be sure, the generally cordial tone of Letter Thirteen is explained by the fact that it belongs to the period between Plato's second and third journeys. In a way, this is a surprise twist all in itself: the final letter in the collection is by far the *earliest* of those we can clearly date. All the other letters directly connected to Dion and Dionysius, at any rate, refer to the time *after* Plato's final departure. Letter Thirteen, then, belongs to a time before the ultimate collapse of Plato's relationship with Dionysius, and perhaps that fact will be enough to assuage some readers' concerns about its carefree tone—after all, Plato must at *some* time have been on friendly terms with the tyrant. But with all we have learned about the shabby way Dionysius treated Plato's loyal acolyte, Dion, and the fuss Plato has consistently made about the unwavering, principled stand he took against that shabby treatment, the dating of this letter to the time between Plato's second and third visits to Sicily—that is, during the time of Dion's lengthy exile—cannot alleviate all of our concern about the cheery tenor of this letter to "Dionysius, tyrant of Syracuse."

Lest we be too quick to take solace in the thought, promoted by the unusual superscription, that this letter may be a forgery, Plato begins immediately by offering to Dionysius assurance that the letter is genuine. Which of the conflicting claims are we to believe: the mysterious note alleging the letter's spuriousness or the author's opening profession of its genuineness? Plato was confident in Letter Three that an authentic work of his could be distinguished from a forgery by "those capable of discerning [his] style," or perhaps "judging [his] character" (316a4–6). It seems the intimacy of our knowledge of Plato is to be put to the test in this final chapter: Letter Thirteen challenges us to make a determination, on the basis of the style or character of its author, as to whether that author could have been Plato himself.

Plato says that "the beginning of this letter" is to be the "token" of its authenticity. Could this refer to Plato's characteristic salutation? Could it even refer, an extreme paradox, to the very note denying the letter's authenticity? Let us settle here for the simplest interpretation: Plato proves to Dionysius that the letter is from him by beginning with a story, the details of which virtually no one but the two of them would have known. Plato fondly recalls a feast Dionysius had put on during his time in Syracuse. Among the details he includes in his reminiscence are Dionysius's jovial friendliness toward him at the time, the beauty of the youth by whose side Plato sat, and especially some witty repartee between the youth and the tyrant. The youth, impressed by some witty or elegant phrase Dionysius had turned, observed that the tyrant must be benefiting in "wisdom" by his relationship to the philosopher; to which Dionysius replied that he "straightaway . . . was benefited" from the moment he invited Plato to come from Athens (360a3–b5). The idea seems to be that Dionysius's reputation is enhanced by the mere notion of his being associated with Plato, the eminent (political) philosopher.

Plato follows his story by expressing a wish that its essence "must be preserved," so that the mutual benefit of their relationship "may always increase" (360b5–6). Juxtaposed to this passage, with its depiction of the tyrant's feast filled with witticisms and beautiful youths, Plato's huffy denunciation in Letter Three of Dionysius's salutation to Apollo—"Rejoice and preserve a tyrant's life of having pleasure!" (316b6)—begins to ring hollow. At any rate, Plato's contemptuous reproof of "Syracusan tables," through which we suffered patiently in Letter Seven (326b6–d6), does not echo here in Letter Thirteen. Have we been misled about how best to "judge" Plato's "character"? Is it precisely because Dionysius knows better than most what the "real" Plato is like that this vignette will be, to him, such an unmistakable token of his authorship? The question here comes down to the matter of the mutual benefit to which Plato refers. If Plato simply endorses Dionysius's use of their highly publicized relationship for the sake of Dionysius's reputation, and if Plato seeks nothing more in return than the proverbial Syracusan delights, Letter Thirteen presents a major puzzle, to say the least, for our interpretation of the *Letters*.

There is more to it than that, of course. Plato immediately explains his intention to continue to benefit Dionysius by reference to some texts he is sending along: "both some of the Pythagorean things and some of the divisions" (360b7–8). Plato continues to encourage

Dionysius toward serious philosophy—Pythagorean and, as it would seem, Eleatic. In addition, Plato sends along a pupil of Eudoxus, who has spent time with students and comrades of Isocrates and Bryson. This man, Helicon of Cyzicus, Plato thinks will be of interest both to Dionysius and to Archytas (360b8–c5). He is hopeful that, already, less than a year since his departure from Syracuse (361c7–d3), Archytas has arrived at the tyrant's court (cf. 338c5–d1). Plato's concern is not only for Dionysius, then: in the first place, there is the benefit Archytas and Helicon may enjoy from discourse with one another; there is also the advantage available to Helicon in the form of the tyrant's beneficent friendship; and this service Plato has done for Helicon may in turn constitute a favor to Helicon's teachers and other associates—Eudoxus, Isocrates, Bryson—who are also solicitous for Helicon's well-being. Nor are we to forget that Plato's decision to maintain his ties with Dionysius by making his third and final journey was said to be for the sake of preserving Archytas's ties to the Syracusan court (339e1–3). Letter Thirteen confirms what we have been saying on the basis of several other letters, including the postscript to Letter Two: Plato was intensely active in benefiting his philosophic friends.

Where does the philosophic education of Dionysius himself fit into these affairs? Plato recognizes that Dionysius may not even have the time to study with Helicon at all. The "lack of leisure" from which Archytas was said to suffer in Letter Nine is at least as great for Dionysius. If anything, it seems Plato was hopeful that Archytas's sojourns in Syracuse could afford *him* greater leisure to spend time with people like Helicon. The problem is not that Dionysius is altogether ill suited to philosophy. Plato has said in Letter Seven that Dionysius "is not ill-natured with respect to the ability to learn, having an amazing love of honor" (338d6–7; cf. 314d3–4, 328a1–7, 333d4–7, 339e4). But Plato was also very clear in that same letter that intellectual virtue alone, unaccompanied by moral or character virtue, is totally inadequate (343e3–344b1). Plato's praise for Helicon is based on the fact that he is not only smart or "graceful" regarding the thought of Eudoxus, but—what is really rare—that he is graceful generally, and seems rather to be of "good character" than "bad character"—and even still, Plato is wary of trusting him (360c2–d7). Dionysius's own problem, as Plato has it, was that same love of honor that also made him a good learner (338d7–339a3). It is clear throughout the *Letters*, for example, that Dionysius was unendingly jealous of the favor Plato showed to Dion and Dion's comrades and desperately desirous of gaining the reputation of being the most highly esteemed by Plato (318c4–6, 319a4–6, 329d3–6, 330a3–6, 349e4–8). This jealous love of honor was so great as to make the genuine pursuit of philosophy impossible for Dionysius (345c2–d5; see also 344d3–345a1).

If Plato was so wary even of someone as promising as Helicon, he cannot have been willing to put much trust in Dionysius's love of philosophy (see 328b2–5). Plato does not, then, restrict himself, in his attempt to "benefit" the tyrant, to sending along books and scholars. For one thing, Plato appeals directly and repeatedly to Dionysius's concern for honor. He is happy to use Dionysius's love of honor, to play on it for the sake of keeping a hold on the tyrant's tenuous interest in philosophy and, therewith, his attachment to Plato (360e2–3). But even this is a problematic strategy, the difficulty being most evident in Letter Two. There, Plato says as clearly as one could wish that his purpose in Syracuse was to use his relationship with Dionysius so that "philosophy would be honored even among the multitude" (312a1–2). But that means that Plato, too, is seeking honor in this relationship: he needs Dionysius to show publicly that he has become enthralled by Plato and his philosophic education. It will not do, then, to flatter the tyrant endlessly for his philosophic ability, to make him believe he has no *need* of Platonic philosophy, and thus to make a show of fawning on the tyrant without receiving anything in return. The whole passage in Letter Two wherein Plato is wrangling with Dionysius over the seemingly petty matter of who should be seen honoring the other first is a testament to the seriousness of this problem (312b5–d1). Getting Dionysius to honor Platonic philosophy was so critical to Plato's project of promoting philosophy in Syracuse that, in the end, Dionysius's unwillingness to honor Plato seems to have been decisive in the failure of Plato's undertaking (309b4–5, 312a2–b2, 341b3–4, 345b7–c3).

Since Plato cannot rely sufficiently on leveraging Dionysius's love of honor, he must engage in still other means of maintaining his usefulness to the tyrant. In Letter Thirteen, this is reflected in the rapid decline in subject matter from philosophy—whether for the sake of wisdom or honor—to material gifts Plato sends to Dionysius and his family. There is still a tinge of something loftier in Plato's helping Dionysius to acquire a fine sculpture of the god Apollo (361a1–4)—here, Plato seems to make himself useful as a liaison for Dionysius to the cosmopolitan center of fine arts and culture that is Athens. Plato then turns to a description of gifts that he has sent to the women and children of the tyrant's household, beginning with another sculpture, this one for Dionysius's wife, in gratitude for the care she took of Plato during his stay, particularly during a bout of illness (361a4–7). With this, we enter even further into the corporeal and quotidian: Plato's illness, his friendly relationship with the members of Dionysius's family, remind us of the little things with which everyone, even Plato, must deal, the minor and minute affairs and challenges that must be navigated every day. Here is an example of what Dion never understood: one will never succeed by insisting that everything and everyone must be held to the standard of the loftiest ideals; the individual is weak and needs help, and so must be ready to propitiate others in accordance with custom (321b5–c1, 327b4–6). Finally, Plato sends along sweet wine and some honey "for [Dionysius's] children," with apologies that he did not get back to Athens in time to send figs or myrtle-berries—the season having passed and the berries having rotted—and a promise to do better in the future (361a7–b3). (Are we not prompted by this detail to reflect on what other propitious moments Plato may have missed in Athens for the sake of his "occupation" in Sicily—moments in the cultivation, not of fruit, but of philosophy in young minds?) It seems Plato is sending some plants to Dionysius along with everything else, perhaps so that the tyrant can grow his own figs and berries. The letter carrier Leptines "will tell [Dionysius] about the plants (*phutōn*)" (361b3–4). This last appearance of any word related to "nature" (*phusis*) stands in stark contrast to the discussion of "the nature of the first" in Letter Two, which that letter's carrier, Archytas's companion Archedemus, was to explain to the tyrant. This contrast between Platonic instruction in the "highest and first" things and instructions on caring for plants brings out Plato's willingness in Letter Thirteen to do what Dion was constitutionally unable to do (321b5–c1): to engage with Dionysius on a level far below that of Plato's genuine interest and concern for the sake of cultivating something bigger and more important in Syracuse.

Letter Thirteen's next revelation, however, contradicts much more glaringly the impression we have received from the rest of the *Letters*. Plato now explains how he "got the money for these things," as well as for "certain taxes for the city": from Leptines (361b4–c1), which in turn proves to mean that he got it from Dionysius himself (362b6–c2). This introduces the longest section of the letter, in which we learn in detail of the financial arrangements between Plato and Dionysius. Plato documents in this letter a number of expenses for the sake of which he has been drawing, or may yet need to draw, from a considerable reserve of funds that Dionysius and his agents maintain in Athens. The expenditures discussed include civic duties such as the outfitting of triremes and choruses (361b4–8, 362a2–5), dowries Plato must pay out to the husbands of his grandnieces (361c7–e4), gifts to friends (363a1–4), some additional discretionary funds (361b8–c1) that Plato used to pay in part for the sculptures and other thoughtful gifts he is now sending along (361a1–b2), and, planning ahead, a tombstone for his own mother (361e4–5). It is to be noted that in each and every one of the other letters to Dionysius (Letters One, Two, and Three), Plato explicitly emphasizes his disdain for the wealth prized by tyrants, and his concern lest people be allowed or encouraged to draw the conclusion that Plato consorted with Dionysius merely for the base purpose of acquiring money (309b8–c5, 310a2–7, 312c4–6, 317c8–d4, 318d4–e4; see also 333d4–7, 334b3–4, 335a5–c1). The *Letters* opens with the staunch and indignant denial that Plato was at the court of Dionysius as a Simonides, a wise man at the doors of the rich; but it closes with a Polaroid of Plato with his hand in the Syracusan cookie jar.

The shock worsens the more we examine the tone and direction of the discussion. Having itemized his expenses, Plato makes a point of providing some counsel to Dionysius: the tyrant must "habituate and compel" everyone who deals with his finances to be as meticulous as Plato himself has been in reporting their expenditures (362c5–e1). This counsel constitutes a glaring violation of the pedagogical principle Plato vaunted in Letter Seven: that he absolutely refuses to counsel anyone "concerning any of the greatest things in his life, such as the acquisition of money or the care of body or soul," unless that person's daily life and habits meet Plato's rigorous standards of decency and self-discipline (331a5–b7). Indeed, Plato seems to have paid for this breach of his principle, as we see when we examine the details of Letter Seven in light of the suggestion that Plato may have been motivated in part at least by the prospect of financial gain. To appreciate this, let us take note of two patterns that emerge from such an examination of Letter Seven.

First, we find that, in the description of Plato's third and final visit—a description that extends from the end of the second digression to the end of the letter—Plato's concern for Dion is repeatedly cast in terms of Dion's *property*, which Dionysius has flagrantly stolen (345c4–d1; cf. 317e7–318c1). Plato estimates that Dion's estate was worth some hundred talents—an enormous sum—and cites his desire to keep that money in Dion's hands as the only reason he agreed to stay in Syracuse after learning that Dionysius's desire for philosophy was superficial (347a6–b3). In other words, the possibility emerges that Plato's loyalty to Dion had something to do with his virtually boundless wealth along with his being an adoring zealot of Platonic philosophy, and, relatedly, his conviction that excessive attachment to one's own wealth was a moral vice (327a5–b4, 335a2–c2, 355a8–c5). (Here we may make reference to some disputed ancient accounts according to which it was Dion who provided the funds with which Plato purchased the land that became the Academy; Diogenes Laertius 3.20.) Dionysius, at any rate, used Plato's concern for Dion's property as leverage for the duration of Plato's final stay, until Plato finally gave up hope altogether (348a2–3, 349c5–7, 350b3–5). For his part, Plato maintains that the civil war in Syracuse could have been avoided if only Dionysius had relented and restored Dion's estate to its rightful owner—without that, Plato lost the will or the ability to hold Dion off (350d5–e2). The whole ending of the letter is a condemnation of the tyrannical grasping for wealth (351a5–c1). But, in light of Letter Thirteen, we are brought to wonder whether Plato's frustration with Dionysius's tyrannical grasping was not made especially sharp by the financial loss to Plato himself that resulted from the tyrant's confiscation of Dion's property.

The second thing we notice about Letter Seven in light of Letter Thirteen's emphasis on Plato's financial needs is that, despite Plato's lessons to him in household management, Dionysius seems to have done a very poor job at managing his finances. When Dionysius finally decided to liquidate Dion's estate, he did so in a haphazard and unprofitable way (347c8–e5). Moreover, the final collapse of Plato's position in Syracuse is precipitated by a terrible political-economic decision made by Dionysius. He "undertook, against the customs of his father, to reduce the wages of his senior mercenaries"—already a sign that he had found himself in bad financial shape—and when this plan predictably failed by turning the mercenaries against him, Dionysius caved in completely to their demands, costing himself more money in the end than if he had done nothing at all (348a4–b5). The chaos surrounding this debacle elevated the danger to Plato to unbearable levels, and he finally contrived to flee—his philosophic friend Archytas plays the deus ex machina in this drama (350a5–b3). But it was Dionysius's terrible squandering of his finances that crushed any hope of meaningful restitution to Dion.

The final and most distressing shock of Letter Thirteen comes toward the end, when Plato mentions, in veiled terms, some scheme in which he is conspiring with Dionysius against Dion (362e2–8). The evidence in this letter overwhelmingly suggests that Plato's whole association with the Syracusan regime was pursued and maintained, in large part at least, out of concern to acquire financial support, including from Dion (361d7–e1). But if the *Letters* is a book artfully composed and arranged by Plato himself, this massive, revelatory twist at the end must have been intended. Why would Plato do such a thing? We must think more broadly about the effect of Letter Thirteen on the reader. Immediately, it gives the impression that the beans have at last been spilled. A cynical or hostile reader might rush to conclude that all of Plato's huffing and puffing about the evils of avarice and the harmfulness of wealth has been a hypocritical attempt to cover up the truth about his affairs in Syracuse: he was always out for the money. But reflection on the details Plato provides impels the candid reader to a more sympathetic conclusion. What was the money used for, after all? Was it not for the sake of Athens, in the form of payments for liturgies and other taxes? For the discharge of Plato's civic and familial duties in taking care of his orphaned nieces and building a tomb for his mother? Was Plato not merely following his own advice to Archytas in Letter Nine, doing his best to pay his dues to his fatherland and his family? Are these not worthier uses for the money than the dissolute tyrant would have found on his own? And if Plato spends some of this money on gifts for the tyrant, shall we not be pleased that at least he buys him a sculpture of Apollo? Plato allows readers to judge him to have been naive in underestimating the moral or practical cost of depending on a tyrant for financial support; but the angry denunciation of Dionysius's tyranny with which the *Letters* began is likely to resonate in the reader's memory, and since this denunciation came in fact at the later date, the reader may well take Plato at his word that his experience with Dionysius taught him certain lessons the hard way (309b6–7).

What must be recalled beyond this is the *reason* Plato's financial needs were so great. He was supporting not only himself, and not only his extended family, but also certain friends, whose names—especially those of Speusippus and Cebes—remind us of the true core of Plato's life in Athens. It was the life of the Academy, the support for his philosophic friends' ability to live the philosophic life, that put Plato in the position of needing to raise funds in places like Syracuse. The need for this was made as clear as anyone could wish with the case of Erastus and Coriscus in Letter Six. What we get in addition in Letter Thirteen is the sudden, brief reminder of the immense dedication of time and energy involved in Plato's (probably not lucrative) composition of his dialogues: this is the only letter in which any of Plato's dialogues (the *Phaedo*) is referred to directly (363a5–8). We may note that, in Letter Seven, it is following his narration of Dionysius's squandering of Dion's assets that Plato laments the failure of his efforts to come "to the aid of philosophy and of friends" (347e6–7). The choice to end the *Letters* with the shocking revelation of Plato's enrichment at Dionysius's hands may be intended partially to overshadow the question of why the pursuit and promotion of philosophy should be thought to excuse the lengths to which Plato was willing to go for this cause. Like Letter Two, Letter Thirteen also has a short "postscript," which follows what otherwise seems to be Plato's final valediction, "be strong" (363c9). The very last piece of business in the *Letters* refers to a man "set free" by Plato in Syracuse. We are thus reminded of the political position Plato seems to have held there (cf. 309b2–3), and of all the questions that remain about how he used it.

If anything is clear from the *Letters* it is that Plato's dedication was to protecting the life and public reputation of philosophy; we are given no reason to doubt that, unless the cause of philosophy needed material support, Plato's concern for honor or money was quite limited or subsidiary (321a3–4, 333d4–7, 334b3–4, 361d1–2). Considering the bustle of traffic between Athens, Syracuse, and Tarentum that we observe, even in Letter Thirteen alone, we must conclude that Plato succeeded in finding a safe place for many of his students and friends to become acquainted with new ideas and brilliant minds, to discuss, to think, and to write. Almost his last counsel to Dionysius in the *Letters* is to "philosophize, and urge on the other youths" toward philosophy, "and offer fond greetings to your fellow-spherists" (363c9–d1)—a reminder of Plato's education of Dionysius in the matter of the "little sphere" in Letter Two (312d2–3). What for Plato was evidently most important was not that Dionysius himself make great progress in philosophy, but that Dionysius's interest in philosophy contribute to the blossoming of the philosophic life in Syracuse. The goal was not the regime of the *Republic*, but rather that, with the help of Dionysius, "through [Plato], philosophy would be honored even among the multitude."

Plato's Secret Sign

Letter Thirteen, like several others in the collection, contains reflections on the difficulty of ascertaining the genuineness and authorship of the letter itself—a curious bit of irony (or prescience?) given the controversy over authenticity into which the *Letters* has descended in recent centuries. Following the disclaimer that the letter is not by Plato, Letter Thirteen begins with a "token" of proof that it *is* by Plato. And then this matter of the "token," the *sumboulon*, by which the genuineness of the letter is to be recognized by Dionysius, is taken up once more toward the end of the letter, after all the minutiae of Plato's and Dionysius's financial arrangements have been thoroughly reported. Plato says that he has already agreed with Dionysius on a secret sign by which he will distinguish "those letters [he] would send in seriousness": "A god begins the serious letter, gods the less [serious]" (363b1-6). The suggestion is that Plato has shared with Dionysius his secret monotheistic philosophic doctrine, a flagrantly impious rejection of the traditional Greek pantheon, and that the signals he gives to Dionysius reflect the tyrant's initiation into these Platonic theological mysteries.

The device is hopelessly clumsy. Plato knows, as we have seen from Letter Two, that it would be folly to reveal dangerous secrets, or the passwords to those secrets, in a letter, which one cannot protect against exposure once it has been sent. In fact, in almost comically sharp contrast to Letter Two, Plato not only fails to tell Dionysius to burn this letter after reading it—a directive that one might think would have been well advised given the cascade of ticklish financial revelations Letter Thirteen contains—but ends the letter by telling the tyrant to keep a copy of it (363e4-5). And yet Plato makes an emphatic point in Letter Thirteen about the untrustworthiness and changeability of human beings, including human beings much closer in disposition and turn of mind to Plato himself than to Dionysius (360d1-7). To be precise, Plato says that almost all human beings are "easily changeable"; he excepts "some very few, and with respect to few things." It is not possible that Plato thought simple "passwords" like the one that he proposes in this letter could be reliable or effective. This discussion of his secret password arrangement with Dionysius in Letter Thirteen should be compared, moreover, to the parallel passage about the secrecy of letters in Letter Twelve. There Plato says to Archytas that there is no need for them to remind or to exhort each other about the necessity of "guarding" their correspondence (359e1-2). Perhaps, then, the monotheism signal that Plato here claims to share in secret with the tyrant—but which, as we have noted, is a very poorly kept secret indeed—is itself something of a smoke screen.

The "password" passage in Letter Thirteen does, however, make an illuminating point about Platonic writing. For Plato here explains the reason why any secret device should be necessary in his writing at all. "There are many directing [me] to write," Plato explains, "whom it is not easy to refuse openly" (363b4–5). Plato indicates that he produces his less "serious" writings because he is *compelled* to do so (cf. 344c1–d2). This passage is followed immediately by a reference to a number of different people who are already spreading elaborate stories about Plato and Dionysius (363b7–c3). This is already, then, the problem of rumor that pervades the first several letters, and which Letter Two suggests rather clearly is a major reason for Plato's having written the *Letters* at all. It seems that the whole Platonic project, which belongs to "a Socrates become beautiful and new," may be Plato's response to an abiding political necessity for him to give an account of himself and his philosophy to the world.

Conclusion

The *Letters* is about Plato's promotion and defense of philosophy, which was perennially endangered in his day. To defend philosophy in writing was always a problem, because, as Plato reminds us more than once in the *Letters*, it is difficult to write about philosophy. The "labor pains," which the student must endure in wrestling with the most challenging cosmological and theological problems and all their moral implications, are, in Plato's words, "responsible for all evils." To cast writings about these subjects out into the world without sufficient thoughtfulness on this point would be to become responsible for many evils oneself. Plato, for his part, says that he therefore declined to write about the "highest and first things concerning nature" altogether. And even if we grant that this is something of an exaggerated claim insofar as Plato *did* write about these things for such readers as "are themselves capable of finding them out through a small indication," we can at least recognize something of the extent of Plato's self-restraint in writing about them by contrasting the Platonic with the Aristotelian corpus. Perhaps teacher and student differed fundamentally in this case on the question of the possibility of writing safely about natural philosophy, or perhaps Aristotle found that the success of Plato's project of promoting philosophy opened up possibilities that had not existed for Plato himself. Whatever the case, Aristotle evidently thought it reasonable to go further than Plato did in writing about these subjects, and this remains among the most striking and significant differences between these two philosophic giants.

But Plato *did* develop his own brilliant and novel way of writing and speaking about philosophy. The possibility Plato discovered and made use of was a result of the Socratic emphasis on the examination of the "What is?" questions regarding the moral and political things. On one hand, the Socratic project of examining and refuting commonsense opinions regarding justice and virtue involved Socrates and his students in perhaps *more* danger than was typical for Greek philosophers even at this time. On the other hand, this same focus on moral and political questions allowed Plato to highlight the fact that these very questions—which anyone must admit are of the deepest and most urgent importance to human beings, especially once one has been shown by Socrates how deficient one's supposed answers had been—are not likely to be susceptible of any resolution unless one will engage in a quest for wisdom regarding the human things. The shining ideal of philosophic rule in the *Republic* was a way of defending philosophy by saying that the happiness or fulfillment we seek in justice, virtue, piety, and generally in devotion to moral or political causes is in fact the subject of yet unanswered *questions* about the good—and insofar as the answers to those questions are actively sought nowhere but in philosophy, philosophy appears to offer the only possible path to the happiness and fulfillment we seek. The true philosopher, in Plato's presentation, is the truly just man, the true statesman, the paragon of true piety. If it is the regime that is to arrange our affairs appropriately for the sake of our fulfillment, then it is the philosopher, who has examined and discovered the ideas of the good and the just, who is supremely qualified to establish and govern the regime.

To be sure, Plato also gave ample indication in his *Republic* that the possibility of philosophic rule is infinitesimal if it exists at all. Even aside from the many obstacles to the establishment of philosopher-rulers, which we have mentioned, there is the question of whether, according to Plato's Socrates, the real, defective regime *taken over* by philosophers has any hope of becoming the perfectly good, perfectly virtuous city Socrates holds up as an ideal. It seems rather that this philosophically corrected regime will at best be made as closely *akin* to the genuinely ideal or best regime as possible, but we never learn in what ways or how greatly the approximation must differ from the model (471c2–473e5, 500d4–501c3, 540d1–541b1). But this does not alter the fact that Plato has allowed the *Republic* to give the *impression* that his philosophic utopia might be a real possibility, or at any rate that it would be a tremendous boon to humanity if philosophy and rule should ever, anywhere coincide. By portraying Socrates's main interlocutors, Glaucon and Adeimantus, as having been persuaded that the appearance of philosopher-rulers is thus to be hoped for, Plato indicates his awareness that the *Republic* will leave many readers under the same impression and with the same hope.

There is some sense in saying that Dion represents the danger, which Plato invites by publishing the *Republic*, of creating devoted Glaucons. Dion and Glaucon are of course different. Dion seems to be more fully the "timocratic" man than Glaucon (see *Republic* 548d6–549a7), less at home in a democracy; Dion is more active and less thoughtful, perhaps less erotic, or in any case less musical. But it is the way in which Dion gets carried away by Plato's rhetoric concerning the ideal of philosophic rule that is the point here. Plato eventually had to reckon with the danger that the reputation of philosophy in general, and of Platonic philosophy in particular, might be badly tarnished by someone like Dion, who hopes too ardently for the profound fulfillment Plato has described under philosopher-kings, and who has the will and the resources to make a serious—and sure to be disastrous—attempt at bringing it about.

Dion was likely a great ally and supporter of Plato for twenty years following their initial meeting. When Dionysius the Elder died, and Dion saw at last, as he thought, the possibility of philosophic rule present itself in Syracuse, Plato came to be in a difficult bind. The problem with declining Dion's invitation was not only that the reputation of Platonic philosophy would thus be yoked to whatever catastrophe Dion might orchestrate on his own. There was also the problem that Plato would have publicly turned his back on this man, to whom he owed some considerable debt, when Dion's hope had only been to accomplish what Plato himself had always famously said would be best for all humanity. If Plato should accept the invitation, he would of course be involving himself and his reputation much more directly in the dangerously imprudent venture. But at least in this case he might be seen as having nobly failed, which is better than to be seen as having coldly rebuffed his friend and repudiated his own doctrine. And after all, what if Dionysius should turn out to have some genuine interest in philosophy? Would it not be a boon to those seeking to live the philosophic life, to Plato and his friends, for Plato to have made such a powerful man his student and admirer?

It seems clear enough from the *Letters* that Plato made an earnest attempt to make Syracuse a comfortable place for philosophers. The fact that he was at work on "preludes to the laws" during the earliest, most hopeful phase of his visit—that he was attempting something apparently more closely akin to the regime of the *Laws* than to that of the *Republic*—helps us to recognize that the *Laws* itself, like the *Letters*, was intended in part to serve as a kind of antidote to the *Republic*. The *Laws* is an attempt to provide a more realistic, more concrete and practical proposal than the dangerously utopian ideal of the *Republic*. That Plato was willing to devote such enormous effort to the production of a writing concerning things that must not be "the most serious things" to a "serious man" shows how greatly this antidote was needed.

And let us not understate the extent to which Dion was after all on to *something* in recommending Dionysius as a prospective student for Plato. Plato lets it be known in the *Letters* that the young tyrant was neither without aptitude nor without some genuine interest in philosophy. But Dion had failed to appreciate *just how rare* it is for a human being to become a philosopher—something Plato's Socrates stresses in the *Republic* (503b3–10). Dionysius had the advantage of a tremendous love of honor spurring him on toward intellectual achievement. But he seems not to have had enough of an independent, philosophic drive to articulate and to resolve the philosopher's deepest, most intractable problems. And, perhaps worse, Dionysius was too averse to the cultivation of a virtuous character and sound daily habits. Such character and habits are, of course, always a prerequisite of serious, dedicated study. Still more important, Plato insists that a student's natural kinship with the elements of a "good nature," a commitment to attaining the highest fulfillment promised by moral virtue, is necessary for anyone who is to follow the path of Platonic philosophy through to the end.

Plato's establishment of diplomatic relations between Dionysius and Archytas may have been his most important political achievement in the whole Syracusan affair. These friendly relations were doubtless good for Plato's and Archytas's students and friends, at least for a time. Other than that, it is rather an understatement to say that nothing much went well for Plato in this endeavor. But surely, Plato must have approached the entire attempt with the understanding that such would be the likely outcome. The true silver lining here, if it is appropriate to speak of it in that way, is Plato's writing and publication of the *Letters* itself. On one level, the *Letters* is Plato's attempt to "set the record straight" on his involvement in Syracuse, to give his own account of what happened, to salvage the reputation of Platonic philosophy from the wreckage of this dark period in Syracusan history. This was indeed a difficult task, given the problem of rumor or slander that besets Plato throughout this text. But on a deeper level, the *Letters* is Plato's attempt to clarify the meaning of his lifelong project of promoting and defending the reputation of philosophy, of seeking to make philosophy "honored even among the multitude."

Works Cited

Aalders, G. J. D., and H. Wzn. 1972. "Political Thought and Political Programs in the Platonic Epistles." In *Pseudipigrapha I*, edited by Kurt von Fritz, 144–75. Geneva: Fondation Hardt.

Albinus. 1865. "The Introduction of Albinus to the Dialogues of Plato." In *The Works of Plato: A New and Literal Version*, vol. 6, edited by George Burges, 315–22. London: Henry G. Bohn.

Alcinous. 1865. "The Introduction of Alcinous to the Doctrines of Plato." In *The Works of Plato: A New and Literal Version*, vol. 6, edited by George Burges, 241–314. London: Henry G. Bohn.

Alfarabi. 1962. *Philosophy of Plato and Aristotle*. Translated by Mushin Mahdi. Ithaca, NY: Cornell University Press.

Altman, William H. F. 2010. "The Reading Order of Plato's Dialogues." *Phoenix* 64:18–51.

Altman, William H. F. 2012. *Plato the Teacher: The Crisis of the Republic*. New York: Lexington Books.

Apelt, Otto. 1918. *Platons Briefe*. Leipzig: Felix Meiner.

Bentley, Richard. 1838. *The Works of Richard Bentley*. Vol. 3. Edited by Alexander Dyce. London: Francis Macpherson.

Bentley, Richard. 1874. *Dissertations upon the Epistles of Phalaris, Themistocles, Socrates, Euripides, and upon the Fables of Aesop*. Edited by Wilhelm Wagner. Berlin: S. Calvary.

Bloom, Allan. 1991. *The Republic of Plato*, 2nd ed. New York: Basic Books.

Bluck, R. S. 1960. "The Second Platonic Epistle." *Phronesis* 5:140–51.

Boedeker, Deborah, and David Sider. 2001. *The New Simonides: Contexts of Praise and Desire*. Oxford: Oxford University Press.

Brandwood, Leonard. 1990. *The Chronology of Plato's Dialogues*. Cambridge: Cambridge University Press.

Brisson, Luc. 1992. "La *Lettre* VII de Platon, une autobiographie?" In *L'invention de l'autobiographie d'Hésiode à Saint Augustin*, edited by Marie-Françoise Baslez et al., 37–46. Paris: Presses de l'École Normale Supérieure.

Brisson, Luc. 1993. *Platon: Lettres*. Paris: Flammarion.

Brumbaugh, Robert S. 1988. "Digression and Dialogue: The *Seventh Letter* and Plato's Literary Form." In *Platonic Writings, Platonic Readings*, edited by Charles L. Griswold Jr., 84–92. New York: Routledge.

Brunt, P. A. 1993. "Plato's Academy and Politics." In *Studies in Greek History and Thought*, 228–43. Oxford: Oxford University Press.

Burnyeat, Myles. 1999. "Utopia and Fantasy: The Practicability of Plato's Ideally Just City." In *Plato 2: Ethics, Politics, Religion, and the Soul*, edited by Gail Fine, 297–308. Oxford: Oxford University Press.

Burnyeat, Myles, and Michael Frede. 2015. *The Pseudo-Platonic Seventh Letter*. Edited by Dominic Scott. Oxford: Oxford University Press.

Bury, R. G. 1929. *Plato: With an English Translation*. Vol. 7. Loeb Classical Library. Cambridge, MA: Harvard University Press.

Caskey, Elizabeth Gwyn. 1974. "Again—Plato's Seventh Letter." *Classical Philology* 69:220–27.

Cherniss, Harold. 1962. *The Riddle of the Early Academy*. Oakland: University of California Press.

Christy, John Paul. 2010. "Writing to Power: Tyrant and Sage in Greek Epistolography." PhD diss., University of Pennsylvania.

De Blois, L. 1979. "Some Notes on Plato's Seventh Epistle." *Mnemosyne* 32:268–83.

Dickey, Eleanor. 1997. "The Ancient Greek Address System and Some Proposed Sociolinguistic Universals." *Language in Society* 26:1–13.

Dillon, John. 2003. *The Heirs of Plato: A Study of the Old Academy (347–274 BC)*. Oxford: Oxford University Press.

Diogenes Laertius. 1972. *Lives of Eminent Philosophers*. Edited by R. D. Hicks. Loeb Classical Library. Cambridge, MA: Harvard University Press.

Dornseiff, Franz. 1934. "Platon's Buch 'Briefe.'" *Hermes* 69:223–26.

Edelstein, Ludwig. 1966. *Plato's Seventh Letter*. Leiden: Brill.

Engen, Darel. 2004. "The Economy of Ancient Greece." EH.net Encyclopedia, edited by Robert Whaples. July 31, 2004. http://eh.net/encyclopedia/the-economy-of-ancient-greece.

Evelyn-White, Hugh G. 1914. *Hesiod: The Homeric Hymns and Homerica*. Loeb Classical Library. Cambridge, MA: Harvard University Press.

Field, G. C. 1930. *Plato and His Contemporaries: A Study in Fourth-Century Life and Thought*. New York: Haskell House.

Fontenrose, Joseph. 1978. *The Delphic Oracle: Its Responses and Operations*. Oakland: University of California Press.

Friedlander, Paul. 1969. *Plato: An Introduction*. Princeton, NJ: Princeton University Press.

Galen. 1914. *Corpus Medicorum Graecorum*. Vol. 9.1. Edited by Johannes Mewaldt et al. Berlin: Teubner.

Granger, Herbert. 2000. "Metaphysics Z.11.1036b28, αἰσθητόν or αἰσθητικόν?" *Classical Quarterly* 50:415–23.

Grote, George. 1867. *Plato and the Other Companions of Sokrates*. Vol. 1. London: John Murray.

Gulley, Norman. 1972. "The Authenticity of the Platonic Epistles." In *Pseudipigrapha I*, edited by Kurt von Fritz, 103–30. Geneva: Fondation Hardt.

Guthrie, W. K. C. 1978. *A History of Greek Philosophy*. Vol. 5. Cambridge: Cambridge University Press.

Hackforth, R. 1913. *The Authorship of the Platonic Epistles*. Manchester: Publications of the University of Manchester.

Harward, J. 1932. *The Platonic Epistles: Translated with Introduction and Notes*. Cambridge: Cambridge University Press.

Heath, Thomas. 1981. *A History of Greek Mathematics*. Vol. 1. New York: Dover Publications.

Heidel, William Arthur. 1976. *Plato's Euthyphro with Introduction and Notes and Pseudo-Platonica*. New York: Arno Press.

Holzberg, Niklas. 1986. *Der antike Roman: Eine Einführung*. Munich: Artemis Verlag.

Holzberg, Niklas. 1994. *Der griechische Briefroman: Gattungstypologie und Textanalyse*. Tübingen: Gunter Narr Verlag.

Howald, Ernst. 1923. *Die Briefe Platons*. Zurich: Verlag Seldwyla.

Howland, Jacob A. 1991. "Re-Reading Plato: The Problem of Platonic Chronology." *Phoenix* 45:189–214.

Huffman, Carl A. 2005. *Archytas of Tarentum: Pythagorean, Philosopher, and Mathematician King*. Cambridge: Cambridge University Press.

Hull, Andrew. 2019. "Sleepless in Syracuse: Plato and the Nocturnal Counsel." In *Plato at Syracuse: Essays on Plato in Western Greece*, edited by Heather L. Reid and Mark Ralkowski, 215–30. Haverhill, MA: Parnassos Press.

Iamblichus. 1975. *De vita Pythagorica liber*. Edited by Ludwig Deubner and Ulrich Klein, Berlin: Teubner.

Irwin, Terrence H. 2009. "The Inside Story of the Seventh Platonic Letter: A Sceptical Introduction." *Rhizai* 6:7–40.

Kahn, Charles H. 1992. "Vlastos's Socrates." *Phronesis* 37:233–58.

Kahn, Charles H. 1996. *Plato and the Socratic Dialogue: The Philosophic Use of a Literary Form*. Cambridge: Cambridge University Press.

Kahn, Charles H. 2015. Review of *The Pseudo-Platonic Seventh Letter*, by Myles Burnyeat and Michael Frede. *Notre Dame Philosophical Reviews: An Electronic Journal*. ndpr.nd.edu/news/the-pseudo-platonic-seventh-letter.

Keyser, Paul. 1992. "Stylometric Method and the Chronology of Plato's Works." *Bryn Mawr Classical Review* 3:58–74.

Kline, Morris. 1972. *Mathematical Thought from Ancient to Modern Times*. Vol. 1. Oxford: Oxford University Press.

Lane, Melissa. 1999. "Plato, Popper, Strauss, and Utopianism: Open Secrets?" *History of Philosophy Quarterly* 16:119–42.

Ledger, Gerald R. 1989. *Re-Counting Plato: A Computer Analysis of Plato's Style*. Oxford: Oxford University Press.

Lennartz, Klaus. 2018. "'To sound like Plato': Profiling the Seventh Letter." In *Animo Decipiendi? Rethinking Fakes and Authorship in Classical, Late Antique, and Early Christian Works*, edited by Antonio Guzmán and Javier Martinez, 65–88. Groningen: Barkhuis Publishing.

Levison, M., A. Q. Morton, and A. D. Winspear. 1968. "The Seventh Letter of Plato." *Mind* 77:309–25.

Lewis, V. Bradley. 2000. "The Seventh Letter and the Unity of Plato's Political Philosophy." *Southern Journal of Philosophy* 38:231–50.

Lewis, V. Bradley. 2012. "Letters." In *The Continuum Companion to Plato*, edited by Gerald A. Press, 67–69. London: Bloomsbury.

Lewis, V. Bradley. 2017. "The Authenticity of Plato's Seventh Letter." *Classical Review* 67:355–57.

Lloyd, G. E. R. 1990. "Plato and Archytas in the *Seventh Letter*." *Phronesis* 35:159–74.

Molyneux, John H. 1992. *Simonides: A Historical Study*. Wauconda, IL: Bolchazy-Carducci Publishers.
Momigliano, Arnaldo. 1971. *The Development of Greek Biography*. Cambridge, MA: Harvard University Press.
Morrison, A.D. 2013. "Narrative and Epistolarity in the 'Platonic' Epistles." In *Epistolary Narratives in Ancient Greek Literature*, edited by Owen Hodkinson et al., 107–31. Leiden: Brill.
Morrow, Glenn R. 1962. *Plato's Epistles: A Translation with Critical Essays and Notes*. 2nd ed. Indianapolis: Bobbs-Merrill.
Morton, A. Q., and A. D. Winspear. 1967. "The Computer and Plato's 'Seventh Letter.'" *Computers and the Humanities* 1:72–73.
Nails, Debra. 1992. "Platonic Chronology Reconsidered." *Bryn Mawr Classical Review* 3:314–27.
Nails, Debra. 1993. "Problems with Vlastos's Platonic Developmentalism." *Ancient Philosophy* 13:273–91.
Nails, Debra. 2002. *The People of Plato: A Prosopography of Plato and Other Socratics*. Indianapolis: Hackett.
Nails, Debra. 2006. "The Life of Plato of Athens." In *A Companion to Plato*, edited by Hugh H. Benson, 1–12. Hoboken, NJ: Blackwell.
Nehamas, Alexander. 1992. "Voices of Silence: on Gregory Vlastos' Socrates." *Arion* 2:157–86.
Novotný, František. 1930. *Platonis Epistulae commentariis illustratae*. Brno: Filosofická fakultá.
Pangle, Thomas L. 1980. *The Laws of Plato*. Chicago: University of Chicago Press.
Pangle, Thomas L. 1987. "Editor's Introduction." In *The Roots of Political Philosophy: Ten Forgotten Socratic Dialogues*, edited by Thomas L. Pangle, 1–20. Ithaca, NY: Cornell University Press.
Pappas, Nickolas. 2017. Review of *The Pseudo-Platonic Seventh Letter*, by Myles Burnyeat and Michael Frede. *Classical Review* 67:39–45.
Plato. 1907. *Platonis Opera*. Edited by John Burnet. 5 vols. Oxford: Clarendon Press.
Post, L. A. 1925. *Thirteen Epistles of Plato: Introduction, Translation, and Notes*. Oxford: Oxford University Press.
Post, L.A. 1927. "The Date of the Second Platonic Epistle." *Classical Review* 41:58–59.
Post, L. A. 1930a. "Plato, Epistle VI 322D." *Classical Review* 44:116.
Post, L. A. 1930b. "The Seventh and Eighth Platonic Epistles." *Classical Quarterly* 24:113–15.
Price, A. W. 2016. Review of *The Pseudo-Platonic Seventh Letter*, by Myles Burnyeat and Michael Frede. *Philosophy* 91:450–53.
Proclus. 1873. *Procli Diadochi in primum Euclidis Elementorum librum commentarii*. Edited by Gottfried Friedlein. Berlin: Teubner.
Reid, Heather L., and Mark Ralkowski, eds. 2019. *Plato at Syracuse: Essays on Plato in Western Greece*. Haverhill, MA: Parnassos Press.
Richards, Herbert. 1911. *Platonica*. London: Grant Richards.

Rosenmeyer, Patricia A. 2001. *Ancient Epistolary Fictions: The Letter in Greek Literature*. Cambridge: Cambridge University Press.

Ryle, Gilbert. 1966. *Plato's Progress*. Cambridge: Cambridge University Press.

Sanders, Lionel Jehuda. 2008. *The Legend of Dion*. Toronto: Edgar Kent.

Sauppe, Hermann. 1866. "Commentatio critica de Platonis quae feruntur epistolis praecipue tertia septima et octava." *Göttingische gelehrte Anzeigen* 1:881–92.

Sayre, Kenneth M. 1988. "Plato's Dialogues in Light of the *Seventh Letter*." In *Platonic Writings, Platonic Readings*, edited by Charles L. Griswold Jr., 93–109. Abingdon: Routledge.

Sayre, Kenneth M. 1993. "Why Plato Never Had a Theory of Forms." In *Proceedings of the Boston Area Colloquium in Ancient Philosophy*, vol. 9, edited by J. J. Cleary and W. Wians, 167–99. Leiden: Brill.

Schofield, Malcolm. 2000. "Plato and Practical Politics." In *The Cambridge History of Greek and Roman Political Thought*, edited by Christopher Rowe and Malcolm Schofield, 293–302. Cambridge: Cambridge University Press.

Schofield, Malcolm. 2006. *Plato*. Oxford: Oxford University Press.

Smith, William. 1867. *A Dictionary of Greek and Roman Biography and Mythology*. Vol. 3. Boston: Little, Brown.

Solmsen, Friedrich. 1969. Review of *Plato's Seventh Letter*, by Ludwig Edelstein. *Gnomon* 41:29–34.

Souilhé, Joseph. 1931. *Platon: Lettres*. In *Oeuvres complètes*, vol. 13.1. Paris: Les Belles Lettres.

Stannard, Jerry. 1960. "Plato, 'Ep. II', 312A." *Phronesis* 5:53–55.

Strauss, Leo. 1952. *The Political Philosophy of Hobbes*. Chicago: University of Chicago Press.

Strauss, Leo. 1964. *The City and Man*. Chicago: University of Chicago Press.

Strauss, Leo. 2000. *On Tyranny*. Chicago: University of Chicago Press.

Strauss, Leo. 2001. *Hobbes' politische Wissenschaft und zugehörige Schriften—Briefe*. Vol. 3 of *Gesammelte* Schriften, edited by Heinrich Meier. Stuttgart: J. B. Metzler.

Susemihl, Franz. 1891. *Geschichte der griechischen Litteratur in der Alexandrinerzet*. Leipzig: B.G. Teubner.

Syme, Ronald. 1972. "Fraud and Imposture." In *Pseudipigrapha I*, edited by Kurt von Fritz, 1–17. Geneva: Fondation Hardt.

Szlezak, Thomas Alexander. 2019. Review of *The Pseudo-Platonic Seventh Letter*, by Myles Burnyeat and Michael Frede. *Areté* 31:257–71.

Tarrant, Harold. 1983. "Middle Platonism and the Seventh Epistle." *Phronesis* 28:75–103.

Tarrant, Harold. 1993. *Thrasyllan Platonism*. Ithaca, NY: Cornell University Press.

Taylor, A. E. 1926. *Plato: The Man and His Work*. London: Methuen & Co Ltd.

Tigerstedt, E. N. 1974. *The Decline and Fall of the Neoplatonic Interpretation of Plato*. Helsinki: Societas Scientarum Fennica.

van der Waerden, Bartel L. 1961. *Science Awakening*. Oxford: Oxford University Press.

von Fritz, Kurt. 1971. "The Philosophical Passage in the Seventh Platonic Letter and the Problem of Plato's 'Esoteric' Philosophy." In *Essays in Ancient Greek Philosophy*, edited by John P. Anton and George L. Kustas, 408–47. Albany: SUNY Press.

Westerink, L. G., ed. 1962. *Anonymous Prolegomena to Platonic Philosophy*. Amsterdam: North-Holland Publishing Company.

Wohl, Victoria. 1998. "Plato avant la lettre: Authenticity in Plato's Epistles." *Ramus* 27:60–93.

General Index

Translation Index

The following index is divided into three parts. The first contains proper names, the second lists forms of familiar address as well as forms of salutation and valediction, and the third is a general index of subjects. The Stephanus pages listed in each entry refer to passages in which that name, word, or phrase is used explicitly. Numbers in boldface refer to the numbers of the letters.

An asterisk next to a Stephanus page number indicates that the word appears more than once in that section of text. By necessity, the Stephanus page numbers given in the margins of this translation do not match exactly their location in the Greek edition to which they refer, and the page numbers in this index refer to the latter. As a result, one will often find a word said in this index to appear within a given Stephanus page in the first lines of the following one (or, more rarely, in the last lines of the preceding).

Each entry in this index refers to a Greek word or family of words, a primary example of which is given in transliteration (except for proper names). Since many Greek words are incapable of being rendered consistently by the same English word, many entries in the index list several English words before giving the Greek. For any given appearance of the Greek word to which an entry refers, any of the English words supplied may have been used in the translation. In instances where I was compelled to deviate even from the English words so listed, I have indicated in parentheses both the specific Greek word appearing at that place in the text and the corresponding English word used in the translation.

It should be stressed that each entry will generally list occurrences of both the Greek word indicated and related Greek words. For example, the entry for the noun "letter (*epistolē*)" also lists appearances of the verb *epistellō*, "to send a letter." Likewise, related words differing, say, by the addition or change of a prefix are usually listed together under the same entry without explicit mention of the fact—for instance, the entry for "sending (*pempō*)" includes instances of the closely related verb *apopempō*, which will have been rendered in translation by some form of the English word "send," or by a phrase containing that word.

Names

Familiar Address, Salutations, and Valedictions

Subjects

Printed in the USA
CPSIA information can be obtained
at www.ICGtesting.com
LVHW091922011123
762786LV00021B/68/J